DATE DUE

			PRINTED IN U.S.A.

Authors & Artists for Young Adults

ISSN 1040-5682

R

Authors & Artists for Young Adults

VOLUME 8

Laurie Collier,
Editor

 **Gale Research Inc.** · DETROIT · LONDON

The paper used in this publication meets the minimum requirements of
American National Standard for Information Sciences—Permanence Paper for
Printed Library Materials, ANSI Z39.48-1984. ∞™

Copyright © 1992
Gale Research Inc.
835 Penobscot Bldg.
Detroit, MI 48226-4094
All rights reserved.

Library of Congress Catalog Card Number 89-641100
ISBN 0-8103-7583-4
ISSN 1040-5682

Printed in the United States of America

Published simultaneously in the United Kingdom
by Gale Research International Limited
(An affiliated company of Gale Research Inc.)

Contents

Introduction

Authors and Artists for Young Adults is a reference series designed to bridge the gap between Gale's *Something about the Author*, created for children, and *Contemporary Authors*, intended for older students and adults.

Authors and Artists for Young Adults is aimed entirely at the needs and interests of the often overlooked young adults. We share the concerns of librarians who must send young readers to the adult reference shelves for which they may not be ready. *Authors and Artists for Young Adults* will give high school and junior high school students information about the lives and works of their favorite creative artists—the people behind the books, movies, television programs, plays, cartoons, and animated features that they most enjoy.

The scope of *Authors and Artists for Young Adults* will cover artists in various genres and from all over the world whose work has a special appeal to young adults today. Some of these artists may also be profiled in *Something about the Author* or *Contemporary Authors*, but their entries in *Authors and Artists for Young Adults* are tailored specifically to the information needs of the young adult user.

Entry Format

Each volume of *Authors and Artists for Young Adults* will furnish in-depth coverage of about twenty authors and artists. The typical entry consists of:

— A detailed biographical section that includes date of birth, marriage, children, education, and addresses.

— A comprehensive bibliography or filmography including publishers, producers, and years.

— Adaptations into other media forms.

— Works in progress.

— A distinctive essay featuring comments on an artist's life, career, artistic intentions, world views, and controversies.

— References for further reading.

— Extensive illustrations, photographs, movie stills, manuscript samples, book covers, and other relevant visual material.

A cumulative index to featured authors and artists appears in each volume.

Compilation Methods

The editors of *Authors and Artists for Young Adults* make every effort to secure information directly from the authors and artists through personal correspondence and interviews. Sketches on living authors and artists are sent to the biographee for review prior to publication. Any sketches not personally reviewed by the biographee are marked with an asterisk (*).

Highlights of Forthcoming Volumes

Among the authors and artists planned for future volumes are:

Isaac Asimov	Peter Dickinson	Jill Paton Walsh
Margaret Atwood	John L. Goldwater	Jayne A. Phillips
Avi	Deborah Hautzig	Jane Pratt
Lynda Barry	William Least Heat-Moon	Ayn Rand
Peter Benchley	Robert Heinlein	Anne Rice
James Blish	Janni Howker	Ntozake Shange
Marion Zimmer Bradley	Hadley Irwin	Scott Spencer
Robin F. Brancato	Shirley Jackson	Amy Tan
James Cameron	Paul B. Janeczko	Mildred D. Taylor
Stephen J. Cannell	Dean R. Koontz	Julian F. Thompson
Agatha Christie	Ursula K. LeGuin	John Rowe Townsend
Sandra Cisneros	Linda Lewis	Bill Watterson
Tom Clancy	Lael Littke	Simon Wiesenthal
Chris Crutcher	Barry Lopez	Jack Williamson

The editors of *Authors and Artists for Young Adults* welcome any suggestions for additional biographees to be included in this series. Please write and give us your opinions and suggestions for making our series more helpful to you. Direct your comments to: Editors, *Authors and Artists for Young Adults*, Gale Research Inc., 835 Penobscot Building, Detroit, Michigan 48226-4094.

Authors & Artists for Young Adults

Vivien Alcock

Personal

Born September 23, 1924, in Worthing, England; daughter of John Forster (a research engineer) and Molly (Pulman) Alcock; married Leon Garfield (a writer), October 23, 1947; children: Jane Angela. *Education:* Attended Ruskin School of Drawing and Fine Arts, Oxford, 1940-42, and Camden Art Centre. *Politics:* Liberal. *Religion:* Church of England. *Hobbies and other interests:* Painting, patchwork, reading.

Addresses

Home—59 Wood Lane, London N 6 5UD, England. *Agent:* John Johnson Ltd., Clerkenwell House, 45-47 Clerkenwell Green, London EC1R 0HT, England.

Career

Writer of books for juveniles and young adults. Artist, Gestetner Ltd. (duplicating firm), London, England, 1947-53; manager of employment bureau, 1953-56; secretary, Whiltington Hospital, London, 1956-64. *Military service:* British Army, ambulance driver, 1942-46. *Member:* Authors Society.

Awards, Honors

Travelers by Night was named to the *Horn Book* Honor List, 1985; *The Monster Garden* was named *Voice of Youth Advocate* best science fiction/fantasy book of 1988.

Writings

The Haunting of Cassie Palmer, Delacorte, 1980.
The Stonewalkers, Delacorte, 1981.
The Sylvia Game: A Novel of the Supernatural, Delacorte, 1982.
Travellers by Night, Methuen, 1983, published as *Travelers by Night,* Delacorte, 1985.
Ghostly Companions: A Feast of Chilling Tales (collection of ten ghost stories), Methuen, 1984.
The Cuckoo Sister, Methuen, 1985.
The Mysterious Mr. Ross, Delacorte, 1987.
The Monster Garden, Delacorte, 1988.
The Thing in the Woods, illustrated by Sally Holmes, Hamish Hamilton, 1989.
The Trial of Anna Cotman, Delacorte, 1990.

Adaptations

The Sylvia Game was adapted for television and broadcast on BBC-TV, 1983.
The Haunting of Cassie Palmer was the basis of a television series produced by TVS (Television South), 1984.

Travellers by Night was adapted for television and broadcast on BBC-TV, 1984, and was the basis of a television series produced by TVS, 1985.

The Cuckoo Sister was the basis of a television series produced by BBC-TV, 1986.

■ Sidelights

Vivien Alcock is the author of ten action-packed books of mystery and fantasy that are very popular with teenage readers, especially in Alcock's native England. Reviewers have praised Alcock for creating gripping and suspenseful tales involving intriguing characters that sensitively reflect many of the emotions and experiences of her young readers. Alcock is also recognized as an author whose sense of humor is as evident in her books as her ability to captivate and entertain. Writing in the *Times Literary Supplement*, Elaine Moss describes Alcock as a "writer who can command plot, character, nuance, and dialogue with a precision and sensitivity that sets her firmly among the elite of English fantasy authors for the young."

Alcock's childhood was not an ideal storybook tale. Shortly after Alcock's birth, her parents separated. Alcock and her two sisters lived with their mother in Worthing, a picturesque seaside town. Always weak and frail, Alcock's mother, Molly, became extremely ill and died when Alcock was ten years old. "As long as I can recall my mother was ill and we didn't question her much," Alcock noted in an interview for *Authors & Artists for Young Adults (AAYA)*. "When I was ten she went into the hospital finally, and I didn't see her again. So, I don't remember her clearly. In a way I wove dreams around this romantic invalid lying in her bed."

After their mother's death, Alcock's father arranged for the three girls to live with a guardian, a doctor, in Devizes, a market town in Wiltshire, England. Life in Devizes was quite a change for Alcock and her sisters. The guardian and his unmarried, adult daughter seemed very strict to Alcock. "Our guardian, Doctor Mackay, was near retirement when we went to live with him," explained Alcock. "He seemed very imposing and a bit frightening to us. His daughter, though very kind in many ways, had a terrible temper and used to shout at us. We didn't get on very well with her for years. She never kissed us goodnight, which my mother and grandmother had done. She later told us that she didn't know how long we would be with her and thought it unfair to win our love. Though it was a misunderstanding, to us it seemed that she

didn't care for us. She was also a firm church-goer and, though we were brought up Church of England, we had never been to church until we moved to Devizes."

Contributing to her unhappiness and her sense of not belonging to the type of family she longed for was the fact that Alcock occasionally felt emotionally separated and inferior to her two sisters. Sylvia, Alcock's elder sister by three years, became more of a mother-figure than a sister. Perhaps because they were very much alike, her middle sister was closer to Sylvia than to Vivien—leaving Alcock feeling very much alone. She recalled her feelings: "They were both bigger than me, with curly hair, pink cheeks and blue eyes. They learned to read before I did. They learned to swim before I did. They were chosen to be angels in the school nativity play, while I was disguised as a sheep somewhere at the back of the stage. It was difficult not to feel like an insignificant shadow trailing behind two bright sisters."

Belle and Charlie discover that hiding an elephant in a small town is very hard to do.

After years of trying to cope with the many tumultuous events that greatly changed her childhood and life, Alcock finally found a outlet for her emotions. Acting on the suggestion of her guardian, Alcock began drawing and writing and immediately derived pleasure from her hobby. She was thrilled to discover something that she loved and that was unique to her. "Our guardian encouraged us to draw and to write, which my mother being ill never had a chance to do," noted Alcock to *AAYA*. "I wrote a lot of verse as a child and I also made up all kind of stories. It is easy to be the hero of a story if you write it yourself. I started telling myself stories in which the heroines were always small and skinny and dark, like me. It was comforting to find out how well they got on, facing up to incredible adventures and danger—as long as I was writing the script. It was a form of escapism, I suppose, just as daydreams are. But I think it was a valuable one.

"I was also unconsciously influenced by my Russian grandmother, who used to tell us amazing tales of her escape from Russia riding a sleigh on a winter night. At the time I thought they were true, but looking back I doubt that they were. I was very fond of my grandmother—she was the steady part of our childhood and more or less looked after us when my mother was unable to cope. She died when I was eight years old."

Another factor that also greatly brightened Alcock's adolescence was her friendship with a fellow classmate. Alcock remarked: "While in Devizes I made a very close friend at school. This made an enormous difference. If I'd been by myself, I'd have been a very unhappy and disturbed child. My friend had three sisters and a brother, all very friendly and lively. Her mother was quite wonderful, and her father was the kind that didn't mind going on all fours to let the youngest ride on his back. They were very welcoming and warm people—the sort of family I would have liked to be part of. My friend was a very popular girl at school and in a way protected me.

"I was a painfully shy child and had been bullied in the past. I remember quite clearly running away with what seemed all of the children after me. I came across the wire netting of the tennis courts, so there was no escape. I turned around and screamed that I'd kill the first one who touched me. After that they kept away from me, they thought I was weird."

Alcock's education was quite normal for a middle-class child growing up in England. She especially loved reading, writing, and art. "I was fond of the usual children's books such as *The Jungle Stories, The Secret Garden, Peter Pan,* and of course *Alice in Wonderland,*" Alcock remembered. "Then a little later we were given books on myths, which I was fascinated with, and a marvelous illustrated book of Chinese folktales. It had the kind of velour cover you can draw on with your finger, and it smelled, as some print does, deliciously exotic. As I grew older I began reading Jane Austen and the Brontes with enormous pleasure. My guardian had a mixed collection of books we had access to, and when I was fourteen I read Turgenev's *Fathers and Sons* as well as *John Halifax, Gentleman* and the works of Victorian writer Mrs. Henry Wood. I was fairly catholic in my taste."

After graduation from the British equivalent of American high school, Alcock was unsure of which direction her life should take—should she develop her writing talents or should she pursue a career as an artist? Her father strongly urged her to attend a university and study English. However, Alcock loved to draw and paint and thought art school might be more satisfying. In the end, Alcock started attending classes at Oxford University's Ruskin School of Drawing and Fine Arts. Alcock enjoyed her classes and was doing very well until World War II broke out and she enlisted in the British Army.

Alcock recalled her involvement in World War II to *AAYA:* "Volunteers started off in an initial training camp, which could be fairly hellish at times. The uniforms were pretty grim and it was also the first time I slept in a dormitory with twenty-four other people. Because I could drive, thank heavens, I was given special training to become an ambulance driver. I was first assigned in Wales, then in Corwall, and as the war progressed I went all over Belgium and France until V-Day when we moved up to Germany.

"When I became an ambulance driver, I gave up writing stories for a time. It was not that we were always so busy. We would often sit doing nothing for hours, just waiting in case we were called. But somehow it was difficult to settle down to work when one might have to leave in a hurry. In Belgium, the trains from the front always came at night. We were told to rest on our bed fully dressed, even down to our army boots, so that we should be ready when the signal came. Then we would drive in convoy to Ostend Station, park on the platform and wait behind the wheel, ready to switch on our engines as soon as the train entered the station. When the train stopped, Belgian stretcher-bearers loaded the wounded soldiers

VIVIEN · ALCOCK

The Mysterious Mr Ross

Felicity's friendship with a strange young man jeopardizes her relationships with other people in a small seaside town.

onto the ambulance so quickly that we hardly saw them. They were just voices in the night. As soon as the back door slammed you'd have to drive off. It was an interesting experience and I was never near action enough to be frightened."

Besides finding the army an interesting experience it also introduced her to her future husband, Leon Garfield. Alcock explained: "I met my husband in Belgium toward the end of the war. He was in the Medical Corps and we met in an army canteen. He was being towed in by a girl I particularly disliked. She came over to our table to show off her handsome conquest. Leon was extremely good looking when he was young—he still is. He was carrying a roll of cartridge paper under his arm. I asked him to show me his drawings, and we started to talk about art. He was wonderful company. He

was very fond of making puns and had a wonderful sense of humor. He was, however, hopeless at short-cuts. Whenever we went out for a walk and he decided to take a short-cut, we'd end up in ghastly bogs up to our knees in mud. It was definitely love at first sight but also quite a pleasant feeling to whip him away from this very smug little girl.

"Like me Leon could not decide whether he wanted to be an artist or a writer. He could draw excellent faces, they were expressive, well-drawn and rather Leonardesque. But the bodies looked as if he had not done enough art classes. I said so very tactfully. In the end he became the writer and I became the commercial artist."

Alcock and Garfield married a year after their discharge from the service and moved to London. Alcock worked as a wheel-pen artist at a duplicating firm while Garfield was employed at a hospital and wrote in his spare time. Alcock was very happy. As she recalled: "I loved London. I loved the fact that not everyone knew everyone else. In Devizes gossip was rife and you couldn't wear a peculiar dress or go somewhere without everyone gossiping about you—in London no one cared. It was free. I liked the city life, the galleries, the theaters, the cinemas, and the people—lots of people. We used to mainly go see Shakespeare's plays because Leon had always doted on him. For our holidays, we used to go up to Stratford-on-Avon. We usually chose a week when we could see three different plays, and during the daytime we'd go on the river in a punt. It was lovely."

In 1964, Alcock gave birth to her daughter, Jane Angela. Although she continued to paint as a hobby, Alcock left her job so she could care for her child full time. She loved reading to Jane and eventually started making up her own stories that completely captivated her young daughter. About this same time, Garfield's writing career was proving successful. After his third book was published, Garfield left his job at the hospital and turned to writing full time, becoming a respected and award-winning author of over forty books for children and juveniles.

One day, Alcock shared an idea she had for a book with her husband and suggested he use the idea for his next book. When Garfield decided against using the concept, Alcock resolved to write the tale herself. So, inspired by her daughter's interest in her stories, Alcock starting writing again, launching what would become a rewarding career.

"Careers often seem to happen almost by accident," Alcock noted to *AAYA*. "When I left school, I wanted to be either a writer or an artist. Chance (in the form of an entrance exam needing more Latin than I possessed) sent me to art school rather than to the university. Chance (in the form of a small daughter who wanted to be told stories, rather than have them read to her) turned me to the idea of writing. I like writing for children because I love telling stories of adventure and fantasy."

Alcock's first book, *The Haunting of Cassie Palmer*, is a tale about the seventh child of a seventh child who has spiritual powers. Cassie Palmer has unhappily inherited her magical abilities from her mother and she longs to be a normal and average teenager—just like her friends. However, one day, on a dare, Cassie conjures up a ghost who refuses to leave her alone. A reviewer for the *Bulletin of the Center for Children's Books* described Alcock's *The Haunting of Cassie Palmer* as "an impressive first novel from a British writer, with a fusion of realism and fantasy that is remarkably smooth." And Dudley Carlson remarked in *Horn Book* that in *The Haunting of Cassie Palmer* Alcock "achieves a good balance between family tensions and financial worries, on the one hand, and supernatural uncertainties, on the other; the result is a satisfying brew."

As in this first novel, all of Alcock's novels contain elements of fantasy and the supernatural. For example, in Alcock's second novel, *The Stonewalkers*, lonely and friendless Poppy Brown pours her feelings out to a statue that suddenly comes to life. Unfortunately, the statue is mean and destructive and Poppy struggles to stop the statue's trail of terror. Alcock explained her thoughts on writing a story about a statue that comes to life to *AAYA*: "I have always been fascinated by statues. When I was a child we used to go on visits to a house with an enormous garden, subdivided into patches. I used to wander off in that garden as far as possible and one day, in a shadowy corner, I saw what I took then to be a real ghost. The leaves were moving so this white figure seemed to move with them and my heart jumped. Then I realized that it was a statue, it must have weighed three tons. I went back to see it over and over again and began to imagine that the statue was moving and that I was seeing it in different spots in the garden.

"Then in art school we often drew lots of beautiful men from plaster-casts. It sounds childish now, but back then if I arrived early at school, I would go up to those statues and look at them very closely. If you are close enough and press your nose on the nose of the statue, you'll notice that it looks like the statue's eyes are moving. You can do that with your own face in the mirror. It's a fascinating thing, it's as if the eyes take on a life of their own—they separate from you. The combination of all those experiences made me think of writing a story about statues that come to life. I wanted them to be without human feelings because they looked like humans but utterly lacked any humanity. They capture the two girls in order to copy them, in order to learn how to be human beings." In a *School Library Journal* review of *The Stonewalkers*, Anita C. Wilson wrote: "The author skillfully creates a sense of escalating horror. The blending of suspenseful fantasy and elements of the contemporary problem novel works remarkably well here, and may appeal to children not ordinarily attracted to fantasy literature."

Critics continue to praised Alcock's following books. Whether it be the suspenseful mystery involving the supernatural and art forgery in *The Sylvia Game: A Novel of the Supernatural*, the exciting attempt of two circus children to save an old elephant from the slaughterhouse in *Travellers by Night*, the exciting collection of stories found in *Ghostly Companions: A Feast of Chilling Tales*, the fascinating tale of separated sisters in *The Cuckoo Sister*, the untold story dramatically revealed in *The Mysterious Mr. Ross*, the experiments in genetic engineering in *The Monster Garden*, or the evil and secrecy in *The Trial of Anna Cotman*, Alcock's books have been recognized for their intriguing stories and endearing characters. Geoffrey Trease commented in the *Times Literary Review* that "Alcock is unsentimental, but there is an unmistakable depth of feeling in her deft handling of her very human and imperfect characters. She is writing of fear and courage, exploring the ambivalent relationships of parent and child, boy and girl, boy and boy. The contemporary juvenile dialogue rings true, and there is felicity in the descriptive phrasing."

Alcock shared with *AAYA* some of her interesting and insightful thoughts on writing in this manner: "Although I have a liking for dramatic and sometimes fantastic plots, I try to make my characters as real as possible, and their relationships true. I suppose, like all writers, I am influenced to some extend by my own experience, though I do not draw on it consciously. My heroines are no longer always small and skinny and dark. I suspect there is a little of me still lurking at the bottom of all the characters I create, blown up out of all recognition.

I find I tend to write about children who are facing some great change or difficulty in their lives, and who learn to grow through it to a greater understanding of themselves and other people. I do not apologize for having happy endings. I firmly believe that children are resilient and resourceful, and will make their own happiness somehow if given a chance. The end of childhood is not necessarily when the law decides it shall be.

"In trying to invent characters, you have to look at people more closely, try to guess what they are thinking and what they are likely to say, and how the world looks through their eyes. Even in producing a disguised version of yourself as a heroine, you learn at least what strengths and virtues you would most like to have, and sometimes they are unexpected ones. I like my characters to be human, to have the same fears and uncertainties that I had, or their triumphs seem phoney—unsatisfying.

"I don't set out to instruct or preach, but it is impossible to write without one's view showing. I can only hope that my heart and my morals are in the right place. Although I am more of a pessimist, I don't want to infect my young readers with pessimism. To show evil winning out or even worse, a sort of middle-age pessimism about life and the state of the world, is very damaging for children. They are our only hope for a possible way out of the mess we are in. Even if we believe the world is bound to destroy itself with pollution, atomic weapons and such, it's unfair to worry children with impending disasters because they are the hope of our future."

Alcock described her writing process to *AAYA* in this manner: "I usually write in the morning. Sometimes in longhand but mostly straight onto the typewriter. I usually have a beginning and I roughly know the end but I don't work out the middle because it would be boring. I mostly know how a story is going to end. Sometimes it changes but usually it doesn't.

"I always get stuck and lose interest after the first impetus runs out—about a third of the way through. Sometimes I will introduce a new character to give me an extra fillip, or I will reread the last chapter and perhaps cut it in half or altogether because that gets me started writing again.

"Once, while writing *Travellers by Night*, I changed the whole idea completely. I started with the idea of a mysterious stranger who comes to a small seaside town. I couldn't decide what to do with him. The story seemed to slip through my fingers and I decided to have two ex-circus children befriend him. Somehow this started me off thinking about an elephant and I ended up writing a story about two circus children who kidnap an elderly elephant they both love, in an attempt to save it from the slaughterhouse. They traveled by night, hid by day, and sneaked Tessie the old elephant in a safari park. I have never tried to hide an elephant. I can remember, however, hiding my favorite cat under my blankets at bedtime, and with a bit of imagination.

"Five years later, I finally wrote about my mysterious stranger in a book called *The Mysterious Mr. Ross*. I wanted it to be by the seaside because I had been a seaside child myself. I knew the sort of person I wanted him to be: young, pale, and appealing. The sort of person you couldn't help liking, yet with something a little odd about him so that curiosity and rumors start among the elderly people of the guest house. And I liked the idea of a child befriending a man against whom the adults are gradually turning. I first tried to write *The Mysterious Mr. Ross* in the first person with a boy as the narrator. I could not quite do it. I felt I didn't know enough about the boy to portray him from inside. I went back to a girl's point of view, and that became the Felicity character.

"I rather like taking a boy's point of view occasionally. I have done it with short stories. It's easier perhaps because one doesn't show development so much. It's more a sketch of a character.

"After I finished *The Mysterious Mr. Ross*, I felt like doing something lighthearted and wrote *The Monster Garden*. I always loved the idea of monsters. I thought it would be amusing to write a Frankenstein-type story for children but you cannot very well have children go around graveyards and dig up bodies. It's too fantastic. So, I turned to genetic engineering. I knew nothing about the subject and got a very simple book for lay people, which gave me a vague idea about the subject. A friend of mine also arranged for me to meet her husband who was a micro-biologist and her son who was involved in genetic engineering. I very early realized that I would have to start from something fairly small like jello. That's why Monnie develops into a jelly-like creature that grew up. Except for its appearance I based the Monnie's behavior on a toddler's behavior. The creator's first horror starts when she realizes how vulnerable her creation is. Just like a child he wants to hold her hand when going to sleep and so forth. The little girl who is the narrator is named Frankie Stein as a tribute to Mary Shelley, but this is a reversal—a monster who is loved and cared for. I am quite fond of Monnie.

"It is not easy to remember where an idea comes from. I usually think of something and let my mind drift. With *The Cuckoo Sister*, I remembered that my daughter was upset by the ending of *The Beauty and the Beast* when she first heard the story. She could not understand why that furry animal had to turn into a stupid boy. Perhaps that is why I became interested in what happens after happy endings. Was the maiden who kisses the frog disappointed after he turned into a prince? Or if a family paid a ransom to kidnappers to have their child back, would the child ever dare to be rude and bad-tempered again? Would he be afraid that the parents regretted their sacrifice? Or supposing like in *The Cuckoo Sister*, a baby daughter was stolen from her pram and given back to the parents thirteen years later. How would the parents feel? And if they had another daughter how would she feel having a sister after being an only child for twelve years? As I thought about all those possibilities I became fascinated by the relationship of the two children and decided I wanted to write a story about them.

"In *The Trial of Anna Cottman* I further explored the motif of isolation, though in a different way. I was dealing more with the idea of secrecy and how evil can be bred in secrecy. This question of honor as a bright shining ideal is very interesting. As a child, because of the literature we read, it's a very glittering and attractive thing to see the hero give his word of honor and never break it, whatever the circumstances. It can also be quite damaging if you carry it to the extreme. I remember when I was in the army, a girl I hardly knew was having terrible headaches because she had fallen on her head from her bicycle. She was terrified to go to the doctor; she thought they would put in her in some asylum. She made me promise not to tell anyone about her headaches and, though I promised, I told an officer because I thought that if I didn't say anything she might get an abcess in her brain and maybe die. As a responsible adult I did the right thing and yet I broke a solemn promise to her. On one hand I feel that we need people who never, never break their word, but on the other I am aware that it can be quite damaging. And what happens if in life anyone suits themselves as to whether they keep or break a promise? It's quite an interesting problem.

"One of the things I was furious about at the time was [British Prime Minister Margaret] Thatcher changing the secrecy laws. You can no longer, now, claim that you leaked something because it was in

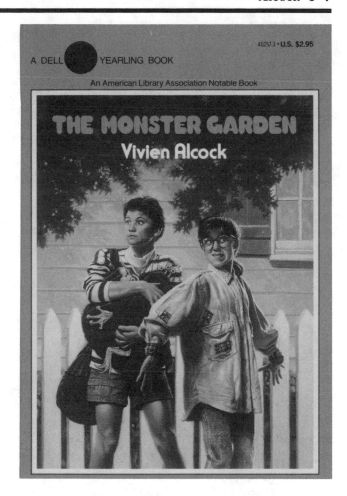

Frankie Stein's brush with genetic engineering leads to strange complications in Alcock's 1988 novel.

the public interest. The whole idea of any secret society binding you to them and getting you more and more involved [is] terribly dangerous.

"I tried to make [the character] Anna Cottman as good as possible because I was a bit tired of writing about very human heroines with their faults. They are much more interesting characters to write about but I wanted to see if I could write about a basically good character. Anna is not simple, she is bright but very naive and trusting, and [I wondered] could I make her convincing on those bases?"

Alcock and her husband live in a house in the Highgate section of London where both continue to write. "Leon has a large study downstairs and I work in a room upstairs in a windowed corner. The sun comes through and it's lovely. We often meet to exchange bits of transcript and check each other's work to know if we are going off the rails."

■ Works Cited

Alcock, Vivien, in an interview with Catherine Courtney for *Authors & Artists for Young Adults*.

Bulletin of the Center for Children's Books, May, 1982, p. 161.

Carlson, Dudley, *Horn Book*, June, 1982, p. 294.

Moss, Elaine, "Ghostly Forms," *Times Literary Supplement*, November 20, 1981, p. 1354.

Trease, Geoffrey, "Curdling the Blood," *Times Literary Supplement*, July 23, 1982, p. 788.

Wilson, Anita C., *School Library Journal*, May, 1983, p. 68.

■ For More Information See

BOOKS

Something about the Author, Gale, Volume 38, 1985, Volume 45, 1986.

PERIODICALS

New York Times Book Review, September 11, 1983.

Times Literary Supplement, July 23, 1982; November 8, 1985; September 4, 1987; April 15-21, 1988.

Sue Ellen Bridgers

■ Personal

Born September 20, 1942, in Greenville, NC; daughter of Wayland Louis (a farmer) and Elizabeth (Abbott) Hunsucker; married Ben Oshel Bridgers (an attorney), March 17, 1963; children: Elizabeth Abbott, Jane Bennett, Sean MacKenzie. *Education:* Attended East Carolina University, 1960-63; Western Carolina University, B.A. (summa cum laude), 1976.

■ Addresses

Home—64 Savannah Dr., Sylva, NC 28779. *Office*—P.O. Box 248, Sylva, NC 28779.

■ Career

Writer, 1970—. Member of board of directors, North Carolina Center for Public TV, Chapel Hill, NC, 1984—, Jackson County Library, Sylva, NC, 1985—, and North Carolina Humanities Council, 1990—.

■ Awards, Honors

Breadloaf Writers' Conference fellowship, 1976; *Boston Globe-Horn Book* Award for fiction, Christopher Award, named to American Library Association list of best books for young adults, all 1979, and American Book Award nomination, 1981, all for *All Together Now;* American Book Award nomination, 1983, for *Notes for Another Life;* ALAN Award, Assembly on Literature for Adolescents of the National Council of Teachers of English, 1985, for her outstanding contributions to young adult literature.

■ Writings

YOUNG ADULT NOVELS

Home before Dark (originally appeared in *Redbook*), Knopf, 1976.
All Together Now, Knopf, 1979.
Notes for Another Life, Knopf, 1981.
Permanent Connections, Harper, 1987.

OTHER

Sara Will (adult novel), Harper, 1985.

Contributor of stories to magazines, including *Redbook, Ingenue, Carolina Quarterly,* and *Mountain Living.* A collection of Bridgers's manuscripts is housed at Western Carolina University's Hunter Library.

■ Sidelights

A native of North Carolina, Sue Ellen Bridgers writes novels mainly for and about young adults on

A BANTAM STARFIRE BOOK

AN ALA BEST BOOK FOR YOUNG ADULTS
"Exceptional....Superb writing and skillful portrayal of human relationships."—Horn Book

ALL TOGETHER NOW

Sue Ellen Bridgers
Author of NOTES FOR ANOTHER LIFE

Bridgers's 1976 novel explores the complex relationship between a lonely twelve-year-old girl and an older, distrustful retarded man.

the troubled path to adulthood and maturity. She draws nostalgically upon her own experience in small southern towns, where people know and care about one another and where most inhabitants are kin, to probe the complexities of family relationships. Suggesting that Bridgers has "an ear for the authentic talk of teenagers and a heart for the way they feel," Bettie Cannon remarks in the *Los Angeles Times:* "Perhaps because of her life in one of those small Appalachian towns where family and friends seem to matter, she has tapped into a phenomenon in American life. Through her perceptive writing Bridgers wants, it seems, to help teen-agers love themselves." Lauding Bridgers's accomplishments as a writer, Alice Digilio remarks in the *Washington Post Book World* that she "can bring a scene or the memory of some adolescent yearning or frustration into sharp and vivid focus.

In her prize-winning novels for young people she has confronted many of life's most demanding trials—accidents, the death of parents, social rejection, the realignment of family—and she has done so with a clear-eyed toughness."

Winner of the 1985 ALAN Award from the Assembly on Literature for Adolescents of the National Council of Teachers of English for her outstanding contributions to young adult literature, Bridgers contemplates the past and its link to the present in her fiction. "We Southerners have a 'thing' about history," she says in "My Life in Fiction" in the *ALAN Review,* "and this abiding need to look backwards for lessons to live by has affected me profoundly." Using North Carolina as a setting for most of her fiction, Bridgers indicates in "Stories My Grandmother Told Me" in the *ALAN Review* that a "writer pins down a place, identifies and defines it, gives the reader directions to it." For her, that place is North Carolina, "not because what we know best is easiest to write about," she says. "To the contrary, the knowing makes it hard. That terrain that touches us deepest, that moves us most, is the most difficult to capture, but the most necessary. This is the map of my memory, the place I want to understand well and to illuminate completely. I want to show you my vision. I want to see it for myself."

While not autobiographical, Bridgers's fiction does rely heavily upon memory and the emotions connected to it; an ability to recall and to articulate feelings and sensations is a hallmark of her work. "Memory comes to us floating on smells; it pierces our bustling days with incongruous sounds, makes us pause at a name, an address, a postcard, a photograph, a baby bonnet, a china plate...," she writes in an essay for *Something about the Author Autobiography Series.* "Sometimes we can't even discern the stimulus; suddenly we are captured by a memory, locked into another time and, for a moment, we are someone we used to be." Her earliest memory is the astonishing recollection of being drawn, at the age of eighteen months, closer and closer to a face she later realized was that of her great-grandmother who was bedridden at the time and died soon thereafter. For Bridgers, memory and fiction are closely linked. Discussing an early story about a grandfather's death and the feelings of his family toward him, Bridgers explains in "My Life in Fiction" how, years later, she realized that the story was actually true, that she had tapped into "one of the most crucial issues of my life." She continues: "What amazes me is that I unwittingly recorded so much truth in that small work of fiction and refused to acknowledge it. It is an argument for how much memory must lie at the root of fiction, even when we do not intend it or recognize it."

Bridgers grew up near both her parents' families in North Carolina. "We were surrounded by kin," relates Bridgers in her autobiographical essay. "The lessons of such an upbringing are both difficult and joyful. There were perhaps too many eyes focused on us and yet there was an abundance of concern and well-intentioned affection. We learned to be proud of our heritage; we knew the unyielding, powerful hold of family." Born and raised in small southern towns, where families remain for generations and legal links become blood ties, and where kinship is frequently identified in "times removed" from a common ancestor, Bridgers indicates that it was important to identify her connection to other people: "I can't remember a time when I wasn't interested in my connection to other people. 'How is this person kin to me?' was one of my favorite questions."

Bridgers remembers that as a child, she "lived between two houses"—that of her father's father, a carriage builder who added to his sprawling house often and haphazardly as his family grew, and the "symmetrical, open, deep" house in which her mother grew up. The families were as different as their homes, and Bridgers recalls that despite many happy memories at her paternal grandparents' home, "the 'feel' of the house was nonetheless one of strict discipline, of self-control, of judgments passed down with sighs and frowns." Conversely, her maternal grandparents' home "was a house for the imagination. In the window seat in the living room I was Jo reading and scribbling as in *Little Women*. On a chaise lounge in the front bedroom I died many deaths. Before a dresser mirror I preached sermons that began with biblical texts and wandered into fairy tales, liberally strewn with bits of poetry and nursery rhymes.... In this house emotions ran high.... Here family life was exposed. Here I was afraid and yet loved. Here I was valued and accepted, but I felt responsibilities too."

Bridgers's desire to become a writer originated early. According to her autobiographical essay, she "always wanted to be a writer," and believes that it probably stemmed from being read to as a child—an activity she adored. In "My Life in Fiction" she acknowledges that stories have mesmerized her throughout her life: "Having been captivated by fairy tales and Bible stories, by my family history, even my own fiction, I am a prisoner of phrases like

'in the beginning' and 'let me tell you about the time.'" In her autobiographical essay she considers the "revelation" of her life to have been when she correlated the "printed curves and angles in the books at home with the alphabet" she was learning at school in the first grade and she realized that she, herself, could write.

Bridgers composed poetry during her grammar school days, much of it about holidays, and had several of her poems published by the local newspaper. She relates in her autobiographical essay, though, the one point in her youth at which she realized she would become a writer: "I remember being in the car with Mother driving when I was twelve or thirteen. I remember the intersection at which we stopped for the light to change. The sensations of that moment—the lights from the service station on the corner, the other cars, the hum of our engine—are still with me. I was talking about the future the way young people do, wanting one minute to be a teacher, the next an engineer. I thought perhaps I would be a nurse. 'Oh, Sue Ellen,' she said almost sternly, as if to make finally clear what she had always known, 'you are going to be a writer.'" While a student at East Carolina University, she volunteered as a typist for the school's literary magazine. Assessing her own work in light of the contributions made by others, she began to submit her own poems, essays, and stories, and eventually became the journal's book review editor.

Bridgers deferred her plans to become a writer when she left school to marry Ben, who was then an English instructor, and start a family. Regarding the postponement of her education and writing career until her family needed her less, she recalls in her autobiographical essay that despite whatever irritation she may have felt at having so little time for her professional goals, "I loved the people in my care. I had responsibilities to them. There were only so many hours in the day and just having done what seemed essential, I always fell into bed exhausted. There was no time, no place for myself." However, she did begin to read the work of women writers in an attempt to determine "how they managed their lives"; and she attended feminist gatherings but soon realized she had neither the time nor the energy for activism. She found time to write stories, though, many of which were published in small North Carolina magazines; and she returned to school to finish her degree, which she received in 1976—the same year she published her first novel, *Home before Dark*. Marriage and motherhood may have delayed her career as a

Bridgers drew upon some painful childhood memories to write this 1981 novel about the effects of mental illness upon a family.

writer, but her award-winning work has generated much critical acclaim. Defining "family life as the core of my writing," Bridgers explains in "Stories My Grandmother Told Me": "I have a personal past, a family history that, while providing me with fertile creative ground, also provides me with awesome responsibility."

Preparing for her trip to the Breadloaf Writers' Conference in Vermont, where she was awarded a fellowship, Bridgers received the first copy of *Home before Dark* from Knopf. She recalls in her autobiographical essay that she "felt quite detached from it [and] a little disappointed with myself because I wanted to get really excited about this tangible evidence of my success." While at the conference, she showed the book to author Toni Morrison, "who carefully turned it over in her hands as if testing the feel of it before saying, 'A book is a good thing.' That was what I needed to hear—not that I was wonderful to have written it or that it was an extraordinary accomplishment, but simply that with it, I had joined the ranks of those with an opportunity for doing a good thing. It is, beyond all else, what we are striving for."

Home before Dark is about James Earl Willis, who returns with his wife and children to his native North Carolina home after spending years as migrant workers in Florida. The tobacco farm of his youth now belongs to his younger brother, who lets the family live in a cabin on the property. James's wife Mae has difficulty adjusting to a more stationary life; and when she dies in a lightning storm, fourteen-year-old Stella must assume the responsibilities of making the cabin a home. When her father marries Maggie Grover, Stella refuses to move from the cabin to Maggie's home. And although the cottage represents her first experience with establishing roots, Stella matures and eventually joins her father and his new wife, arriving at their home just before nightfall.

Suggesting that "no summary can convey the tremendous integrity" of *Home before Dark*, Barbara Helfgott adds in the *New York Times Book Review:* "The author speaks with a voice that is intensely lyrical yet wholly un-selfconscious. Character and theme have been developed with such painstaking attention that each episode seems inevitable and right." Praising Bridgers's "perceptive, masterful writing," Sally Holmes Holtze calls *Home before Dark* an "outstanding first novel," adding in *Horn Book* that Bridgers's "unique insights are expressed in profound metaphors, and she creates haunting images." According to Linda Bachelder in *English Journal*, the novel is "flawlessly written and loaded, like the great Southern novels, with gothic humor and with fascinating characters."

Bridgers writes about how people are connected emotionally to one another, about the fragility of some of those connections as well as the endurance of others. In *All Together Now*, which won the *Boston Globe-Horn Book* Award, the Christopher Award, and was nominated for the American Book Award, she presents the stories of several different characters from the point of view of each. Twelve-year-old Casey Flanagan spends the summer with her grandparents while her mother works and her father is fighting in the Korean war. She meets Dwayne Pickens, a retarded man who had once been a childhood friend of her father. Because Dwayne doesn't like or trust girls, Casey tries to dress and look like a boy. By summer's end, Dwayne discovers that although Casey is a girl, he still looks forward to seeing her again the next summer. Writing in *Horn Book,* Kate M. Flanagan believes that the novel is "exceptional not only for its superb writing and skillful portrayal of human relationships but for its depiction of a small southern town where everyone knows everyone and neighbors care enough to rally in times of trouble." According to Katherine Paterson in the *Washington Post Book World,* "It is a book about simple people learning how to love, and because love is a difficult task for the wisest of us, these simple people botch and bungle but never quite give up." Paterson adds that Bridgers "has certainly written a lovely book—a book for all of us who crave a good story about people we will come to care about deeply." Calling the book "the deceivingly effortless writing of an artist at work," Dana G. Clinton remarks in the *Christian Science Monitor,* that "long after the story ends, the haunting force of harmony stays with the reader and attests to the power of the tale and the mastery of its teller."

Critics praise Bridgers for writing realistically about the thoughts, emotions, and behavior of her characters. "Unlike many who write for young adults," states Doris Betts in a *Washington Post Book World* review of *Notes for Another Life,* "Sue Ellen Bridgers affirms the earned sweetness of life without ever pretending it has a cream center or sugar coating." *Notes for Another Life,* for example, deals with the effects of mental illness on a family; and although the novel is not autobiographical, Bridgers does draw on personal experience for it. "When I was eleven my father suffered his first debilitating bout with mental depression," writes Bridgers in her autobiographical essay. "The treatment of mental illness was too modern a science for our rural area, and Mother's desperation to find him help led her to a psychiatrist in Raleigh. She drove Daddy to Raleigh twice a week and finally he was hospitalized there. Periodically over the next fifteen years he was hospitalized, treated with medication and shock treatments until he was able to function, then sent home for a period of time during which he farmed and carried on some semblance of normality before slipping back into a catatonic, depressed state that one again required hospitalization. The effects of his illness on each of us children were individual and private."

Notes for Another Life, which earned Bridgers her second American Book Award nomination, is about thirteen-year-old Wren and her older brother Kevin who live with their grandparents because

their father is mentally ill and their mother cannot cope with existing circumstances. In a *Voice of Youth Advocates* review, Joan L. Atkinson calls the novel "superbly written," adding: "Topics of contemporary interest—suicide, mental illness, divorce, living with loss—are placed in the context of family living so skillfully that they appear as universal rather than contemporary themes. There is genius in the development of so many rounded characters in a medium length novel. . . . Its picture of an adolescent brother and sister deeply concerned for and never failing each other is hard to find in literature and is entirely believable."

Critics appreciate Bridgers's vivid characterizations, especially the females in her fiction who show both spiritual and physical strength. According to Betts, "Bridgers endorses the survival of

An angry teen learns how much certain members of his family mean to him when he almost loses them in Bridgers's 1987 novel.

family love and values, which nearly always are stronger in women than men." Yet because of the element of female self-sacrifice in *Notes for Another Life,* Janet French considers the novel "a propaganda vehicle for female domesticity" in a *School Library Journal* review. However, also in *School Library Journal,* Joan L. Atkinson contends that "far from being a 'propaganda vehicle for female domesticity,' [the novel] says that family life is multi-faceted—a mix of love and loss, of responsibilities accepted and rejected, of forces controllable and out of hand, of disappointment and support.... To me the book says that both men and women struggle to find that delicate balance between self-actualization and care for the meaningful others in their lives. But its more important message is that people need inner resources, stamina and will to live fully." Bridgers relates in her autobiographical essay that she did not "think consciously about dealing with a feminist issue" when she was writing the novel; but she realizes that "the choices the mother Karen makes reflect a growing urgency on the part of women to refuse entrapment." Declaring, "I am more aware than ever before of my opportunities to make choices," Bridgers adds, "My family heritage burdened and blessed me with an accumulation of maxims, dictated certain behavior, a life view which it is finally my choice to accept as my own or to reject."

In *Permanent Connections,* Bridgers tells the story of seventeen-year-old Rob Dickson, who is not happy about having to accompany his father to North Carolina to visit his uncle who is hospitalized with a broken hip. Angry and withdrawn, Rob must stay in North Carolina with his partially senile grandfather and his agoraphobic aunt while his uncle recuperates. One stormy evening, Rob has a terrible argument with his grandfather and storms out of the house. After they search for one another all night, Rob begins to realize how much he means to his family and how much his family means to him. "Fine characterization, realistic situations, and wonderful descriptions throughout make this one of Bridgers' best works," comments a *Kliatt* contributor. According to a reviewer in *Publishers Weekly,* "This marvelous book movingly evokes the tortured feelings of young people, and the viewpoints of their elders, who are coping as best they can.... Readers of all ages will be moved by its rich characterizations and universal themes." Praising Bridgers's "masterful" descriptions, Barbara Chatton writes in *School Library Journal* that "there is no miraculous happy ending here, but

instead a clear and healthy beginning of understanding."

Bridgers indicates in her autobiographical essay that each of her novels has originated with a particular "visionary moment, a scene that came to me spontaneously with images so potent I couldn't shake free of them." Her books also begin with the characters themselves. "Technically the characters always come first and then the kind of people they are dictates what they do, just as you and I are products of heredity and environment," says Bridgers in the "Stories My Grandmother Told Me." In her only novel thus far for adults, *Sara Will,* the title character came to her suddenly and completely developed. "I encountered *Sara Will* in my mind, one of those wonderful moments of visualization that has marked almost all my beginnings, and I knew immediately who she was," says Bridgers in "My Life in Fiction."

Sara Will is about a spinster in her fifties who lives with her widowed sister in the aging house in which their parents died. Their lives are changed when Fate Jessop, the brother-in-law of their dead sister, brings his unwed teenage niece Eva and her baby to live there. The narrative ricochets between past and present, filling in the backgrounds of the disparate people who eventually establish an extended, three-generation family. Writing in *Library Journal,* Jeanne Buckley calls *Sara Will* "a quietly moving book of affirming love." And in a *Booklist* review, Sally Estes considers it "a beautifully written, ultimately heartwarming gem of a novel." According to Bridgers in "My Life in Fiction," during the writing of the novel, her own personal life was in upheaval. While she was trying to be an adequate parent to teenagers, her semi-invalid father had become bedridden, her grandmother had died, and her best friend had committed suicide. "So I struggled to get started again," says Bridgers. "Fruitless days passed when I couldn't let go of my own grief enough to let Sara share in it. She wanted to. Finally, I let myself enter her world, and she, until that moment as rigid as a beanpole, bent down to start my healing. I will always love her for it."

Pamela Sissi Carroll, who has written the first doctoral dissertation on Bridgers, considers her to rank with writers of the Southern Renaissance because of the importance in her work of place, memory, and family, and because of her use of language. "Literary analysis of Bridgers' novels not only reveals the merit of her fiction," maintains Carroll. "It also suggests that the genre of young adult literature has matured enough to allow for specialization; that is, Bridgers should not only be respected as a writer of young adult literature, but also as a writer of fine Southern literature." Praising her use of language, Ted Hipple remarks in the *ALAN Review* that her writing "often causes a reader to return to a metaphor or a paragraph to marvel again at the exquisite marriage of language and meaning." And expressing gratitude that Bridgers writes for teenagers, Hipple concludes: "They deserve their literary giants, too; in Sue Ellen Bridgers, they have one."

■ Works Cited

Atkinson, Joan L., "Mote in the Eye," *School Library Journal*, January, 1982, p. 57.

Atkinson, J. L., review of *Notes for Another Life*, *Voice of Youth Advocates*, October, 1981, p. 20.

Bachelder, Linda, "Looking Backward: Trying to Find the Classic Young Adult Novel," *English Journal*, September, 1980, pp. 86-89.

Betts, Doris, "Themes and Variations on Family Life," *Washington Post Book World*, November 8, 1981, p. 17.

Bridgers, Sue Ellen, "My Life in Fiction," *ALAN Review*, fall, 1990, pp. 2-5.

Bridgers, S. E., "Stories My Grandmother Told Me," *ALAN Review*, Part 1, fall, 1985, pp. 44-47, Part 2, winter, 1986, pp. 53-55, 61.

Bridgers, S. E., *Something about the Author Autobiography Series*, Volume 1, Gale, 1986, pp. 39-52.

Buckley, Jeanne, Review of *Sara Will*, *Library Journal*, January, 1985, pp. 98-99.

Cannon, Bettie, "A Troubled Teen Discovers Family Roots and His Way," *Los Angeles Times*, October 3, 1987.

Carroll, Pamela Sissi, "Southern Literature for Young Adults: The Novels of Sue Ellen Bridgers," *ALAN Review*, fall, 1990, pp. 10-13.

Chatton, Barbara, review of *Permanent Connections*, *School Library Journal*, March, 1987, pp. 168-69.

Clinton, Dana G., "Summer Witness to Forces of Love," *Christian Science Monitor*, May 14, 1979, p. B6.

Digilio, Alice, "Sentimental, Seduction," *Washington Post Book World*, February 16, 1985.

Estes, Sally, review of *Sara Will*, *Booklist*, January 1, 1985, pp. 602-3.

Flanagan, Kate M., review of *All Together Now*, *Horn Book*, April, 1979, pp. 197-98.

French, Janet, review of *Notes for Another Life*, *School Library Journal*, September, 1981, p. 133.

Helfgott, Barbara, review of *Home before Dark*, *New York Times Book Review*, November 14, 1976, p. 40.

Hipple, Ted, "Sue Ellen Bridgers: An Appreciation," *ALAN Review*, fall, 1990, pp. 8-9.

Holtze, Sally Holmes, review of *Home before Dark*, *Horn Book*, April, 1977, pp. 165-66.

Paterson, Katherine, "Learning to Love," *Washington Post Book World*, May 13, 1979, pp. K1, K4.

Review of *Permanent Connections*, *Kliatt*, May, 1988, p. 2.

Review of *Permanent Connections*, *Publishers Weekly*, January 16, 1987, p. 75.

■ For More Information See

BOOKS

Children's Literature Review, Volume 18, Gale, 1989.

Contemporary Literary Criticism, Volume 26, Gale, 1983.

Dictionary of Literary Biography: American Writers for Children since 1960; Fiction, Gale, 1986.

Hipple, Ted, *Presenting Sue Ellen Bridgers*, Twayne, 1990.

Milner, Joseph O., *Children's Literature: Annual of the Modern Language Association Group on Children's Literature and the Children's Literature Association*, Volume 10, edited by Francelia Butler, Yale University Press, 1982.

PERIODICALS

Best Sellers, November, 1981.

Catholic Library World, March/April, 1987.

Children's Literature, Volume 10, 1982.

English Journal, September, 1981.

Horn Book, October, 1979.

Kirkus Reviews, May 15, 1979.

New York Times, December 4, 1979.

New York Times Book Review, November 14, 1976; April 29, 1979; November 2, 1980; November 15, 1981; July 26, 1987.

School Library Journal, January, 1977; May, 1979; September, 1981.

Voice of Youth Advocates, December, 1985.

Washington Post Book World, November 9, 1980; November 7, 1982.

World of Children's Books, spring, 1978.

—Sketch by Sharon Malinowski

Bruce Brooks

■ Personal

Born September 23, 1950, in Richmond, VA; son of Donald D. Brooks and Lelia Colleen Collins; married Penelope Winslow, June 17, 1978; children: Alexander. *Education:* University of North Carolina at Chapel Hill, B.A., 1972; University of Iowa, M.F.A, 1980. *Politics:* "Certainly." *Religion:* "Lapsed Baptist." *Hobbies and other interests:* Music, nature study, sports, reading.

■ Addresses

Home and office—11208 Legato Way, Silver Spring, MD 20901.

■ Career

Writer. Has worked variously as a letterpress printer, newspaper and magazine reporter, and teacher.

■ Awards, Honors

The Moves Make the Man was named a best book of 1984 by *School Library Journal,* a notable children's book by the American Library Association,

and a notable book of the year by the *New York Times,* 1984, received a *Boston Globe-Horn Book* Award and Newbery Honor from the American Library Association, both 1985; *Midnight Hour Encores* was named a best book of 1986 by *School Library Journal,* a best book for young adults in 1986 by the American Library Association, a *Horn Book* Fanfare Honor List book in 1987, a teacher's choice by the National Council of Teachers of English in 1987, a young adult choice by the International Reading Association in 1988, and an American Library Association/*Booklist* best of the eighties book for young adults; in 1989 *No Kidding* was named a best book for young adults by the American Library Association, an American Library Association/*Booklist* young adult editor's choice, a best book by *School Library Journal,* and a notable children's trade book in Social Studies; *Everywhere* was named a notable children's book by the American Library Association and a best book by *School Library Journal.*

■ Writings

FICTION

The Moves Make the Man, Harper, 1985.
Midnight Hour Encores, Harper, 1986.
No Kidding, Harper, 1989.
Everywhere, HarperCollins, 1990.
What Hearts (stories), HarperCollins, 1992.

NONFICTION

On the Wing: The Life of Birds from Feathers to Flight Scribner, 1989.
Predator, Farrar, Straus, 1991.

Nature by Design, Farrar, Straus, 1991.

■ Sidelights

Bruce Brooks is an award-winning novelist whose books, including *The Moves Make the Man, Midnight Hour Encores, No Kidding,* and *Everywhere,* have been described by reviewers as intelligent and thought-provoking. Christine McDonnell, writing in *Horn Book,* praised the "strong voice, unusual characters, and powerful emotional ties" exhibited in Brooks's stories. *Publishers Weekly* contributor Leonard Marcus was equally enthusiastic, deeming the author's works "impassioned, [and] often psychologically complex." Critical attention to these aspects of his work pleases Brooks who, in an interview with *Authors & Artists for Young Adults (AAYA),* remarked, "We are capable as readers of a wild and intricate world of thought and response and feeling—things going on in different layers at the same time. I hope to write books that involve all those layers of the thinking and feeling in my reader." To produce such responses, Brooks tackles sophisticated topics and avoids straightforward conclusions to his novels. He told *AAYA:* "I leave my books open-ended on purpose, because I want my readers to continue to think about the characters. I want the characters to come to life in the imaginations of the readers."

Citing the age of his characters, critics have christened the author a young adult or children's writer. Brooks accepts this tag ambivalently. He explained to *AAYA,* "I'm delighted to be called a children's book author. I'm thrilled that kids read my work, and I wouldn't trade my life in the world of children's literature for any authorial life I can imagine. I sincerely would not. At the same time I'm not going to call myself any 'kind' of writer; I'm not going to put any label on myself, because tomorrow I might want to write something that's completely inappropriate for kids to read, or I might want to write a book of monosyllables for kids below one year of age. I want to be free." Another reason Brooks avoids the children's author categorization is because he believes his works hold meaning for a diverse audience. "I don't feel I write books *about* kids, exactly; I feel I write books about families and friends—ultimately (this sounds corny) about love and the way it works between people," Brooks pronounced in an essay in *Speaking for Ourselves: Autobiographical Sketches by Notable Authors of Books for Young Adults.*

Yet, in an interview with Marcus, Brooks admitted that his first four fictional works have adolescent

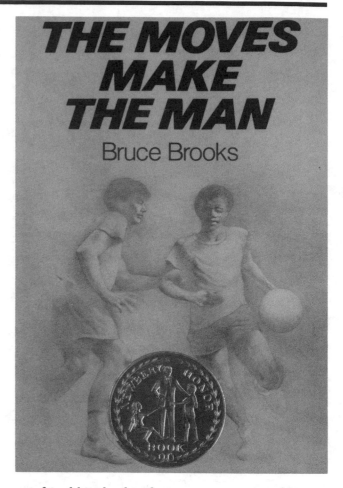

A friendship develops between two teenage athletes despite the tense racial climate of 1950s North Carolina in this 1985 Newbery Honor Book.

protagonists "because my own childhood is still something I am very much wondering about." After his parents divorced when he was six years old, Brooks shuttled back and forth between homes in Washington, D.C. and North Carolina. The locations and the families contrasted; Brooks told *AAYA* that he faced the demands of adapting to life both with his father's "smaller, urban-oriented family" and the "larger Southern clan" on his mother's side. In addition the author attended various schools and was often forced to move in the middle of the year. Although originally somewhat shy, Brooks drew on his strengths to adapt to his itinerant existence. He recalled, "I never really had the chance to patiently develop a long-term relationship with kids, so I was always having to grab what I could and make friends fast. Because of that I think I overcame my shyness and was a very vivacious kid. I was always a good talker, was always a funny storyteller, was always a good mimic—language for me was a fascinating tool. I discovered that I could really be myself in words."

In his interview with *AAYA* Brooks described how moving between the North and South and lacking permanent roots in either location affected him. "Belonging to both worlds but not belonging completely to either was really an experience that made me an observer and a student of social situations; it made me learn how to apply myself to people and activities and to figure out how to belong, after figuring out which natural parts of me belonged and which parts did not." Yet this upbringing also lent itself to a certain amount of alienation. The author continued: "I could never really relax and just say 'Ah, this is me, I'm among my peers.' I was never among my peers. I was always somewhat different from everyone else. I was always the Yankee kid in the South, and when I went back to the North I was always the Southern kid. It led me to simply be very watchful."

This tendency to observe and listen provided source material for Brooks when he began writing fiction. For example, during the 1950s and 60s the author's moves between the North and South allowed him a unique perspective on the burgeoning civil rights movement. Brooks was accustomed to racially mixed schools in Washington, D.C. However, in North Carolina he attended all-white schools and witnessed segregation—the enforced separation of black Americans from white in housing, education, and social situations—that was especially prevalent in the southern and border states. In 1954 seventeen of forty-nine American states permitted the practice. Brooks joined his mother's extended family in North Carolina in the wake of the 1954 landmark case *Brown v. Board of Education of Topeka,* which pronounced segregated schools inherently unequal. The ensuing movement to break down the barriers of racial discrimination—a process first enacted in public schools—was called integration, but despite the program, racial separation and tension remained prevalent.

This entrenched system of racial inequality is the background for Brooks's first novel, *The Moves Make the Man.* However, the author did not merely record his own experiences on paper; he deliberately created characters with backgrounds different than his. Explaining this approach in his interview with *AAYA,* Brooks remarked, "I make a very conscious effort not to use experiences or events in my life as models or direct inspiration for my work. That doesn't mean that behind my back—in the back of my mind—there isn't some unconscious inspiration; certainly there is. It's just that I have trust in my imagination, whereas I distrust the autobiographical tendency in me and in writing in general. I don't feel that my books are going to be good for being confessional, and I don't feel like I need to ask people to read through some kind of a therapeutic revision of my own history. I like to think that, hey, I've made up a *story* people will want to read, and to me the story happens completely in terms of the characters. It's important to me as a writer to feel the story flow through the characters in the situation in which *they* find *themselves.*"

In *The Moves Make the Man* the two main characters find themselves in an interracial friendship during the late 1950s in North Carolina. The tense racial climate at the time, however, is not conducive to such a relationship. Transcending the norms of segregation, the two boys discover that their racial differences prove subordinate to other aspects—both positive and negative—of their relationship. The story is related by basketball enthusiast Jerome Foxworthy, a thirteen-year-old black boy who spends a large portion of his summer vacation writing a chronicle of his experiences with Bix, his runaway friend. Jerome first saw Bix the previous summer in a baseball matchup between Bix's all-white team and the black team that Jerome's brother was coaching. Despite Jerome's general dislike for baseball, he is amazed by Bix's athletic ability, his technical knowledge about the position of shortstop, and his obvious dedication to the sport. Jerome hopes to meet Bix during a picnic after the game, but the shortstop has already left, and Jerome assumes he will never see the boy again.

Shortly before the school year begins Jerome learns that, as a result of legislation to integrate the schools in the town, he alone has been ordered to attend an all-white junior high school. There he hopes to join the basketball team, but his efforts are thwarted by the bigoted coach who purposely overlooks Jerome's talent. Instead of attempting to fight this injustice, Jerome continues to play basketball by himself at an isolated court. Even this activity is halted, though, when Jerome's mother is hospitalized after an accident, leaving him and his three brothers to divide the housekeeping chores. Since he is assigned the task of cooking, Jerome enrolls in the home economics class at school to hone his culinary skills and is surprised to find that Bix is also in the class. When the boys become partners in class, Jerome notices a change in Bix's personality; instead of the confident ballplayer Jerome had witnessed the previous summer, Bix seems to be a psychologically troubled boy.

Initially Jerome and Bix have little contact outside of school, but one night the two run into each other at the secluded basketball court. Bix is engrossed in an imaginary game, and Jerome approaches him, offering to teach him the fundamentals of basketball. Armed with natural athletic ability, Bix learns quickly but, to the annoyance of Jerome, he refuses to incorporate fake moves into his repertoire of basketball skills. Bix reasons that fakes are akin to cheating or lying, and if you can't win without them, the game is not worth playing. As the boys continue to meet at the court, Jerome gradually learns about Bix's unstable family situation. Confined to a hospital and recovering from a nervous breakdown, Bix's mother has left the boy at home with an insensitive stepfather who refuses to take Bix to see her.

Determined to visit his mother, Bix—with his sharpened basketball skills—proposes a deal to his stepfather, a former college basketball player. If Bix beats him at a game of one-on-one, his stepfather must let him visit his mother. Jerome serves as the referee in the heated contest, which Bix wins after he resorts to using fakes. Excited about his victory and eager to introduce his new friend to his mother, Bix asks Jerome to go along on his visit. However, the reunion is not what Bix anticipated, and the unexpected result stuns both boys. Unable to cope, Bix runs away, while Jerome is left trying to sort out the jarring events by recording them on paper.

The Moves Make the Man earned enthusiastic critical reception; it was named a Newbery honor book and won a *Boston Globe-Horn Book* Award. Yet Brooks confessed that such praise was not as heady as might be expected for a first-time novelist. At the time the awards were bestowed, Brooks explained, "I hadn't written a word of fiction in three years. I'd been working out the story on my second book, *Midnight Hour Encores*, for three years mentally, but I had not written anything because I was too busy earning a living, and I had a new child. So when the award came, I felt like a hypocrite. Here everybody was saying 'Oh, brilliant new writer' and I didn't *feel* like a *writer*. I felt like an editor of a newsletter on communications skills, because *that* was what I was doing with my life. So in a way my life didn't change after the awards for *The Moves Make the Man;* they were wonderful but *The Moves Make the Man* was old news—I'd written that book three years before."

Regardless of his contradictory feelings, Brooks's success afforded him new opportunities in his career. He told *AAYA* that "because *The Moves*

Fatherhood inspired Brooks to write this 1986 story about a sixteen-year-old music prodigy's coming-of-age.

Make the Man had done well, my wife and I together were able to say: On the strength of that let's take a chance. Let's borrow some money and see if you can write your second book that you've gotten all worked out and see if that does well too. Then, when that book comes out, we'll try and push it through and do a third book and a fourth and see what happens and see if we can piece together a living where you're a writer. So *The Moves Make the Man* coming out allowed me to take the really reckless adventure of trying to put together a life of writing rather than a life of trying to squeeze my writing in around the edges of a full-time job."

For Brooks's next, and equally successful, venture he produced *Midnight Hour Encores*, a story narrated by Sibilance (Sib for short), a sixteen-year-old musical prodigy who chose her name when she was eight years old. Sib, whose parents separated when she was one day old, lives with her father, Taxi, in Washington, D.C. Though her father repeatedly offers her the chance, Sib has no desire to meet her mother, and she maintains a relatively distant and secretive relationship with Taxi; she refuses to acknowledge or appreciate her father's emotional overtures. The self-absorbed Sib, one of the top-ranked cello players in the world, is wrapped up in her practices, competitions, and concerts. Music critics have deemed Sib's playing style "arrogant and cunning," a phrase that she admits also describes her personality. There are few cello players Sib admires or who can teach her at her level. However, after a concert circuit reporter tells her about a former Soviet child prodigy named Dzyga who, nearly forty years earlier, won the same international competitions Sib has, she listens to a recording of the Russian and realizes she has unearthed a possible mentor.

Unfortunately her new idol has not been seen or heard from in several decades. Sib suspects he made disparaging remarks about the Russian government and, as punishment, his work and recordings have been suppressed. Ever persistent, Sib vows to locate a recent album on which the cellist is featured and contact him through the record company. One day a clerk at a record store she frequents gives her a contraband album and, listening to it at home, Sib recognizes Dzyga's playing style. She sends a tape of herself playing hoping that Dzyga will be impressed by her talent and offer to teach her. Several months later Sib receives an audition offer from the Phrygian Institute, a new music school in California that boasts of an Eastern European virtuoso on its faculty. The letter alludes to a certain musical composition she recorded on her tape for Dzyga, so Sib is certain he is the faculty member. Sib wishes to attend the audition in order to meet Dzyga even though she has been accepted at Juilliard, a school in New York City with a renowned music program.

In an attempt to keep her plan a secret from her father, Sib tells him she wants to go to California to meet her mother. The ever-complying Taxi agrees, but informs his daughter that they will travel across the country by car. The trip allows Taxi the chance to provide a reluctant Sib with an accelerated course in 1960s lore complete with a Volkswagen van and music of the era. Sib initially thinks Taxi is using this education in the mood of the 1960s to explain why her mother left; eventually, though, she realizes that Taxi is trying to explain himself and his own fear of losing her. Nonetheless, Sib clings to her notion that she is a self-made young adult and shies away from Taxi's attempts at emotional bonding, even though her attitude hurts his feelings.

Upon arriving in California and dropping his daughter off at her mother's house, Taxi seems so distraught at the separation that Sib belatedly experiences pangs of emotion and guilt. Nonetheless they part, with Taxi—who has discovered the real reason for the trip—promising to attend Sib's audition. Upon meeting her mother, Connie, Sib is surprised by how different she is from her father. A fashionable, astute woman, Connie runs a successful business and seems the antithesis of a 1960s flower child. Despite her pent-up anger at her mother for abandoning her, Sib likes Connie and enjoys her stay in California. She even falls in love with her mother's male secretary, Martin, whose most important contribution to Sib is teaching her that her success and general well-being have resulted not entirely from her self-sufficiency, but also from her father's love. Sib ponders this information before her recital for the institute's faculty. At her audition, Sib finally sees Dzyga. Inspired by his appearance, she dazzles the audience with some of her best playing and, as an encore, improvises a light-hearted, snappy tune—to the dismay of those who expect formality in such a situation—which serves as a tribute to her father. *Midnight Hour Encores* ends as Sib decides what school to attend and, consequently, which parent to live with.

Midnight Hour Encores was favorably received by critics. Deeming the work "another terrific book" for Brooks in *Washington Post Book World* review, author Katherine Paterson acknowledged the welcome complexity of *Midnight Hour Encores*. "This is a book the reader will have to fool around with, poke into, and tell in his own accents," Paterson insisted. Although several reviews of the book focused on the novel's emotional coming-of-age slant, Brooks remarked in his interview with *AAYA* that "to me *Midnight Hour Encores* is about being a father. I wrote that book in the year after my son was born. The most important thing in my life was being a father. None of it was the same as Taxi's experiences, but a lot of the same feelings about fatherhood applied, and my curiosity about the future—of what you get when you invest certain things in the very early days of your child's life—inspired my imagination to come up with those characters and that story."

For Brooks's next literary enterprise he again tackled a sophisticated topic, but also took a calculated risk by switching from first-to third-person narration and setting his story in the future. *No Kidding* presents a portrait of life in twenty-first century Washington, D.C., where alcoholics constitute sixty-nine percent of the population and nearly fifty percent of the chronic drinkers are under treatment. The problem has so overwhelmed social agencies that upon turning twelve years old, a child can recommend that a parent be committed to a rehabilitation institute. In Brooks's bleak representation of the future, the population has declined drastically and forty percent of the city's homes are empty. This has occurred not only because many people believe getting drunk is more important than family life, but also because the cathode-ray tubes in television sets cause sterility. One of the most pronounced reactions to these societal ills has come from organized religion. Various denominations have united to condemn alcohol and those who use it.

Alcoholism has so permeated society that programs have been instituted in schools to handle alcoholic offspring, more commonly referred to as AOs. Schools are categorized according to whether the

Brooks's 1989 futuristic novel presents a bleak world in which alcoholics constitute more than half the population.

curriculum is geared to AOs or non-AOs. The children of alcoholics are defined by that status first, rather than as individuals. Therefore, all behavior of AOs is considered a product of their exposure to alcoholism, and certain tenets have been established that explain actual or expected reactions to most situations. For example, one principle is: "The Alcoholic Offspring cherish the illusion of control over all lives that touch them." *No Kidding*'s main character, Sam, is a prime illustration of this dictum. The fourteen-year-old has assumed responsibility of his family since his father left to join a religious order.

Complicating Sam's formidable task is his mother's alcoholism, which makes her unable to properly care for Sam or his younger brother, Ollie. After trying in vain to care for his mother at home, Sam has resorted to temporarily institutionalizing her. In addition, he has placed his brother Ollie—who is unaware his mother is an alcoholic—with foster parents, the Bigelows. As the story opens, Sam, who is now of the legal age to retain custody of his mother, decides to bring her home. He manages to get her a job and an apartment, but must decide whether or not to reunite the entire family. Sam wavers on the issue of bringing his brother home, because he wonders if Ollie, a rather enigmatic boy, will be better off with the Bigelows. At the end of the book, Sam's mother manipulates events to generate the outcome, giving Sam the chance to assume the role of a child once again.

Brooks brought intimate knowledge of alcoholism to *No Kidding;* his own mother suffered from the addiction. As for how her affliction affected him, Brooks admitted to *AAYA* that it is a "question I'll be answering for the rest of my life. It certainly would be artificial of me to say I wasn't intrigued with all the questions about alcoholism and its affect on kids because of my own experience. *No Kidding* certainly came out of that fascination and the ongoing insight that I'm having. Really though, none of the characters in the book—I was very careful about this—are like me particularly. They're not going through the same things I've been through; certainly my experience as a kid isn't like theirs. I think one of the reasons I wrote *No Kidding* the way I wrote it was to take a lot of societal things to their extreme expressions and to indicate some future pitfalls of our current tendencies to institutionalize private problems. But I really started thinking about Ollie and Sam and their mother and their father and their society in their own terms. To me it wasn't a book about an issue, it wasn't a book about my life, it was a book about those characters."

Brooks's next book, *Everywhere*, is a shorter novel targeted at a younger audience, but it still contains the complex thoughts and ideas that mark the author's works. In *Everywhere*, a nameless young protagonist frets about his beloved grandfather who has suffered a heart attack and is near death. The reticent young boy, who has been known to sit motionless for prolonged periods of time, has enjoyed a special relationship with his grandfather. He recalls how the two would spend hours building things in a garage workshop and how his grandfather would accommodate him by always wearing the bow tie his grandson picked out even if it clashed with his shirt. When a local nurse arrives to tend to the grandfather, she brings her nephew Dooley to cheer up the boy. Dooley suggests that they perform a soul-switching ceremony; he insists that by killing an animal—that somehow resembles the sick man—in a ceremony, the boy's grandfather will be saved. During the course of the story, the boy ponders his grandpa's fate, his own mortality, and the ethical question of taking one life to save another.

Commenting about *Everywhere* during his *AAYA* interview, Brooks explained that he meant it to be a "subtle and complex book" and added, "I hope that doesn't argue against its being meaningful to a nine-year-old." Expanding on this idea the author stated, "I like all of my books to be easy to read, and yet at the same time I don't like them to be over in a flash. I like them to be subtle and complicated, and I like the ramifications to continue to intrigue people." Because of this philosophy, Brooks feels that his books are suitable for a diverse audience. "I never think of children as my readers when I write," he remarked. "I don't think of adults as my readers when I write. I'm completely wrapped up in the story and in the act of somehow communicating to someone. I don't define a child in my mind as a reader. I never once in any of my books have made a single change, nor have been asked to make a single change by any of my editors, expressly because the books were intended for kids."

With his fictional works, Brooks has achieved substantial success, and while he labored for many years before being published, he points to his persistence and love of writing as the reasons he can keep producing books. He recalled in his interview with *AAYA*: "I know that from the time I was about twelve or thirteen, all I really wanted to do was to spend my life writing novels, and it never

The relationship between a young boy and his beloved grandfather is threatened in this 1990 work.

occurred to me that I couldn't. I could sit down and write, and *that's* what defines you as a writer, not that you've achieved a certain level of income or prestige or anything like that. When you're thirteen—at least when I was thirteen—you didn't know about things like income and prestige. You knew about what you liked to do, and what I liked to do most was write."

Brooks's keen observational skills were conducive to a writing career. He suggested in *AAYA* that "most writers have that element of being a spy in their characters. We are all a bunch of spies. How else would we be so good in mimicking different people's voices and knowing what certain gesture a minor character would use exactly at a certain moment to express something that we want our readers to perceive without having to spell it out for them? How would we know that, if we weren't really good watchers, really good empathizers, who knew how people felt? I think that writers pay incredibly precise attention to things. We notice why things happen, how things happen, and that makes us able to stage the mechanics of lives in print."

Writing books has been a happy enterprise for Brooks, but he realizes that future success is not assured. He told *AAYA* that "one of the nice things about being a writer is also the biggest challenge about being a writer: you're always going to be a beginner as soon as you finish something. You wrap up one book and immediately you are rookie again, because you've never written your next book. You start all over, and you're fresh and you're challenged and you're green, and you don't yet know how to solve all the problems that are going to come up. You're going to have to gain wisdom and technique as you write, so that you can take care of these new challenges. It's a constantly refreshing recurrence of being a beginner. That keeps me from being goal-oriented. My goal is to be able to write my next book. That's it."

Commenting on his future plans, Brooks concluded in his *AAYA* interview: "In my work I want to go places I haven't been, to figure out ways of seeing things that I haven't experienced before, and to see things in ways that I haven't seen them. Writing is really an adventure. That's what I like about it. It is completely adventurous. My life is nothing but one adventure after the next, and I stand in the middle of my life with, for me, a very nice balance of control and curiosity. I don't know what's going to happen when I decide to write my next book. That keeps me feeling very alive, keeps me feeling very much that I'm not just going through the motions, but that I'm *living* while I'm writing."

■ Works Cited

Brooks, Bruce, essay in *Speaking for Ourselves: Autobiographical Sketches by Notable Authors of Books for Young Adults*, edited by Donald R. Gallo, National Council of Teachers of English, 1990, p. 34.

Brooks, Bruce, *Everywhere*, HarperCollins, 1990.

Brooks, Bruce, interview with Mary Ruby for *Authors & Artists for Young Adults*, conducted September 25, 1991.

Brooks, Bruce, *Midnight Hour Encores*, Harper, 1986.

Brooks, Bruce, *No Kidding*, Harper, 1989.

Brooks, Bruce, *The Moves Make the Man*, Harper, 1985.

Marcus, Leonard, interview with Bruce Brooks for *Publishers Weekly*, July 29, 1990, pp. 214-215.

McDonnell, Christine, "New Voices, New Visions: Bruce Brooks," *Horn Book*, March/April, 1987, pp. 188-190.

■ For More Information See

PERIODICALS

Horn Book, January/February, 1986.

New York Times Book Review, January 4, 1987; June 25, 1989.

Washington Post Book World, November 9, 1986.

—Sketch by Mary K. Ruby

Alice Childress

■ Personal

Surname is pronounced "*chill*-dress"; born October 12, 1920, in Charleston, SC; married second husband, Nathan Woodward (a musician and composer), July 17, 1957; children: (first marriage) Jean (Mrs. Richard Lee). *Education:* Attended public schools in New York, NY.

■ Addresses

Home—New York, NY. *Office*—Beacon Press, 25 Beacon St., Boston, MA 02108. *Agent*—Flora Roberts, Inc., 157 West 57th St., Penthouse A, New York, NY 10019.

■ Career

Actress, director, novelist, and playwright. Began theater career as an actress, with first appearance in *On Strivers Row*, 1940; actress and director with the American Negro Theater, New York City, 1941-52; actress in stage plays, including *Natural Man*, 1941, and *Anna Lucasta*, 1944; directed and performed in her own play, *Florence*, 1949; also performed on Broadway and television. Lecturer at universities and schools; member of panel discus-

sions and conferences on black American theater at numerous institutions, including New School for Social Research, 1965, and Fisk University, 1966; visiting scholar at Radcliffe Institute for Independent Study (now Mary Ingraham Bunting Institute), Cambridge, MA, 1966-68; playwright-scholar in residence, Cambridge University, 1966-68. Member of governing board of Frances Delafield Hospital. *Member:* PEN, Dramatists Guild (member of council), American Federation of Television and Radio Artists, Writers Guild of America East (member of council), Harlem Writers Guild.

■ Awards, Honors

Obie Award for best original Off-Broadway play, 1956, for *Trouble in Mind;* John Golden Fund for Playwrights grant, 1957; Rockefeller grant, 1967; *A Hero Ain't Nothin' but a Sandwich* was named one of the outstanding books of the year by *New York Times Book Review,* 1973, and a best young adult book of 1975 by American Library Association; Woodward School Book Award, 1974, Jane Addams Children's Book Honor Award for young adult novel, 1974, National Book Award nomination, 1974, and Lewis Carroll Shelf Award, University of Wisconsin, 1975, all for *A Hero Ain't Nothin' but a Sandwich;* Childress was named honorary citizen of Atlanta, GA, 1975, for opening of the play *Wedding Band;* Sojourner Truth Award, National Association of Negro Business and Professional Women's Clubs, 1975; Virgin Islands Film Festival Award for best screenplay, 1977, for *A Hero Ain't Nothin' but a Sandwich;* first Paul Robeson Award for outstanding contributions to the performing arts, Black Filmmakers Hall of Fame, 1977, for *A Hero Ain't Nothin' but a Sandwich;* "Alice Childress Week" officially observed in Charleston and Columbia, SC, 1977, to celebrate opening of the play *Sea Island Song; Rainbow Jordan* was named one of the best books by *School Library Journal,* 1981, one of the outstanding books of the year by *New York Times,* 1982, and a notable children's trade book in social studies by National Council for the Social Studies and Children's Book Council, 1982; Coretta Scott King Award honorable mention, 1982, for *Rainbow Jordan.*

■ Writings

Like One of the Family: Conversations from a Domestic's Life, Independence Publishers, 1956, reprinted with an introduction by Trudier Harris, Beacon Press, 1986.
(Editor and contributor) *Black Scenes* (collection of scenes from plays), Doubleday, 1971.
A Hero Ain't Nothin' but a Sandwich (young adult novel; also see below), Coward, 1973.
A Short Walk (adult novel), Coward, 1979.
Rainbow Jordan (young adult novel), Coward, 1981.
Many Closets, Coward. 1987.
Those Other People, Putnam, 1989.

PLAYS

Florence (one-act play), produced in New York City at American Negro Theater, 1949.
Just a Little Simple (based on Langston Hughes's short story collection *Simple Speaks His Mind*), produced in New York City at Club Baron Theater, September, 1950.
Gold through the Trees, produced at Club Baron Theater, 1952.
String (one-act play; based on Guy de Maupassant's story "A Piece of String"; also see below), produced Off-Broadway, 1969.
Mojo: A Black Love Story (one-act play; also see below), produced in New York City at New Heritage Theater, 1970.
Trouble in Mind (produced Off-Broadway, 1955), revised version published in *Black Theater: A Twentieth-Century Collection of the Work of Its Best Playwrights,* edited by Lindsay Patterson, Dodd, 1971.
Mojo [and] *String,* Dramatists Play Service, 1971.
Wedding Band: A Love/Hate Story in Black and White (produced in Ann Arbor, MI, 1966; also see below), Samuel French, 1973.

When the Rattlesnake Sounds (children's play), illustrated by Charles Lilly, Coward, 1975.
Let's Hear It for the Queen (children's play), Coward, 1976.
Sea Island Song, produced in Charleston, SC, 1977.
(With husband, Nathan Woodard) *Gullah,* produced in Amherst, Massachusetts, 1984.
(With Woodard) *Moms: A Praise Play for a Black Comedienne* (based on the life of Jackie "Moms" Mabley), produced Off-Broadway, 1987.

Also author of *Martin Luther King at Montgomery, Alabama,* music by Woodard, 1969; *A Man Bearing a Pitcher,* 1969; *The African Garden,* music by Woodard, 1971; *Vashti's Magic Mirror;* and *The Freedom Drum,* music by Woodard, produced as *Young Man Martin Luther King* by Performing Arts Repertory Theater (on tour), 1969-71.

SCREENPLAYS

Wine in the Wilderness: A Comedy-Drama, Dramatists Play Service, 1969.
Wedding Band (based on her play of the same title), American Broadcasting Companies (ABC-TV), 1973.
A Hero Ain't Nothin' but a Sandwich (based on her novel of the same title), New World Pictures, 1978.
String (based on her play of the same title), Public Broadcasting Service (PBS-TV), 1979.

Contributor of plays, articles, and fiction to numerous books, including *Black American Literature and Humanism,* University of Kentucky Press, 1981; *Black Women Writers (1950-1980): A Critical Evaluation,* Doubleday-Anchor, 1984; *The Young American Basic Reading Program,* Lyons & Carnaham, 1972; *Success in Reading,* Silver Burdette, 1972; and *Keeping the Faith,* edited by Pat Exum. Contributor of plays and short stories to anthologies, including *The Best Short Stories by Negro Writers: An Anthology from 1899 to the Present,* edited by Langston Hughes, Little, Brown, 1967; *Plays to Remember,* Macmillan, 1968; *Best Short Plays of 1972,* edited by Stanley Richards, Chilton, 1972; *Best Short Plays of the World Theater, 1968-1973,* edited by Richards, Crown, 1973; and *Anthology of the Afro-American in the Theater: A Critical Approach,* edited by L. Patterson, Publishers Agency, 1978. Contributor of plays, articles, and reviews to periodicals, including *Masses and Mainstream, Black World, Freedomways, Essence, Negro Digest,* and the *New York Times.* Author of "Here's Mildred" column in *Baltimore Afro-American,* 1956-58.

■ Sidelights

Alice Childress is a novelist and playwright known for her sensitive characterizations of poor and downtrodden people coping with a harsh and often bigoted environment. Writing about the experiences of black people in America, Childress has deliberately chosen not to write about those who have triumphed in a hostile world. "I recall teachers urging me to write composition papers about Blacks who were 'accomplishers,'" she said in *Children's Literature Review* "—those who win prizes and honors by overcoming cruel odds; the victory might be won over racial, physical, economic, or other handicaps but the end result had to inspire the reader/audience to become 'winners'.... I turned against the tide and to this day I continue to write about those who come in second, or not at all."

Like many contemporary minority writers, Childress rejects the idea that good writing must describe what critics often call "universal experience." She commented in *Children's Literature Review:* "We are told that 'the best' is that subject matter applicable to the whites of the world; to the same extent it may acceptably touch upon the Black experience. That measure of 'universality' and 'common experience' places shackles on a writer's pen." Childress argues that, in a traditionally white literary market, black writers carry a burden that white writers do not encounter. While most writers wish to win approval for their work, black writers have often felt an additional pressure to use their fiction to elicit approval or acceptance for their race. Reacting to the negative images left behind by centuries of racial stereotyping and intolerance, some black writers have become caught up with the unlikely burden of demonstrating the human worth of their characters to a possibly hostile white readership. In framing his or her work to be positive and palatable to a white audience, an individual writer's experience and insight can be neglected. "Too often," Childress said in *Children's Literature Review*, "we Black writers are image-building for others to measure our capability, acceptability, or human worth."

Some black writers, Childress continued, attempt to avoid this image-building trap by de-emphasizing the effects of race and racism on their literary creations. "I've heard some of us say, 'I am not a Black writer, I'm a *person*, an *artist*.' I've never heard any whites decry being *white* for fear that being *white* and a *person* might cancel one or the other." The author believes that black literature

need not be a reaction to—or denial of—discrimination, but should effectively express the individual writer's knowledge of the world—including its discrimination. "Politically I see my Black experience, my characters, and myself in very special circumstances," Childress stated in *Children's Literature Review.* "A Black writer *is a person* and there should be no room for contradiction. The twisted circumstances under which we live is grist for the writing mill."

In accord with her artistic principles, Childress's novels and plays affirm the experiences of the kind of life she knew in her childhood in Harlem, a section of New York City that became one of the largest black communities in the United States. In *Something about the Author* (SATA), Childress described the people she grew up with—and chooses to write about—as "the poor, genteel, and sensitive people who are seamstresses, coal-carriers, candy-makers, sharecroppers, bakers, baby care-takers, housewives, foot soldiers, penny candy sellers, vegetable peelers who are somehow able to sustain within themselves the poet's heart, sensitivity and appreciation of pure emotion, the ability to freely spend tears and laughter without saving them up for a rainy day. I was raised by and among such people living on the poorest blocks in Harlem."

Born in 1920 in Charleston, South Carolina, Childress moved to Harlem at the age of five. Although she attended grade school in Harlem and three years of high school in Harlem, Childress says she received most of her education from the world around her. She credits her grandmother, Eliza, who raised her, with a good deal of her intellectual development. Eliza, an avid storyteller, related to her granddaughter the history of her mother Annie, Childress's great-grandmother. Annie was born into slavery, and she did not know about the emancipation of slaves after the Civil War because her "owners" did not bother to tell her; she remained a slave until civil law belatedly forced the slaveholders to free her. Other members of Annie's family had been sold before the emancipation, and since she had no one to take her in, the slaveholders brought the thirteen-year-old girl to Charleston and abandoned her there. Eventually a kind white woman, Anna Campbell, took Annie into her home. When Annie became pregnant with the child of Anna Campbell's son, the young sailor deserted Annie, Anna, and his newborn child, Eliza. The three women continued to live together until Anna's death. In her will, Anna left her house to Annie and Eliza, but since laws of the time did

Ruby Dee starred in a 1972 adaptation of *Wedding Band: A Love/Hate Story in Black and White*, Childress's controversial play concerning a ten-year love affair between a black woman and a white man.

not allow black heirs to inherit if white heirs existed, Anna's distant relatives claimed the house. Annie later married and raised a large family, but poverty made it difficult for her children to stay in school. Yet even though Eliza was taken out of school in the fifth grade to help support the family, she found time to educate herself.

Telling Annie's story was difficult for Eliza since it chronicles so much inhumanity and injustice, and Childress is not nostalgic about her own or her family's past. "There is nothing grand, fine or right about going hungry, standing on the receiving end of persecution or being any other kind of loser," she emphasized in *SATA*, "except coming through such experiences with your head held up ready for the next round." Nonetheless, Childress believes that the past is a central force in the present and defines herself and her work accordingly. "Events from the distant past, things which took place before I was born, have influence over the content, form, and commitment of my work. I am a descendant of a particular American slave, my great grandmother, Annie."

Inspired by her grandmother's storytelling, Childress became interested in theater and, in 1941, joined the American Negro Theater in Harlem. She established herself as an actress, performing in such plays as *On Strivers Row* and *Natural Man* in the early 1940s. In 1944 she worked with many famous actors in the opening cast of Philip Yor-

dan's *Anna Lucasta*, including Ossie Davis, Ruby Dee, and Sidney Poitier. Poitier, as quoted by Trudier Harris in the *Dictionary of Literary Biography*, commented about his acquaintance with Childress in the late 1940s: "I learned more from her than I did from any other person I knew during that period of my life—things about life that no one else ever took the time to explain. She opened me up to positive new ways of looking at myself and others, and she encouraged me to explore the history of black people." During her eleven years with the American Negro Theater, Childress served as performer, drama coach, director, member of the board of directors, and, temporararily, as the personnel director. During this time Childress was also raising Jean, a daughter from her first marriage, and working at various jobs to support herself and her child.

In 1949 the American Negro Theater produced Childress's first play, *Florence*, which she wrote, starred in, and directed. In this one-act play a black woman and a white woman strike up a conversation through an iron grille in a Jim Crow railroad station (a station segregated between blacks and whites by state law). Mama, the black woman, whose daughter, Florence, has been unsuccessful in her attempts to become a professional actress, plans to go to New York to bring her daughter home. Mrs. Carter, the white woman, condescendingly promises to find Florence a job as a domestic, and continues to demonstrate her bigotry and stereotyping throughout their encounter. After talking to Mrs. Carter, Mama cancels her trip to New York and sends the ticket money to Florence with a note—"Keep trying." The play succeeds in capturing the dignity of "the genteel poor," according to *Dictionary of Literary Biography* contributor Rosemary Curb, who elaborated that "the simple, direct plot played out in a drab setting provides the opportunity for Mama's strength of character to shine." Although the play was performed in a small loft in Harlem with limited seating space, it elicited favorable critical attention and established Childress as a playwright.

Combining themes from *Florence* with characters and ideas from American writer Langston Hughes's story *Simple Speaks His Mind*, Childress wrote a play entitled *Just a Little Simple*, which was produced at the Club Baron Theater in 1950. Childress made further strides in the theater when, in 1952, her play *Gold through the Trees* became the first play by a black woman to be professionally produced on the American stage.

Childress's own experiences in the theater formed the basis of *Trouble in Mind*, her play about one woman's fight for artistic integrity as an actress in a play about racial tensions. In the 1955 production, the lead character Wileta, an experienced and knowledgeable actress, believes that the play's script is ill-conceived with regard to the motivation of her character—a black mother who illogically sends her son out into the hands of an angry mob. When the white director of the play lightly dismisses her insight, Wileta heads a cast walk-out. Under pressure, the director calls the script-writer back to make the changes to the script that Wileta suggested. Curb maintained that in this production Childress ironically gave in to pressures to create an audience-pleasing "happy ending" for her play. In a later published version the director does not reappear at the play's end, and the cast is apparently left without jobs after the walk-out. In its early version, *Trouble in Mind* ran for ninety-one performances at the Greenwich Mews Theater in New York. When it won the Obie Award for the best original Off-Broadway play in 1955, Childress became the first woman ever to have won the award. The play was optioned for Broadway production, but, viewed as a commercial risk, it was never produced.

During the 1960s Childress wrote *Wedding Band: A Love/Hate Story in Black and White*, first produced at the University of Michigan in Ann Arbor in 1966. The play is the story of a ten-year-old love affair between a black woman and a white man. Living in South Carolina during World War I, they cannot marry because of state laws prohibiting interracial marriage. No one from among their families, friends, or neighbors supports the relationship between Herman and Julia, and the ostracization has worn on both of them. As the play opens, Herman brings Julia a wedding ring which she must wear on a chain under her clothes. The couple fantasizes about escape, but because they are poor, they can find no feasible alternative to their situation. During a visit with Julia, Herman becomes feverish with influenza. Julia's landlady refuses to get medical help, not wishing to be implicated in their illegal bond, and even Herman's mother waits until dark to take him to a doctor. The resentments generated between families and friends by the relationship over the past ten years explode over Herman's sick bed, and a provoked Julia hurls racial insults at his family as they take him away. When a dying Herman returns to Julia with two tickets for a steamer to New York, Julia locks everyone else out of her apartment and holds him as he dies, letting him dream he is sailing to New York.

Wedding Band does not paint a comfortable picture of life in America. Harris summarized that the play's "dialogue is replete with racial and ethnic insults and uglinesses, and the backdrop provided is war and influenza. Characters go about their lives under impossible circumstances at worst, and trying ones at best." Without offering resolution, romance, or heroism, *Wedding Band* represents both love and hate, humanity and inhumanity in a racially divided society. Julia, for example, feels deep love and respect for Herman and at the same time "tormented revulsion from him as part of the community which has victimized her people," *Nation* critic Harold Clurman remarked. Many reviewers commented that despite the decades that have passed since the abolishment of laws against interracial marriage, the play continues to hit a nerve in audiences of all races.

Wedding Band was, according to Curb, almost too honest and sensitive to be commercially successful. "Neither white producers nor black revolutionary theater groups were likely to relish the dramatic portrait of an interracial love affair in *Wedding Band* at the time it was written. In contrast to the violent 'kill whitey' plays that stole the media spotlight during the height of the black revolution, the plays of Childress never condone needless hostility or defensive machismo." Childress herself commented in *SATA* that *Wedding Band* was "a play I did not want to write.... I really did not wish to beat the drum for an interracial couple and yet there they were in front of me, not giving a damn about public opinion of this day or that past day."

Wedding Band received excellent reviews for its Ann Arbor run, but was never produced on Broadway. It was six years before a major production, directed by Childress and Joseph Papp, was produced at the New York Royal Shakespeare Festival. Ruby Dee, who starred in the play's Ann Arbor and New York productions as well as the 1973 film produced for television, commented on Childress's career, as quoted by Harris: "There is a tragedy involved here that cannot be underestimated. Alice Childress is a splendid playwright, a veteran— indeed a pioneer. She has won awards, acclaim, and everything but consistent productions. It is difficult to think of a play by a white writer earning the reviews that *Wedding Band* earned in 1965 and having to wait until 1973 to reach the New York stage. It proves one thing: We may salute and savor the glory of the black theatrical pioneer, but in a land where materialism is all-important, the real salutes take longer." When ABC ran the screenplay on network television, several local stations refused to air it, and others tried to avoid controversy by showing it after midnight when viewership was at a minimum.

Although mainstream theater and film continued to resist Childress's work, during the 1960s and 1970s she was increasingly welcomed into academic and critical circles, appearing frequently on television and at universities to speak about black artists in the American theater. In recognition of her outstanding contribution to drama, she received a two-year appointment at the Radcliffe Institute for Independent Study and was the playwright-scholar in residence at Cambridge from 1966 to 1968. Childress also took time to travel, making extensive trips to the Soviet Union in 1971, China in 1973, and Ghana, West Africa, in 1974.

During this period, Childress was approached by Ferdinand Monjo, an editor and author of children's books, who suggested that she write a book

Childress traces a young boy's search for identity in a violent urban environment in this novel from 1973.

for young people about drugs, since she was interested in the subject. The result was her multi-award-winning young adult novel *A Hero Ain't Nothin' but a Sandwich,* the story of Benjie, a thirteen-year-old boy dangerously close to heroin addiction. As he relates at the start of the novel, Benjie's childhood has apparently been lost to the ghetto: "Now I am thirteen, but when I was a chile, it was hard to be a chile because my block is a tough block and my school is a tough school. I'm not trying to cop out on what I do or don't do cause man is man and chile is chile, but I ain't a chile no more. Don't nobody wanta be no chile cause, for some reason, it just hold you back in a lotta ways." Benjie's mother, Rose, working to support him and his grandmother, lacks the time to guide him. Her new boyfriend, Butler Craig, tries to reach out to Benjie, but Benjie has been alone too long to trust this new element in his mother's life. After experimenting with other drugs, Benjie shoots heroin on a friend's dare. Betraying himself by nodding off in school, he is sent to a rehabilitation program, but upon his release, he promptly steals from his family to buy more heroin. In an attempt to steal a neighbor's toaster, Benjie nearly falls from a roof. Butler saves him from the fall and in doing so earns Benjie's trust, presenting real hope for a meaningful relationship between them. At the end of the story, Butler waits at the rehabilitation center where Benjie has an appointment, leaving the reader to decide whether Butler's intervention is enough to bring Benjie around.

Benjie's story unfolds through his own narrative and the narratives of a variety of people around him, including his teachers, principal, pusher, mother, friends, and Butler. Elbert R. Hill commented in *Children's Novels and the Movies* that the "first person narration is particularly effective in bringing out the uncertainty and ambiguity the various characters feel about their own identities; their stories provide an effective parallel to Benjie's own confusion and uncertainty." These uncertainties even invade the structure of Benjie's education. One of his teachers, Nigeria Greene, is a modern-thinking black man whose highest priority is to teach his students to take pride in being black. While Greene daily emphasizes his own scorn for white values, his social position as a teacher places him almost as far outside his students' circle as if he were white. In contrast to Greene, Bernard Cohen is a white middle-class liberal who wants to teach his students the traditional subjects. Cohen fears that thinking like Greene's will put him out of a job, and although he is generally well-intentioned, he is absorbed, like Greene, with justifying what he is doing. Although each man has an understandable individual perspective, as educators they are shamelessly neglecting Benjie. Harris summarized, "Greene must put Benjie's addiction in the context of his [black] nationalism, and Cohen must put it in the context of his status as a martyr going against all odds to teach children in the ghetto. The principal sees the bust as an embarassment to his career ... None of them really cares for Benjie as Benjie. And he feels that."

Walter the pusher's narrative gruesomely parallels the self-justifying stands of Benjie's educators. Walter believes that if he wasn't selling drugs to the kids in the neighborhood, somebody else would be. His chilling logic is portrayed as a reflection of American materialism. "Me, I say screw the weak and screw the power. If it's free enterprise, then let it be free.... All them that wanta die let em put a five in my pocket, and I'll help em to slowly make it on outta here, with a smile on their face ... and one on mine." Childress admits to having second thoughts about including the drug dealer's point of view in a children's novel. "I was tempted to remove 'The Pusher' from *A Hero Ain't Nothin' but a Sandwich*," she said in *Children's Literature Review*. "The villain was too persuasive, too good at self-defense, too winning in his sinning; however, he is the toughest form of street temptation, so I let him live." The sympathetic view of Walter also demonstrates that to Childress the problem is not one isolated villain, but a network of influences in the environment that produces such villains. Ortiz commented that "there are no evil characters in the book, though there are evil consequences: a perfect example of hating the sin, but not the sinner."

A Hero Ain't Nothin' but a Sandwich offers the message that someone must get beyond political, economic, and selfish contexts, and think about the welfare of the particular child. The human side of Benjie that Greene and Cohen neglect is rapidly becoming lost to the toughness of the streets and to heroin. Ortiz summarized that Childress, "without condoning or relieving [Benjie] of the responsibility which is rightfully his, shows him becoming a junkie, but does not lose sight of the fact that he is a child who is hurting, in trouble, and worthy of our sympathy." The only character in the novel who seems able and willing to respond to the complexity of Benjie's personality and needs is Butler Craig, who is, according to Alleen Pace and Kenneth L. Donelson in *Literature for Today's*

Young Adults, "one of the noblest creations in young adult fiction."

Although Childress won many literary awards for *A Hero Ain't Nothin' but a Sandwich*, the book was also banned by several school libraries—and reinstated in one Long Island, New York library only by order of the Supreme Court in 1983. Unlike adults who wish to protect young people from harsh realities, Childress believes that her open look at drug use among kids is one way to fight the problem. Since "the art of living cannot be taught or learned by rote," she commented in *Literature for Today's Young Adults*, children should learn about the drug scene at home and at school, where they can safely learn to exercise their judgement before they encounter the actual temptation. Having corresponded with kids who have opted not to take drugs, Childress has faith in young people's capacity to decide correctly when they are armed with knowledge. "Their letters let me know that 'cinema verite' in writing, exposes the land mines and booby traps to be found on the contemporary scene," Childress asserted in *Literature for Today's Young Adults*.

Childress also wrote two plays for young people during the 1970s. *When the Rattlesnake Sounds* is a one-act play depicting a scene in the life of Harriet Tubman, the nineteenth-century abolitionist and pioneer of the Underground Railroad, a network that helped hundreds of slaves to escape to the North. The play depicts a single event in which Tubman and two other women work as laundresses in order to make money for the Underground Railroad. When one of the women voices second thoughts about taking part in this dangerous project, Tubman encourages her with stories and a hymn. Zena Sutherland commented in *Bulletin of the Center for Children's Books* that even though there is little action in this short play, Childress's "deftness" in developing "characters and background in so brief and static a setting" creates deeply moving drama. *Horn Book* contributor Mary M. Burns called the play "a poignant celebration of courage, a beautifully crafted work."

On a very different note, in 1976 Childress adapted the nursery rhyme "The Queen of Hearts" into a play for children to perform called *Let's Hear It for the Queen*. In the adaptation Childress added a score for a rock band, and provided new motivational dimensions, including the perspective of the knave of hearts who stole the tarts, and the insensitivity of the king for not giving the tarts to the knave in the first place.

AVON BOOKS · 0-380-58974-5 · (CANADA $3.95) · U.S. $2.95

She's too brave to be a child, too scared to be a woman.

Rainbow Jordan

By Alice Childress

Author of A HERO AIN'T NOTHIN' BUT A SANDWICH

"RAINBOW JORDAN is a beautiful book!"
The New York Times

Childress's award-winning 1981 novel explores the turbulent life of a mature fourteen-year-old as she faces the break-up of her family.

Childress's 1979 adult novel, *A Short Walk*, chronicles the life of Cora James from her birth in 1900 to her death in mid-century. Cora, the daughter of a wealthy white boy she never meets and a poor black girl who dies in childbirth, wanders through her life, marrying, divorcing, becoming a card dealer in a gambling house, and joining a minstrel show. The chronicle of Cora's life is at the same time a sojourn through American history, highlighting such events as Jamaican black nationalist leader Marcus Garvey's "back-to-Africa" movement of the 1920s and the Great Depression of the 1930s. *Washington Post* contributor Joseph McLellan observed that although the novel is not easily summarized, Cora's "wandering has been through some interesting scenery, and instead of a conclusion the reader has come to know a human being—complex, struggling valiantly and totally believable." American novelist Alice Walker maintained in her *Ms.* review of *A Short Walk* that the novel lacks passion, but still commands respect. "Chil-

dress's is a *mature* intelligence, and the novel is rich with the fullness of her experience as a black woman in America—and as an extremely aware and political person."

In 1981 Childress returned to young adult fiction with her novel *Rainbow Jordan*, the story of Rainbow, a mature urban fourteen-year-old girl, and the two adults in her life: Kathie, her free-spirited twenty-nine-year-old mother, and Josephine, a fifty-seven-year-old dressmaker. Through the narratives of all three women, the reader learns that Kathie is an intermittently employed go-go dancer who frequently takes off with new boyfriends, leaving Rainbow to be picked up by a social worker. Josephine provides a home for Rainbow during the periods when her mother has abandoned her. Although Rainbow has experienced a great deal of hardship at Kathie's hands—beatings, poverty, neglect, and abandonment—she loves her mother and excuses her behavior. But while Rainbow represents her mother as a beautiful woman, Josephine's narratives compare Kathie, with her long wigs and excessive make-up, to "a 'lost girl' out of a TV show about crime and prostitution."

Rainbow Jordan's central drama lies in the relationship that develops between Rainbow and Josephine, a relationship that substitutes—or supplements—the flawed relationship between Kathie and Rainbow. As the novel begins, Rainbow, who is at a very vulnerable stage of adolescence, is abandoned once again by her mother. In addition, Rainbow's boyfriend is pressuring her to have sex with him, and she has begun to shoplift. Josephine, whose husband has recently deserted her, is also vulnerable. Although Rainbow has never liked to be placed in Josephine's "interim home," the respect and grace with which the older woman treats her gradually secures Rainbow's trust. Both women eventually find in each other the comfort and strength they need to make their way through their difficult lives. At the novel's end, Rainbow has decided to stay on with Josephine for six months in order to give her mother time "to get her head together," and Josephine, as Rainbow's guardian, meets with her teachers to enroll her in a sex education class.

Critics responded enthusiastically to *Rainbow Jordan*, especially applauding Childress's characterizations of the three women. Anne Tyler, writing for the *New York Times Book Review*, commented, "Rainbow's story moves us not because of the random beatings or financial hardships, but because Rainbow needs her mother so desperately that she will endlessly rationalize, condone, overlook, forgive. She is a heartbreakingly sturdy character, and *Rainbow Jordan* is a beautiful book." The social phenomenon of parental neglect portrayed in *Rainbow Jordan*, according to Geraldine Wilson in *Interracial Books for Children Bulletin*, is handled with a humanistic view of the individual lives involved. "The themes are painful, but Childress handles them well, resolving the difficult conflicts in realistic sensitive, direct fashion and in ways that seem consistent with the characters." Observers also noted that, as in most of her work, Childress's profound understanding of individual characters presents a realistic, but affirming picture of America's "have-nots." "Childress's value to parents," Carole E. Gregory wrote in her *Black Enterprise* review of *Rainbow Jordan*, "is that she understands the best of rural and urban experiences pertaining to the care of black children. Her message is clear. Any concerned, loving adult may 'mother' someone else's child."

Reviewers also praised Childress's skillful use of expressive and often poetic idiomatic language. "Using the African-based language forms characteristic of the Black community, Childress energizes her characters," Wilson maintained. "The language has intensity, pith, rhythm, volume, stillness. In places it sparkles." Sally Holmes Holtze remarked in the *School Library Journal* that in *Rainbow Jordan* "the language is so polished that in doubt Rainbow speaks differently from when she is sure of herself."

Childress attributes her fiction-writing style to her experience in theater. She explained in *SATA*: "When I'm writing a book, I visualize it all on stage. I'm very pleased when critics say my novels feel like plays. I've learned to lean on theater instead of breaking with it. . . . When writing a novel or a play I act out all the parts. I've actually gotten up, walked around and played out a scene when I've run into difficulty with the writing." Along with several other commentators, John T. Gillespie remarked in his book *More Juniorplots: A Guide for Teachers and Librarians* that "Alice Childress' experience as playwright and actress is revealed in the brilliant characterization and dialogue" of her novels.

Childress continued her quest for open discussion of difficult subjects with her 1989 novel *Those Other People*, a story about young people faced with conveying their "differences" to an unsympathetic social world. Jonathan, a gay seventeen-year-old boy, has been unable to "come out" to his family or come to terms with being homosexual in a homophobic culture. He teaches a high school computer class in which the only two black students, Tyrone and Susan, are being harassed by a vocal racist student. When another student, Theodora—a fifteen-year-old girl undergoing psychiatric treatment to cope with being sexually molested as a child—is sexually assaulted by the physical education teacher, Jonathan, Tyrone, and Susan are the only witnesses. In order to help each other, each of these characters must confront exposure to social discrimination. *School Library Journal* contributor Kathryn Havris maintained that although the plot is somewhat contrived to bring these characters together, "Childress has presented the problems and reactions with a competence that deserves reading."

Childress has won a vast array of awards for her uncompromising artistic and social integrity in drama and fiction throughout a long career. In 1975, when *Wedding Band* opened in Atlanta, Georgia, she was made an honorary citizen of the city. When her musical play, *Sea Island Song*, opened in Charleston, South Carolina, in 1977, both Charleston and Columbia, South Carolina, observed "Alice Childress Week" in her honor. For her screenplay *A Hero Ain't Nothin' but a Sandwich*, produced by New World Pictures in 1978, the Black Filmmakers Hall of Fame presented her with the first Paul Robeson Award for outstanding contributions to the performing arts. Among its many other awards, *A Hero Ain't Nothin' but a Sandwich* received a Coretta Scott King Award honorable mention in 1982. But, despite a large group of devoted admirers of her contributions to theater and children's fiction, Childress has not had the kind of recognition one might expect. Trudier Harris commented: "Ever busy and ever refusing to compromise her creative principles, Childress's reputation as a writer has been somewhat obscured; she calls herself 'one of the best known of unknown persons.' She has not received much critical attention despite her consistent productivity in a wide variety of genres. Theater histories make only passing mention of her, even though she was in the forefront of important developments in that medium. Literary critics have virtually ignored her short fiction, children's books, and novels."

Childress has been dedicated to social justice throughout her career, promoting it not only through her writing but also by her activity in schools, community affairs, theater projects, union work, and by her aid to young black women playwrights. Her own experiences as a black woman committed to exposing injustice, both as a dramatist and as a writer, often left her feeling isolated during her youth. Childress remarked in *Children's Literature Review* that she turned from acting because "racism, a double blacklisting system, and a feeling of being somewhat alone in my ideas caused me to know I could more freely express myself as a writer ... and yet. My stories and plays were usually labeled controversial and some were banned." Nonetheless, Childress feels she has reaped meaningful rewards from her lifetime of struggles. "Happily, I managed to save a bit of my youth for spending in these later years," she said in *Contemporary Authors*. "If we hang on to that part within that was once childhood, I believe we enter into a new time dimension and every day becomes another lifetime in itself. This gift of understanding is often given to those who constantly battle against the negatives of life with determination."

■ Works Cited

Burns, Mary M., review of *When the Rattlesnake Sounds, Horn Book,* June, 1976, p. 301.

Children's Literature Review, Volume 14, Gale, 1988, pp.85-94.

Childress, Alice, "The People behind the Books: 'A Hero Ain't Nothin' but a Sandwich," *Literature for Today's Young Adults,* by Alleen Pace Nilsen and Kenneth L. Donelson, Scott, Foresman, 1980, p. 427.

Clurman, Harold, "Theatre," *Nation*, November 13, 1972, p. 475.

Contemporary Authors, New Revision Series, Volume 27, Gale, 1989, pp. 100-103.

Dictionary of Literary Biography, Gale, Volume 7: *Twentieth-Century American Dramatists*, 1981, pp. 118-124, Volume 38: *Afro-American Writers after 1955: Dramatists and Prose Writers*, 1985, pp. 66-79.

Gillespie, John T., *More Juniorplots: A Guide for Teachers and Librarians*, R. R. Bowker Company, 1977, pp. 51-74.

Gregory, Carole E., review of *Rainbow Jordan, Black Enterprise*, December, 1981, p. 22.

Kathryn Havris, review of *Those Other People, School Library Journal*, February, 1989, pp. 99-100.

Hill, Elbert R., "A Hero for the Movies," *Children's Novels and the Movies*, edited by Douglas Street, Ungar, 1983, pp. 236-43.

Holtze, Sally Holmes, review of *Rainbow Jordan, School Library Journal*, April, 1981, p. 137.

McLellan, Joseph, review of *A Short Walk, Washington Post*, December 28, 1979.

Nilsen, Alleen Pace and Kenneth L. Donelson, "Life Models: Of Heroes and Hopes," *Literature for Today's Young Adults*, second edition, Scott, Foresman, 1985, pp. 208-57.

Ortiz, Miguel A., "The Politics of Poverty in Young Adult Literature," *The Lion and the Unicorn*, Volume 2, fall, 1978, pp. 6-15.

Something about the Author, Volume 48, Gale, 1981, pp.50-56.

Tyler, Anne, "Looking for Mom," *New York Times Book Review*, April 26, 1981, pp. 52-53 and 69.

Walker, Alice, "A Walk Through Twentieth-Century Black America," *Ms.*, December, 1979, pp. 46-47.

Wilson, Geraldine L., review of *Rainbow Jordan, Interracial Books for Children Bulletin*, Volume 12, Nos. 7 & 8, 1981, pp. 24-5.

■ For More Information See

PERIODICALS

New Yorker, November 19, 1979; February 23, 1987.

New York Times Book Review, November 11, 1979.°

—*Sketch by Sonia Benson*

Pat Conroy

■ Awards, Honors

Anisfield-Wolf Award, Cleveland Foundation, 1972, for *The Water is Wide*; Lillian Smith Award, best novel from the South, 1980, and nomination, Robert Kennedy Book Award, Robert F. Kennedy Memorial, 1981, both for *The Lords of Discipline*.

■ Writings

The Boo, McClure, 1970.
The Water is Wide, Houghton, 1972.
The Great Santini, Houghton, 1976.
The Lords of Discipline, Houghton, 1980.
The Prince of Tides, Houghton, 1986.

Also author of *The Citadel*, 1967.

■ Adaptations

The Water Is Wide was produced as *Conrack* by Twentieth-Century Fox in 1974; the musical *Conrack* was adapted for the stage by Granville Burgess, and first produced Off-Off Broadway at AMAS Repertory Theater, November, 1987; *The Great Santini*, starring Robert Duvall, Michael O'Keefe, and Blythe Danner, was produced by Warner Brothers in 1979; *The Lords of Discipline*, starring David Keith, was produced by Paramount in 1983; *The Prince of Tides*, starring Nick Nolte, Kate Nelligan, and Barbra Streisand, was produced and directed by Streisand for Columbia, 1991.

■ Personal

Born October 26, 1945, in Atlanta, GA; son of Don (a military officer) and Frances "Peggy" (Peck) Conroy; married Barbara Jones, 1969 (divorced, 1977); married Lenore Gurewitz, March 21, 1981; children: (first marriage) Megan; Jessica, Melissa (stepchildren); (second marriage) Susannah; Gregory, Emily (stepchildren). *Education:* The Citadel, B.A., 1967.

■ Addresses

Office—c/o Old New York Book Shop, 1069 Juniper St., Atlanta, GA 30309. *Agent*—Julian Bach Literary Agency, 747 Third Ave., New York, NY 10017.

■ Career

Writer. Taught high school English in Beafort, SC, and general studies for one year on Daufuskie Island, SC.

■ Sidelights

Best-selling novelist Pat Conroy has drawn on the experiences of his often-traumatic Southern youth to create stories that are complex, colorful, tragic, and sometimes, horrific. The son of a career Marine fighter pilot, Conroy often found himself at odds with both his father's expectations and his own desire to carve out a niche for himself. As a result, his novels are full of themes and situations that reflect the negative, long-term effects such a condition may foster. While some critics have found Conroy's autobiographical slant melodramatic at times, others view the author's personal approach as illustrative of a uniquely Southern writing style that combines storytelling with a well-defined sense of drama, tradition, and ethics. Conroy "writes about virtues we neglect, to our diminishment," asserted poet James Dickey in *Esquire*, "courage, brotherhood, and victory over the difficult obstacles to authentic manhood."

Pat Conroy was born in Atlanta, Georgia, the oldest son in a family of seven children. A self-described "military brat," Conroy spent much of his childhood in transit as his father moved from posting to posting. The family eventually settled in Beaufort, South Carolina, near the Paris Island Marine base. A city of great beauty and innate Southern tradition, Beaufort became a sanctuary for Conroy, a place he could finally call home. In 1963, Conroy graduated from Beaufort's high school and, at his father's insistence, enrolled in South Carolina's military college, The Citadel. Conroy's adjustment to life at The Citadel was difficult. In an interview with Joyce Leviton of *People*, Conroy admitted that at one point during his plebe year, he had called his father and begged to come home. Donald Conroy would not allow it, saying, "If you come home, you'll be a pansy."

After graduating from The Citadel, Conroy decided to forgo a military career in favor of teaching high school. "I paid my dues to the military with my life with Dad," he explained to Leviton, adding that his father "went to Vietnam twice. Any war my father supported I took a good hard look at." Conroy returned to Beaufort and began teaching English at the same high school he had graduated from a few years before. Things had changed in Beaufort from the days when Conroy was a student, however. The student body had been integrated (although the faculty was still all white) and tensions were high. Conroy often found himself at odds with an unyielding faculty, as well as newly integrated students who were suspicious of both his Southern upbringing and the motivation behind his offers of assistance. Frustrated by conditions at school and worried about losing his draft deferment status, Conroy began looking for alternative employment.

Conroy applied to the Peace Corps, but never got a response. On the advice of a friend, he then applied for and got a teaching job on Daufuskie Island, a small enclave off the South Carolina coast. In many ways, the island was terribly isolated; most of the residents were fishermen who had little or no contact with the mainland. Conroy's students were nearly all illiterate; many thought Daufuskie Island was the center of the United States. Some students did not know the name of their own country, that they lived on the Atlantic Ocean, or that the world was round. They did, however, expect their new teacher to be fairly self-sufficient; that meant being able to set a trap, skin a muskrat, and plant okra. By adopting some atypical teaching techniques, Conroy was able to make headway with his students. Despite this progress, however, Conroy was dismissed after a year, ostensibly for disregarding the dictates of the local school board. Conroy was very bitter about both his firing and the school board's refusal to hear his ideas. "I sent the [school] superintendent a letter telling him his school was a garbage dump," Conroy disclosed to Leviton.

Conroy had married widow Barbara Jones during his year on Daufuskie Island. After his dismissal, things became rather difficult at home; Conroy's wife was pregnant, and no job offers were forthcoming. In desperation, Conroy began to write a book about his time on the island. His efforts eventually became the autobiographical novel *The Water is Wide*. Upon finishing the book, Conroy was told that he would need an agent in order to sell it. After some searching, he came up with the name of New York agent Julian Bach. Conroy called Bach on a typically busy day, an experience he recalled for Sam Staggs of *Publishers Weekly*. According to Conroy, Bach was "as rude as any son-of-a-bitch could possibly be on the telephone. He would hardly listen to me without interrupting. But he heard 'black children on an island' and he snapped 'Just send me your manuscript. I'm so tired of people like you who call me everyday. I don't know why I'm talking to you. Send it up and I'll read it when I get time.'"

There was just one problem with the manuscript— it had been written in longhand. Since he could not type, Conroy enlisted the help of family and friends. Each person agreed to type one chapter.

While this was a great help to Conroy, it also posed another dilemma. "I had forgotten to tell them to use the same type of paper," he admitted to Staggs, "so there was onionskin, yellow foolscap, long sheets, short ones, some with lines—well, we put this unbelievable thing together and shipped it off to Julian. He read it, thinking it was the most adorable hayseed thing he had ever seen—and he sold it." Almost as soon as Bach agreed to represent him, however, Conroy began to have doubts about the agent's credibility. He wrote a letter to Bach in which he asked (among other things) if the the agent had "ever done this kind of work before." A few days later, Bach responded with his own long letter in which he detailed his agency's history and clients. Listed among the writers Bach represented were John Fowles and the estate of Charles Dickens. According to Staggs, Barbara Conroy read Bach's letter first; as she gave it to her husband, she wryly noted, "You poor dumb son-of-a-bitch; [Bach] just mauled you." "I felt utterly humiliated," Conroy later confessed.

Despite this awkward beginning, Conroy and Bach quickly established a very productive working relationship. In the years that followed the publication of *The Water is Wide*, Conroy wrote a series of semi-autobiographical novels. Not everyone was enamored of his efforts, however. Some members of Conroy's family felt that his books were too personal and revealing. Others objected to his frank depiction of sexuality and sometimes harsh use of language. Conroy told Staggs that his Aunt Helen phoned to complain about *The Lords of Discipline*. When Conroy asked how far into the novel she had actually read, Aunt Helen replied, "Page four and I've never been so embarrassed." Conroy was eventually able to reconcile much of his family with his writing career, in part due to a series of successful screen adaptations of his novels. (Donald Conroy, for example, was initially infuriated at the suggestion that he was the role model for Bull Meecham in *The Great Santini*; Robert Duvall's sympathetic depiction of the character in the 1979 film adaptation changed the elder Conroy's mind to such an extent that he began to sign his Christmas cards "The Great Santini.")

Critics have been quick to point out that much of Conroy's work closely reflects his Southern upbringing and his early association with military life. Both of these influences are detectable in Conroy's first book, *The Boo*. In *The Boo*, Conroy tells the story of Lieutenant Colonel Thomas Nugent Courvoisie, Assistant Commandant of Cadets at The

Conroy's first autobiographical novel depicts a young teacher's often frustrating struggle to reach a group of isolated students.

Citadel from 1961 to 1968. Although Conroy personally felt that *The Boo* was "one of the worst written books in the history of the English language," it nevertheless captured the essence of the love affair between Courvoisie, his cadets, and the school's traditions and history. Robert Willingham, Jr., writing in the *Dictionary of Literary Biography*, noted that while *The Boo* "in style and format is little removed from juvenilia, the language generally bland or affected, transitions weak or nonexistent," the book still manages to "presage the later Conroy with its wry humor ... the iconoclasm balanced with a certain respect for authority." In light of Conroy's later publishing successes, it is interesting to note that he personally paid for the first printing of *The Boo* by securing a loan from his hometown bank. "I can't tell you how naive I was," Conroy told Staggs. "I thought I had discovered the secret of getting your books published. I said to myself 'This is easier than I thought. I think I'll be a writer.'"

The years that preceded the events chronicled in *The Water Is Wide* allowed for a maturation of sorts, both with respect to Conroy's literary style and his perception of himself and his world. After graduating from The Citadel, Conroy traveled to Europe. While there, he visited a great many historic sights, including the former Nazi concentration camp at Dachau. These visits, combined with Conroy's earlier experiences in the South during the first years of the civil rights movement, fed the flame of the author's growing cynicism. Conroy became more and more convinced that "the world was a colorful, variegated grab bag of bastards." This point of view is conspicuous in the

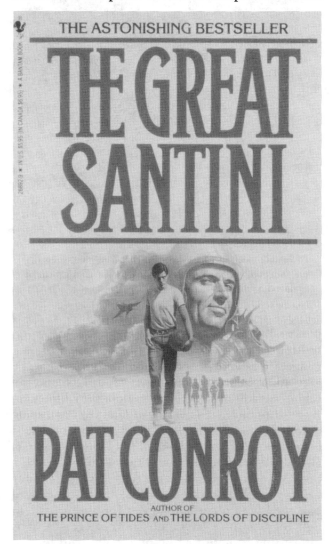

THE ASTONISHING BESTSELLER

THE GREAT SANTINI

PAT CONROY

AUTHOR OF
THE PRINCE OF TIDES AND THE LORDS OF DISCIPLINE

The bitter relationship between a teenage boy and his authoritarian father is at the heart of Conroy's 1976 novel.

narrative of *The Water is Wide.* On one level a scathing attack on educational hypocrisy, the novel is also a warning against youthful hubris. Conroy wrote: "I saw the necessity of living and accepting bullcrap in my midst. It was everywhere. In the teacher's manuals, . . . in school boards, in the community, and most significantly, in myself. I could be so self-righteous, so inflexible when I thought that I was right or that the children had been wrong. I lacked diplomacy and would not compromise."

Critical response was generally favorable to Conroy's first autobiographical tale. Anatole Broyard, writing in the *New York Times Book Review,* called *The Water Is Wide* a "hell of a good story." He added: "Mr. Conroy's modesty will not allow him to claim much for his year at Yamacraw, but he did get his pupils to listen to Beethoven and Brahms by alternating them with James Brown. He also opened their minds to an outer world they had never even conceived of. And, most memorable of all, he taught them to trust a white man and believe he cared about them." Jim Haskins, also writing in the *New York Times Book Review,* found some flaws in the text. He noted that Conroy "does not provide any of the badly needed alternative suggestions for alleviating or controlling the stifling ignorance that is an ever-present part of the American education scene." Haskins added, however, that the book nevertheless offers "interesting insights and observations about the processes of black Southern rural education from a young white Southerner's point of view."

Conroy's next work is also one of his most personal. *The Great Santini* focuses on the work and family life of Bull Meecham, a colonel in the U.S. Marine Corps. Bull runs his family like a Marine unit, much to the open dislike of his teenage son Ben. This father-son war of words eventually leads to the quiet rebellion of his wife Lillian and the other Meecham children. The core of the novel concerns the long-term ramifications of Bull's "double life," or his struggle to reconcile his duties as a Marine with his role as a husband and father. This conflict is exemplified in Bull's relationship with his oldest son, who is a nice, if not exactly driven, young man. For Bull, it is not enough that his son is a well-liked basketball star; it is also not acceptable that Ben rebels against many of the ideals his father holds dear.

The tension between father and son comes to a head during a one-on-one basketball game, when Ben manages to beat Bull. Partly in anger, partly in shock, Ben tells his father: "Do you know, Dad,

Robert Duvall and Michael O'Keefe play a brutal game of one-on-one basketball in the 1979 film adaptation of *The Great Santini*.

that not one of us here has ever beaten you in a single game? Not checkers, not dominos, not softball, nothing." Bull is unable to lose even this minor contest gracefully; his response is to ridicule his son's victory and spend the remainder of the night shooting practice baskets in the dark. This incident, and others that precede it, are illustrative of the fact that there are few truces in the Meecham family, and even fewer moments when they can be truly honest with one another.

In their reviews of *The Great Santini*, most critics were drawn to the strong autobiographical currents in the book. "In a novel that displays keen insight into family life on a military base, author Pat Conroy appears to be writing his autobiography," wrote James M. Hutchins of *Best Sellers*. He added that Conroy "also delves into the conflicts that are seemingly endemic to a 'lifer's' family.... *The Great Santini* is a fine, sensitive novel." A reviewer for *Virginia Quarterly Review* was equally laudatory, finding that the strength of the book "is its realism.... The dialogue, anecdotes, and family atmosphere are pure Marine.... At the heart of the book is the search of the eighteen-year-old son to

find himself while learning to understand and love his rigidly authoritarian Marine father, *The Great Santini*. A good novel and enjoyable reading."

Military life is also at the center of Conroy's next book, *The Lords of Discipline*. In *The Lords of Discipline*, Conroy takes the reader inside the fictional world of the Carolina Military Institute, a trip guided by senior cadet Will McLean. A large part of the novel traces the friendship between Will and his roommates: Mark Santoro, Dante "Pig" Pignetti, and Tradd St. Croix. The four young men have been together since their plebe year; as a result, their alliance is a special one, based on common experience, love, and trust. When Will is asked to unofficially protect the Institute's first black cadet, he runs afoul of the Ten, a secret association bent on maintaining the purity of the institution—racial purity included. Will's private war with the Ten spills over into all aspects of his life, including his relationships with his roommates and a mysterious young woman he has come to love. Will soon learns that his search for answers to the identity of the mysterious vigilante group exacts a high cost—one that even-

THE MAGNIFICENT NATIONAL BESTSELLER

THE LORDS OF DISCIPLINE

PAT CONROY

AUTHOR OF
THE PRINCE OF TIDES AND THE GREAT SANTINI

Conroy's 1980 novel explores the turbulent events at a fictitious Southern military academy in the 1960s.

tually includes betrayal, disillusionment, and death.

Critical response to *The Lords of Discipline* was mixed. Harry Crews of the *New York Times* "read the first 200 pages thinking that this is not only a very good book, but also one so memorable and well-executed that it would become the yardstick against which others of its kind are measured. Alas, the next 300 pages proved this not so." Crews's main complaint was that Conroy's plot turns become too convoluted in the second half of the book. The critic continued: "The story has more twists than a snake's back. There are reversals inside reversals. . . . But I was not surprised. . . . Simply put, Conroy's creative energies are sidetracked during the course of this book. Ultimately, he is more interested in posing and solving clever puzzles than in developing the character of the human beings inside those puzzles."

Washington Post Book World reviewer Frank Rose disagreed. He declared Conroy's handling of character and plot a "personal triumph." "What Conroy has achieved is two-fold: his book is at once a suspense-ridden duel between conflicting ideals of manhood and a paean to brother love that ends in betrayal and death," Rose continued. "Out of the shards of broken friendship a blunted triumph emerges, and it is here . . . that the reader finally comprehends the terrible price that any form of manhood can exact. . . . All this in a novel that virtually quivers with excitement and conviction. . . . Will's tale sounds less like a work of fiction than a cry from the heart—except, of course, that it is so tightly bridled, Conroy having learned the importance of order, and mystery, and control, those ideas that stand at the center of the military mystique."

Conroy followed *The Lords of Discipline* with what many critics consider his most ambitious work, *The Prince of Tides. The Price of Tides* is the sprawling tale of the Wingo family, a complex group of personalities whose fortunes run the gamut from glorious to sublimely tragic. Father Henry Wingo is a shrimper who often masks his deep love for his wife and children with anger and physical abuse. His wife Lila is a lyrically beautiful woman whose dreams reach far beyond the limits of a shrimper's salary. Their three children form a complex group: eldest son Luke is an earthy straight-talker; twins Tom and Savannah share an emotional bond that is tested by a number of cataclysmic twists of fate. The three young people are spiritually bound by both a deep and abiding love for their parents and the grim understanding that their own emotional survival depends largely upon one another.

Conroy shuttles the action of the novel between the Wingos' South Carolina island home and Manhattan. Tom narrates the family story at the request of his suicidal sister's psychiatrist, Susan Lowenstein (who eventually becomes Tom's lover and confidant). As the story opens, Tom is in early middle age; he has been fired from his high school coaching job and has learned that his wife Sallie, a successful doctor, is having an affair. Most of the other Wingos have also faired poorly: Henry is in jail on a drug smuggling charge, Savannah is in a semi-catatonic state following a failed suicide attempt, and Luke is dead. Only Lila has emerged unscathed, a condition owed to her successful manipulation of various people and events.

When Tom agrees to relate the family history, he also frees some dark family secrets. Child and spousal abuse, rape, robbery, murder—these things all figure prominently in Tom's memories; there is also a great deal of love, excitement, success, and benign eccentricity. Tom states: "The truth is this: Things happened in my family, extraordinary things. I know families who live out their entire lives without a single thing of interest happening to them. I have always envied those families. The Wingos were a family that fate tested a thousand times and left defenseless, humiliated, and dishonored. But my family also carried some strengths into the fray, and these strengths let almost all of us survive the descent of the Furies." By the end of the novel, some of the family rifts have been mended. Tom is reunited with his sister and father; his marriage survives as well. These reconciliations have come at a high price, however, particularly for Tom. He muses: "I knew that deliverance often requires the kiss of Judas as a prelude; there are times when betrayal can be an act of love in itself."

Many critics gave *The Prince of Tides* mixed reviews. "Never does Conroy settle for one word when he can pack in a dozen. . . . All the characters love each other so wildly that they just go nutty, or they hate each other with a hate that cannot be measured. It's Confederate prose like this that gave Southern writing a bad name," wrote a reviewer for *People*. R. Z. Sheppard of *Time* was less harsh, noting that while Conroy "can be shameless in his extravagances of language and plot," he nevertheless "consistently conveys two fundamental emotions: the attachment to place and the passion for blood ties." And Gail Godwin, writing in the *New York Times Book Review*, asserted that while "the ambition, invention, and sheer energy of this book are admirable," other readers "will be turned off by the turgid, high-flown rhetoric that the author must have decided would best match his grandiose design." In 1990, Conroy worked with Barbara Streisand on the script for the movie adaptation of *The Prince of Tides*. Conroy commented of the experience: "We got along splendidly. I kept waiting for her to yell at me or something, hurt my feelings, but she never did. It was the best collaboration I've ever had."

In an essay for *Commonweal*, David Toolan wrote that Conroy's novels "track but a single life, one boy's rite of passage—through the betrayals of high school, college, first job, and marriage—to an adult ethic of honor and loyalty." While the autobiographical aspects of Conroy's novels confirm the spirit of this definition, the author's personal view of his work is much simpler. "I'm incredibly shallow," Conroy told Staggs. "I write a straight story line. . . . But most important, I do the thing Southerners do naturally—I tell stories. I always try to make sure there is a good story going on in my books." Conroy has also admitted to a streak of sentimentalism that "weakens me as a writer, but preserves me as a person." Despite this weakness (or perhaps because of it), Conroy has been able to turn to turn some of the more bitter aspects of his life into engaging tales. When asked where he sees himself in the pantheon of "Southern writers," Conroy replied: "Critics call me a popular novelist, but writing popular novels is not what urges me on. If I could write like Faulkner or Thomas Wolfe, I surely would. . . . Each book has been more ambitious. I'm trying to be more courageous."

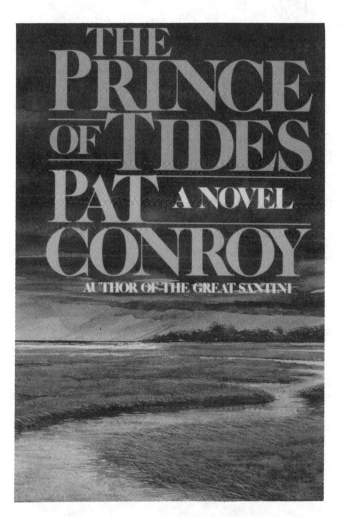

Tom Wingo narrates the often tragic history of his complex family in this 1986 best-seller.

■ Works Cited

Broyard, Anatole, "Supererogating Down South," *New York Times Book Review,* July 13, 1972, p. 33.

Conroy, Pat, *The Great Santini,* Houghton, 1976.

Conroy, Pat, *The Prince of Tides,* Houghton, 1986.

Conroy, Pat, *The Water is Wide,* Houghton, 1972.

Contemporary Literary Criticism, Volume 30, Gale, 1984, pp. 76-80.

Crews, Harry, "The Passage to Manhood," *New York Times,* December 7, 1980, pp. 12, 43.

Dictionary of Literary Biography, Volume 6: *American Novelists since World War II, Second Series,* Gale, 1980, pp. 55-58.

Esquire, December, 1984, p. 128.

Godwin, Gail, review of *The Prince of Tides, New York Times Book Review,* October 12, 1986, p. 14.

Haskins, Jim, "Rural Education Sea Islands Style," *New York Times Book Review,* September 24, 1972, p. 10.

Leviton, Joyce, "Shaping His Pain Into Novels, Pat Conroy Gets His Reputation, His Fortune—and His Revenge," *People,* February 2, 1981, pp. 67-69.

Premiere, December, 1991, p. 90.

Review of *The Prince of Tides, People,* November 10, 1986, p. 8.

Rose, Frank, "The Martial Spirit and the Masculine Mystique," *Washington Post Book World,* October 19, 1980.

Sheppard, R. Z., review of *The Prince of Tides, Time,* October 13, 1986, p. 97.

Staggs, Sam, "Pat Conroy," *Publishers Weekly,* September 5, 1986.

Toolan, David, "The Unfinished Boy and His Pain," *Commonweal,* February 22, 1991, pp. 127-131.

■ For More Information See

BOOKS

Authors in the News, Volume 1, Gale, 1976.

PERIODICALS

Chicago Tribune, November 25, 1986.

Chicago Tribune Book World, October 19, 1980; September 14, 1986; October 19, 1986.

Los Angeles Times, February 19, 1983; October 12, 1986; October 19, 1986; December 12, 1986.

New York Times Book Review, September 24, 1972; December 7, 1980.

Washington Post, October 23, 1980.

Washington Post Book World, October 12, 1986.

—Sketch by Elizabeth A. Des Chenes

Jim Davis

Cartoonists Society, Newspaper Features Council, Screen Actors Guild/American Federation of Television and Radio Artists, Newspaper Features Council, Cartoon Art Museum of California (member of board of directors), Museum of Cartoon Art, Ball State Alumni Association, Muncie Civic Theatre (member of board of directors, 1974-76).

■ Personal

Born James Robert Davis, July 28, 1945, in Marion, IN; son of James William (a farmer) and Anna Catherine (Carter) Davis; married Carolyn L. Altekruse (formerly an elementary school teacher), July 26, 1969; children: James Alexander. *Education:* Attended Ball State University, 1963-67, B.S., 1986.

■ Addresses

Home—Muncie, IN. *Office*—Paws, Inc., R.R. 1, Box 98-A, Albany, IN 47320; and United Feature Syndicate, Inc., 200 Park Ave., New York, NY 10166.

■ Career

Groves & Associates, Muncie, IN, artist, 1968-69; free-lance advertising artist, 1969-78; assistant to "Tumbleweeds" cartoon strip author Tom Ryan, 1969-78; writer and cartoonist of "Garfield," and later "U.S. Acres," comic strips, syndicated internationally by United Feature Syndicate, 1978—; Paws, Inc. (art base for Garfield merchandising), Albany, IN, founder, 1981. *Member:* National

■ Awards, Honors

Outstanding Young Men of America Award, 1972; National Cartoonists Society, Reuben Award for best humor strip, 1982, 1986, 1990, Segar Award, 1985, Cartoonist of the Year, 1990; Golden Plate, American Academy of Achievement, 1983; Marketing Hall of Fame award, American Marketing Association (southern California chapter), 1983; Sagamore of the Wabash Award, State of Indiana, 1984; National Academy of Television Arts and Sciences ("Emmy") Award for outstanding animated program, 1984, for *Garfield on the Town,* 1985, for *Garfield in the Rough,* 1986, for *Garfield's Hallowe'en Adventure;* named Volunteer of the Year by Indiana Council of Fund Raising Executives, 1985; Forest Conservationist of the Year, Indiana Wildlife Federation, 1990; Hoosier Pride Award, 1990; Arbor Day Award, National Arbor Day Foundation, 1990; Distinguished Alumnus Award, American Association of State Colleges and Universities. Honorary doctorates from Ball State University and Purdue University, both 1991.

■ **Writings**

"GARFIELD" COMIC STRIP COLLECTIONS

Garfield at Large, Ballantine, 1980.
Garfield Gains Weight, Ballantine, 1981.
Garfield, Bigger than Life: His Third Book, Ballantine, 1981.
Garfield Weighs In, Ballantine, 1982.
Garfield Treasury, Ballantine, 1982.
Here Comes Garfield (based on the television special; also see below), Ballantine, 1982.
Garfield Takes the Cake, Ballantine, 1982.
Garfield Sits around the House, Ballantine, 1983.
Garfield on the Town (based on the television special; also see below), Ballantine, 1983.
Garfield Eats His Heart Out, Ballantine, 1983.
The Second Garfield Treasury, Ballantine, 1984.
Garfield Tips the Scales, Ballantine, 1984.
Garfield Loses His Feet, Ballantine, 1984.
Garfield: His Nine Lives, Ballantine, 1984.
Garfield Makes It Big, Ballantine, 1985.
Garfield Rolls On, Ballantine, 1985.
Garfield in Disguise, Ballantine, 1985.
The Third Garfield Treasury, Ballantine, 1985.
Garfield Out to Lunch, Ballantine, 1986.
The Unabridged, Uncensored, Unbelievable Garfield Book, Ballantine, 1986.
Garfield Food for Thought, Ballantine, 1987.
The Fourth Garfield Treasury, Ballantine, 1987.
A Garfield Christmas (based on the television special; also see below), Ballantine, 1987.
Garfield Swallows His Pride, Ballantine, 1987.
Garfield Goes Hollywood (based on the television special; also see below), Ballantine, 1987.
Garfield Rounds Out, Ballantine, 1988.
Garfield's Thanksgiving (based on the television special; also see below), Ballantine, 1988.
The Garfield How to Party Book, Ballantine, 1988.
Garfield World-wide, Ballantine, 1988.
Garfield Chews the Fat, Ballantine, 1989.
Babes and Bullets, Ballantine, 1989.
The Fifth Garfield Treasury, Ballantine, 1989.
Garfield Goes to Waist, Ballantine, 1990.
Garfield Hangs Out, Ballantine, 1990.
Garfield on the Farm, Ballantine, 1990.
Garfield's Feline Fantasies, Ballantine, 1990.
Garfield's Judgment Day, story adapted by Kim Campbell, illustrated by Mike Fentz and others, Ballantine, 1990.
Garfield Takes Up Space, Ballantine, 1991.

"U.S. ACRES" COMIC STRIP COLLECTIONS

U.S. Acres Counts Its Chickens, Pharos Books/ Ballantine, 1987.
U.S. Acres Goes Half Hog!, Pharos Books, 1987.

U.S. Acres Rules the Roost, Pharos Books, 1988.
U.S. Acres I: I Wasn't Hatched Yesterday, Berkley Publishing, 1989.
U.S. Acres Runs Amuck, Pharos Books, 1989.
(Creator) Jim Kraft, *U.S. Acres: The Big Camp Out,* designed and illustrated by Betsy Brackett and others, Bantam, 1989.
(Creator) Kraft, *U.S. Acres: Wade Dives In,* designed and illustrated by Brackett and others, Bantam, 1989.
U.S. Acres: It's a Pig's Life, Berkley Publishing, 1989.
U.S. Acres: Hold That Duck, Berkley Publishing, 1989.
(Creator) Kraft, *U.S. Acres: Beware! Rooster at Work,* designed and illustrated by Brett Koth and others, Bantam, 1989.
(Creator) Kraft, *U.S. Acres: Sir Orson to the Rescue,* designed and illustrated by Koth and others, Bantam, 1989.
U.S. Acres, Berkley Publishing, 1990.
U.S. Acres: Take This Rooster, Berkley Publishing, 1990.
(Creator) Kraft, *U.S. Acres: Happy Birthday Sheldon!,* designed and illustrated by Koth, Larry Fentz, and Dwight Ferris, Bantam, 1990.
Wade's Haunted Halloween, Bantam, 1990.
U.S. Acres Hams It Up, Pharos Books, 1990.
Counting Sheep, Berkley Publishing, 1990.

JUVENILES

(Illustrator) Shep Steneman, *Garfield: The Complete Cat Book,* Random House, 1981.
(Illustrator) Emily P. Kingsley, *Garfield the Pirate,* 1982.
Garfield Mix and Match Storybook, Random House, 1982.
(Illustrator) *Garfield the Knight in Shining Armor,* Random House, 1982.
Garfield Counts to Ten, Random House, 1983.
Garfield in Space, Random House, 1983.
Garfield Goes Underground, Random House, 1983.
(Illustrator) Jack Harris, *Garfield Goes to a Picnic,* Random House, 1983, published as *Garfield's Picnic Adventure* (also see below), Western Publishing, 1988.
(With M. Fentz and Dave Kuhn) *Garfield A to Z Zoo,* Random House, 1984.
(With M. Fentz and Kuhn) *Garfield Book of the Seasons,* Random House, 1984.
(Illustrator) *Garfield Water Fun,* Random House, 1985.
(With L. Fentz and M. Fentz) *Garfield Goes to the Farm,* Random House, 1985.

My Little Pony through the Seasons, illustrated by Kathy Allert, Random House, 1985.

(Illustrator) Kate Klimo, editor, *Garfield Touch-&-Go-Seek: Things to Touch, See, & Smell,* Random House, 1986.

(Creator) Norma Simone, *Garfield, the Fussy Cat,* Western Publishing, 1988.

Garfield's Night before Christmas, Putnam, 1988.

(Creator) Kraft, *The Great Christmas Contest,* illustrated by Paws, Inc., Bantam, 1988.

(Creator) Leslie McGuire, *Garfield and the Space Cat* (also see below), Western Publishing, 1988.

Garfield and the Haunted Diner: A Lift-the-Flap Book, Putnam, 1989.

Garfield and the Tiger, Western Publishing, 1989.

Garfield in the Park, Western Publishing, 1989.

(Creator) Simone, *Garfield the Big Star* (also see below), Western Publishing, 1989.

Happy Birthday, Garfield, Western Publishing, 1989.

Garfield's Furry Tales, Putnam, 1989.

Garfield, the Easter Bunny?, Putnam, 1989.

Garfield's Longest Catnap, Western Publishing, 1989.

(Creator) Kraft, *A Most Special Easter Egg: From the Creator of Garfield,* illustrated by Paws, Inc., Bantam, 1989.

Let's Play Ball!, Bantam, 1989.

(Creator) Simone, Harris, and McGuire, *Garfield Stories: Including The Big Star, Garfield's Picnic Adventure, Garfield and the Space Cat,* Western Publishing, 1990.

(Creator) Kraft, *Garfield: Mini-Mysteries,* illustrated by Kuhn and M. Fentz, Western Publishing, 1990.

Scary Tales, Grosset & Dunlap, 1990.

(With Sharryl Davis Hawke) *London,* Raintree Publishers, 1989.

New York, Raintree Publishers, 1990.

ANIMATED TELEVISION SPECIALS

Here Comes Garfield, Columbia Broadcasting System (CBS-TV), 1982.

Garfield on the Town, CBS-TV, 1983.

Garfield in the Rough, CBS-TV, 1984.

The Garfield Hallowe'en Special, CBS-TV, 1985.

Garfield in Paradise, CBS-TV, 1986.

Garfield Goes Hollywood, CBS-TV, 1987.

The Garfield Christmas Special, CBS-TV, 1987.

Garfield's Thanksgiving Special, CBS-TV, 1988.

Garfield—His Nine Lives, CBS-TV, 1988.

Babes and Bullets, CBS-TV, 1989.

Garfield's Feline Fantasies, CBS-TV, 1990.

Garfield Gets a Life, CBS-TV, 1991.

OTHER "GARFIELD" BOOKS

(With Bill Tornquist) *The Garfield Trivia Book,* Ballantine, 1986.

(With Carol Wallace) *The Garfield Book of Cat Names,* Ballantine, 1988, also published as *The Garfield Cat Naming Book,* 1988.

(Creator) Kraft, *Garfield: The Me Book: A Guide to Superiority, How to Get It, Use It, and Keep It,* illustrated by Koth, Ballantine, 1990.

Garfield Postcard: Birthday, Ballantine, 1990.

■ Sidelights

Anyone who has picked up the comics page of a newspaper or visited the humor section of a bookstore will be familiar with Jim Davis's lasagna-scarfing, cantankerous cartoon cat Garfield. Appearing in newspapers across the United States and in dozens of countries around the world, Garfield has also become a familiar face on merchandise ranging from t-shirts to bookmarks and as the star of animated television specials. But even though his creation has made him a millionaire, Davis has not allowed his celebrity to change him in any way. "Everything I did cannot erase the fact that I am an Indiana farm boy," he tells *People* writer Mary Vespa. "Except for the media attention, precious little has changed."

The origin of Davis's love for cartooning can be traced back to his childhood on a farm in Fairmont, Indiana. He spent much of his time there sick in bed. When Davis "was 7 months old," reports Vespa, "he developed severe asthma. It kept him inside and almost killed him when he was 9; it plagued him until he was in college." In order to alleviate some of the boredom, Davis's mother encouraged him to draw. "She's the one who got me started," the cartoonist explains. "She'd give me a paper and pencil and make me try to draw. I'd draw someone, and as soon as I learned to spell, I'd have them saying something. Then I started drawing boxes and in second or third grade, it was cartooning."

Continuing to practice his hobby in high school, Davis created a cartoon strip he called "Herman." In college, the cartoonist decided to add practicality to creativity, majoring in both art and business, but not doing very well in either. His low grades persuaded him to leave school and seek gainful employment, which turned out to be an entry level job at an advertising agency earning $1.60 per hour. Even so, Davis tells *Forbes* writer John Heins, "I liked advertising . . ., but my ulcer didn't." After working in the art department for a year and a half,

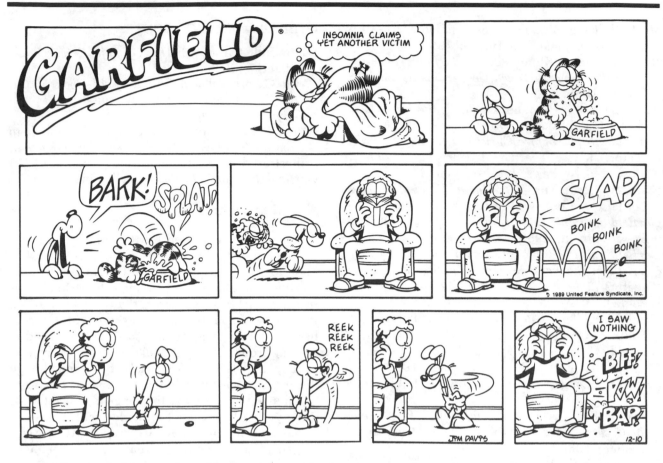

Garfield's renowned laziness, love of food, and distaste for dogs dominate this strip from Davis's 1991 *Garfield Takes up Space*. (Garfield reprinted by permission of United Feature Syndicate Inc.)

he quit his job to work for cartoonist Tom Ryan, drawing backgrounds for that artist's humorous look at Westerns called "Tumbleweeds." Ryan acted as a mentor to Davis, teaching him many of the basics in writing and drawing cartoon strips.

With Ryan's help, Davis was encouraged to create his own strip, "Gnorm the Gnat." Davis describes the strip to *Los Angeles Times* contributor Paul Galloway: "Some of the characters were fruit flies. They have a life expectancy of about three weeks, and they are very nervous and insecure, as you can imagine. They never worried about long engagements. Freddy Fruit Fly would say 'Bill me' when he bought something." The concept did not appeal much to the cartoon syndicates that buy new cartoon ideas. Davis tried to sell "Gnorm the Gnat" for five years before finally giving up on it. It seemed that nobody wanted to read about angst-ridden insects.

By this time Davis was wondering if he had a future in cartooning. He and his wife Carolyn, who sold Tupperware to help make ends meet, struggled by with a twenty-year-old Chevrolet and a few thousand dollars a year. "Carolyn never doubted I would get syndicated," Davis tells Vespa. "She provided a great home life and a lot of support. It was blind faith on her part." So Davis kept up his resolve and set out to create a new strip idea. He still wanted to write some kind of comic strip about animals. "I wanted to keep working with animals because they have the advantage of not being either white or black, male or female, young or old," he relates to Galloway. "I didn't want ... to be controversial." Like George Gately, the creator of "Heathcliff," and the late B. Kliban, whose meatloaf-shaped felines are still immensely popular, Davis took advantage of the lack of cartoon cats at the time. "I noticed the popularity of dogs.... There was Snoopy, Marmaduke, Fred Bassett—a lot of dogs but hardly any cats."

So Davis created his cat character Garfield by borrowing the name and much of the personality from his grandfather, John Garfield Davis. Originally, however, the central character of Davis's strip was Jon Arbuckle, Garfield's bumbling owner and the object of the cat's surly temper and needle-sharp claws. But Davis soon realized that Garfield was the real star of the cartoon, and so he focussed his attention on developing the feline's distinctive personality. He also changed Garfield's appearance, making his body smaller and his arms and legs longer so his character was more mobile; and he made the eyes larger and more expressive.

After fine-tuning "Garfield" for about a year, Davis felt he was ready to submit it as a proposal to the syndicates. The first two, Chicago Tribune-New York News and King Features, turned Davis down, but United Feature Syndicate liked the cartoonist's idea, signing him to a ten-year contract and immediately distributing "Garfield" to forty-one newspapers. Initially, the success of the new strip seemed in jeopardy. J. D. Reed notes in *Time* that newspapers "in Chicago, Salt Lake City and Little Rock, Ark., canceled the strip after test runs. But irate readers forced all three papers to reinstate it." United Feature capitalized on this incident by using it to promote the popularity of "Garfield," and the strip soon became the fastest-growing in the country.

It was Garfield's unapologetically rude and self-indulgent personality that produced the strip's most memorable lines: "I'm not fat, I'm undertall"; "Cats don't ask. Cats take"; "I never met a lasagna I didn't like"; "Big, fat, hairy deal"; and many others. As a contrast to Garfield's surly temperament, Davis introduced Nermal, "the world's cutest kitten," and Odie, a good-natured but extremely slobbery mutt. Odie's drooling tongue has been the object of a number of Garfield's pranks, since it is long enough and elastic enough to stretch around Odie's head or tie into knots. At times, Garfield's jokes on Odie have fallen flat when his victim was simply too pea-brained to notice them. Nermal's refusal to adopt a proper feline attitude despite Garfield's attempts to instruct him has also been the cause of frustration for the cartoon star.

Despite these few setbacks, however, Garfield has remained set in his ways. He will eat anything in Jon's house that does not move and refuses to diet—in one episode he became so fat that his legs no longer reached the floor; he sleeps as much as possible; and if Jon crosses him he will shred his owner's clothes to ribbons. "One reason Garfield is interesting for cat lovers," Davis explains to Toby Kahn and Sarah Moore Hall in *People*, "is that he confirms what they've always suspected about cats. In Garfield they see his human aspects—his refusal to diet, his inability to walk through a room without knocking things over, and his total pursuit of warm places to curl up and sleep. He champions a lot of unpopular causes, like anti-jogging, and what's more, he doesn't apologize for them."

Davis's main goal in writing "Garfield" is to be entertaining. "I feel a responsibility to keep 'Garfield' good and fluffy," he relates to *Contemporary Authors New Revision Series* interviewer Jean W. Ross. "I feel like we're balancing the scales just a bit with some of the very real, very depressing things going on. In fact, the harder the times, the more popular the comics page, from what I've noticed. They were very, very popular during the Great Depression; that was their heyday. And even today, with the economic recession or the military conflicts, it seems like people come back to the comics page again and again. I feel someday comics will take their rightful place as a piece of Americana. It's not exactly art, it's not exactly writing, it's *cartooning*. We invented it, and even now nobody does it better. If you look at a comics page in a foreign newspaper, by and large it will be American strips. Cartooning will come into its own. Its getting more and more attention, and that's good."

"My single biggest break toward national recognition," declares Davis in a *Publishers Weekly* article by John F. Baker, was the first Garfield book, *Garfield at Large*. Baker relates how Davis "had roughed out a book dummy, using six month's worth of strips, and taken it to United Feature to see if they could get any publisher interest in it. When he got home to Indiana there was a letter awaiting him from Ballantine's then editor-in-chief Nancy Coffey." Coffey had seen the strip in Philadelphia newspapers and was already a fan.

Garfield and Odie enjoy a lighthearted moment.
(Copyright © 1978 United Feature Syndicate Inc.)

She eagerly accepted Davis's book and published it in 1980. *Garfield at Large* sold hundreds of thousands of copies. Somewhat ironically, *Garfield at Large* appeared on the *New York Times* best-seller list even before the strip appeared in a New York City newspaper. Davis's next breakthrough was being the first author to have more than two books on the *New York Times* trade-paperback best-seller list at the same time. At one point, seven of his books were on the list in one week. Finally, "Garfield" became internationally popular with translations appearing in Europe, Africa, Australia, and Asia.

The immense success of "Garfield" has caused it to be compared at times to Charles Schulz's now classic strip "Peanuts." When asked by Ross whether there was any rivalry between him and Schulz, Davis responded, "No. Charles Schulz is a legend in his own time. He is by far the most widely syndicated cartoonist and he's been doing 'Peanuts' for [more than forty] years now. We are with the same syndicate ... so Sparky—as we call him—has been a big help as well as a big inspiration for me. I think, as far as comparing the two characters, nobody dislikes Snoopy. He's a free spirit, the humor is gentle, and everybody loves him as well as the whole cast of characters—with the possible exception of Lucy; I'd like to meet her in a dark alley sometime. Garfield, on the other hand, is a little more abrasive. I don't think he can count as many followers as Snoopy can, but he's not out to make a lot of friends. In fact, it's the texture to his personality, I think, that gives him his appeal." Schulz has been an idol of Davis's since he was a child, and Davis remarks to Baker that "'Snoopy and the Red Baron' is probably the greatest sequence of strips that was ever done." Some of Davis's other favorite cartoonists include Mort Walker, author of "Hi and Lois" and "Beetle Bailey," and "B.C." creator Johnny Hart.

Some cartoonists would call Davis a "big foot artist," meaning his drawings are simple and rely on caricature, rather than the more detailed drawings of a "wrinkle artist." Davis explains some of the reasons for his approach to Ross: "Some newspapers have been shrinking the size of comics. There simply isn't the room for the detail that there used to be. I also like to draw a cartoon as one would tell a joke. I keep the characters in the same position; I use very little background if any—usually I use the table top. That allows the eye to travel through the strip without having to stop and start and look at any art work or tricky variation on character angle. I use as few words as possible so

A collection of Davis's popular "U.S. Acres" comic strips.

that people can read through a strip smoothly in three frames and laugh as if they were being told a joke. It's timing; it's bomp, bomp, ta-*domp*. If the eye doesn't stop, if it doesn't have to linger over a lot of words, you can get the spontaneous laugh. Otherwise you've lost your timing, you've lost your humor in a way. So I like to keep the art simple. Initially I kept the art simple because I'm a simple artist. . . . It was Mort Walker that called me the big foot cartoonist. And he's a big foot cartoonist."

Davis feels that he is a better joke writer than artist. "I've always had to work very, very hard at the art. I love the art. When I draw, time stands still. I really enjoy drawing. I've had to concentrate very hard on it, though, to try to improve my art. . . . My strong point is frankly the writing— writing the strip, writing for some of the books, and also writing the TV shows. Since I know the character so well, since I've been doing the Garfield gags for so many years, he really does exist in my mind. Therefore it's very easy for me to anticipate what he'll do in given situations."

As more "Garfield" books came out and the strip's popularity continued to soar, the cartoon character began to diversify. Garfield and his friends went to Hollywood to film several television specials for the Columbia Broadcasting System. The voice for Garfield in the animated shows is provided by Lorenzo Music, whose sleepy, low-key voice once was used for Carlton the doorman on the series "Rhoda" and is the perfect compliment to Garfield's laid-back personality. In addition to his television appearances, "Garfield" has branched out into nonfiction books for children, such as *Garfield: The Complete Cat Book*, a book instructing children how to take care of their pet cat, and a counting book, *Garfield Counts to Ten*.

Garfield's fame has led naturally to merchandising, and in this area Davis proved to have a natural gift. Learning from the salesmen who sold his cartoon strip, Davis entered the spin-off business, adding drawings of Garfield—along with some of his wise cracks—to just about every item imaginable. To help him with his growing operation, Davis founded Paws, Inc., in 1981. The company has a large support staff to help in the production and sales of "Garfield" products, all of which are personally overseen by their creator. "The thought of rubber-stamping [the merchandise] isn't for me," Davis says in the *People* article. "I have a real conscience about licensing." At first, Davis's group aimed its products at a very specific audience, eighteen to thirty-four-year-old mothers, whom they believed to be the biggest fans of the rotund cat. Davis later

Davis and Garfield celebrate their success with a poolside toast.

discovered, however, that "Garfield" appealed to a much broader spectrum of people, from young children and college students to cat-hating men who liked the strip because they felt it justified their claims about felines.

Paws, Inc., also has a staff of several artists who assist Davis with drawing the strip, books, and merchandise illustrations. Still, Davis keeps an eye on everything that concerns his creation. "I used to work eighty to a hundred hours a week," the cartoonist tells Ross. "Now with a lot of staff help, I'm down to probably sixty or seventy. A day starts around seven and goes to five, with an hour break for lunch. Then usually three, four, or five nights out of the week I'm writing something for the feature. I get back at it about eight and work until ten or eleven. On weekends, if I can find some time away, I slip back to the studio or slip out somewhere quiet to do some more writing. As far as what I do during the course of the day, a lot of times I talk on the phone, meet on new licensing projects, talk to licensees, travel—on an average I probably travel a week out of the month promoting the feature or else working on the TV show in California and going to trade shows." Although some of the "Garfield" books for children have been written and illustrated by other writers and artists, Davis has a hand in all of them. He still writes all the "Garfield" strips and collections and creates the scripts, story boards, and layouts for all of the television specials.

By the mid-1980s, Davis had his hands more than full with his writing of "Garfield" and management of Paws, Inc. Asked by Ross at the time whether he would consider doing another strip, Davis replies, "No. I can't imagine doing anything else. Of course I've always thought about other comic features. If something like that comes about, of course it'll be going to a market we can't reach with 'Garfield,' going to children or some other audience we don't have now. If I feel like we're not saying or doing enough for entertaining, or because of the size of the staff to make sure we always have work, we may pursue something like that." Davis did eventually start a new strip which he called "U.S. Acres." The strip is set on a farm and involves the shenanigans of the barnyard animals, including the central character, Orson the Pig, a baby chick named Sheldon who refuses to come out of his shell, and a paranoid duck named Wade who—because of his fear of water—insists on wearing an inner tube at all times. Although not nearly as popular as "Garfield," "U.S. Acres" has had some success and a number of comic collections have been published over the last few years based on the strip.

As an Indianan who was raised on a farm, it is not surprising that Davis should come up with a strip like "U.S. Acres." His creation of a feline cartoon character also stems from his childhood on the farm, where his family owned twenty-five cats, though Garfield is not based on any particular pet. Today, Davis does not own a cat because his wife is allergic to them. The Davis family still lives in Indiana, where they own a home, a studio, and thirty acres of land. "A frugal millionaire," nevertheless, according to Reed, "Davis . . . traded in his 1962 Chevrolet and bought a 1979 Lincoln Continental with 30,000 miles on it" when "Garfield" first began to pay off. "'I still couldn't bring myself to get a new one,' he says. Some day he might even break down and get a dog." "The major changes," Davis tells *Forbes* writer John Heins, "have been freedom to travel, not having to look at price tags, affording a little nicer wine and having lobster as much as I like."

"The best part of [my success]," Davis concludes in his interview with Ross, "is getting to draw cartoon strips. That's all I've ever wanted to do. And I think if I do anything in the service of the readers, it's to provide some humor, make them feel a little better. That's the reason I started the whole thing anyway. My favorite fan letters are those that say I brightened that reader's day a little bit. If I can make someone laugh, smile, or just think a nice thought, then I've accomplished my job. Cartooning is entertainment, and if 'Garfield' serves that purpose, then I've accomplished what I wanted to do. That, for me, is the biggest thrill."

■ **Works Cited**

Baker, John F., "PW Interviews Jim Davis," *Publishers Weekly*, March 13, 1981, pp. 6-7.

Contemporary Authors New Revision Series, Volume 16, Gale, 1985.

Galloway, Paul, *Los Angeles Times*, November 14, 1982.

Heins, John, "Garfield Galore," *Forbes*, November 21, 1983, pp. 326, 328.

Kahn, Toby, and Sarah Moore Hall, "The Market Is Going to the Cats as the Fur Flies over Retailing Millions," *People*, November 17, 1980, pp. 106-109.

Reed, J. D., "Crazy over Cats," *Time*, December 7, 1981, pp. 72-79.

Vespa, Mary, "Garfield Goes Hollywood—with Jim Davis on His Cattails—for Feline Fame and Fortune," *People*, November 1, 1982, pp. 88-92.

■ **For More Information See**

PERIODICALS

Cartoonist Profiles, December, 1978.

Chicago Sun-Times, November 2, 1978.

New York Times Book Review, July 27, 1980.

Sunday Record (New Jersey), February 20, 1983.

[Sketch verified by Kim Campbell, secretary to Jim Davis.]

Leon Garfield

Personal

Born July 14, 1921, in Brighton, Sussex, England; son of David Kalman (a businessman) and Rose (Blaustein) Garfield; married Vivien Dolores Alcock, October 23, 1948; children: Jane Angela. *Education:* Attended grammar school in Brighton, England. *Politics:* "Somewhere between Labour and Liberal." *Religion:* Jewish.

Addresses

Home—59 Wood Lane, Highgate, London N6, England.

Career

Writer. Whittington Hospital, London, England, biochemical technician, 1946-66; part-time biochemical technician in various hospital laboratories in London, 1966-69. *Military service:* British Army, Medical Corps, 1940-46; served in Belgium and Germany. *Member:* International PEN.

Awards, Honors

Gold medal from Boys Clubs of America, 1966, for *Jack Holborn*; Guardian Prize, 1967, for *Devil-in-the-Fog*; Carnegie commendation, 1967, *Boston Globe-Horn Book* Award, 1968, and Phoenix Award, 1987, all for *Smith*; Carnegie honour book, 1968, for *Black Jack*, and 1970, for *The Drummer Boy*; *Mister Corbett's Ghost* named Best Illustrated Book by the *New York Times*, 1968; Carnegie Medal, 1970, and Greenaway commendation, 1970, both for *The God beneath the Sea*; Greenaway commendation, 1972, for *The Ghost Downstairs*; Whitbread Award, 1980, for *John Diamond*; *Boston Globe-Horn Book* Award, 1981, for *Footsteps*; Federation of Children's Book Groups Award, 1981, for *Fair's Fair*; Maschler Award runner-up, 1985, for *Shakespeare Stories* and for *The Wedding Ghost.*

Writings

FICTION

Jack Holborn, Constable, 1964, Pantheon, 1965.
Devil-in-the-Fog, Pantheon, 1966.
Smith, Pantheon, 1967.
Mister Corbett's Ghost, Pantheon, 1968.
Black Jack, Longmans, Green, 1968, Pantheon, 1969.
The Restless Ghost: Three Stories, Pantheon, 1969.
Mr. Corbett's Ghost and Other Stories, Longman, 1969.
The Drummer Boy, Pantheon, 1969.
The Boy and the Monkey, F. Watts, 1969.

The Strange Affair of Adelaide Harris, Pantheon, 1971.

The Captain's Watch, Heinemann, 1972.

The Ghost Downstairs, Pantheon, 1972.

Lucifer Wilkins, Heinemann, 1973.

The Sound of Coaches, Viking, 1974.

The Prisoners of September, Viking, 1975.

The Pleasure Garden, Viking, 1976.

An Adelaide Ghost, Ward Lock, 1977.

The Confidence Man, Kestrel, 1978, Viking, 1979.

The Night of the Comet: A Comedy of Courtship Featuring Bostock and Harris, Delacorte, 1979.

Footsteps, Delacorte, 1980, (published in England as *John Diamond*, Kestrel, 1980).

The Mystery of Edwin Drood (based on the unfinished manuscript by Charles Dickens), Deutsch, 1980, Pantheon, 1981.

King Nimrod's Tower, Lothrop, 1982.

Fair's Fair, Doubleday, 1982.

The Writing on the Wall, Methuen, 1982, Lothrop, 1983.

The House of Cards, Bodley Head, 1982, St. Martin's, 1983.

Tales from Shakespeare, Gollancz, 1984.

The King in the Garden, Lothrop, 1984.

The December Rose, Viking, 1987.

The Empty Sleeve, Delacorte, 1988.

Blewcoat Boy, Delacorte, 1988.

Young Nick and Jubilee, Delacorte, 1989.

The Saracen Maid, Simon & Schuster, 1991.

"APPRENTICES" SERIES

The Lamplighter's Funeral, Heinemann, 1976.

Mirror, Mirror, Heinemann, 1976.

The Cloak, Heinemann, 1976.

Moss and Blister, Heinemann, 1976.

The Dumb Cake, Heinemann, 1977.

Tom Titmarsh's Devil, Heinemann, 1977.

The Fool, Heinemann, 1977.

Rosy Starling, Heinemann, 1977.

The Valentine, Heinemann, 1977.

Labour in Vain, Heinemann, 1977.

The Enemy, Heinemann, 1978.

The Filthy Beast, Heinemann, 1978.

The Apprentices (contains all 12 of the "Apprentices" series books), Viking, 1978.

EDITOR

Baker's Dozen: A Collection of Stories, Ward, Lock, 1973, published as *Strange Fish and Other Stories*, Lothrop, 1974.

The Book Lovers, Ward, Lock, 1976.

A Swag of Stories, Ward, Lock, 1978.

(With Edward Blishen, and author of introduction) Charles Dickens, *Sketches from Bleak House*, illustrations by Mervyn Peake, Methuen, 1983.

OTHER

(Reteller with Blishen) *The God Beneath the Sea* (based on Greek mythology), Longman, 1970, Pantheon, 1971.

(With David Proctor) *Child o' War: The True Story of a Boy Sailor in Nelson's Navy*, Holt, 1972.

(Reteller with Blishen) *The Golden Shadow* (based on Greek mythology), Pantheon, 1973.

The House of Hanover: England in the Eighteenth Century, Seabury Press, 1976.

Contributor of stories to *Winter's Tales for Children, 4*, Macmillan, 1968, and *The Restless Ghost and Other Encounters and Experiences*, edited by Susan Dickinson, Collins, 1970. Contributor of play to *Miscellany Four*, edited by Edward Blishen, Oxford University Press, 1967.

■ Adaptations

Devil-in-the-Fog, Smith, and *The Strange Affair of Adelaide Harris* were filmed for British television; *Black Jack* was filmed in 1979; *John Diamond* was filmed for television by the British Broadcasting Corp. (BBC) in 1981; *Jack Holborn* was filmed by Taurus Film in 1982 and broadcast on German television; *The Ghost Downstairs* was filmed for television in 1982; *The Restless Ghost* was filmed for television in 1983; *The December Rose* was filmed for television by the BBC in 1986; *The Ghost Downstairs* is available on cassette tape, with Clifford Norgate reading the text, from G. K. Hall, 1987.

■ Sidelights

"God knows why I write," Leon Garfield once stated, "except that I feel restless when I don't." After working twenty years as a biochemical technician at a London hospital and writing in his spare time, Garfield began selling his novels in the mid 1960s. His first book, *Jack Holborn*, a tale of a stowaway boy on an eighteenth century pirate ship, set the tone for many of his later books, which are often set in historical times, feature young characters, and have the fast-paced adventure characteristic of such writers as Charles Dickens, Robert Louis Stevenson, and Henry Fielding. Mary Wadsworth Sucher writes in *English Journal*: "Rich in atmosphere, character, and style, with the gusto of a Dickens or a Sterne, Garfield's elaborate and

Leon Garfield

JACK HOLBORN

Now an exciting television series

Piracy and adventure fill Garfield's 1964 novel, in which a young orphan unknowingly stows away on a pirate ship and is forced to join the crew.

witty tales are full of surprises, courage of survival, and hope for the future."

Garfield was born in the English town of Brighton, where his interest in writing stories began when he was young. His early works were inspired by Edgar Allan Poe, Tolstoy, Lewis Carroll, and other classic writers, with Garfield trying to develop a style of his own which incorporated elements from the humorous and the gothic. His hometown of Brighton was also an influence on his writing. The town's eighteenth century architecture appears many times in Garfield's books set during that period of history. After serving six years in the British Army's Medical Corps during World War II, Garfield became a biochemical technician at a London hospital, where he worked for some twenty years.

Five years of research into eighteenth century seafaring resulted in 1964 in the publication of Garfield's first novel, *Jack Holborn,* a tale of piracy and adventure. The author explains in *Horn Book* that he had wanted to write a sea adventure set in the eighteenth century but knew little about the time or about maritime life. "At last I looked into Swift and Defoe for some appropriate nautical information," Garfield writes. "They were both very strong in it, and they appeared to get their effects from vivid personal experience. I was very depressed . . . until I discovered that both had got their information straight out of an old sailing manual from which, in places, they had copied word for word. They knew no more about the sea than I did. . . . It was the most encouraging discovery I have ever made. From there on, though [writing the novel] was never plain sailing, it was at least navigable."

Originally written as an adult novel, an editor at the British publishing house of Constable thought *Jack Holborn* would work better as a juvenile novel. "She suggested that, if I would be willing to cut it," Garfield recalls in Justin Wintle and Emma Fisher's *The Pied Pipers,* "then she'd publish it as a juvenile book. And of course, though I'd vowed I'd never alter a word, once the possibility of its being published became real, I cut it in about one week."

Jack Holborn is a young orphan who has never known his parents or his real name. When he stows away aboard the *Charming Molly,* he thinks of it as an exciting chance to see the world. Only when the ship is out at sea does he realize his mistake: he has stowed away on a pirate ship. Forced to join the crew, Jack endures storms, naval battles, shipwreck, and a trek through the African jungle before he returns home to a murder trial at the Old Bailey.

Jack Holborn was a success for Garfield. Margaret Sherwood Libby of *Book Week* calls it "a taut, tough and exciting story, complicated but so well-told that it held me to the last page." "It's done with such terrific good nature and flair," states the *Virginia Kirkus Service* reviewer, "that you begin by liking Jack, whose instincts are good, and wind up enjoying the whole teeming book." Marcus Crouch in *The Nesbit Tradition: The Children's Novel in England, 1945-1970* claims that "Garfield seems to have had no 'prentice period. His first book, *Jack Holborn,* has all his characteristic qualities. . . . The ingredients are all conventional enough. It is the author's expert chemistry—appropriately he is a biochemist by calling—which makes the unpromising materials react to produce tension and atmosphere." *Jack Holborn* was adapted as a film and a television series. With the success of the book, Garfield left his hospital job to become a full-time writer.

In *Devil-in-the-Fog*, Garfield's second novel, a young boy who works in a traveling show may well be the real heir to a baronet. Told in a style compared by several critics to that of Charles Dickens, the story is complicated, humorous, and an intriguing mystery. Margery Fisher in *Growing Point* calls the novel "a strange book, more than life-size and yet life-like for the feelings and attitudes of the characters: a book to leave firmly out of categories and accept thankfully for what it is—a masterpiece." *Devil-in-the-Fog* won the first *Guardian* Award for children's fiction.

With *Smith*, Garfield again turned to a Dickensian story, this time telling of a young pickpocket in eighteenth century London who steals a document from an elderly gentleman. When the gentleman is later murdered, Smith is charged with the crime. Meanwhile, the stolen document is the target of underworld thieves who wish to retrieve it. Naomi Lewis in *New Statesman* calls the book "an electrifying experience," while Margery Fisher claims it is "an outstanding book.... A book ... rich in the furnishings of historical fiction which offers also such a fascinating and such a valid study of human beings." Crouch believes that "Garfield's craft is at its most brilliant, and is most at the command of his theme, in *Smith*.... It is not just a masterly exercise in story-telling, but a book through which the reader shares in the triumphs and disasters of Smith and his admirable sisters."

Smith was followed by *Black Jack*, another novel set in eighteenth century England and focusing on the criminal underworld of the time. The story begins with the hanging of the notorious highwayman, Black Jack. Through the use of a hollow metal tube inserted in his throat, Black Jack cheats death by strangulation and escapes to continue his life of crime. It is only through the relationship between Tolly, an orphan boy, and the mad girl Belle, that Black Jack comes to a realization of the power of love.

According to David Rees in the *School Librarian*, "Garfield's best work is to be found in *Smith* and *Black Jack*, both exciting adventure stories." Other critics echo this assessment. "There is a richness about [*Black Jack*], both in physical detail and in human feeling, that makes it a notable contribution to the genre of the historical novel," according to a reviewer for the *Times Literary Supplement*. Gor-

don Parsons in the *School Librarian and School Library Review* praises those qualities Garfield displays in the novel: "A mastery of gripping openings, the rich Dickensian characterization, the nightmare atmosphere of impending doom and threatening mystery which inform the narrative, the wryly humorous and vivid imagery.... A magnificent novel."

Other Garfield books set in the eighteenth century include such novels as *The Sound of Coaches*, the story of a coachman's son who discovers his true identity, *The Prisoners of September*, set in a grim and chillingly violent Revolutionary France, and *Blewcoat Boy*, in which two orphans convince a pickpocket to pose as their father so that they can qualify for charity assistance. In an article for *Children's Literature in Education*, Garfield talks about his use of historical settings in his novels, particularly his use of England in the eighteenth century. He reveals that in "spite of all my research and caution over detail, I don't really write historical novels. To me, the eighteenth century—or my idea of it—is more a locality than a time. And in this curious locality I find that I can represent quite contemporary characters more vividly than I could otherwise." The eighteenth century was not chosen "by caprice," Garfield continues. "I preferred the discipline of classicism to the freedom of romanticism. Just as Alan Garner admits that he uses fantasy as a crutch, so I use the classical form."

To give his historical settings accuracy, Garfield does not crowd his fiction with details of the period. Rather, Garfield tells Wintle and Fisher, he mentions only "such details as [are] unusual enough to be noticed and remarked on.... After all, if one writes a contemporary novel, one does not go into details of garbage collection, the price of dustbins, or what a doctor wears." Speaking of Garfield's historical fiction, a reviewer for the *Times Literary Supplement* claims that "Garfield's sense of the past is at once precise and imaginative, and his presentation of it is entirely convincing because his interest is concentrated, not on the accidentals of behaviour, but rather on the unchanging human heart."

In many of his books, Garfield has also revealed a special fondness for ghost stories. He has written several of them, including *Mr. Corbett's Ghost*, *The Restless Ghost*, and *The Ghost Downstairs*, while ghosts figure prominently in many of his other stories. In *Jack Holborn*, for example, the ghost of a madman haunts the crew. Garfield's ghosts are sometimes the spirits of the dead and sometimes creations of a guilty character's troubled conscience. One of his most successful ghost stories has been *Mr. Corbett's Ghost*, the story of an apothecary's apprentice, Benjamin, who wishes that his stern boss were dead. When he meets a man who can grant wishes, but at a price, Benjamin discovers that his wish is not all that he hoped it would be. Mr. Corbett's ghost haunts him, making his life worse than before. "I would say, and not lightly, that [this novel] can be compared to *A Christmas Carol*," John Rowe Townsend states in his *A Sense of Story: Essays on Contemporary Writers for Children*.

In the "Apprentices" series of 12 books, Garfield writes for a younger age group about boys and girls learning various trades in eighteenth century England. Each book tells a brief tale of an apprentice who struggles toward maturity while gaining insight into the often deceptive nature of the world. "On one level," writes Sheila A. Egoff in *Thursday's Child: Trends and Patterns in Contemporary Children's Literature*, "the stories are straightforward, exciting, and, at times, comic narratives.... There are as well other levels of meaning—highly symbolical, often allegorical—and these are sometimes elusive.... The motifs of light and dark, or friendship and love, not romantic love, but the divine love of compassion, forgiveness, and rebirth, are creatively varied and skillfully interwoven." Writing in the *Times Literary Supplement*, Lance Salway finds the "Apprentices" books to be a "remarkable combination of precise historical detail and timeless characterization.... The series as a whole is an achievement that matches the best of Leon Garfield's more prestigious work."

While he has used historical settings in many of his stories, Garfield has also written historical nonfiction. In *The House of Hanover*, he presents a look at the Georgian Period of English history. "Taking the brilliant device of viewing the period through the portraits of its leading figures," writes Anne Wood in *Books for Your Children*, "[Garfield] proceeds to follow this through literally by making the entire book an account of a visit to the National Portrait Gallery. It is brilliantly done, never flagging for a second in breathless interest and amusement.... *The House of Hanover* must surely be one of the most entertaining introductions, not just to the artistic life of a particular period but to the relationship between art and life in any age, ever written."

In *Child O' War: The True Story of a Boy Sailor in Nelson's Navy*, Garfield joined with David Proctor to present the story of the British Navy's youngest

A notorious eighteenth-century English criminal, Black Jack, escapes his own hanging and eventually finds love in this 1968 Carnegie Honor Book.

recruit ever, Sir John Theophilus Lee, who enlisted at the age of five and served in the Napoleonic wars. Based on Lee's own memoirs, "an endlessly boring document," as Catherine Storr describes it in *New Statesman*, *Child O' War* is a compact recounting of the life and times of the British war hero. Storr calls the resulting work "a compassionate and witty short book which should do more to illustrate to the young what horror lies behind the brave front of war than all the diatribes contrived by moralists and preachers."

With Edward Blishen, Garfield turned to the imaginary past of the ancient Greek myths, writing two books which fuse the myths into a single continuous narrative. The first of these books is *The God Beneath the Sea*, which retells such stories as the agony of Prometheus, the fall of Hephaestus, and the opening of Pandora's box. The authors' intricate interweaving of many disparate tales was especially appreciated by critics. Writing in *Con-*

Garfield's affinity for ghost stories is apparent in this 1969 work, which has been compared to Dickens's *A Christmas Carol.*

temporary Review, Peter Geoffrey Townsend finds that "the manner in which many of the better known myths are put within a dramatic framework and given a coherence, both chronological and psychological, is indeed probably the greatest achievement of the book." Similarly, Ted Hughes, writing in *Children's Literature in Review,* states that "there have been many retellings of Greek myths for children but this interweaving of about twenty of them must be among the best." In their afterword to the book, Garfield and Blishen explain that one of their chief aims was to present the Greek myths in the "literary voice of our own time." Several critics found the book's writing to be exceptional. "Its language," Barbara Wersba writes in the *New York Times Book Review,* "is like a mosaic of fiery, precious jewels; and its interwoven plots are brilliantly handled.... They are only

myths, yet they seem to be a total dream-history of the world."

In *The Golden Shadow,* Garfield and Blishen again retell classic Greek myths in a single narrative, this time joining the stories through the device of an old storyteller who travels ancient Greece and tells of the events he witnesses. "It is an interesting device, and a successful one, as if the authors had imaginatively become this archetypal figure," Gerard Benson writes in *New Statesman.* Much of the book focuses on Heracles, recounting the story of his long and heroic life. "This is in no way a conventional retelling of the deeds of a strong-arm bully whose heroism is measured in monsters slain and enemies lying dead in heaps," Judith Vidal Hall explains in *Children's Book Review.* "It is every bit as idiosyncratic an interpretation as the previous book, concerned more with the hero as a man than a superman, and questioning the nature of heroism itself." Shulamith Oppenheim in the *New York Times Book Review* calls *The Golden Shadow* "a gem of a book," while Benson concludes that the book is "utterly modern in its writing and still Greek in feeling."

Garfield has also written a collection of stories based on the plays of William Shakespeare, a writer he much admires. In *Shakespeare Stories,* he retells classic Shakespearean dramas in short story form. "Garfield," writes Stanley Wells in the *Times Literary Supplement,* "seeks to convey in prose narrative the experience, not of reading the twelve plays that he includes, but of seeing them performed." The intricate plotting of the original plays, and the many sides to the characters, are captured in Garfield's stories. "They are not pale reflections of the plays," Wells states, "not introductions to the study of Shakespeare, but fresh creations with a life of their own." D. J. R. Bruckner in the *New York Times Book Review* simply believes that "Garfield's performance in *Shakespeare Stories* is masterly."

Looking over the whole of Garfield's written production, Sucher sees a close correlation between the author's life and art. "Much of Garfield's writing," Sucher states, "seems to result from his own active, varied life—his scientific study, his Army Medical Corps experience, his interest in the eighteenth century and Shakespearean drama, and his fondness for language, along with 'much reading of a very *few* books.'" Garfield's prose style, Sucher believes, has its roots in the literature of the nineteenth century. She writes: "His highly visual, colorful writing makes one think of Fielding or even Stevenson, but he is most often compared to

The twelve volumes of Garfield's Apprentices series, which describe various eighteenth century English trades, are collected in this 1978 work.

Dickens and Thackeray in his handling of characters and intricate plots and in his propensity to use a definite time and place (eighteenth century London) as the setting for most of his novels."

Wood finds a strong moral stance in Garfield's fiction. All of his books, she writes, "deal in some way with an atmosphere of concentrated evil shot through with possibilities for good.... The overwhelming contribution of his books is that they deal in that old-fashioned quality, morality. At the centre of each story is a young person, a boy usually, whose life is impinged upon by mysterious forces for good and evil, their rightness or wrongness obscured by different shows and pretences or seemingly accidental occurrences.... These are not historical novels in the accepted sense. An interpretation of history is certainly not what they are about. An interpretation of life perhaps."

Rees notes that Garfield often employs allusion in his novels, quoting from or paraphrasing such earlier writers as Joseph Conrad, Thomas Love Peacock, and Jane Austen. Garfield also borrows or re-employs scenes and characters from the books

of earlier writers. "One is not accusing him of plagiarism, or pallid imitations of the real thing," Rees clarifies. "[Garfield] has a remarkable ability to transmute these bits of other authors into something that is wholly his own; his style is in fact highly individual, and, at its best, an excellent instrument for his purposes. Parody (even self-parody), irony, a kind of grotesque humour, and a fine eye for the ridiculous are its hallmarks."

Speaking to Wintle and Fisher, Garfield discusses writing for young people. He explains first of all that "one does not write *for* children. One writes so that children can understand. Which means writing as clearly, vividly, and truthfully as possible. Adults might put up with occasional lapses; children are far less tolerant. They must never be bored; not for an instant. Words must live for them; so must people. That is what really matters, and it entails believing entirely in what one writes and having a real urgency to convince the reader that it is absolutely, utterly true."

Arguing for the importance of children's literature in an article for *Horn Book,* Garfield declares: "The suggestion that writing for children always requires a smaller mental effort than other kinds [of writing] is surely most careless.... And the trouble with these hasty and mildly scornful attitudes to children's books is that they make it more difficult for us all to recognize a surely essential truth: that no good comes from thinking of literature as divided into a negligible junior field, and senior field that is alone worth considering seriously. Surely literature is a continuous matter, from childhood onward? With children's books, readers are created for all books whatever."

Rhodri Jones sees a similar importance in children's literature, an importance particularly evident in Garfield's own children's novels. Writing in *The Use of English*, Jones claims that Garfield's novels "deal with the same kind of themes as adult literature, but in terms that children can understand. By identifying with the heroes, children can appreciate the moral choices that arise, and can see that the world is not entirely black and white but varying shades of grey. When they go on to read Shakespeare, Dickens, George Eliot or Jane Austen, they are prepared for similar complexities of feelings and responses to character and situation. If they do not go on to read these classics, they have had a valuable and easily approachable substitute."

Garfield's books have won him recognition as one of England's most outstanding children's writers. Garfield, according to Geoffrey Trease in *New Statesman*, "quickly established himself by general acclamation as one of the most gifted and individual writers for the older child. He has staked out a special corner for himself; one is tempted to say 'a graveyard plot,' so macabre is his fancy, but that description would belie the vitality, the exuberant gusto, with which he claps his skeletal grip upon the bristling nape and sends his delicious frissons down the spine." Writing in the *Children's Book Review*, C. S. Hannabuss states that "the richly styled atmospherics of Leon Garfield form one of the salient literary features in the landscape of the last decade and a half of children's books.... [His] tales of misty derring-do, replete with coincidental encounters and nightmare villainies that work an insidious chemistry on the imagination of the reader, will remain on booklists for a long while." "Of all the talents that emerged in the field of British writing for children in the 1960s," writes Townsend, "that of Leon Garfield seems to me to be the richest and strangest. I am tempted to go on and say that his stories are the tallest, the deepest, the wildest, the most spine-chilling, the most humorous, the most energetic, the most extravagant, the most searching, the most everything."

■ For More Information See

BOOKS

Blishen, Edward, editor, *The Thorny Paradise: Writers on Writing for Children*, Kestrel Books, 1975.

Butts, Dennis, editor, *Good Writers for Young Readers*, Hart-Davis, 1977.

Children's Literature Review, Volume 21, Gale, 1990.

Contemporary Literary Criticism, Volume 12, Gale, 1980.

Crouch, Marcus, *The Nesbit Tradition: The Children's Novel in England, 1945-1970*, Ernest Benn Limited, 1972.

Egoff, Sheila, G. T. Stubbs, and L. F. Ashley, editors, *Only Connect: Readings on Children's Literature*, Oxford University Press, 1969.

Egoff, Sheila A., *Thursday's Child: Trends and Patterns in Contemporary Children's Literature*, American Library Association, 1981.

Eyre, Frank, *British Children's Books in the Twentieth Century*, 1971, Longman Books, 1971, revised edition, 1979.

Fisher, Margery, *Classics for Children & Young People*, Thimble Press, 1986.

Inglis, Fred, *The Promise of Happiness: Value and Meaning in Children's Fiction*, Cambridge University Press, 1981.

Meigs, Cornelia, editor, *A Critical History of Children's Literature*, revised edition, Macmillan, 1969.

Townsend, John Rowe, *A Sense of Story: Essays on Contemporary Writers for Children*, Lippincott, 1971.

Tucker, Nicholas, *The Child and the Book: A Psychological and Literary Exploration*, Cambridge University Press, 1981.

Wintle, Justin and Emma Fisher, *The Pied Pipers*, Paddington, 1974.

PERIODICALS

Books for Your Children, summer, 1976.

Book Week, October 31, 1965.

Children's Book Review, December, 1973, autumn, 1974.

Children's Literature in Education, July, 1970, November, 1970, March, 1973, Volume 9, number 4, 1978, Volume 21, number 1, 1990.

Contemporary Review, December 3, 1971.

English Journal, September, 1983.

Growing Point, December, 1966, July, 1967, September, 1969, May, 1970, September, 1980.

Horn Book, December, 1968, February, 1971.

Junior Bookshelf, October, 1973.

Lion and the Unicorn, fall, 1978.

New Statesman, May 26, 1967, May 16, 1969, June 2, 1972, May 25, 1973.

New York Times Book Review, May 2, 1971, February 3, 1974, February 26, 1986.

School Librarian, May, 1988.

School Librarian and School Library Review, March, 1969.

Signal, May, 1971.

Times Educational Supplement, February 19, 1982.

Times Literary Supplement, November 24, 1964, May 25, 1967, December 5, 1968, October 30, 1970, June 15, 1973, July 5, 1974, July 7, 1978, April 26, 1985.

The Use of English, winter, 1971, summer, 1972.

Virginia Kirkus Service, October 15, 1965.

Jean Craighead George

York City, employee, 1944-45, artist and reporter, 1945-46; continuing education teacher in Chappaqua, NY, 1960-68; *Reader's Digest*, Pleasantville, NY, staff writer, 1969-74, roving editor, 1974-80; author and illustrator of books and articles on natural history. *Pageant* (magazine), New York City, artist. *Member:* League of Women Voters, P.E.N., Dutchess County Art Association.

■ Personal

Has also written as Jean George; born July 2, 1919, in Washington, DC; daughter of Frank Cooper (an entomologist) and Mary Carolyn (Johnson) Craighead; married John Lothar George, January 28, 1944 (divorced January 10, 1963); children: Carolyn Laura, John Craighead, Thomas Luke. *Education:* Pennsylvania State University, B.A., 1941; attended Louisiana State University, Baton Rouge, 1941-42, and University of Michigan. *Politics:* Democrat. *Hobbies and other interests:* Painting, field trips to universities and laboratories of natural science, modern dance, white water canoeing.

■ Addresses

Home and office—20 William St., Chappaqua, NY 10514. *Agent*—Curtis Brown Ltd., 10 Astor Place, New York, NY 10003.

■ Career

International News Service, Washington, DC, reporter, 1942-44; *Washington Post and Times-Herald*, Washington, DC, reporter, 1943-44; United Features (Newspaper Enterprise Association), New

■ Awards, Honors

Aurianne Award, American Library Association (ALA), 1956, for *Dipper of Copper Creek*; Newbery Medal honor book award and ALA notable book citation, both American Library Association, 1960, International Hans Christian Andersen Award honor list, 1962, Lewis Carroll Shelf citation, 1965, and George G. Stone Center for Children's Books Award, 1969, all for *My Side of the Mountain*; Woman of the Year, Pennsylvania State University, 1968; Claremont College award, 1969; Eva L. Gordon Award, American Nature Study Society, 1970; *Book World* First Prize, 1971, for *All upon a Stone*; Newbery Medal, National Book Award finalist citation, German Youth Literature Prize from West German section of International Board on Books for Young People, and Silver Skate from Netherlands Children's Book Board, all 1973, and listing by Children's Literature Association as one of ten best American children's books in two hundred years, 1976, all for *Julie of the Wolves*; School Library Media Specialties of South Eastern New York Award, 1981; Irvin Kerlan Award, University of Minnesota, 1982; University of Southern Mississippi award, 1986; Grumman

Award, 1986; Washington Irving Award, Westchester Library Association, 1991; Knickerbocker Award for Juvenile Literature, School Library Media Section, New York Public Library Association, c. 1991.

■ **Writings**

UNDER NAME JEAN GEORGE, WITH JOHN L. GEORGE; SELF-ILLUSTRATED JUVENILE NOVELS

Vulpes, the Red Fox, Dutton, 1948.
Vison, the Mink, Dutton, 1949.
Masked Prowler: The Story of a Raccoon, Dutton, 1950.
Meph, the Pet Skunk, Dutton, 1952.
Bubo, the Great Horned Owl, Dutton, 1954.
Dipper of Copper Creek, Dutton, 1956.

SELF-ILLUSTRATED JUVENILE NOVELS

(Under name Jean George) *The Hole in the Tree,* Dutton, 1957.
(Under name Jean George) *Snow Tracks,* Dutton, 1958.
(Under name Jean George) *My Side of the Mountain,* Dutton, 1959.
The Summer of the Falcon, Crowell, 1962.
Red Robin, Fly Up!, Reader's Digest, 1963.
Gull Number 737, Crowell, 1964.
Hold Zero!, Crowell, 1966.
Water Sky, Harper, 1987.
On the Far Side of the Mountain, Dutton, 1990.

JUVENILE NOVELS

Coyote in Manhattan, illustrated by John Kaufmann, Crowell, 1968.
All upon a Stone, illustrated by Don Bolognese, Crowell, 1971.
Who Really Killed Cock Robin? An Ecological Mystery, Dutton, 1971.
Julie of the Wolves, illustrated by John Schoenherr, Harper, 1972.
All upon a Sidewalk, illustrated by Bolognese, Dutton, 1974.
Hook a Fish, Catch a Mountain, Dutton, 1975.
Going to the Sun, Harper, 1976.
The Wentletrap Trap, illustrated by Symeon Shimin, Dutton, 1978.
The Wounded Wolf, illustrated by Schoenherr, Harper, 1978.
River Rats, Inc., Dutton, 1979.
The Cry of the Crow, Harper, 1980.
The Grizzly Bear with the Golden Ears, illustrated by Tom Catania, Harper, 1982.
The Talking Earth, Harper, 1983.

Shark beneath the Reef, Harper, 1989.
Missing 'Gator of Gumbo Limbo: An Ecological Mystery, HarperCollins, 1992.

"THIRTEEN MOONS" JUVENILE NONFICTION SERIES

The Moon of the Salamanders, illustrated by Kaufmann, Crowell, 1967, new edition illustrated by Marlene Werner, HarperCollins, 1992.
The Moon of the Bears, illustrated by Mac Shepard, Crowell, 1967, new edition illustrated by Ron Parker, HarperCollins, 1993.
The Moon of the Owls, illustrated by Jean Zallinger, Crowell, 1967, new edition illustrated by Wendell Minor, HarperCollins, 1993.
The Moon of the Mountain Lions, illustrated by Winifred Lubell, Crowell, 1968, new edition illustrated by Ron Parker, HarperCollins, 1991.
The Moon of the Chickarees, illustrated by Schoenherr, Crowell, 1968, new edition illustrated by Don Rodell, HarperCollins, 1992.
The Moon of the Fox Pups, illustrated by Kiyoaki Komoda, Crowell, 1968, new edition illustrated by Norman Adams, HarperCollins, 1992.
The Moon of the Wild Pigs, illustrated by Peter Parnall, Crowell, 1968, new edition illustrated by Paul Mirocha, HarperCollins, 1992.
The Moon of the Monarch Butterflies, illustrated by Murray Tinkelman, Crowell, 1968, new edition illustrated by Kam Mak, HarperCollins, 1993.
The Moon of the Alligators, illustrated by Adrina Zanazanian, Crowell, 1969, new edition illustrated by Michael Rothman, HarperCollins, 1991.
The Moon of the Gray Wolves, illustrated by Lorence Bjorklund, Crowell, 1969, new edition illustrated by Catalano, HarperCollins, 1991.
The Moon of the Deer, illustrated by Zallinger, Crowell, 1969, new edition illustrated by Sal Catalano, HarperCollins, 1992.
The Moon of the Moles, illustrated by Robert Levering, Crowell, 1969, new edition illustrated by Rothman, HarperCollins, 1992.
The Moon of the Winter Bird, illustrated by Kazue Mizumura, Crowell, 1969, new edition illustrated by Vincent Nasta, HarperCollins, 1992.

"ONE DAY" JUVENILE NONFICTION SERIES

One Day in the Desert, illustrated by Fred Brenner, Crowell, 1983.
One Day in the Alpine Tundra, illustrated by Walter Gaffney-Kessell, Crowell, 1984.

One Day in the Prairie, illustrated by Bob Marstall, Crowell, 1986.

One Day in the Woods, illustrated by Gary Allen, Crowell, 1988.

One Day in the Tropical Rain Forest, illustrated by Allen, HarperCollins, 1990.

OTHER NONFICTION

Spring Comes to the Ocean (juvenile), illustrated by John Wilson, Crowell, 1965.

Beastly Inventions: A Surprising Investigation into How Smart Animals Really Are (juvenile), self-illustrated, McKay, 1970, published in England as *Animals Can Do Anything*, Souvenir Press, 1972.

Everglades Wildguide, illustrated by Betty Fraser, National Park Service, 1972.

(With Toy Lasker) *New York in Maps, 1972/73*, New York Magazine, 1974.

(With Lasker) *New York in Flashmaps, 1974/75*, Flashmaps, 1976.

The American Walk Book: An Illustrated Guide to the Country's Major Historic and Natural Walking Trails from New England to the Pacific Coast, Dutton, 1978.

The Wild, Wild Cookbook: A Guide for Young Wild-Food Foragers (juvenile), illustrated by Walter Kessell, Crowell, 1982.

Journey Inward (autobiography), Dutton, 1982.

How to Talk to Your Animals, self-illustrated, Harcourt, 1985 (also see below).

How to Talk to Your Dog (originally published in *How to Talk to Your Animals*), self-illustrated, Warner, 1986.

How to Talk to Your Cat (originally published in *How to Talk to Your Animals*), self-illustrated, Warner, 1986.

OTHER

Tree House (play; with music by Saul Aarons), produced in Chappaqua, NY, 1962.

(Illustrator) John J. Craighead and Frank C. Craighead, Jr., *Hawks, Owls, and Wildlife*, Dover, 1969.

Contributor to books, including *Marvels and Mysteries of Our Animal World*, Reader's Digest Association, 1964. Contributor of articles on natural history and children's literature to periodicals, including *Audubon, Horn Book, International Wildlife*, and *National Wildlife*. Consultant for science books.

George's manuscripts are held in the Kerlan Collection at the University of Minnesota, Minneapolis.

■ **Adaptations**

My Side of the Mountain was adapted as a film starring Teddy Eccles and Theodore Bikel, Paramount, 1969; *Julie of the Wolves* was adapted as a recording, read by Irene Worth, Caedmon, 1977; *One Day in the Woods* was adapted as a musical video, with music by Fritz Kramer and Chris Kubie, Kunhardt Productions, 1989.

■ **Work in Progress**

The First Thanksgiving and *To Climb a Waterfall*, with paintings by Thomas Locker, for Philomel; *The Fire Bug Connection: An Ecological Mystery*, for HarperCollins.

■ **Sidelights**

Since 1948 Jean Craighead George has given young readers many fascinating glimpses of nature, earning a reputation as "our premier naturalist novelist," according to *New York Times Book Review* contributor Beverly Lyon Clark. Writing

$1.50 | J58
$1.75 in Canada

A Harper Trophy Book

Winner of the 1973 Newbery Medal

JULIE OF THE WOLVES

Jean Craighead George

Pictures by John Schoenherr

A summer trip to Alaska inspired George to write this Newbery Medal-winning tale of survival.

first with her husband and later alone, she penned studies of animals, such as *Dipper of Copper Creek,* as well as adventures of young people learning to survive in wilderness, like her Newbery Medal-winning novel *Julie of the Wolves.* Her books are distinguished by authentic detail and a blend of scientific curiosity, wonder, and concern for the natural environment, all expressed in a manner critics have described as both unsentimental and lyrical. Action, vividly drawn settings, and believable characters invigorate her stories. Observed Karen Nelson Hoyle in an article in *Dictionary of Literary Biography,* George "elevates nature in all its intricacies and makes scientific research concerning ecological systems intriguing and exciting to the young reader."

George and her twin brothers, John and Frank, grew up spending their summers on land her father's family had farmed for generations. Her ancestor John Craighead had settled in southern Pennsylvania in 1742, and members of the family

George's 1959 Newbery Honor Book describes a runaway teenage boy's adventures in the wilderness.

had lived in the area, which came to be known as Craigheads, ever since. A love for nature and literature was part of the Craighead heritage. In her autobiography, *Journey Inward,* George wrote: "My father had been born in a handsome Victorian house above the Yellow Breeches Creek, at the center of Craigheads. As a boy he explored the meadows and woods, discovering where the skunks lived and the copperheads denned. When he was sent to Harrisburg to go to high school, he awakened to new worlds with the discovery of the literary classics in the library of a great-aunt. During his high school years he read his way from the door around the room and back again. Years later he told me that the library had indeed inspired him to go to college and get his Ph.D. After eight generations, since increased to eleven, John Craighead's love of the land was still inherent, and Dad studied forestry and entomology. Every summer while I was growing up, when Dad went west to supervise his field research stations, my mother, John, Frank and I moved to the Victorian house, which was up the road from Dad's and Mother's farm. During these summers we too learned to follow the skunks, the snakes and the birds; and in the old house, I read the classics myself."

Always drawn to the outdoors, George fished, played softball, swam, caught frogs, and rode hay wagons with her brothers. Homely tasks such as sewing and canning bored her, but being with the twins had its own drawbacks. "They dominated not only me but the entire family and community," she recalled. "Besides being A students, John and Frank were responsible for beginning the sport of falconry in the United States, and while in high school they wrote articles about it for the *Saturday Evening Post* and the *National Geographic.* They were athletes and artists as well. In the summer they initiated all the exciting endeavors, from climbing down the rainspouts during nap time to spelunking. The group of fans who continually followed them included grown men as well as boys and girls. Even in those early days at Craigheads, they had begun to build a way of life which in later years would be looked on with envy by job-locked people who saw their falconry, river running and grizzly-bear research as a kind of American wish fulfillment. With two such brothers, a younger sister *had* to be a writer to find her niche and survive."

George began writing in her youth and published her first books in the late 1940s, a few years after marrying John George. The couple had met while

Sam Gribley receives survival lessons from Bando, a wandering folk singer, in the 1968 film version of *My Side of the Mountain.*

John was serving in the U.S. Navy during World War II and were married a mere four months later. "I was ready to marry," George explained in *Journey Inward.* "All of me except for that spark in the far right-hand corner that makes each one of us different from everyone else. In that far corner, my own belief in myself as a writer still held out. My solution would be to open up that corner and include John in it." Thus George's first books appeared under both their names. They were animal biographies often based on firsthand experiences with wild creatures that became family pets—at least temporarily. The first, *Vulpes, the Red Fox,* was written when John was still serving in the Navy. George wrote much of the book and illustrated it, relying in part on John's notes from interviews with a dog trainer who hunted foxes. Later the couple got firsthand information when they adopted "a young fox pup who denned in our fireplace and draped herself around my shoulders when I typed." Recalled George, "John brought to the book his observations of birds and animals and

occasionally tapped out a paragraph. The collaboration to me was a sorely needed bond between two people who were more or less strangers and were separated most of the time by the war."

Episodes with subsequent pets provided material for other books, and the couple always seemed to have at least one wild pet in their household. Some joined the family during the Georges' summers in the woods, where John studied birds for his doctoral dissertation. The owl that became the subject of *Bubo, the Great Horned Owl,* for instance, was given to them when he was too young to fly and lived with the Georges at their research site in southeastern Michigan. Later he accompanied them to their quarters at Vassar College, north of New York City, where John was teaching. Such company often eased the hardships of raising a family on John's small academic salary. The apartment they shared at Vassar, just after their first baby was born, had cramped, dark bedrooms and lacked a washing machine; but when George saw Bubo there, she "heard the wind in the beech trees outside, and smelled the green scent of their leaves" and decided that "the apartment would be just fine." Over the years George has kept more than one hundred seventy wild animals and birds; most of them eventually returned to their natural habitats.

Although their writing partnership was successful—the Georges won the American Library Association's Aurianne Award for best nature writing with their 1956 book, *Dipper of Copper Creek*—other aspects of the couple's marriage were not always harmonious. George wanted children very much, yet for six years she remained childless. When at last she became successfully pregnant she rejoiced—until her husband, watching her being wheeled to the delivery room, told her to give him a boy. He was disappointed and she felt guilty when the child turned out to be a girl. The first months of parenthood taxed the couple as well, for Carolyn Laura George—renamed "Twig" because "she's so small she's not even a branch on the family tree"—cried every night. "John was losing weight, I was tired and irritable. I wondered if our lives would ever be normal again," George wrote in her autobiography. Finally her pediatrician suggested she stop bottle-feeding Twig and feed her whatever she would eat from her parents' plates. "Peace descended upon us. We slept from ten to six. I stopped resenting John for escaping to the lab all day. I found time to be mother, wife, artist, hostess, listener and typist for John's lectures, and loved every minute of it."

Later George began to have second thoughts about her life. She loved being close to nature while her husband studied his birds, but she began to feel more acutely the weaknesses in her marriage. The couple rarely discussed their emotions or needs; conversation was often limited to the affairs of the day and interesting wildlife observations. John's academic salary was meager for a growing family, yet he procrastinated over finishing his dissertation, which would make him eligible for promotion. George found herself pressuring him to finish it. "And so I did what I didn't want to do. I pushed him each day to dictate something while I typed it out. I felt aggressive and unfeminine, but I heard my brothers telling me at the time I met John, 'You'll have to push him. He's a talented guy and smart, but he needs to be pushed or he blocks.'"

Thoughts about writing solo continued to recur despite the guilty feelings they caused. Finally, after she had tried to assist John in a confrontation with another professor, George reached a turning point. "I cannot do anything more for John," she thought. "He must do it for himself. In the end no one can help anyone else. It's time I started writing in my own name and in my own way and let John be what he is without me. I closed my eyes, feeling the guilt mount. John was enjoying the public lectures and the awards and honors we shared. An amusing and authoritative speaker, he often told audiences how we had written the animal biographies. I had been glad for him. I loved seeing my handsome husband take the leading part in the show we had produced together. But now I had to ask myself whether he knew it was only a part. It seemed to me that he was beginning to believe *he* wrote those books. I shook my head, ashamed of having such thoughts. What difference did it make? We were man and wife, companions and lovers." But already George was planning a novel of her own, which eventually became *My Side of the Mountain.*

Several years passed before *My Side of the Mountain* was published, but when it finally appeared in 1959 it was warmly received. A survival story about a teenage boy who runs away to the woods to live off the land for a year, the novel won a number of awards and widespread praise. Variously evaluated as "delightful," "extraordinary," "excellent," and "splendid," the first-person account describes Sam Gribley's self-sufficient wilderness life in detail, including the hollowed-out tree that becomes his home, his capture and training of the female peregrine falcon he names Frightful, and his various woodland recipes. Writing in *Horn Book,* Karen Jameyson commented on the book's premise: "When Sam explains, in his determined, quietly exuberant way that he has decided to leave his New York City home with a penknife, a ball of cord, an ax, some flint and steel, and forty dollars to go to live on the old Gribley land in the Catskill Mountains, the plan sounds a bit cockamamie. It also sounds mighty appealing."

The book's combination of authoritative nature lore, adventure, and fine writing impressed even those reviewers who questioned a few details. Several critics, for instance, found it incredible that Sam's family would let him go so easily. Sam leaves in spring, and it is Christmas before his father seeks him out. In *Journey Inward* George revealed that Sam's departure had given her some trouble, too. When she first conceived the story, she knew she "was going to write the story of a boy who lives off the land for a year—a story of survival, resourcefulness and ingenuity." But she didn't know how "to get the boy out into the wilderness in the

Sam takes his pet raccoon Gus with him to the woods, and while there he also captures and trains a baby falcon.

twentieth century without everyone looking for him." The answer came to her shortly after her husband lost his post at Vassar College. Worn out from caring for three children while John looked for another job, she thought, "'If I could just run away for a few hours.' ... I closed my eyes and went back to my childhood. I could see the falcons shooting across the sky like crossbows, could smell the wild garlic in the pot of mussel soup Dad was serving in a turtle shell. I could feel the crisp snap of a sagittaria tuber between my teeth and hear John and Frank call from the river that they had a mess of catfish for dinner. That's how I get Sam Gribley into the woods, I thought. He runs away as I am doing now. He even tells his father he is going to go, as I had told my mother when I was a kid and marched off into the night—only to turn around

and come back. His father will expect him back ... but Sam Gribley won't turn around. He'll make it."

Reviewers agreed that once Sam reaches his destination the story becomes captivating. In a 1990 *New York Times Book Review* article, Rafael Yglesias recalled how Sam's struggles were "depicted with a clean realism, fascinating detail and economical suspense," making the novel "a cross between the ultimate Boy Scout manual and the runaway passages of 'Tom Sawyer.'" The 1969 film version was also well received, but even so, Jameyson maintained, "the book has unquestionably snared its share of fans on the strength of its literary allure alone." The book was also a runner-up for the coveted Newbery Medal.

Professional success aside, the Georges' marriage continued to deteriorate. Although the family was living in southeastern New York, John took a job in Washington, D.C., and started commuting, coming home only on weekends. George began confiding in another friend whose marriage was in trouble. The couple argued frequently, and John blamed her for their problems. Finally George began to see a counselor. During a painful period of awakening, she began to accept that her marriage was ending. "My whole world was turning around," she wrote in *Journey Inward.* "Everything was not my fault. I was a person after all. I had my own importance. And I was still growing and changing." Observed her psychiatrist, "You have outgrown your husband." On her way home from the divorce, which was completed in Mexico, George felt unburdened. "Now I would be both breadwinner and housewife," she reflected. "Alone I could do it; with a man I became resentful when I had to mow the lawn, repair the plumbing, earn the living. My grandmother had once said she did not mind washing the floors, she just did not want anyone to see her doing it. I did not mind doing a man's work when there was no man around to harm."

With the divorce came a tighter budget, for John provided only one hundred fifty dollars per month, and George's income as a writer fluctuated. She learned to solve financial problems in new ways and gained a new outlook on her career. Once, after a particular article she had worked on for months was rejected, George had to ask the grocer for more time to pay her bill. To her surprise, she recalled in her autobiography, he consented graciously. "'I know writers don't get weekly checks,'" he said. "I was touched by his kindness and also by his respect for a writer. Somehow I had taken a hard line on my profession; I had to make good and there were to be no excuses."

Gradually life settled down to a comfortable rhythm. "Friends and animals, and an open house for the children's friends, made my life pleasant and lively," she wrote. "As I became more professional I enjoyed writing more and more. When I sold an article we celebrated; when I did not, we went back to chili con carne and cornmeal mush. The canoe was our recreation—cheap, simple and beautiful. The elusive peace of mind I had sought was descending upon me."

As George's children grew more independent, her own independence grew. Once, research trips had been family outings; now she began to go alone. In *Journey Inward* she recounted the mixed feelings with which she set out on one early excursion:

"The backpack had leaned against the bedroom wall all winter waiting for me. June came and I was out backpacking—alone. As I rolled up the car windows and locked the doors, I could feel my resolve begin to crumble. Couldn't I do my research for a book about black bears in the Smoky Mountains just as well with a companion as without? A moment ago I had known why I couldn't. Now I did not. Four steps down the trail I turned and looked back at the visitors' tower. Friendly people moved in clusters up the ramp for a look at the view. I stared at them a long while, then slowly turned and began to walk. The kids were growing up; this summer they were off to camp. The time had come to walk alone."

Once begun, the Smoky Mountain hike had its own rewards. "To my right and left the Smoky Mountains rolled out in summits and troughs like the waves of a seascape. More than two hundred different species of trees breathed out a vapor that rose like smoke, and had given the mountains their name. The dripping mixture of greens was so fecund that I could all but feel new creatures coming into being. I stopped now and then to make a note and then walked on. A winter wren sang; gray boulders gleamed in the light; all around me in the mystic vat of the soil, bacteria were at work recycling the debris of the forest to sustain the higher kingdoms of the plants and animals. The miraculous accidents of DNA that brought the human being and the forest into existence seemed almost understandable as I walked the trail. [Naturalist and writer Henry David] Thoreau was right: in the wilderness one had the ability to make sense of it all ... almost."

In 1968 George was named Woman of the Year by Pennsylvania State University; the university president stated that her "personal life and professional achievements and community service" exemplified the university's objectives. "I was both thrilled and moved by the honor," she reflected in her autobiography. "I, a divorced woman, exemplified the objectives of Penn State? Was one's personal life at last indeed one's own? Even after all these years of being a single parent, I felt very insecure about my status. I could not shake off two centuries of intolerance toward divorce. And yet it had been the right decision. John had a son, a home, a wife who worked in the Home Economics School at the university and did not invade his work world as I had done. John was moving out of his cage even as I was moving out of mine."

One summer George and her younger son, Luke, made a journey to Alaska, which strongly shaped her Newbery Medal-winning novel, *Julie of the Wolves.* The two had gone to Barrow to learn about wolf behavior from a scientist doing a study there. They also got some unplanned lessons in native culture. Early in their stay, for example, they were exploring the town's footpaths and met an Inuit boy who beckoned to them. "We followed him to the wall of ice on the beach, up ice steps to a floe and looked down on a sealskin boat shaped like a willow leaf," George wrote in *Journey Inward.* "The daylight filtering through it made it glow like a crescent moon. Beside the boat lay a gargantuan bowhead whale. I gasped to behold this creature of the ocean, which diminished the men to mice. Dressed in white parkas, pants and boots, the whalers were butchering the great mammal. Its spirit seemed to have passed into them, so reverently did they carve. 'My father's,' said the boy with enormous pride. Standing on the ice with the whale before me, the dark blue ocean curving toward the top of the earth, I experienced a deep welling-up of emotion that disconcerted me. I dismissed it, not understanding what was happening, and concentrated on the men who were laying open the great whale. Later I would learn that I had been observing a two-thousand-year-old ritual of carving the whale for distribution among the Eskimo people. Until the mid-nineteenth century when white whalers all but wiped it out, the bowhead had constituted not only food but religion, culture and history for the Eskimo. . . . Within a few hours the great whale was reduced to a jawbone fifteen feet long and a vertebra the size of a girder. The crew then began to gently rock the great carcass until it moved, then slid it toward the sea. Slowly and gently, they towed it out into deep water. As the great skeleton sank the men bowed their heads and once more I felt an emotion I could not cope with. 'We give the spirit of the whale in those bones back to the sea,' the boy said, 'so she will give us more. Whales are very rare. For years my father did not see even one whale.'" George later met a young Inuit woman and her husband, a girl whose character shaped that of the heroine of *Julie of the Wolves* and from whom she learned more about Inuit life.

George also absorbed a wealth of information about wolves during her stay in Alaska. She learned about the mated pair of dominant wolves, called "alphas," in each pack, and how wolves communicate. Repeatedly she tried to use wolf signals to interact with a captive female, who at first ignored George but finally responded. She discovered that wild wolves will approach a human who is on hands and knees but not one who is standing. And eventually she saw beyond the surface organization of the pack. Contrary to what she had been told, "the wolf pack was not the follower of the alpha male wolf," George wrote in *Journey Inward.* "Rather, it was one living organism made up of complex parts, all working toward the survival of the whole. There were reproductive parts, planning and thinking parts, parts that supported the planning and thinking. The pack was held together by a tripart language that ran like blood through an organism made up of individuals capable of changing and adapting to the environment; or even of dying out if necessary—all but a male and a female—until the environment changed again. A single wolf is not a wolf, just as a totally solitary human being is not truly human."

George's newfound knowledge found expression in *Julie of the Wolves,* which describes the adventures of an Eskimo girl who becomes lost on the tundra while running away from an unhappy marriage.

This much-anticipated 1990 sequel follows Sam as he searches for his sister and is reunited with his falcon.

When her father disappears on a hunting expedition, Miyax, also known by the English name Julie, is adopted by relatives. At thirteen she marries so she can leave her foster home. Although her husband is slow-witted, the marriage is little more than a formality at first, and Miyax is content living with his family. His forceful attempt to have sex with her, however, frightens her and she leaves him. Remembering her California pen pal's repeated invitations to visit, Miyax sets out across the tundra. When she loses her way in the barren land, she survives by learning how to communicate with a wolf pack and be accepted among them. Her own knowledge of Eskimo ways is also crucial, although gradually she begins to understand that the old ways are dying.

In *Journey Inward* George revealed some of the different responses she received for the book: "I had a call from George Woods, the children's book editor of the *New York Times*. 'Don't you think it's a little much to have the heroine get down on all fours? I mean . . . where's your artistry?' 'It's true,' I told him. 'The scientist at McKinley was approached by wild wolves when he got down on his hands and knees . . .' But my voice trailed off and I said no more. Obviously I had failed to make the wolves convincing. I started another book." But Woods's opinion was not shared by all reviewers. Another call brought the breathtaking announcement that the novel had won the Newbery Medal. Remembered George: "Later that night . . . I went downstairs to pour myself a celebratory drink of bourbon. I opened the refrigerator for ice. There, on the second shelf, lay the book I had been reading when the phone rang. On the kitchen table sat a plate of what I had thought were cookies when I offered them to a neighbor who had dropped in for coffee. They were dog biscuits. It appeared that I had not taken the news as calmly as I imagined; in fact, I was overwhelmed. To me the Newbery Medal meant more than the Nobel or the Pulitzer Prize because it reached into childhood, into those years where books and characters last a lifetime. . . . Even though I had been told that I was an old pro and a Newbery Medal would not rattle me, it did and it still does."

Julie of the Wolves is "George's most significant book," asserted Hoyle in *Dictionary of Literary Biography*. "Focusing on the theme of self-reliance, the plot, character development, and setting are epic in dimension." Other critics joined in praising George's authentic, vivid descriptions and storytelling, her winning characterization, and the book's conservationist slant. According to Brian W.

Alderson, writing in *Children's Book Review*, *Julie of the Wolves* "sustains a powerful case not only for conservation but also for the preservation of man's natural skills" and would appeal to many readers "because of its integrity and its wholly convincing portrayal of its setting." The Children's Literature Association named the novel one of the ten best American children's books in two hundred years.

Native American culture is also a central element in George's novel *The Talking Earth*. Among a Seminole tribe in Florida is Billie Wind, a scientifically minded thirteen-year-old girl who questions her tribe's legends of talking animals. Asked to select her own punishment for doubt, she makes a solitary journey into the Everglades. As Billie learns about survival from her observations of the wildlife, she begins to understand that in showing her where to find food and warning her when danger threatens, the animals have indeed "talked" to her. Writing in the *New York Times Book Review*, Hazel Rochman pointed out the book's conservation message, which "grows naturally out of the excitement and concrete detail of the survival adventure story," and praised George's "lovingly precise language, simple and rhythmic." Susan L. Locke in *School Library Journal* called it "a beautifully written book, strong in characterization, that addresses important issues, but not at the expense of the story."

In 1987 George wrote again about the Arctic in *Water Sky*, the story of a New England teenager who goes to Alaska seeking his missing uncle. During his stay the youth gets an extensive education in the ways of the Arctic ice, the creatures of the land and the sea, and the Inupiat Eskimos. Noting the book's similarities to *Julie of the Wolves*, Clark asserted that *Water Sky* "contains even more insights into Eskimo life than the earlier work" but is less well constructed. "Ecology, ethnology, adventure, romance—there is too much here for one novel, it's true. But Jean Craighead George almost carries it off."

George prompted further comparisons to earlier work with *On the Far Side of the Mountain*, a sequel to *My Side of the Mountain*. Beginning after all of Sam's relatives except his sister Alice have abandoned their attempt to live on the old Gribley land, *On the Far Side of the Mountain* is largely about Sam's efforts to follow a trail his sister has left. Sam's loss of and eventual reunion with Frightful, his peregrine falcon, provide another thread of action that opens and closes the book. In his *New York Times Book Review* article, Yglesias criticized this construction and expressed a wish that George had shown Alice's journey through her own eyes instead of through Sam's. Observed Yglesias, "The power of the beginning and the ending" of the sequel "will be more than enough to satisfy a new generation" of fans, but the middle "suggests there's still nutritious food to be foraged in Sam Gribley's wilds." Other critics were more complimentary. Starr LaTronica, reviewing the book for *School Library Journal*, felt that the sequel "can be enjoyed without the background laid in the first book, and it will inspire many readers to investigate the beginning of Sam's story." Writing in *Booklist*, Deborah Abbott declared that it "surpasses the original in style and substance."

For more than forty years George has shared her love of nature with young people as a writer and illustrator of novels and nonfiction works, winning generations of readers. She has won one of the most prestigious awards in her field, the Newbery Medal, and earned a lasting place in children's literature. Able to satisfy "both the bookish and boisterous child," as Yglesias asserted, books such as *My Side of the Mountain* became contemporary classics. Writing in *Horn Book*, Laura Robb suggested that George's "presentation of animals, the environment, and people has the power to change the lives and thinking of youngsters making their difficult journey to adulthood." Explained the critic, George's works are often "about children searching for independence and self-knowledge." Such a search reflects the author's own lifelong struggles. Like Sam Gribley, George strove to be self-sufficient; like Miyax she learned to make her own way in a hostile environment—a divorced woman in a society where divorce earned reproach. In the end she has proved as resourceful and successful as her characters.

■ Works Cited

Abbott, Deborah, review of *On the Far Side of the Mountain* in *Booklist*, April 1, 1990, p. 1550.

Alderson, Brian W., review of *Julie of the Wolves* in *Children's Book Review*, spring, 1974, p. 18.

Clark, Beverly Lyon, review of *Water Sky* in *New York Times Book Review*, May 10, 1987, p. 26.

George, Jean Craighead, *Journey Inward*, Dutton, 1982.

Hoyle, Karen Nelson, "Jean Craighead George," *Dictionary of Literary Biography*, Volume 52: *American Writers for Children since 1960: Fiction*, Gale, 1986, pp. 168-74.

Jameyson, Karen, "A Second Look: *My Side of the Mountain*," *Horn Book*, July/August, 1989, pp. 529-31.

LaTronica, Starr, review of *On the Far Side of the Mountain* in *School Library Journal*, June, 1990, p. 120.

Locke, Susan L., review of *Water Sky* in *School Library Journal*, March, 1987, p. 158.

Robb, Laura, "Books in the Classroom," *Horn Book*, November/December, 1989, pp. 808-10.

Rochman, Hazel, review of *The Talking Earth* in *New York Times Book Review*, January 22, 1984, p. 24.

Yglesias, Rafael, "Meanwhile, Back in the Catskills," *New York Times Book Review*, May 20, 1990, p. 42.

■ For More Information See

BOOKS

Children's Literature Review, Volume 1, Gale, 1976, pp. 89-94.

Contemporary Literary Criticism, Volume 35, Gale, 1985, pp. 175-80.

Gillespie, John, and Diana Lembo, *Introducing Books: A Guide for the Middle Grades*, R. R. Bowker, 1970.

Viguers, Ruth Hill, *A Critical History of Children's Literature*, revised edition, Macmillan, 1969.

PERIODICALS

Best Sellers, April 15, 1973; August, 1976; July, 1980.

Books, May 19, 1963.

Bulletin of the Center for Children's Books, June, 1960; October, 1966; May, 1968; January, 1972.

Christian Science Monitor, November 2, 1967; November 13, 1969; May 7, 1970; May 6, 1971; December 30, 1971; May 2, 1973; December 5, 1973; January 22, 1975; June 10, 1975; October 8, 1982; December 15, 1982; November 7, 1986, p. B2; April 3, 1987, p. B6.

Elementary English, December, 1982.

Globe and Mail (Toronto), May 2, 1987.

Horn Book, June, 1958; October, 1959; October, 1964; August, 1966; October, 1966; April, 1968; April, 1971; December, 1971; February, 1973; August, 1973; February, 1975; April, 1979; February, 1983; June, 1984.

Los Angeles Times Book Review, August 27, 1989, p. 8.

New York, May 25, 1970.

New Yorker, December 4, 1971.

New York Herald Tribune Book Review, November 1, 1959.

New York Times, February 26, 1979; April 29, 1979.

New York Times Book Review, September 13, 1959; November 18, 1962; November 1, 1964; February 13, 1966; March 3, 1968; May 5, 1968; January 21, 1973; October 13, 1974; June 27, 1976; September 28, 1980; March 25, 1984.

Saturday Review, October 22, 1966; May 15, 1971; April 14, 1973.

Times Literary Supplement, November 23, 1973.

Village Voice, December 25, 1978; February 4, 1986, p. 48.

Washington Post Book World, January 24, 1965; January 7, 1968; May 5, 1968; November 9, 1969; May 9, 1971; November 7, 1971; May 13, 1973; December 8, 1974; March 10, 1981; November 6, 1983; May 14, 1989, p. 18.

Western American Literature, May, 1983.

—Sketch by Polly A. Vedder

Matt Groening

1977-79; *Los Angeles Reader*, Los Angeles, worked variously as circulation manager, editor, writer, cartoonist, and author of "Sound Mix" music column, 1979-84; partner with Deborah Caplan in Life in Hell Cartoon Co. and Acme Features Syndicate, beginning in 1980s; Twentieth Century-Fox Television, Los Angeles, creator and executive producer of *Simpsons* television series, 1989—.

■ Personal

Surname is pronounced *"gray-ning"* ("rhymes with raining"); born February 15, 1954, in Portland, OR; son of Homer (a filmmaker) and Margaret (a teacher) Groening; married Deborah Caplan (his manager and business partner), October 29, 1986; children: Homer, Abraham. *Education:* Evergreen State College, B.A., 1977. *Hobbies and other interests:* Watching badly translated foreign films; nurturing ducks.

■ Addresses

Home—Venice, CA. *Office*—Life in Hell Cartoon Co., 2219 Main St., Santa Monica, CA 90405. *Attorney-Representative*—Susan A. Grode, 2029 Century Park E., No. 3590, Los Angeles, CA 90067.

■ Career

Writer, cartoonist, and business executive. Held numerous odd jobs in Los Angeles, CA, including cemetery landscaper, dishwasher in a nursing home, clerk in recording and copy shops, and ghostwriter/chauffeur to an elderly filmmaker,

■ Awards, Honors

Won short story contest, *Jack and Jill*, 1962; Academy awards from Academy of Television Arts and Sciences, nominations for outstanding writing in a variety program, 1987, 1988, and 1989, for *The Tracey Ullman Show*, nomination for outstanding animated program, 1990, for Christmas program *The Simpsons Roasting on an Open Fire*, awards for outstanding animated program, 1990 and 1991, for *The Simpsons*.

■ Writings

"LIFE IN HELL"

Love Is Hell, privately printed, 1984, revised, Pantheon, 1985.
Work Is Hell, Pantheon, 1986.
School Is Hell, Pantheon, 1987.
Childhood Is Hell, Pantheon, 1988.
Akbar and Jeff's Guide to Life, Pantheon, 1989.
Greetings from Hell, Pantheon, 1989.
The Big Book of Hell, Pantheon, 1990.
With Love from Hell: A Postcard Book, HarperCollins, 1991.

How to Go to Hell, HarperCollins, 1991.

The *Life in Hell* comic strip was privately printed, beginning in late 1970s, appeared in *Wet*, 1978, in *Los Angeles Reader*, 1980-c. 1984, in *L.A. Weekly*, 1984—, and has been syndicated by Groening and Caplan to hundreds of periodicals worldwide through their company, Acme Features Syndicate, beginning in 1980s. Also creator of "Life in Hell" calendars published by Pantheon, 1985-89, and HarperCollins, 1990-91.

"THE SIMPSONS"

The Simpsons, Twentieth Century-Fox Television, appeared as interludes in *The Tracey Ullman Show*, 1987-89, weekly series (with others), 1990—.

The Simpsons Xmas Book (adapted from a screenplay by Mimi Pond) Harper-Collins, 1990.

The Simpsons Rainy Day Fun Book, HarperCollins, 1990.

Greetings from the Simpsons, HarperCollins, 1990.

(With sister, Maggie Groening) *Maggie Simpson's Alphabet Book*, HarperCollins, 1991.

(With Maggie Groening) *Maggie Simpson's Book of Animals*, HarperCollins, 1991.

(With Maggie Groening) *Maggie Simpson's Book of Colors and Shapes*, HarperCollins, 1991.

(With Maggie Groening) *Maggie Simpson's Counting Book*, HarperCollins, 1991.

Simpsons Student Diary, Trielle Publishers (Australia), 1991.

Simpsons Uncenscored Family Album, HarperCollins, 1991.

Simpsons Fun in the Sun Book, HarperCollins, 1992.

Also creator of Simpsons calendars and *Simpsons Illustrated* magazine.

OTHER

(With Steve Vance) *Postcards That Ate My Brain*, Pantheon, 1990.

Also creator, with Vance, of "Postcards That Ate My Brain" calendars. Contributor to periodicals, including *Jack and Jill* and *Film Comment*.

■ Work in Progress

Other possible titles in the "Life in Hell" series include *The Road to Hell, Art Is Hell, Sex Is Hell, Therapy Is Hell, Enlightenment Is Hell, Bowling Is Hell, Hell, Hell, Hell, Good Grief, It's "Life in Hell," The Bigger Book of Hell, The Even Bigger Book of Hell*, and *The Even Bigger than the Previous Even Bigger Book of Hell*. A novel about Southern California—*Hipness and Stupidity*—has also been mentioned.

■ Sidelights

"I had a very typical childhood," said Matt Groening in the *San Jose Mercury News*. "The only difference was that I took notes and vowed never to forget what it was like." Groening's vow helped drive him into cartooning, where he has been taking revenge on his childhood tormentors, and a lot of other pretentious people, for most of his adult life. In his *Life in Hell* comic strip and *Simpsons* animated TV series, Groening lampoons authority figures from playground bullies to classroom and office tyrants, viewing life through the eyes of children and adults who feel doomed, overpowered, or defiantly obnoxious. His best-known creation is Bart Simpson, a smart-mouthed ten-year-old whose hapless family is chronicled on the television show that bears their name. Students across America have shocked their teachers by wearing T-shirts that display the Bart attitude: "'Underachiever'—And proud of it, man!"

Groening was born and raised in Portland, Oregon. Strangely, the names of his childhood family resemble those of the Simpson clan, including father Homer, mother Margaret, and sisters Lisa and Maggie. Groening now suggests that the coincidence was an inside joke that got out of hand. "My whole family was smart and funny," he told the *Boston Globe*, "where the Simpsons are stupid and funny." According to *Mother Jones*, Groening considered his father "the hippest dad in the neighborhood": a man who, during the conformist 1950s, sought out such unusual jobs as cartoonist and creator of short films. Because of his work Homer Groening subscribed to a huge range of general-interest magazines, and accordingly Matt was gazing at the cartoons in the *New Yorker* and *Punch* even before he could read. Soon he was doodling like his dad.

The closest resemblance between the Simpsons and the Groenings would likely be the bickering kids. As the third child out of five, Matt was picked on by an older brother and sister and then picked on his two younger sisters in turn. "It was great," he confessed to the *San Francisco Examiner*. "I had a whole repertoire of lies. Like that there were secret gifts hidden in the basement and if they just went down there I wouldn't shut the lights out and slam the door shut. I learned that you can tell your mother that you're taking your younger sisters to see 'Pinocchio' and actually see 'Barbarella.' My brother was supposed to take me to see 'Bambi' as a kid and we went to see 'Hell Drivers' instead. I was outraged. I had to swear never to tell." For Groening, admirers agree, such childhood memories are amazingly vivid—even intense. "I really do remember being in my crib and being bathed in the sink," he declared in the *Los Angeles Times*. "I remember being that small. At the time, I thought everything was dramatic. I was caught up in the drama of being a kid. . . . Adults have forgotten how scary it is."

Scariest of all for Groening was probably elementary school. He found it a rigid, humorless, uncreative place that had no use for a child whose talent lay in doodling. "I could understand getting sent to the principal's office for dropping an encyclopedia out the window, but I couldn't understand them ripping my cartoons up," he told the *Los Angeles Times*. "I would have been much happier," he later observed, "if I'd known I was going to grow up to write a cartoon book called 'School Is Hell,' and have a cartoon show on TV, if I'd known I was going to make up for all that wasted time sitting in the principal's office, staring at the ceiling and counting the dots in the tiles." To console himself, Groening started keeping a diary in the fifth grade. That way, in years to come, he could examine the record and decide if he'd been right to rebel. "Not too many guys got into trouble today," ran one entry, according to the *Washington Post*. "I did."

Resisting all threats and pleas, Groening remained a nonconformist. He became a fan of satirical comics like Walt Kelly's *Pogo*, Charles Schultz's *Peanuts*, and the notorious *Mad* magazine. With cartooning friends he formed the Creature Club (motto: "I'm Peculiar") and, in their honor, he created the comic-strip villain "Rotten Rabbit." When *Jack and Jill* magazine invited readers to submit their own ending to a story about a boy on Halloween, Groening won a prize for his morbid finale: the boy dies from a bump on the head and swoops down from the attic once a year to join his family for dinner. By high school Groening began to hit his stride. He wrote and cartooned for the school newspaper, hung out with antiwar students from a nearby college, and, with fellow misfits from his high school, formed a sarcastic political party called Teens for Decency and got himself elected student body president. "You are what you are," he told the *Los Angeles Times*, "basically despite school."

When it came time for college, Groening applied to only two: far-off Harvard (he didn't make it) and nearby Evergreen State in Olympia, Washington.

Founded in the late 1960s, Evergreen was a classic hippie school with no tests, no grades, and no classes (they were called seminars). "[It] was heaven for talent," he recalled in the *Los Angeles Times*. "Brilliant teachers really talking about what they were enthusiastic about, no limits on the cameras and tape recorders and media tools you could check out." Groening, who was really too straight to be a hippie, responded to the freedom of Evergreen with a burst of self-discipline. Since he didn't see cartooning as a viable career, he decided to be a writer and soon became editor of the student newspaper. There he met Lynda Barry, an aspiring artist who cartooned on the side and who later created the best-selling strip *Ernie Pook's Comeek*. "Lynda's stuff . . . was unlike anything I'd ever seen before," Groening told the *Washington Post*. "It was funny, wild, had a very strong point of view, and it was obviously what *Lynda* thought was funny. I had been trying to make other people laugh and I found out by looking at Lynda's cartoons that if you make yourself laugh, it's generally good for other people as well." He decided to publish some of Barry's cartoons in the paper and, inspired by her example, published some of his own as well. Cartooning with Barry was fun, but it didn't change Groening's plans: he enjoyed writing comedy, but, by the slick standards of traditional cartooning, he couldn't draw very well. "I didn't expect there to be an audience for what I was drawing," he told the *Washington Post*, "because I didn't see anything drawn that crummy. There was nothing else as crude."

Eager for a writing job after graduation, Groening moved to an apartment in Los Angeles and found himself in hell. "There was one point when my girlfriend broke up with me, my car blew up, I didn't have a job, I couldn't pay my rent, and the guy downstairs kept playing rockabilly full blast at 3 in the morning," he told *Newsweek*. "Even though I turned my speakers face-down on the floor and blasted him back with my superior reggae, he didn't get the picture until I took a cinder block from my bookshelves and dropped it on the floor and knocked out the light fixture in his ceiling." The only writing job that materialized was ghostwriter/chauffeur to a forgotten, eighty-eight-year-old Hollywood filmmaker who was trying to compose his memoirs. Other memorable work included record-store clerk, copy-shop clerk, graveyard landscaper, and dishwasher in a convalescent home.

Faced with explaining his budding career to folks back home, Groening decided to entertain them while cartooning his frustrations away. His life in Los Angeles was reborn as *Life in Hell,* the chronicle of a frustrated, harassed-looking rabbit named Binky. The first *Life in Hell* comic strips were run off on photocopiers, stapled into booklets, and mailed by Groening to old friends. Soon he tried selling some of the booklets to punk patrons of the record store where he worked. "The punks' reactions were pretty much either they liked it or they tore it up," he told *Newsweek,* "which could have meant they liked it too." *Wet* magazine, a pioneer of off-the-wall New Wave graphics, liked the strip enough to run several installments. Groening also tried to interest both of Los Angeles's alternative weeklies in his work, and in 1979 he landed a job with the *Los Angeles Reader.* At first the job must have seemed the latest in a string of humiliations: when he didn't write for the paper, he delivered it in his beat-up car. Within a year, though, *Life in Hell* was a weekly feature of the *Reader,* and Groening's job soon expanded into editor and rock music columnist.

As originally seen in the *Reader, Life in Hell* was a little different from the comic strip fans have come to know and love. Like Groening with his cinder block, Binky came on strong. "First impressions are very important, so SHUT UP and listen to me," the rabbit declared in his debut, now immortalized in *The Big Book of Hell.* "My job here is to teach you the errors of your ways.... It may not do much for YOU, but it makes ME feel a hell of a lot better." Then Binky griped for weeks about the cliches and "trite fad words" he heard in everyday speech. "He was really hostile, ranting and raving, the way I felt," Groening explained in *Rolling Stone.* "After a year of doing the comic strip and not getting much response, I decided to make the rabbit a victim instead of an aggressor. And the second I made the rabbit a victim, people started liking the comic strip. The more tragedies that befell this poor little rodent, the more positive response I got." Binky took his present-day form: a lonely, beleaguered office worker with a nightmarish love life that never brought him anything more than an illegitimate son. The son, Bongo, is a beleaguered school-aged rabbit with only one ear. "That's so you can tell him apart from Binky," Groening explained in the *San Jose Mercury News.* "I thought, 'What could be a more alienated rabbit?'" With the addition of Sheba, Binky's girlfriend (and *not* Bongo's mother), Groening had a cast of characters on whom he could inflict the humiliations of everyday life, including love, work, and childhood.

He set to work with a tenacity that his boss, James Vowell, recalled years later in the *Los Angeles Times.* "I think he's a better artist than [legendary *New Yorker* cartoonist] James Thurber," Vowell said, "and I thought he was in Thurber's league back then. He would practice drawing those characters all the time, thinking carefully and meticulously about how to get the exact line stroke that looks casual but is completely repeatable. I actually think the drawings are exquisitely well done." When a girlfriend dumped Groening, he responded with "Love Is Hell," a thirteen-part comic-strip miniseries that told readers about the nine types of boyfriends (such as Old Man Grumpus, Bigfoot, and Flinchy), nine types of girlfriends (Ms. Vaguely Dissatisfied, Old Yeller, and Sickly), and nine types of relationships (Woman + Wimpy, Brute + Jumpy, and Sourballs vs. The World). He also wrote about a more pressing frustration: having an office job. "Isn't It About Time You Quit Your Lousy Job?" asked one of Groening's favorite strips. "Wake up, chumply. You're not getting any younger. The clock is ticking. You can't just sit there in your cubbyhole while life passes you by."

Groening might still be holed up at the *Reader* if not for Deborah Caplan, who worked in the advertising department and was quick to see his potential. "It didn't take many sales calls before I realized that Groening's comic strip was the major drawing card of the newspaper," she told *People* magazine. Caplan gave Groening love, and, as an added bonus, she helped organize his life. "I started by getting his basics together," she told the *Los Angeles Times,* "getting him out of a horrible part of Hollywood into a beach area and finding ways to market the cartoon and his talent." In the mid-1980s Groening and Caplan quit their jobs and formed the Life In Hell Cartoon Company and Acme Features Syndicate, which syndicated the comic strip and sold all kinds of hell-related products, from posters to T-shirts to coffee mugs. Even before *The Simpsons* became a mass-market phenomenon, Life In Hell Co. was pulling down a six-figure income. "Everyone I know goes, 'Well, if *I* had a Deborah, I could be a success, too," he told the *Times.* "And they're right." The pair were married in 1986, and figurines of Binky and Sheba topped the wedding cake.

The boom in hell made Groening more ambitious, leading to a string of comic miniseries and cartoon books. The first book, *Love Is Hell,* was originally published by Caplan on her own in 1984 and sold more than twenty thousand copies. Its success brought Groening a contract with Pantheon Books,

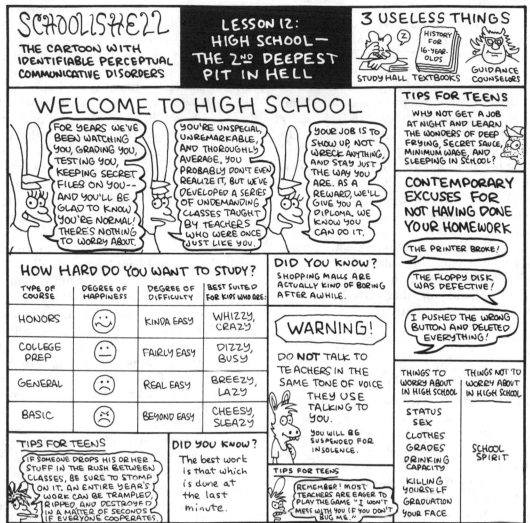

Groening rummaged through high school dumpsters trying to discover the issues concerning teens before beginning this series. (From *School Is Hell*, by Matt Groening. Copyright © 1987. All rights reserved. Reprinted by permission of Pantheon Books, a division of Random House, NY.)

which began by issuing a new edition of *Love Is Hell* in 1985. Further books, each built around a miniseries, were titled *Work Is Hell*, *School Is Hell*, and *Childhood Is Hell*. To gear up for the "School Is Hell" series, Groening ransacked high-school dumpsters for the notebooks and papers that students toss out at the end of the year. The final product surveyed such topics as "Trouble: Getting In and Weaseling Your Way Out" and "How to Drive a Deserving Teacher Crazy." *Childhood Is Hell*, based in part on Groening's fifth-grade diary, included a "Childhood Trauma Checklist" and a tribute to "Your Pal the TV Set." For variety Groening gave an increasing role in *Life in Hell* to gay entrepreneurs Akbar and Jeff, whose insistent-

ly empty grins were somehow as creepy as the frowns on Binky and Bongo. Owners of such thriving small businesses as the Video Hut, the Tofu Hut, and the Reincarnation Hut, Akbar and Jeff offered their advice to the world in *Akbar and Jeff's Guide to Life*. Describing the author's work for the *Los Angeles Times Book Review*, Charles Solomon observed that Groening still wasn't a great artist in traditional terms, but that he had mastered the art of making his simple drawings a vehicle for good writing and sharp wit. "Groening," Solomon declared, "is one of the funniest and most original cartoonists working in the comics today."

All this success invites a question: why would people enjoy seeing Groening's characters act stupid and get humiliated? His answer: it's therapeutic. The characters, he explained in *Rolling Stone*, are "completely at the mercy of the forces that are blowing them around. They know vaguely that something is wrong, but they can't quite put their finger on who to blame or how to solve it." In other words, they're as clueless as the audience, only more so. "People recognize a bit of themselves, but at the same time they can feel totally superior." Not everyone, however, has learned to love hell. People in the newspaper business told Groening that he could sell his work more widely if he made it simpler, and friendlier, and took the "hell" out. A religious young surfer, irked by a strip in which Bongo wonders what God looks like, sent the author a letter warning that "you're going to hell, dude." Groening was unrepentant. "I hope the cartoons amuse you," he told readers of *The Big Book of Hell*, "but if you're one of those people who finds my stuff annoying, that's OK. Luckily for me, being annoying is a blast, too."

The television industry also found Groening a tough bargainer. "I'd get called up by Hollywood producers," he told the *Boston Globe*, "and they'd say, 'What would you like to do in animation?' and I'd talk about how bad TV cartoons were and that I'd like to do something with the same standards as [the 1960s cult favorite] 'Rocky and Bullwinkle'—great writing, great voices, great music. They got all cold and distant after that and claimed that 'Rocky and Bullwinkle' was a failure because it only appealed to smart kids." Groening, who felt that TV viewers were ripe for something new like smart animation, held tight. Finally he got an offer from James L. Brooks, a producer at the adventurous new Fox television network who had a poster from *Life in Hell* on his wall. At first the pair planned to do an animated version of the comic strip, but then Fox laid down its terms: Groening must surrender all legal rights to the characters. "The studio was still getting over the fact that a few years ago it gave George Lucas all the licensing rights to 'Star Wars,'" he explained in the *San Francisco Examiner*. Instead Groening sold Fox the concept for a whole new animated show, with human characters who were nearly as frazzled as his rabbits—"a messed-up American family," as he put it. So were the Simpsons born.

The Simpsons are a blue-collar clan who live in the mythical town of Springfield. As Groening knew, this was also the hometown of the Andersons, an affluent, well-adjusted television family who charmed America during the 1950s in the comedy *Father Knows Best*. The Simpsons, however, look like somebody's parody of a happy TV family. Ten-year-old Bart is irreverent, irrepressible, and usually in trouble. He cheats on tests, sneaks into movies, and never misses a chance to one-up his father. (Bart to Homer, who's moonlighting as a department-store Santa: "You must really love us to sink so low.") Homer is fat, bald, and sometimes grumpy—just a regular guy. He works at a nuclear power plant, where his blunders often put Springfield on the edge of annihilation. (Homer on Bart: "What do we need a psychiatrist for? We know our kid is a nut.") Marge Simpson, wife and mother, is crowned by an enormous blue beehive hairdo. She holds the family together with kindhearted wisdom, although sometimes her advice is a little off target. (Marge to daughter Lisa: "Just smile. Then you'll fit in and you'll be invited to parties and boys will like you and happiness will follow.") Lisa is an eight-year-old genius who's full of common sense, but vaguely smarmy. (Lisa to Bart: "Oh, Bart, you're just like Chilly, the elf who cannot love.") And Baby Maggie "isn't TV-baby-cute; she's just *there*, all wide eyes and sucking noises," wrote Ken Tucker in *Entertainment Weekly*. "At its heart this is guerrilla TV," said Tucker's colleague Joe Rhodes—"a wicked satire masquerading as a prime-time cartoon."

As a television series *The Simpsons* started small—it was a supplement to another prime-time series, *The Tracey Ullman Show*. At first the animation, written, directed, and produced by Groening, was used as fifteen-second lead-ins to commercial breaks; finally it got its own ninety-second segment. There was just enough time for a joke, but the Simpsons characters were clearly established. In one segment, for instance, Marge blithely sang "Rock-a-Bye Baby" to little Maggie, who took the words literally and imagined herself cradled in a tree-top and crashing to the ground. "One of the great things about working with the [Ullman show] was that it was an ongoing experiment and we tried certain things," Groening said in *Animation* magazine. "It was really good preparation for the series." Going to a full-length series, however, was by no means a foregone conclusion: because animation is generally drawn by hand, it requires a lot of time and money. "[It seemed] a huge risk," confessed Fox chairman Barry Diller in *Newsweek*. "We tried hard to say: 'Oh, let's just do four specials. What do we need to rush so fast for?' But an advance screening of the show made him ecstatic. "It's not often I've had this experience—

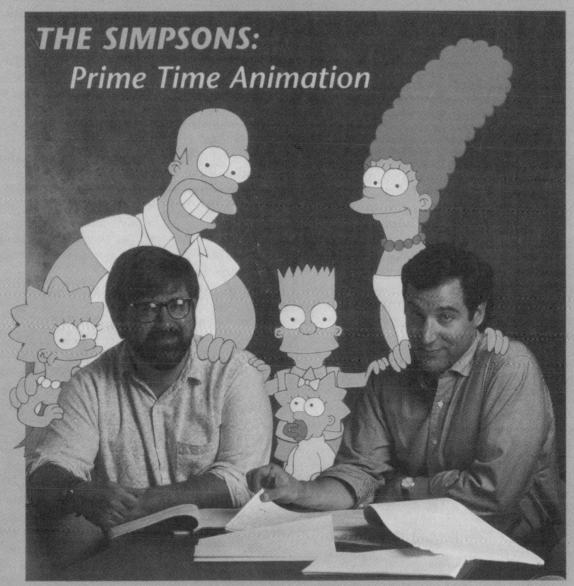

INSIDE: The Little Mermaid, Disney's Underwater Fairy Tale

Originally a supplement to *The Tracy Ullman Show*, *The Simpsons* became one of the first successful prime-time animated series in over twenty-five years after Groening and associates launched it in January 1990. (Groening is shown with Sam Simon, a fellow executive producer.)

the experience of watching something great and praying that the next minute doesn't dash it. And not only having that not happen, but saying at the end: 'This is the real thing! This is the one that can crack the slab for us!'" After the full-length program debuted on Fox in January of 1990, it was soon one of the fifteen most-watched shows on American television—an amazing feat for a fledgling network that still didn't reach one-fifth of the country. *The Simpsons* had become the first successful prime-time animated series in twenty-five years.

In the aftermath, swarms of experts appeared to explain the phenomenal success of the show. Briefly, their reasons could be summarized as quality, teamwork, and timing. Named one of three executive producers of *The Simpsons*, Groening aimed for quality. He wanted animation with enough depth to appeal to grown-ups, animation with characters so vivid that people would forget it was animated, and a situation comedy that would transcend the old sitcom formula of one-liners and easy sentiment. *The Simpsons*, Groening explained in *Animation*, "[is] not in the tradition of most sitcoms. . . . There's great dialogue, I think, but it's not your typical kind of sitcom insult/retort, insult/retort. What we're trying to do is bring a level of intelligence to the dialogue that's missing from virtually every other animated cartoon on television, along with stuff that animation does better than live action—wild, physical comedy and exaggerated sight gags." As he modestly summarized in the Chicago *Sun-Times:* "The amount of care in writing, acting and animation is something you just haven't seen on TV, *ever.*"

To the surprise of Groening—who, as a comic-strip artist, was used to working by himself—the Fox organization largely supported him. "The amazing thing to me is how little compromise there has been," he told the *Philadelphia Inquirer.* "Everybody hears all the horror stories about what it's like to work in television and the industry, but we've had a relatively free hand in the show. The kinds of people who might be adversaries aren't. They're allies. The number-one reason is James L. Brooks. I think his history and reputation and clout is what got *The Simpsons* on the air." An executive with a strong writing background, Brooks helped to create and produce such award-winning television programs as *The Mary Tyler Moore Show* and *Taxi* during the 1970s. He then won several Academy awards as producer, director, and writer of the box-office smash *Terms of Endearment*, a film he saw to completion despite industry claims that it

was destined to fail. "If [*The Simpsons*] were not Matt's dream we would not be doing it," Brooks told *Animation.* "Matt is a genuine comic artist." When *The Simpsons* went full-time, Brooks shared the title of executive producer with Groening.

To make the dream come true, Brooks and Groening drew on a remarkable pool of talent, including two animation teams staff—experts in Los Angeles and a lower-priced support staff in Korea. Suddenly Groening was helping to supervise a flock of animators as they strove to imitate his artfully crude style. "We had a rocky beginning, trying to draw the characters the way I designed them," he told *Entertainment Weekly.* "It's very hard for people who devoted themselves to animated cartoons to break the habit of cuteness. My characters are anti-cute." Scripts also became a team affair as the show recruited a wide array of writing talents, including such alumni of the Ullman show as Sam Simon. Simon, who began his career as a scriptwriter on the hit shows *Taxi* and *Cheers*, had worked increasingly as a producer; his credentials made him the third of three executive producers of *The Simpsons*, along with Groening and Brooks. Scripts began at a story conference, where the trio gathered with the writing staff to swap ideas. Many consultations, read-throughs, and rewrites later, the finished scripts would be shaped by Groening and Simon as they directed the actors who were the voices of the Simpsons.

Groening and Simon, interestingly, had contrasting ideas of what a script might be, as suggested by their interview with *Animation.* "The story moves," Simon observed, "are much . . . broader and wilder than you do in a sitcom. But I think what will make the half-hours work is that they are structurally sound. A problem is introduced, they complicate it, and we resolve it." Groening, whose *Life in Hell* strips often abandon the notion of a beginning, middle, and end, added that "you won't be able to tell where the story is going to end up, in the first five minutes or even the first fifteen minutes." Somehow the two men combined to produce a series that was wild enough to be innovative and structured enough that most of America could understand it. In *American Film*, Groening offered his impression of teamwork, Hollywood-style. "Success in Hollywood," he declared, "is predicated on the ability to be charming in a small room with several people for months at a time." As of the third season Groening is largely in charge of the series.

But beyond production values—as everyone from TV critics to sociologists agreed—*The Simpsons* clicked because the audience was ready for it. The show was seen as a revolt against decades of happy-family sitcoms, from *Father Knows Best* to *The Cosby Show*, that projected a world that was too good to be real. As America faced a long list of stubborn social and economic woes, many of which took a toll on family life, the "messed-up" Simpsons looked surprisingly realistic. "'The Simpsons' is a joke on traditional sitcoms because its characters are so far removed from what's always been depicted as the norm," said Jack Nachbar, a professor of popular culture, in *Newsweek* magazine. "But in actuality, they're closer to the real norm than anything we've ever seen." Like many people in the audience, the Simpsons weren't fulfilled in life; they were lucky to survive it. In one episode Homer is treated like a hero for preventing a nuclear explosion, then has to admit that he pushed the right button by accident. When Bart is menaced by playground bullies, he doesn't win by taking the high road; he teams up with a local gun nut and fights dirty. When he's threatened with flunking out of fourth grade, he studies pathetically hard, and he's delighted to scrape by with a 'D.' And when Lisa suffers from childhood depression, an old musician teaches her how to survive by playing the blues: "The blues isn't about feeling better," he confides, "it's about making other people feel worse." Yet despite all their flaws, bickering, and money troubles, the Simpsons still manage—just barely—to love each other. "Part of the Simpson appeal," Groening said in the Chicago *Sun-Times*, "is the acknowledgement that you can still love the people who drive you crazy."

The popularity of *The Simpsons* created a marketing tidal wave as fans scooped up as many as one million Simpsons products a day, including T-shirts, caps, bubble gum, boxer shorts, and a Bart talking doll. "The only thing they wouldn't let me do is have the doll belch," Groening told *Newsweek*, "but the Bart doll does get to say, 'The kids in TV land are being duped.'" Suddenly the underground cartoonist from hell found himself crossing the country doing high-profile interviews and talking about copyrights and production deals. He tried to stay casual. "We have to do the merchandise because there are bootlegs out there, with T-shirts on crummy material, with ugly humor and art that is atrocious," he told the Chicago *Sun-Times*. "We don't want to cash in and get out. We want to control the merchandise and give people great shows." If Groening had a favorite bootleg it was probably among the wave of "black Bart" T-shirts, which testified to the broad range of Bart's

Perhaps Groening's most popular character is the irrepressible Bart Simpson. (From *Greetings from The Simpsons*™, by Matt Groening Productions, Inc. Copyright © 1990. All rights reserved. Reproduced by permission of HarperCollins, Publishers, NY. The Simpsons ™ and © Twentieth Century-Fox Film Corp.)

appeal. "Nothing I say should be construed as 'My blessing on these shirts,'" he told *Mother Jones*. "But that aside, I think the Simpsons with red dreadlocks is very, very funny."

Not surprisingly, some authority figures didn't find the Simpsons funny at all. Across America principals, teachers, and child psychologists warned that Bart was providing a bad example to the young. Bart's foes included American drug enforcement chief William Bennett, who backed off when he was forced to admit that he had never watched the show. Many blasted the notorious "Underachiever" T-shirt, which was actually banned from some classrooms. "If you read the T-shirt, it says, 'Bart Simpson, quote, underachiever, unquote," Groening observed in the *Des Moines Register*. "[Bart] has been labeled an underachiever and his response to that is that he's proud of it. He didn't call himself an underachiever. He does not aspire to be an underachiever." Besides, as the author told *Mother*

Jones, "Kids are smarter than a lot of adults give them credit for. I feel sorry for authority figures who are troubled by kids having fun."

More than anyone, it seemed, Groening was having fun. "Everybody's got a fantasy of watching television and getting annoyed with it and saying, 'Boy, if I had my own TV show, this is what I would do. And in an extremely easy way, I have arrived at that," he told the *Philadelphia Inquirer.* "We lucked out. I'm real comfortable now. I'm real lucky." As happy as anyone who lives in hell can expect to be, Groening and Caplan remodeled their house near the ocean and began raising their children. "I *have* to be good [as a father]," he told the *San Francisco Examiner.* "I can't do what I'm railing against in my books, so I've painted myself into a corner." He's still friends with Lynda Barry, and in many papers their comic strips run side by side. They give each other coy salutes at the beginning of their cartoon collections (the *Big Book of Hell* hails Barry as the "Funk Queen of North America"). And, most of all, he has learned the true meaning of success. "It means," he told the Chicago *Sun-Times,* "that people who used to beat me up in high school call me up and want to be friends."

■ Works Cited

Barol, Bill, "Binky and Sheba in Hell," *Newsweek,* April 23, 1990, p. 64.

Elder, Sean, "Is TV the Coolest Invention Ever Invented?," *Mother Jones,* December, 1989, p. 28.

Elder, "The Rehabilitation of Bart Simpson," *Mother Jones,* January, 1991, p. 13.

Fallon, D'Arcy, "Matt Groening Draws from Kids' Fears and Pain," *San Francisco Examiner,* November 16, 1988.

Foote, Jennifer, "A Doodle God Makes Good," *Newsweek,* September 28, 1987, p. 70.

Givens, Bill, "'The Simpsons' Marks the Return of Prime Time Adult Animation," *Animation,* fall, 1989, p. 22.

Groening, Matt, *The Big Book of Hell,* Pantheon, 1990.

Hamilton, Tish, "Rabbit Punch," *Rolling Stone,* September 22, 1988, p. 81.

Harrington, Richard, "Drawing on the Humor in Life's Little Horrors," *Washington Post,* December 18, 1988.

Kaufman, Joanne, "*Life in Hell*'s Matt Groening Goes Overboard to Make *The Simpsons* the First Family of TV 'Toons," *People,* December 18, 1989, p. 108.

Krier, Beth Ann, "An Alternative Cartoonist Who Draws the Line," *Los Angeles Times,* August 23, 1987.

Lloyd, Robert, "Cartoon from Hell," *American Film,* October, 1989, p. 112.

Morgenstern, Joe, "Bart Simpson's Real Father," *Los Angeles Times,* April 29, 1990.

Oricchio, Michael, "Hell Ain't So Bad," *San Jose Mercury News,* November 8, 1988.

Reese, Michael, "'A Mutant Ozzie and Harriet,'" *Newsweek,* December 25, 1989, p. 70.

Rense, Rip, "The American Family (Cartoon-Style)," *Philadelphia Inquirer,* February 11, 1990.

Rhein, Dave, "Bart's Philosophy Concerns Some Teachers," *Des Moines Register,* August 26, 1990.

Rhodes, Joe, "The Making of 'The Simpsons,'" *Entertainment Weekly,* May 18, 1990, p. 36.

"'The Simpsons': Cartoon Clan of the Grotesque," *San Francisco Examiner,* January 21, 1990.

Solomon, Charles, Review of *Love Is Hell, Los Angeles Times Book Review,* June 29, 1986, p. 2.

Sullivan, Jim, "Amimation's Answer to the Bundys," *Boston Globe,* January 14, 1990.

Tucker, Ernest, "Success of 'Simpsons' Overwhelms Creator," *Sun-Times* (Chicago), April 15, 1990.

Tucker, Ken, Review of *The Simpsons, Entertainment Weekly,* May 18, 1990, p. 43.

Waters, Harry F., "Family Feuds," *Newsweek,* April 23, 1990, p. 58.

■ For More Information See

PERIODICALS

Austin American-Statesman, May 14, 1990.

Baltimore Sun, March 16, 1990; August 1, 1990.

Booklist, June 15, 1986; February 2, 1987; November 1, 1987; January 15, 1989; August 1, 1989; January 1, 1991.

Boston Herald, January 11, 1990.

Clarion-Ledger (Jackson, MS), July 15, 1990.

Daily News (New York), January 11, 1990; April 10, 1990.

Detroit News and Free Press, March 11, 1990; July 16, 1990.

Florida Times-Union (Jacksonville), July 8, 1990.

Horn Book Guide, July, 1990.

Insight, November 24, 1986.

Los Angeles Times, February 23, 1990.

Los Angeles Times Book Review, December 18, 1988; December 21, 1990.

Miami Herald, May 6, 1990.

News and Observer (Raleigh, NC), April 14, 1990.

Newsweek, May 14, 1990.
New York Post, January 11, 1990; June 28, 1990.
New York Times, February 21, 1990.
Olympian (Olympia, WA), January 20, 1987.
Oregonian, December 19, 1986.
People, January 16, 1989.
Philadelphia Inquirer, May 11, 1990.
Publishers Weekly, May 4, 1990.
Rolling Stone, June 28, 1990.

Saturday Review, March, 1985.
School Library Journal, December, 1990.
TV Guide, March 17, 1990.
Village Voice, February 2, 1988.
Voice of Youth Advocates, April, 1988; June, 1989.
Washington Times, October 21, 1986; May 25, 1990.

—Sketch by Thomas Kozikowski

Ron Howard

Inc. (ABC-TV), 1971-72; played Richie Cunningham on *Happy Days*, ABC-TV, 1974-80. Appeared in episodes of television series, including *The Red Skelton Show, Dennis the Menace, Dobie Gillis, The General Electric Theatre, Playhouse 90, Dinah Shore Show, Five Fingers, Johnny Ringo, Danny Thomas Show, Hennessey, The Twilight Show, Cheyenne, June Allyson Show, The New Breed, The Eleventh Hour, Dr. Kildare, Route 66, The Great Adventure, The Fugitive, The Big Valley, Gomer Pyle, U.S.M.C., The Danny Kaye Show, I Spy, The Monroes, Wonderful World of Disney, Gentle Ben, Mayberry RFD, Land of the Giants, Lancer, Daniel Boone, Judd for the Defense, The F.B.I., Laverne and Shirley, Bonanza, Gunsmoke*, and *Partner for Lassie*. Also made television guest appearances, including *Amanda Fallon, Anson and Lorrie, The Olivia Newton-John Show, A Special Olivia Newton-John, Battle of the Network Stars*, and *The Bob Hope Special*. President of Major H Productions, 1977; co-founder of Imagine Films Entertainment (a production company), 1986. *Member:* Academy of Motion Picture Arts and Sciences, Screen Actors Guild, American Federation of Television and Radio Artists.

■ Personal

Born March 1, 1954, in Duncan, OK; son of Rance (an actor, writer, and director) and Jean (an actress) Howard; married Cheryl Alley (a writer), June 7, 1975; children: Bryce Dallas, Paige Carlyle, Jocelyn Carlyle, and a son. *Education:* Attended the University of Southern California and Los Angeles Valley College.

■ Addresses

Home—Greenwich, CT. *Office*—Imagine Films Entertainment, Inc., 1925 Century Park East, Los Angeles, CA 90067. *Agent*—c/o Michael Ovitz, Creative Artists Agency, 1888 Century Park E., Suite 1400, Los Angeles, CA 90067.

■ Career

Actor, director, and producer. Appeared on stage in *The Seven Year Itch*, Hilltop Summer Theatre, 1956, and in *Hole in the Head*, Bridge Bay Summer Theatre, 1963. Played Opie Taylor on *The Andy Griffith Show*, Columbia Broadcasting System, Inc. (CBS-TV), 1960-68; played Bob Smith on *The Smith Family*, American Broadcasting Companies,

■ Films

ACTOR

The Journey, Metro-Goldwyn-Mayer (M-G-M), 1959.
Five Minutes to Live, Sutton, 1961.
The Music Man, Warner Brothers, 1962.
The Courtship of Eddie's Father, M-G-M, 1963.

Village of the Giants, Embassy Pictures, 1965.

The Wild Country, Buena Vista, 1971.

Happy Mother's Day . . . Love, George, Cinema 5, 1973.

American Graffiti, Universal, 1973.

The Spike's Gang, United Artists, 1974.

The Migrants (television film), CBS-TV, 1974.

The Locusts (television film), ABC-TV, 1974.

Huckleberry Finn (television film), ABC-TV, 1975.

Eat My Dust, New World, 1976.

The Shootist, Paramount, 1976.

More American Graffiti, Universal, 1979.

Act of Love (television film), National Broadcasting Company, Inc. (NBC-TV), 1980.

Bitter Harvest (television film), NBC-TV, 1981.

Fire on the Mountain (television film), NBC-TV, 1981.

Return to Mayberry (television film), NBC-TV, 1986.

DIRECTOR

(And author of screenplay with father, Rance Howard; and actor) *Grand Theft Auto,* New World, 1977.

(And author of screenplay with brother, Clint Howard) *Cotton Candy* (television film), NBC-TV, 1978.

(And executive producer) *Skyward* (television film), NBC-TV, 1980.

(And executive producer) *Through the Magic Pyramid* (television film), NBC-TV, 1981.

Night Shift, Warner Brothers, 1982.

Splash, Buena Vista, 1984.

Cocoon, Twentieth Century-Fox, 1985.

(And executive producer) *Gung Ho,* Paramount, 1986.

Willow, M-G-M/United Artists, 1988.

Parenthood (based on a story by Howard, Lowell Ganz, and Babaloo Mandel), Universal, 1989.

Backdraft, Universal, 1991.

EXECUTIVE PRODUCER

Leo and Loree, United Artists, 1980.

(With Henry Winkler) *When Your Lover Leaves* (television film), NBC-TV, 1983.

(With Tony Ganz and Irv Wilson) *Into Thin Air* (television film), CBS-TV, 1985.

No Man's Land, Orion, 1987.

Vibes, Columbia, 1988.

Clean and Sober, Warner Brothers, 1988.

■ Work in Progress

A love story set in Ireland, starring Tom Cruise and Nicole Kidman.

■ Sidelights

The name Ron Howard invokes the title "Mr. Nice Guy." Americans have watched Howard grow up before their eyes, from the red-headed Opie Taylor on *The Andy Griffith Show,* to the wholesome Richie Cunningham on *Happy Days,* to the successful director of such smash hits as *Splash, Parenthood,* and *Backdraft.* And through it all his public image remains, in essence, that of the "nice" and "normal" boy of his youth. "The real Ron Howard is so benign, so nice, so *normal* that you immediately begin to fantasize about how he, as a long-time Hollywood brat, *should have turned out,*" maintain Ron Givens and Charles Leerhsen in *Newsweek.* Because he has not changed, many people continue to address Howard as the two popular television characters he played. "I know when people say, 'Hi, Richie' or 'Hi, Opie,' they're just joking around," explains Howard in a *New York Times* interview with Stephen Farber. "Most of them are pretty much up to date on who I really am." And according to Farber, "Who he really is today is one of the hottest directors working in Hollywood."

Howard's acting career began at an early age. Both his parents acted, and his father, Rance, was also a

Howard grew up before America's eyes as Opie Taylor on the long-running 1960s sitcom *The Andy Griffith Show.*

writer and director. As an infant and toddler, Howard appeared in summer theater whenever his father developed a role that required a young actor. He made his stage debut at the age of two, playing the role of Rickie Sherman in *The Seven Year Itch*. His film debut soon followed these theater appearances when, at the age of four, he and his father landed small roles in *The Journey*, a film shot in Vienna, which starred Yul Brynner and Deborah Kerr. This led to a larger role in the pilot *Barnaby and Mr. O'Malley*, which was shown on *The General Electric Theater*, then hosted by Ronald Reagan. Overshadowed by the other actors in the pilot, Howard was not even listed in the credits, but at the end of the show "Reagan ad-libbed a line of thanks to 'little Ronny Howard, who did so well in playing the part of Barnaby,'" points out Darlene Arden in the *Saturday Evening Post*. The following day Howard received numerous calls for alternate series in case *Barnaby and Mr. O'Malley* did not make it. Among these many callers was Sheldon Leonard from *The Andy Griffith Show*, "and millions of TV viewers of the 1960s became part of what followed," remarks Arden.

Howard began playing Opie Taylor at the age of six, and resided in the fictional town of Mayberry until he was fourteen. "Before there was Lake Wobegon, there was Mayberry, a cozy country Camelot tucked away in the North Carolina pines," recalls *People* contributor Jane Hall. "Mayberry was that rare, sleepy slice of Americana where Bug Month was a big event, the known world ended at the county line and local eccentrics flourished like wildflowers. Beginning in 1960, millions of Americans escaped to that small-town utopia by way of *The Andy Griffith Show* on CBS, enjoying the shenanigans of Sheriff Andy Taylor, his adorable red-haired son, Opie, lovable Aunt Bee, preternaturally nervous Deputy Barney Fife and thick-skulled Gomer Pyle." After eight seasons in the Nielsen top ten, *The Andy Griffith Show* ended, many of its stars anxious to move on to new projects. Reruns of the show, however, continue to be shown on several stations throughout the country, and have imbued the inhabitants of Mayberry with an almost timeless quality.

"I have fond memories of the series and especially of Andy Griffith," reminisces Howard in his interview with Arden. "Around the reading table I best remember him for telling us that it was important the show be funny, but it had to be funny because the viewer could identify with the characters and not because they thought we were a bunch of hayseeds and dumb hicks." Howard also remem-

Howard as the wholesome and level-headed Richie Cunningham with the rest of the cast of ABC-TV's *Happy Days*.

bers Griffith's hard work, which he came to appreciate even more when he had to play a comparable "straight-man" role as Richie Cunningham in *Happy Days*. He did not always look back on his years as Opie Taylor with such positive feelings, though. "I used to be afraid that I was going to be Opie for the rest of my life," continues Howard in his *Saturday Evening Post* interview. "In fact, there was a time when I pretended *The Andy Griffith Show* didn't exist. The worst thing anyone could ever do would be to call me 'Opie.' *Now* I get the biggest kick out of it; I love it! The show is something I've built on. It's something to be proud of."

In 1986 Howard was able to appear as Opie Taylor one more time in the television movie *Return to Mayberry*, which brought together nearly all the original cast members of *The Andy Griffith* show. "The idea for the reunion was triggered when Griffith, Knotts, and Howard presented an Emmy award together . . .," explains Hall. "'I was surprised at the amount of audience laughter,' recalls Griffith. 'We went out to dinner and talked about doing the reunion.' Griffith found no holdouts among the large cast," continues Hall, and Howard tells her: "I think everybody would have been disappointed not to be asked." In the movie, Opie is the editor of the local paper, married, and an expectant father. "I didn't think the experience would live up to my expectations.... But the feelings are still there," says Howard in his interview with Hall. "Andy was like a wonderful uncle to me," he adds. "He created an atmosphere of hard work and fun that I try to bring to my movies."

After *The Andy Griffith Show*, Howard made guest appearances on numerous television shows, appeared in such movies as *The Music Man* and *The Courtship of Eddie's Father*, and had a recurring role on *The Smith Family*, a dramatic series that ran from 1971 to 1972. It wasn't until 1974, when Howard was twenty years old, that he began playing the level-headed teenage character of Richie Cunningham on *Happy Days*. He was cast in the role after playing a similar character in the 1973 movie *American Graffiti*, and stayed with the show for six years. "*Happy Days* was a wonderful job," states Howard in his *Saturday Evening Post* interview, "though I never was passionate about it as a creative experience. I really loved the friendly people on the show, and I saw it as a way to attain my ultimate goal—directing. What I missed most after leaving the series was not the work but the daily exposure to all those people."

While playing Richie Cunningham on *Happy Days*, Howard continued his film career and began directing, which eventually led him away from acting altogether. The desire to direct was not a new one for Howard—it had been with him since childhood. "When I was about eight," recalls Howard in a *Film Comment* interview with Todd McCarthy, "a magazine reporter asked me, 'What do you want to do when you grow up?' and I said, 'I want to be an actor, writer, producer, director, camera man, baseball player.' That sounds like the kind of cute, pat answer that a kid would develop, but it tells me that I was thinking about branching out in the business, and I was interested in everybody's job." Howard's father also influenced his desire to be on the other side of the camera. "My dad used to direct a lot of stage work," explains Howard in his *New York Times* interview, "so I think I was always interested in more than just acting. And then when I was about 15 or so, I really started becoming obsessed with directing, reading books about it, going to more movies, asking questions of every director I worked for."

This increased interest in directing prompted Howard to begin making and editing short home movies; and on the weekends he worked on a feature film starring Donny Most and Linda Perl. In the midst of all this, Roger Corman approached Howard and asked him to appear in the movie *Eat My Dust*. Although Howard disliked the film, he knew that Corman was supportive of student filmmakers and gave new directors a chance, so he agreed to do the film if Corman would let him direct *'Tis the Season*, a script that he and his father had written. It was not the type of picture Corman wanted to do, but he offered Howard and his father the chance to come up with a new story idea instead. And even if this did not work out, Corman guaranteed Howard at least a second-unit directing job. *Eat My Dust* turned out to be quite a hit, prompting Corman to request that Howard and his father write a sequel. In his *Film Comment* interview Howard outlines Corman's instructions: "I'd like you to make a picture. I'd like it to be a car chase comedy, young people on the run. I want you to be able to star in it, and I want it to be able to be titled *Grand Theft Auto*, and with those givens, if you can come up with a story line, we'll do it."

Howard and his father came up with a suitable storyline, and *Grand Theft Auto* was released in 1977. This was not the first writing the two did together, though. Howard was continually proposing story ideas to his father; he was eight or nine when his father was working on a script for *The Flintstones*, one of Howard's favorite shows, and his father actually used one of his ideas for an episode, sharing the money he earned with his son. *Grand Theft Auto* offered Howard not only the opportunity to write again, but gave him his first chance to direct as well. Corman did not leave much room for creativity, though, and Howard admits in his *Film Comment* interview that *Grand Theft Auto* was not the ideal film for his first directing experience: "It clearly would not have been what I would have chosen as my first film. As an actor, I felt my strength would be scenes, character, and trying to help people evolve performances, and *Grand Theft Auto* was hardly a performance picture. But it turned out to be a great experience for me. I feel that work begets work, and if you can put yourself in the flow, good things will come to you."

Grand Theft Auto is the story of a young couple who must travel to Las Vegas to elope when the girl's millionaire father refuses to consent to the marriage. The film contains numerous car chase scenes, including one in which the Rolls-Royce the couple is driving is chased by a fleet of highway patrol cars, several vans, a school bus, a helicopter, and the cars of many others who hope to win the

Howard and executive producer George Lucas stand amidst the cast of little people who portrayed the Nelwyns in the 1988 mythical-medieval *Willow*.

reward the young girl's father is offering for catching the couple. "Scenes like that would cause many older, more experienced directors to chew on their megaphones," remarks Judy Klemesrud in the *New York Times*. "But to hear Ron Howard talk the whole thing was a piece of cake." Despite his apparent confidence, Howard experienced a few moments of anxiety: "I did get panicky on the first day, though," he admits to Klemesrud. "By lunch time I had done only four or five shots, and according to my schedule I was supposed to do 29 shots. I went off to lunch and thought I wasn't going to cut it. But I did, and everyone was very excited because the kid director got it done on the first day."

Howard's first directing experience only strengthened his desire to make this aspect of filmmaking his main career. "I never really understood the feeling of being totally wiped out before, I didn't know how exciting it could be to solve the problems involved in making a movie," relates Howard in his interview with Klemesrud. "If I had a choice right now, acting or directing, I would direct. As an actor, you don't have the same sense of total commitment to a project that you do when you're the director. As a result, it's not as rewarding."

Lawrence Van Gelder, writing in the *New York Times*, praises Howard's first attempt at directing and claims that he "need take a back seat to no one when it comes to competence in the genre. His debut as a director of feature films may not mark him as an innovator, but neither does it suffer from comparison to its many predecessors."

Howard's directing career continued when he left *Happy Days* in 1980 and accepted an exclusive three-year contract from NBC, which enabled him to become a full-time director and producer. *Cotton Candy*, *Through the Magic Pyramid*, and *Skyward*, starring Bette Davis, were the television feature films Howard completed under this contract. *Skyward* was a coproduction of Anson Williams's Anson Productions and Howard's Major H Productions, which he had formed with other members of his family in 1977. Directing a veteran actress like Davis gave Howard valuable experience that he was able to utilize a few years later when he directed the star-studded *Cocoon*. Davis was wary of the young director, and Howard recounts the development of their working relationship in a *Horizon* interview with Samir Hachem: "I would go up to her to talk, or make a suggestion, and she had this look on her face that said something like, 'What could this child possibly have to say to *me?*' She called me 'Mr. Howard.' I said, 'Call me Ron.' She said, 'No, I'll call you Mr. Howard until I decide if I like you or not.' And I called her 'Miss Davis.' One day, we had a scene and I suggested a new way to do it. She said, 'No, no, I don't think that works at all.' I said, 'Would you give it a shot?' She looked at me and said, 'I'll always try it.' So she did. Then she threw her hands up and said, 'Of course. You're absolutely right. That makes the scene.' I said, 'Thanks, Miss Davis.' She said, 'OK, Ron,' with a pat on the rump, and from that point forward, it was great.''

While at Paramount working on *Skyward,* Howard met Brian Grazer, who produced his next two films, *Night Shift* and *Splash.* Both men were about the same age, making them the youngest people working on the lot at that time. They had what Howard terms in his *Film Comment* interview as "one of those Hollywood lunches," during which Grazer outlined an idea for *Night Shift.* He had read an article about a prostitution ring that was being run out of the New York City morgue and thought it would make a good comedy. Lowell Ganz and Babaloo Mandel, former writers for *Happy Days* who were working with Howard at the time, started working on Ganz's idea and Howard liked the result. "We always got a big kick out of the concept, but I'm not sure that it was a readily accessible idea to a lot of people," reflects Howard in his *Film Comment* interview.

Night Shift enabled Howard to work with Henry Winkler again, who plays Chuck Lumley, a reserved and nondescript morgue supervisor who is transferred to the night shift when his boss's nephew is given his job. Billy Blazejowski, played by Michael Keaton, is Chuck's new and somewhat eccentric assistant who constantly carries a tape recorder to keep track of all the ideas and schemes that his vivid imagination generates. Along with his work troubles, Chuck also has problems with his overweight fiancee who is more interested in food and her numerous diets than she is in him. He simultaneously develops a romantic interest in his neighbor Belinda, played by Shelley Long, who happens to be a wholesome prostitute whose pimp has recently been killed. Billy concocts a plan to help Belinda and her co-workers; and he and Chuck begin running a prostitution ring out of the morgue, offering the women health benefits and a larger percentage of the profits.

"Having grown up on television, Mr. Howard is well-versed in the techniques of staging situation comedy, and he keeps the movie fast and entertaining until the material bogs it down," asserts the *New York Times'* Janet Maslin. Howard sees his many years of acting experience as an added advantage in his directing ventures. "Most importantly," remarks Howard in his interview with Farber, "acting gave me a certain amount of self-confidence. That's not something I'm just brimming over with. Another benefit of my acting background is that it's made me very character-oriented. I'm always concerned about trying to round the characters out. I think audiences respond to characters more than to anything else."

Howard enjoys working with comedic actors like former improvisational comedian Keaton, who was enthusiastically received by audiences and critics alike in *Night Shift.* "I like to work with funny, improvisational actors. And they like to work with me," maintains Howard in his interview with Peter Gethers in *Esquire,* adding: "I'm funny in my own right. I can hold my own with them, but I don't compete. I appreciate." *New York's* David Denby appreciates both the actors and the director of *Night Shift,* calling the movie "an extremely entertaining farce made by some TV people on a holiday. Ron Howard has excellent comic timing and the sense to give his actors some room to breathe in. If he stops thinking of that audience in front of the box and contemplates instead that tougher audience in the theater, he may really soar."

Howard's next movie, *Splash,* originated with a story idea from Grazer; however, it was difficult to find someone willing to do the picture, mainly because of a competing project entitled *Mermaids.* Buena Vista, a subsidiary of Disney, finally agreed to do *Splash,* and the competing project dissolved in financial difficulties. Howard originally had to talk himself into doing *Splash.* "I wasn't sure I wanted to follow *Night Shift* with another comedy, an almost silly comedy," he explains in his *Film Comment* interview. "But I started thinking about the romantic possibilities of the project, and we came up with a new structure.... It became a character comedy, more a love story."

Splash is a romantic comedy involving a mermaid named Madison, played by Daryl Hannah, and lonely bachelor Allen Bauer, played by Tom Hanks. Having rescued Allen from drowning on two previous occasions, once as a young boy and again as a young man, Madison makes her way to the New York harbor in search of him. Because her fin changes into legs when she is out of water, she is able to locate him. Allen has no idea she is a mermaid, and they fall in love; but their happiness

Steve Martin, as Gil Buckman, tangles with his career and family life in the 1989 smash-hit *Parenthood*.

is soon threatened by Kornbluth, a marine scientist determined to prove that Madison is a mermaid. "There are chases, bits of wild slapstick (beautifully executed), and plenty of suspense," observes Denby in his review of *Splash*. "It's been a long time since we've had a good boy-meets-fish, boy-loses-fish, boy-gets-fish story, and this one is fairly irresistible."

The actors involved in *Splash* are quick to acknowledge Howard's "comic instincts and his keen actorly insights" as being the real keys to the movie's success, writes Jim Jerome in *People*. And Hanks tells Jerome that Howard "has seen absolutely everything that can happen on a set, because the man started doing it three months before he was born or something like that.... Ron will be huger than all of us, and we'll really be bitter about it in the future. Ron's the king." *Village Voice* contributor David Edelstein also praises Howard's directing abilities, but maintains that "what keeps *Splash* from being a classic is its lack of invention, its overreliance on formula: despite the wonderful gags and shimmering photography, it's still a Disney movie." Denby, on the other hand, sees the movie as "a contemporary story with a foundation in myth and fantasy," which enables it to be "freer and crazier" than a conventional love story. "Good taste may not be one of the great creative virtues, but in American commercial comedy it's increasingly rare, and Ron Howard has it.... He's a real director—maybe a major talent."

"Howard is some fisherman: he keeps pulling wonderful things out of the sea," points out *Newsweek* reviewer David Ansen. "From the depths off Cape Cod emerged *Splash*, the most delightful of mermaid comedies. Now from the warmer waters of the Gulf Coast comes *Cocoon*, a sweet and satisfying fantasy that reinvents the myth of the Fountain of Youth." The film continues Howard's career as a director of comedies, focusing on strong, effective characters, and adding elements of fantasy and science fiction. It was the strong characters that drew Howard to the film, as well as the distinguished cast that was selected to play them—such veteran actors and actresses as Hume Cronyn, Wilford Brimley, Don Ameche, Jessica Tandy, Maureen Stapleton, and Gwen Verdon. "The characters were the most unique aspect of the script," contends Howard in his interview with Farber. "I had some reservations because of the story's similarities to *Splash*, *Close Encounters*, and *E.T.* In fact, that bothered me quite a bit, but it's so rare that you have an opportunity to work

with these kinds of characters that I decided it was worth doing."

The film revolves around the lives of the inhabitants of a retirement community. A few of the men have been sneaking into their neighbor's empty house to use the pool, unaware of the large pods at the bottom; and one day they emerge from their swim feeling rejuvenated and young again. The pods, which have been retrieved from the ocean by the four mysterious people who recently rented the house, turn out to be aliens left behind from an earlier expedition, and are being revitalized in the pool for the trip home. As the members of the retirement community continue their dips in this "fountain of youth," their ailments disappear, but they put the pods in danger by absorbing so much of the mystical energy meant for them. The four aliens eventually invite the swimmers, and other people from the community, to journey back to their planet; and a choice between eternal life and natural human death must be made.

Howard encouraged the actors to improvise as much as possible, trusting the instincts of his skilled cast. In addition to guiding the performers, he also dealt with the complex special effects and fantasy elements that went into the eighteen million dollar film. Brian Dennehy, who played one of the aliens, tells Farber that Howard "prepares as well as any director I've ever seen, but he doesn't take himself that seriously. He's very easy-going on the set, and yet he can be ruthless in the editing. With many directors it's the opposite, and that's when you're in trouble." Stapleton agrees, claiming that Howard "seems like he's been doing it for years. He has common sense, and you trust a man with common sense." Ansen also sees the common sense that went into the making of the movie: "*Cocoon* is not without its sentimental moments, but Howard has the rare quality of tact. He gives his exemplary cast lots of breathing space. As a fellow actor, he must have rejoiced at the arsenal of talent put at his disposal, and he has the grace and good sense not to force pathos out of scenes already brimming with emotional content."

In his *Horizon* interview, Howard claims to have three strengths as a director: "One, I love collaborating with people, motivating people, and coordinating their ideas with mine. Two, I get along very well with actors, and their input gets me going. Three, I think I have a good sense of storytelling, making sure people aren't confused and knowing what to tell when." All these strengths went into the creation of *Cocoon*, making for a movie that "is crowded, not with high-tech space battles and cliff-hanging plot twists, but with humanity,'' points out Ansen. *New Yorker* reviewer Pauline Kael, on the other hand, believes that although Howard ''is an infectiously good-humored comedy director,... he overworks his 'heart' and his ecumenical niceness'' with *Cocoon* in ''an attempt to provide something for all age groups and all faiths.'' Richard Corliss, though, concludes in *Time:* ''By the end, when these sunset adventurers take an outward-bound voyage toward a peaceful death, or into eternal life, this film has charted its serene course. One hopes that moviegoers will take *Cocoon* to their teenage hearts and make a box-office smash of the summer's sweetest, saddest, most exhilarating fable.''

Howard followed *Cocoon* with *Gung Ho* in 1986, another comedy starring Keaton that looks at the differences between American and Japanese work ethics. He then agreed to work on *Willow*, a special-effects-filled fantasy based on a story written by George Lucas. ''If you took Bible stories and 'Peter Pan' and 'Robin Hood' and the 'Oz' books and the Grimm Brothers' fairy tales and 'Gulliver's Travels' and 'Lord of the Rings' and 'Ran' (and the 'Star Wars' trilogy) and put them in a hopper and spun it around until it was a whirring mess of porridge, you'd have the mythical-medieval *Willow*, or something close to it,'' maintains Kael in her review of the movie. Several critics agree, claiming that *Willow* merely takes many elements from books and other movies and combines them all together. ''In brief,'' explains Denby, ''Lucas has covered his bets. Nothing in this exhausting, clangorous picture makes any sense, but there's lots *of* it, including good and bad sorceresses, love dust, much hacking and hewing, and a whole village of tiny Nelwyns.'' And as far as Howard's directing is concerned, asserts Maslin, he ''appears to have had his hands full in simply harnessing the special effects and keeping the plot straight, and he doesn't bring any particular color or personality to material that supposedly had these things to spare.'' *Willow* is an expansive movie, concludes Maslin, and ''the attempt to stage another huge, ambitious fantasy has a certain nobility even when the film itself does not, so that *Willow* at least creates the sense that its audience is witnessing a legitimate cinematic event.''

Howard's 1989 hit comedy, *Parenthood*, moves away from fantasy and follows the course of his earlier movies, relying heavily on strong characters and a large dose of humanity. The idea for the

The cast of the 1991 special-effects-packed *Backdraft* researched their roles by training at the Chicago Fire Academy and by spending the night in a Chicago fire house.

movie originated when the Howards, Ganz, Mandel, and their numerous offspring were flying to Argentina to film on location for *Gung Ho*. The children were making a mess of the cabin, crying, whining, and throwing up, and this inspired the adults to make a movie about families. Howard, Ganz, Mandel, Grazer, and their wives did research for the movie by making lists of twenty of the most memorable feelings or experiences they had had as parents. Howard believed that if he had enough of these "moments" in the movie, then it would work. "I knew I was making an adult movie this time," asserts Howard in his *Newsweek* interview. "I wanted something that was smarter, tougher, a little more painful in places." Givens and Leerhsen hold that Howard achieves this: "With *Parenthood*, Howard abandons his previous reliance on unalloyed charm and tight narratives, to go darker and deeper. In the film's most didactic moment, the great-grandmother compares the best kind of life, with its ups and downs, to a roller coaster that made her 'so scared and so sick and so excited and so thrilled—all together.' *Parenthood* takes you for that kind of emotional ride."

The movie looks at five generations of the Buckman family in its various family units. Gil, played by Steve Martin, and his family, which includes one son who is having psychological problems and another that likes to butt things with his head, are the nucleus of the movie. Gil's sister Helen, played by Diane Wiest, has been abandoned by her husband and is attempting to raise a rebellious teenage daughter and withdrawn son. His other sister, Susan, played by Harley Kozak, has married a man who insists on raising a super child and begins teaching her karate and square roots when she is only three years old. Larry, played by Tom Hulce, is Gil's only brother, and he shows up unexpectedly with an illegitimate child, a large gambling debt, and a contract out on his life. The father of these grown children and young grandchildren, played by Jason Robards, reluctantly presides over the bunch. "There is something brave and original about piling up most of our worst parental nightmares in one movie and then daring to make a midsummer comedy out of them," points out Richard Schickel in *Time*, adding: "It really shouldn't work, but it does. The movie does not linger too long over any moment or mood, and it permits characters to transcend type, offering a more surprising range of response to events."

Directing a film with such a large number of characters "took the skills of a master juggler,"

acknowledge Givens and Leerhsen. Many of the major stars were only on hand for a limited amount of time, and it was often difficult to get natural performances from the young children in the film. "Because Ron Howard ... has a talent for ensemble hubbub, there may be more good, solid performances in this unlikely context than in any other movie this year," contends Schickel. Ansen concurs, claiming that Howard has "woven this enormous cast into a wonderful ensemble." Terrence Rafferty, however, maintains in the *New Yorker* that the numerous characters and story lines are not unified: "The whole thing has been conceived generically, abstractly, and by the end the filmmakers are rushing from scene to scene tidying up loose ends, to make sure that each little individual drama gets its point across unmistakenly and that they all add up to a correct answer to the essay question 'What is parenthood?'" Ansen praises the movie for its authenticity, though, claiming that "at its best, Ron Howard's *Parenthood* captures better than most contemporary American movies the sheer messiness and tumult of middle-class family life."

It was also a strong family story that attracted Howard to the 1991 special-effects-packed thriller *Backdraft*. The main plot line of the movie involves two brothers fighting to continue the legacy of their fireman father, who died on the job when they were children. Kurt Russell plays Brian McCaffrey, an experienced and cocky fire fighter, and William Baldwin is his younger brother, Stephen, a rookie who can do nothing right in his brother's eyes. While this sibling rivalry is raging, so are a number of mysterious fires that the arson investigator, played by Robert De Niro, is trying to solve. "*Backdraft*, the first major film ever made about firefighters, has a strong cast and some impressive action sequences," describes Brian D. Johnson in *Maclean's*. "Flames—crawling, dancing, leaping and rolling—have never performed with such virtuosity."

The screenplay was written by Gregory Widen, a former fire fighter; and when Howard agreed to direct the film, he decided that he and his actors needed "the Hollywood equivalent of Fire Fighting 101," writes *Premiere* contributor Rob Medich. So, the actors went through a few weeks of training under the instruction of the Chicago Fire Academy, and a number of them spent the night at a Chicago fire station, even helping on fire runs. "I trust actors," Howard informs Medich, "but they are like me. They're outsiders to this world that the writer, Greg, understands quite well. They think they understand, just like I thought I did. But I just felt it'd be useful for everyone to go in there and start thinking about it from their character's perspective. Then they'll be able to come to *me* with inconsistencies and questions and solutions. Because they're very smart about it. Nobody's smarter about the character, ultimately, than the actor.''

During his fire fighting training Howard developed a new respect for the profession. "When you spend time with fire fighters and you really see what they do," explains Howard to a *Premiere* contributor, "you begin to feel compelled to abandon the sort of easy entertainment stuff and really invest the time in the people and their behavior and the reality of the situation.'' During the filming, some of the actors did their own stunt work, and a few real fireman had roles in the film. "I don't think anyone has worked as closely to fire as we did," claims actor Scott Glenn in a *People* interview with Diane Goldner and Robin Micheli. "I had scars and blisters across the hairline and on my eyelids." The authenticity of *Backdraft* prompted many critics to praise the film's special effects. "This is what the big screen and special effects are *for*," relates Denby. "Ron Howard ... treats fire as a living thing. It breathes, hides, roars defiance."

"*Backdraft* is undoubtedly the biggest, fanciest firefighting movie ever made," suggests Maslin. "Crammed with impressive pyrotechnics, this technically ambitious film observes the firefighter's life with boyishly awestruck fascination." Some reviewers, though, criticize the various subplots of the movie and suggest that one solid story line would have been much more effective. "The story, however, fails to ignite," upholds Johnson, adding that "all the smoke in the world ... cannot hide the gaps in the barely comprehensible plot." Maslin agrees to an extent, stating that "while Mr. Howard ably maintains a strong forward momentum, *Backdraft* often feels directionless beneath its overlay of frantic activity." She concludes, however, that Howard "has the kind of technical prowess that allows him to hook the audience immediately with a devastating opening sequence."

Howard's technical abilities, along with his many other skills, have grown over a long and varied career that, unlike his movies, he finds very hard to direct. "I try to manage my career," discloses Howard in an interview with Laura Morice for *Us*, "but it never works because ultimately an idea comes to you—you read a script, see something on television, read a book, talk to somebody at a

Howard behind the scenes during the filming of *Parenthood.*

party—*something* happens—and you start to fall in love. You can't really control it." This makes it difficult to sustain the normal family life that is so important to Howard. He and his wife Cheryl are trying to raise their children to understand that "there are people who do things besides make movies and TV shows," explains Howard in his *People* interview. And this is one of the reasons he moved his family to Greenwich, Connecticut. "His private persona is very much the same as his public image," attests Dennehy in his interview with Farber, "and that's rare in the movie business. He really is sweet, unaffected, almost rural, which is funny, since he spent almost his entire life in Hollywood."

"Sometimes I worry that I'm turning into the Steve Garvey of show business," confesses Howard in his interview with Gethers. "You know, too nice. I thought people would think I was faking it. So a few years ago I went through a period where I thought I should rebel. When I gave an interview, I'd act tough and I'd be sure to swear." This rebellion only lasted for about a week, though. "It really wasn't me," concludes Howard. He similarly told Morice: "Sometimes I still think that maybe I should make myself seem a little more dangerous or complex. But it feels like it's a little more trouble than it's worth. I'm getting to do the movies I want to do. I don't feel held back in any way. The respect is there." "The same warm, affable feeling that infused Mr. Howard's television performances shines through in the movies he has directed," concludes Farber, "and that may be the reason why fans continue to approach him not as a larger-than-life celebrity, but as one of the gang, a pal."

■ Works Cited

Ansen, David, "A Brisk Dip in the Fountain," *Newsweek*, June 24, 1985, p. 70.

Ansen, "Bittersweet Pleasures," *Newsweek*, August 7, 1989, pp. 61-62.

Arden, Darlene, "'Opie' Grows Up," *Saturday Evening Post*, December, 1981, pp. 36-39.

Corliss, Richard, "Everybody into the Pool," *Time*, June 24, 1985, p. 89.

Denby, David, "The Wanderers," *New York*, September 13, 1982, pp. 64, 66.

Denby, "A Dish out of Water," *New York*, March 12, 1984, pp. 90-91.

Denby, "Wallow," *New York*, May 30, 1988, pp. 78-79.

Denby, "Lord of the Earrings," *New York*, June 3, 1991, p. 51-52.

Edelstein, David, "Water Babies," *Village Voice*, March 13, 1984, pp. 48-49.

Farber, Stephen, "Ron Howard Goes from Hot Actor to Hot Director," *New York Times*, June 16, 1985, pp. B21, B25.

Gethers, Peter, "A Night of Vice with Mr. Nice," *Esquire*, December, 1986, pp. 256-260.

Givens, Ron, and Charles Leerhsen, "The Nice Guy Rides Again," *Newsweek*, August 28, 1989, pp. 56-57.

Goldner, Diane, and Robin Micheli, "Closer to the Flame," *People*, June 24, 1991, pp. 111-12.

Hachem, Samir, "The Metamorphosis of Ron Howard," *Horizon*, June, 1985, pp. 21-24.

Hall, Jane, "Going Home to Mayberry," *People*, April 14, 1986, pp. 90-92, 97.

Jerome, Jim, "A Whale of a Tail," *People*, April 9, 1984, pp. 34-39.

Johnson, Brian D., "Fear of Frying," *Maclean's*, June 3, 1991, p. 60.

Kael, Pauline, "The Current Cinema," *New Yorker*, July 15, 1985, pp. 70, 73-75.

Kael, "The Current Cinema," *New Yorker*, May 30, 1988, pp. 77-79.

Klemesrud, Judy, "The Kid Wanted to Direct," *New York Times*, June 22, 1977, p. C13.

Maslin, Janet, "Screen: *Night Shift*, Vice Ring Humor at Morgue," *New York Times*, July 30, 1982, p. C8.

Maslin, "*Willow*, a George Lucas Production," *New York Times*, May 20, 1988, p. C8.

Maslin, review of *Backdraft*, *New York Times*, May 24, 1991, p. C14.

McCarthy, Todd, "Auteur Opie," *Film Comment*, May-June, 1984, pp. 40-42.

Medich, Rob, "Playing with Fire," *Premiere*, April, 1991, pp. 97-102.

Morice, Laura, "Burn Baby Burn," *Us*, June 27, 1991, pp. 41-43.

Premiere, June, 1991, pp. 59-60.

Rafferty, Terrence, "The Current Cinema," *New Yorker*, August 7, 1989, pp. 73-75.

Schickel, Richard, "A Typical, Terrible Family," *Time*, August 7, 1989, p. 54.

Van Gelder, Lawrence, "Screen: For Auto Fans," *New York Times*, September 29, 1977, p. C19.

■ For More Information See

PERIODICALS

Esquire, March, 1984.

New Republic, September 13, 1982; June 17, 1991.

New York, June 24, 1985; March 24, 1986.

New York Times, March 9, 1984; February 15, 1985; March 14, 1986; August 2, 1989; August 13, 1989; August 20, 1989.

People, November 23, 1981; June 3, 1991; June 17, 1991.

Rolling Stone, September 2, 1982.

Time, August 9, 1982.

Village Voice, August 3, 1982; April 1, 1986; May 31, 1988.

Vogue, September, 1984.°

—Sketch by Susan M. Reicha

John Irving

Personal

Born March 2, 1942, in Exeter, NH; son of Colin F. N. (stepfather; a teacher) and Frances (Winslow) Irving; married Shyla Leary (a photographer), August 20, 1964 (divorced, 1981); married Janet Turnbull (a literary agent), June 6, 1987; children: (first marriage) Colin, Brendan; (second marriage) Everett. *Education:* Attended University of Pittsburgh, 1961-62, and University of Vienna, 1963-64; University of New Hampshire, B.A. (cum laude), 1965; University of Iowa, M.F.A., 1967.

Addresses

Agent—Janet Turnbull, Turnbull Agency, P.O. Box 757, Dorset, VT 05251.

Career

Novelist. Windham College (now defunct), Putney, VT, teacher of English literature, 1968-72; University of Iowa, Iowa City, writer in residence, 1972-75; Mount Holyoke College, South Hadley, MA, assistant professor of English, 1975-78. Teacher and reader at Bread Loaf Writers Conference, 1976. Worked variously as a bartender and peanut vendor.

Awards, Honors

Rockefeller Foundation grant, 1971-72; National Endowment for the Arts fellowship, 1974-75; Guggenheim fellow, 1976-77; *The World According to Garp* was nominated for a National Book Award in 1979 and won an American Book Award in 1980; named one of ten "Good Guys" honored for contributions furthering advancement of women, National Women's Political Caucus, 1988, for *The Cider House Rules.*

Writings

Setting Free the Bears (also see below), Random House, 1969.

The Water-Method Man (also see below), Random House, 1972.

The 158-Pound Marriage (also see below), Random House, 1974.

The World According to Garp, Dutton, 1978.

Three by Irving (contains *Setting Free the Bears, The Water-Method Man,* and *The 158-Pound Marriage*), Random House, 1980.

The Hotel New Hampshire (Book-of-the-Month Club main selection), Dutton, 1981.

The Cider House Rules (Book-of-the-Month Club main selection), Morrow, 1985.

A Prayer for Owen Meany (Book-of-the-Month Club main selection), Morrow, 1989.

Also contributor of short stories to *Redbook, Boston Review, Esquire, Playboy,* and other magazines.

■ Adaptations

The World According to Garp was released by Warner Bros./Pan Arts in 1982, starred Robin Williams, Glenn Close, and Mary Beth Hurt, and featured cameo performances by Irving and his sons; *The Hotel New Hampshire* was released by Orion Pictures in 1984 and starred Rob Lowe, Jodie Foster, and Beau Bridges.

■ Work in Progress

Another novel, *Son of the Circus;* screenplays for *The Cider House Rules* and *Son of the Circus.*

■ Sidelights

Counted among the twentieth-century's finest novelists, John Irving is noted for his extraordinary imagination and fondness for meshing the comic and the tragic. He is perhaps best known for his 1978 best-seller, *The World According to Garp.* In addition to earning serious critical acclaim, *Garp* achieved a popular cult status complete with T-shirts proclaiming, "I Believe in Garp." Unlike many contemporary novelists who infuse their works with experimental techniques or highbrow literary content, Irving focuses on the art of storytelling in his works, believing modern literature should be enjoyable and accessible to a wide audience. "I think, to some degree, entertainment is the responsibility of literature," he told Scot Haller in *Saturday Review.* Because of Irving's affection for sweeping, classic storytelling, many critics have likened his fiction to that of nineteenth-century novelists; indeed, he has cited English author Charles Dickens as one of his major influences. Also like much nineteenth-century fiction, Irving's works contain themes of the value of family, the dominance of fate, the helplessness that often accompanies misfortune, and the relationship between art and life. Making him uniquely contemporary is his often unsettling portrayal of such issues as rape, incest, and abortion, elements frequently depicted with a combination of humor and violence. "Fashioning wildly inventive, delightfully intricate narratives out of his sense of humor, sense of dread and sense of duty," wrote Haller, "Irving blends the madcap, the macabre, and the mundane into sprawling, spiraling comedies of life."

Born in 1942 in Exeter, New Hampshire, Irving attended the Phillips Exeter Academy, a college preparatory school for boys where his stepfather was a teacher of Russian history. It was there that Irving discovered his penchant for writing. "When I was fourteen or fifteen I found that I needed to tell stories," he told Larry McCaffery in *Contemporary Literature.* "I was always writing stories and when I finally got to prep school I realized that this was not only a legitimate but an encouraged activity. So very early on it seemed to me the dream of something I might one day do. But I didn't feel I was very good at it. For one thing, I was not a very good student. I did all right in English and history courses, where I could simply read and write. But I was terrible at math, science and language courses—a kind of C plus, B minus type of student." Besides writing, Irving expressed passion for only one other subject—wrestling. A member of Exeter's wrestling team, he "was aggressive," recounted his mother, Frances, in R. Z. Sheppard's cover story on Irving for *Time.* "His senior year he won every match."

THE NATIONAL BESTSELLER!
NOW A MAJOR MOTION PICTURE FROM WARNER BROS.

THE WORLD ACCORDING TO *Garp*

JOHN IRVING
AUTHOR OF THE HOTEL NEW HAMPSHIRE

POCKET
45217-7
$3.95

Irving described his best-selling 1978 novel as "an artfully disguised soap opera."

Though seemingly unrelated, writing and wrestling were uniquely connected for Irving: "One reason I got an early start as a writer," he told Haller, "is that I was able to put in long hours when I was young. As a wrestler I was used to training. There's a certain boring routine to staying in shape, and it's a practice for writing, which is about seven-tenths tedious work, a kind of daily maintenance."

Looking back on his youth, Irving recounts having a relatively happy childhood. "The only suffering … occurred when … I knew I wanted to be a writer," the author told Thomas Williams in the *New York Times Book Review*. "How lonely that was! There was nothing like majoring in French or going to law school or medical school to look forward to; I had a terrible sense of how different I was from all my friends, and I didn't want to be different at all. No kid wants to be different. We learn to cultivate and make use of how 'different' we are as we get older." Perhaps because of his acute awareness of being unlike his peers, Irving is remembered as being quite serious in his youth. His mother said to Sheppard: "He was not an exuberant or over-enthusiastic child, although I don't think it's quite accurate to label him as an introvert. I think he kept a lot of things to himself." Reflected the author, as quoted by Sheppard, "I couldn't wait to grow up. … I was a humorless kid. I was not an entertainer; I was very grim."

Irving graduated from Phillips Academy in 1961 with goals of wrestling and writing novels. Rejected by the University of Wisconsin, he attended the University of Pittsburgh for a year "because of the coach," Irving told Sheppard. He later attended the University of New Hampshire, where he recalls being restless. "I felt that I had not got anywhere," Irving said to Sheppard. He was encouraged, though, by a professor and writer, John Yount. "It was so simple," Irving told Sheppard. "Yount was the first person to point out to me that anything I did except writing was going to be vaguely unsatisfying."

In 1963 Irving elected to attend the University of Vienna. Expressing the importance of foreign travel, he told Sheppard, "It is good … for a writer to go to a place where everything is novel, where you can't even take the butter for granted, where the mayonnaise comes in a tube instead of a jar, where you are made to notice even the trivial things—especially the trivial things." "You need to *get away*, to go outside of yourself to see clearly not so much where you are as where you've *been*," the author further explained to Gabriel Miller in *John Irving*. "And there's nothing like that exposure to

something [new]. I'm not speaking personally—I mean as a writer, that is the advantage and the value to me of places far away." While in Vienna, Irving began writing a novel about cowboys who stage a rodeo in New England, but he abandoned it. He toured Europe by car and motorcycle, meeting a variety of people, including painters, poets, and, quite memorably, a man with an old trained bear, "an animal," according to Sheppard, "that would prowl his future books."

Just before the end of his European trip, Irving married painter Shyla Leary, a former Radcliffe student whom he had met in Cambridge before he left for Vienna. Upon returning to the United States, he re-enrolled in the University of New Hampshire, later writing two stories that were published in magazines. Graduating in 1965, the same year his son Colin was born, Irving went on to the University of Iowa Writers' Workshop to work on his master of fine arts degree. He studied under writers Vance Bourjaily and Kurt Vonnegut, Jr., supporting himself and his family by working as a bartender and selling peanuts and pennants at football games. Also during his stint at the University of Iowa, Irving wrote his first novel, *Setting Free the Bears*.

Set entirely in Europe, *Setting Free the Bears* details the horrors of war and a youth's troubled ascent into manhood. Narrated by young Austrian student Hannes Graffe, the book focuses on the narrator's friend Siggy Javotnik, who keeps a journal telling of his family's encounters with enslavement, violence, and dehumanization during and after World War II. "Metaphorically [Siggy] associates his oppressed forebears with the animals in the Heitzinger Zoo of Vienna," noted Hugh M. Ruppersburg in the *Dictionary of Literary Biography*. "His fantasy of freeing the animals and thus avenging his family's fate lies at the novel's core." *Setting Free the Bears* met with positive critical reaction and sold 6,228 copies, a number considered good for a first novel.

With the money earned from *Setting Free the Bears*, the Irvings moved to Putney, Vermont, where they bought a house and Irving taught English at the now-defunct Windham College. From 1969 to 1971 the author spent time in Vienna to work on the screenplay of *Setting Free the Bears*, and, while there, his second son, Brendan, was born. Though the film project did not pan out, the experience Irving gained during the venture provided him with materials for his next novel.

The Water-Method Man, published in 1972, centers on the failed life of Fred "Bogus" Trumper, a blundering but likeable man who searches for spiritual satisfaction. Trumper is in a relationship with a woman named Tulpen, but he dwells on his past unsuccessful marriage and his failed attempt at being a husband. In addition to feeling deficient in such other roles as father, son, and doctoral student, Trumper is made to feel inadequate by a urinary tract disorder that makes urinating and intercourse painful. "Urination and sex are necessary functions of life," noted Ruppersburg. "Trumper can have neither without serious pain, which warps his attitude toward love and life in general." A sound mixer for a New York filmmaker, Trumper even becomes the subject of a movie focusing on his failed life. With a diary he is keeping and an Old Norse poem he is translating, however, Trumper begins to make sense out of his life so that, by novel's end, he is at peace with himself and his world. "In *The Water-Method Man,*" noted Miller, "Irving manages with great success to assemble the disparate fragments of a man's life into a moving, rich, and satisfying whole." Despite receiving positive reviews, the book met with moderate sales.

For the three years following the publication of *The Water-Method Man,* Irving was a writer in residence at the University of Iowa. Though he found some writing success by contributing stories to magazines, he was generally dissatisfied with his career: "I felt I'd *been* to Iowa," the author expressed to Greil Marcus in a *Rolling Stone* interview. "I'd gotten a lot out of it, I'd liked it fine. But now I wasn't wrestling so well anymore. I was getting *beaten up.* I was feeling old, physically. I was *sick of* teaching. I didn't want to *do it anymore.* I was restless, aimless. We lived in four houses over a three year period in the same dull city, Iowa City. I thought I was gonna die a death of boredom."

At this rather discouraging point in his life, Irving wrote *The 158-Pound Marriage,* a book about two married couples who decide to swap mates. "The motive in such an arrangement is supposed to be wholly sexual, with a complete lack of emotional involvement," explained Ruppersburg. "Unfortunately for the couples involved, [hurting] becomes the point of it all; their four-way relationship produces far more pain than pleasure." One couple, consisting of the unnamed narrator and his wife, Utch, perceive the swap as a way of relieving boredom. The other couple, Severin and Edith, see the situation as a means of saving their marriage.

Weaving an intricate pattern of lies, the characters become decidedly cruel, ultimately wreaking devastating emotional pain upon one another. "Jealousy, anguish, hostility are rampant," noted Ruppersburg. Discussing the book with Marcus, Irving proclaimed, "The book is about lust and rationalization and restlessness: I decided I wanted to write a really dark tale of sexual intrigue; in the end nobody would know *anything* about each other." Described by Miller as "Irving's most corrosive work," *The 158-Pound Marriage* was also the best reviewed of his first three novels. Unfortunately, the book sold a disastrous 2560 copies.

By 1974, "John Irving had written three novels, and nobody knew it," wrote Haller. Irving expressed to the reviewer: "I resented like hell that I didn't make enough money from writing to live on. I come from a middle-class family, and I really hated coming into my middle thirties feeling very much a professional at what I did and still scrounging around. I didn't want to be rich, but I goddam well wanted enough money to afford myself."

Irving began another teaching post, working from 1975 to 1978 as an assistant professor of English at Mount Holyoke College. Also at this time, "I began to hear from Random House [the publishers of Irving's first three books] that I had a 'track record,'" he told McCaffery. "This track record was described thusly: 'John Irving can be counted on for some serious critical reviews and diminishing sales. He's a sort of arty-farty writer who's going to be read by other writers and by people at universities, but he's too hard to understand for people in the mainstream.' I resisted that view, saying, Hey, this is *your* track record, not mine." Blaming Random House's inability to properly promote his books, the author took the first chapters of his next novel (which, incidentally, were received coolly by Random House) to Dutton. Impressed with Irving's work in progress, Dutton offered the author a $20,000 advance for the book as well as a $150,000 commission for a following novel. "For the first time the writer returned home to work without having to worry about money," proclaimed Sheppard. Indeed, with the 1978 publication of *The World According to Garp*—which would sell more than three million copies—Irving would never worry about financial security again. He told Richard West in a *New York* interview that with *Garp* he had achieved his lifelong goal: "I was finally able to become a full-time writer."

The World According to Garp, explained its author in a *Washington Post Book World* article, is "an

Jodie Foster, Rob Lowe, and Beau Bridges starred as members of the eccentric Berry family in the film adaptation of *The Hotel New Hampshire.*

artfully disguised soap opera. The difference is that I write well, that I construct a book with the art of construction in mind, that I use words intentionally and carefully. I mean to make you laugh, to make you cry; those are soap-opera intentions, all the way." A lengthy family saga, *Garp* focuses on nurse Jenny Fields, her illegitimate son, novelist T. S. Garp, and Garp's college-professor wife and two sons. Considered by some to be highly disquieting, *Garp* explicitly explores the violent side of contemporary life. Episodes involving rape, assassination, mutilation, and suicide abound, but these horrific scenes are always injected with comedy. As Irving expressed in the *Los Angeles Times*, "No matter how gray the subject matter or orientation of any novel I write, it's still going to be a comic novel."

Preoccupied with the perilousness of life, Garp wants nothing more than to keep the world safe for his family and friends. Ironically, Garp is the one who ultimately inflicts irreversible harm on his children, illustrating Irving's point that "the most protective and unconditionally loving parents can inflict the most appalling wounds on their children," Pearl K. Bell noted in *Commentary*. While Garp is obsessed with protecting his family and friends, his mother's obsession involves promoting her status as a "sexual suspect"—a woman who refuses to share either her life or her body with a man. Through her best-selling autobiography, *A Sexual Suspect*, Jenny becomes a feminist leader. Her home turns into a haven for a group of radical feminists, the Ellen James Society, whose members have cut out their tongues as a show of support for a young girl who was raped and similarly mutilated by her attackers. Both Garp and Jenny eventually are assassinated—she by an outraged antifeminist convinced that Jenny's influence ruined his marriage, he by an Ellen Jamesian convinced that Garp is an exploiter of women because of a novel he wrote about rape. Discussing these characters in a *Publishers Weekly* interview with Barbara A. Bannon, Irving remarked, "It mattered very fiercely to me that [Garp and Jenny] were people who would test your love of them by being the extremists they were. I always knew that as mother and son they would make the world angry at them."

Dealing with such issues as rape, feminism, and sexual roles, *Garp* has been hailed for its sensitivity to women. *Nation* contributor Michael Malone wrote, "With anger, chagrin and laughter, Irving anatomizes the inadequacies and injustices of traditional sex roles. . . . The force behind a memorable gallery of women characters—foremost among them, Garp's famous feminist mother and his

English professor wife—is not empathy but deep frustrated sympathy." Irving explained to Ann Japenga in the *Los Angeles Times*, though, that his "interest in women . . . is really very simple. . . . I see every evidence that women are more often victims than men. As a novelist I'm more interested in victims than in winners." In fact, Irving strongly disagrees with critics who call *Garp* a sociological or political novel. He told McCaffery: "Obviously now when people write about *Garp* and say that it's 'about' feminism and assassination and the violence of the sixties, they're ignoring the fact that I lived half of the sixties in another country. I don't know anything about the violence of the sixties; it's meaningless to me. I'm not a sociological writer, nor should I be considered a social realist in any way."

Irving also takes exception with critics who describe *Garp* as a semiautobiographical work, even though similarities between Garp and Irving abound. For example, both men are professional writers, both display a penchant for wrestling, and both have two sons of whom they are extremely protective. Reviewer Bell wrote that in *Garp* Irving "indulges in elaborate games of allusion to his own life and career, as though taunting the reader to guess what has been made up, what taken whole from life." Even Irving's son Colin told Haller: "My father's a lot like Garp as a parent, very protective. . . . And the book sounds like him, if you've ever heard him tell a story at the dinner table. The tone is the same." Colin was quick to point out to Haller, though, that "*Garp* is in no way autobiographical. I mean, *I* didn't even know some of the things that went through his head until I read *Garp*." In fact, as Irving told Williams, "I make up all the important things. I've had a very uninteresting life. I had a happy childhood. I'm grateful for how ordinary my life is because I'm not ever tempted to think that something that happened to me is important simply because it happened to me. I have no personal axes to grind; I'm free, therefore, to imagine the best possible ax to grind—and I really mean that: that's a significant freedom from the tyranny and self-importance of autobiography in fiction." The author summarized in the *Washington Post Book World*, "As a story, my life would put you to sleep before I got out of grammar school."

The World According to Garp was heralded as Irving's finest and most original work. *New Republic* contributor Terrence Des Pres observed that "nothing in contemporary fiction matches it." The critic continued: "Irving tells the story of Garp's family with great tenderness and wisdom. By tracing the relationship between wife and husband, and then again between parents and children (and how these two sets intersect to cause catastrophe), Irving is able to handle a large range of human hope and fear and final insufficiency. He is excellent in his portrait of Garp's sons, Duncan and Walt, whose view of their father is often hilarious, whose dialogue is true without fail, and whose vulnerability in a world of numberless hurtful things causes Garp a brooding, prophetic dread.''

Several reviewers compliment in particular the narrative flow of *Garp*. "Reading *Garp* was like listening to Homer's account of the Trojan War told in a singsong monotone," wrote Doris Grumbach in *Saturday Review*. "I relished every page, every line, of the imaginative feast." *New York Times Book Review* critic Richard Locke comment-

Irving's controversial 1985 novel dealt with a variety of sensitive issues, including abortion.

ed: "Irving has a natural narrative gift, and even when the plot is not as cosmic as it tries to be, one can't help wondering what will happen to these people next and reading on." Other reviewers praise the originality and credibility of Irving's characterizations. "What does matter about *The World According to Garp* is the captivating originality of the characters, the closely drawn entirety of the life that Irving bestows upon them, and the infectious love he feels for these emanations of his head," wrote Bell. Concurred Locke, "The characters ... compel our sympathy. We feel with them—strongly—in the midst of their family lives and lusts and disasters." *New York Times* reviewer Christopher Lehmann-Haupt added, "The way he filters [the book's violent events] through his hero's unique imagination, we not only laugh at the world according to Garp, but we also accept it and love it."

"Not everyone who read *Garp*," however, "responded to the novel's fun and games," remarked Sheppard. "Many readers were offended by Irving's mating of the truly tragic and grotesquely comic." Irving responded in his interview with Haller, "People who think *Garp* is wildly eccentric and very bizarre are misled about the real world.... I can't imagine where they've been living or what they read for news. Five out of seven days I find things in the *New York Times* that seem to me far less explainable than the rather human behavior in *Garp*." He similarly remarked to Williams, "In just the same way that I don't see comedy and tragedy as contradictions ... I don't see that unhappy endings undermine rich and energetic lives."

The majority of reviewers embrace Irving's fictional world—violence and all. "If the events seem at times to be too brutal and terrible, if too many violences seem to have been heaped upon already suffering and bloodied persons, that is the way it is," wrote Grumbach. "Garp writes and lives as he finds the world. And because John Irving is so subtle and persuasive a writer, we believe in his fictional world." Bell concluded: "Remarkably, none of the slaughter and mayhem that erupt with such bloody frequency in *The World According to Garp* seems sensationalistic or even melodramatic. Irving has taken a capacious and demanding view of his task as a storyteller, and carried it out with sober compassion, adventurous ingenuity, and great intelligence."

Garp was nominated for a National Book Award in 1979 and, when released in paperback, earned an American Book Award. Additionally, the book was made into a highly successful film starring Robin Williams as Garp and Glenn Close as Jenny. Irving did not feel comfortable with the notion of writing the screenplay for *Garp* and let someone else adapt the work for film; he did, though, appear in a bit part in the movie as a wrestling referee.

Within *The World According to Garp* is a piece of writing by Garp, "The Pension Grillparzer," described by Locke as "a short narrative ... [that] glows at the heart of *The World According to Garp* like some rich gem or flower." This brief but compelling tale formed the outline for Irving's next work, *The Hotel New Hampshire.* Irving explained to West: "I realized while writing 'Pension' that I wanted to write about hotels—not realistically, as I was doing at the time, but metaphorically. I also wanted to keep the voice of 'Pension,' a straightforward first-person narrative told from a child's point of view that a child could understand. It would be a novel about childhood, about growing up and how the impressions children have of themselves and those closest to them change as they grow older. It is the most fairytale-like novel I have done in that it relies the least on one's understanding of the real world."

Although rich in fairytale-like qualities, *The Hotel New Hampshire* explores such adult issues as incest, terrorism, suicide, freakish deaths, and gang rape, all pervaded by Irving's trademark macabre humor. A family saga like *Garp, The Hotel New Hampshire* spans nearly four generations of the troubled Berry family. Headed by Win, a charming but irresponsible dreamer who is ultimately a failure at innkeeping, and Mary, who dies in the early stages of the novel, the Berry family includes five children: Franny, Frank, Egg, Lilly, and John, the narrator. While Egg perishes along with his mother, the remaining children are left to struggle through childhood and adolescence. Irving described the family this way to West: "[*The Hotel New Hampshire*] takes a large number of people and says in every family we have a dreamer, a hero, a late bloomer, one who makes it very big, one who doesn't make it at all, one who never grows up, one who is the s— detector, the guide to practicality, and often you don't know who these people will be, watching them in their earlier years."

Along with a colorful array of subsidiary players (including an old trained bear and a flatulent dog), the Berrys eventually inhabit three hotels: one in New Hampshire, one in Vienna, and one in Maine. According to Irving, the hotels are symbols for the passage from infancy to maturity. "The first hotel is the only real hotel in the story," Irving told

West. "It is childhood. The one in Vienna is a dark, foreign place, that phase called adolescence, when you begin leaving the house and finding out how frightening the world is. ... The last one is no hotel at all. ... It is a place to get well again, which is a process that has been going on throughout the novel."

Since it followed such a successful work, *The Hotel New Hampshire* naturally invited comparisons to its predecessor. "There is no question in my mind it's better than *The World According to Garp*," Irving proclaimed to West. "It certainly is every bit as big a book, and it means much more. It's a more ambitious novel symbolically but with a different point of view, deliberately narrower than *Garp.*" Irving nevertheless anticipated that critics would reject the novel. As he told Wendy Graetz in the *Chicago Tribune Book World:* "There will be people gunning for me—they'll call the book lazy, or worse—sentimental. But getting bad press is better than no press. It's better to be hated than to be ignored—even children know that."

Critics' opinions largely fulfilled Irving's dismal prediction. *Chicago Tribune Book World* contributor Judith Rossner, for example, noted, "I found an emptiness at the core of *The Hotel New Hampshire* that might relate to the author's having used up his old angers and familiar symbols without having found new reasons for his rage and different bodies to make us see it." Haller wrote: "*The Hotel New Hampshire* could not be mistaken for the work of any other writer, but unfortunately, it cannot be mistaken for Irving's best novel, either. It lacks the urgency of *Setting Free the Bears*, the bittersweet wit of *The 158-Pound Marriage*, the sly set-ups of *Garp*. The haphazardness that afflicts these characters' lives has seeped into the storytelling, too." Sheppard offered this view: "[Unlike Garp's story,] John Berry's story is not resolved in violent, dramatic action, but in a quiet balancing of sorrow and hope. It is a difficult act, and it is not faultless. The dazzling characterizations and sense of American place in the first part of the novel tend to get scuffed in transit to Europe. There are tics and indulgences. But the book is redeemed by the healing properties of its conclusion. Like a burlesque *Tempest, Hotel New Hampshire* puts the ordinary world behind, evokes a richly allusive fantasy and returns to reality refreshed and strengthened." *New Republic* contributor Jack Beatty concluded: "We all want to check in to the Hotel New Hampshire. It is 'the sympathy space' where we can be fully known and yet fully loved, and where a powerful imagination holds us fast and won't let us die."

Irving followed *The Hotel New Hampshire* with a sixth novel, *The Cider House Rules*. Originally intended to be a saga of orphanage life in early twentieth-century Maine, the book became, instead, a statement on abortion. The issue of abortion arose during Irving's research for the novel, when he "discovered that abortion was an integral part of the life of an orphanage hospital at that time," he remarked in the *Los Angeles Times*. Irving conceded in that same article, "This is in part a didactic novel, and in part a polemic. I'm not ashamed of that.... But I remain uncomfortable at the marriage between politics and fiction. I still maintain that the politics of abortion came to this book organically, came to it cleanly."

Evoking the works of Victorian novelists such as Dickens and Charlotte Bronte, *The Cider House Rules* is set in an orphanage in dreary St. Cloud, Maine, where the gentle, ether-addicted Dr. Larch and his saintly nurses preside lovingly over their orphans. Larch also provides illegal but safe abortions, and although he is painfully aware of the bleak existence that many of the orphans endure, he doesn't encourage expectant mothers to abort. As he states in the novel, "I help them have what they want. An orphan or an abortion." One unadopted orphan in particular, Homer Wells, becomes Larch's spiritual son and protege. Larch schools Homer in birth and abortion procedures and hopes that Homer will one day succeed him at the orphanage. When Homer comes to believe that the fetus has a soul, however, he refuses to assist with abortions. A conflict ensues and Homer seeks refuge at Ocean View apple orchard, located on the coast of Maine.

The book's title refers to the list of rules posted in Ocean View's cider house regarding migrant workers' behavior. Several critics acknowledge the significance of rules, both overt and covert, in the lives of the characters. *Los Angeles Times* critic Elaine Kendall wrote, "Much is made of the literal Cider House Rules, a typed sheet posted in the migrant workers dormitory, clearly and politely spelling out the behavior expected by the owners of the orchard.... Sensible and fair as these rules are, they're made to be broken, interpreted individually or ignored entirely, heavily symbolic of the social and moral codes Irving is exploring." *New York Times* reviewer Christopher Lehmann-Haupt noted that Dr. Larch follows his own rules and that "the point ... is that there are always multiple sets of rules for a given society. Heroism

The hero of Irving's 1989 novel believes himself to be an instrument of God for whom nothing in life is accidental or purposeless.

lies in discovering the right ones, whether they are posted on the wall or carved with scalpels, and committing yourself to follow them no matter what."

Despite the various rules and moral codes Irving explores, critics tend to focus on abortion as the central issue of *The Cider House Rules*. They express different opinions, however, concerning Irving's position on the abortion issue. *Time* critic Paul Gray decided that *The Cider House Rules* "is essentially about abortions and women's right to have them." Kendall, on the other hand, maintained, "Though Dr. Larch's philosophy justifying his divided practice is exquisitely and closely reasoned, the abortion episodes are graphic and gruesome, as if Irving were simultaneously courting both pro-choice and right-to-life factions." *New York Times Book Review* contributor Benjamin DeMott offered this view: "The knowledge and sympathy directing Mr. Irving's exploration of the [abortion] issue are exceptional. Pertinent history, the specifics of surgical procedure, the irrecusable sorrow of guilt and humiliation, the needs and rights of children—their weight is palpable in these pages."

In general, *The Cider House Rules* was favorably reviewed. Several critics believed it is Irving's most worthwhile novel. "By turns witty, tenderhearted, fervent and scarifying, *The Cider House Rules* is, for me, John Irving's first truly valuable book," wrote DeMott. "The storytelling is straightforward—not the case with his huge commercial success, *The World According to Garp*. . . . The theme is in firm focus—not the case with *The Hotel New Hampshire*. . . . The novelist's often-deplored weakness for the cute and trendy, although still evident, is here less troubling." Lehmann-Haupt concurred: "[Irving's] novels have tended to sprawl both in tone and focus, but in *The Cider House Rules* he has positively streamlined his form. . . . The familiar elements of the macabre, the violent and the cute all seem more controlled and pointed, more dedicated to the end of advancing Mr. Irving's story toward a definite and coherent resolution. . . . *The Cider House Rules* has greater force and integrity than either of its two immediate predecessors. It's funny and absorbing and it makes clever use of the plot's seeming predictability."

Following the publication of his next book, *A Prayer for Owen Meany*, Irving remarked in a 1989 *Time* interview that he is "moved and impressed by people with a great deal of religious faith." "Jesus has always struck me as a perfect victim and a perfect hero," Irving explained to Michael Anderson in the *New York Times Book Review*. What impresses him most is that Christ is aware of his own destiny: "That is truly a heroic burden to carry," he told Phyllis Robinson in the *Book-of-the-Month Club News*. Similarly, in *A Prayer for Owen Meany*, a novel that examines good and evil—especially the capacity of each to be mistaken for the other—Irving's memorable Christ-like hero knows his destiny, including the date and circumstances of his death. Small in size but large in spirit, the young Owen Meany has a distinctive, high-pitched voice caused by a fixed larynx. Throughout the novel, Irving renders Owen's speech in upper case, a feature suggested to him by the red letters in which Jesus's utterances appear in some editions of the New Testament. Professing himself an instrument of God, Owen believes that nothing in his life is accidental or purposeless. For example, although the foul ball hit off Owen's bat kills the mother of his best friend, Johnny Wheelwright, the incident ultimately reveals to Johnny the identity of his father. The story of Owen and Johnny's adolescence and friendship is recalled and narrated by Johnny, who eventually comes to believe in God because of Owen. "No one has ever done Christ in the way John Irving does Him in *A Prayer for Owen Meany*," wrote Stephen King in the *Washington Post Book World*. "This is big time, friends and neighbors."

In a 1989 *Time* review, Sheppard pointed out that "anyone familiar with Irving's mastery of narrative technique, his dark humor and moral resolve also knows his fiction is cute like a fox." Sheppard suggested that despite its theological underpinnings, the novel "scarcely disguise[s] his indignation about the ways of the world" and actually represents "a fable of political predestination." Although finding the book flawed in terms of its structure and development, Robert Olen Butler maintained in Chicago *Tribune Books* that it nevertheless contains "some of the elements that made *The World According to Garp* so attractive to the critics and the best-seller audience alike: flamboyant, even bizarre, characters; unlikely and arresting plot twists; a consciousness of contemporary culture; and the assertion that a larger mechanism is at work in the universe." In the estimation of Brigitte Weeks in the *Book-of-the-Month Club News*, "John Irving is a reader's writer, and *A Prayer for Owen Meany* is a reader's novel, a large, intriguing grab bag of characters and ideas that moves the spirit and fascinates the mind. . . . There is no one quite like him."

Offering a general assessment of Irving's work, Sheppard wrote in his cover story, "Irving's philosophy is basic stuff: one must live willfully, purposefully and watchfully. Accidents, bad luck, . . . and open windows lurk everywhere—and the dog really bites. It is only a matter of time. Nobody gets out alive, yet few want to leave early. Irving's popularity is not hard to understand. His world is really the world according to nearly everyone." In an interview with Michael Priestly for the *New England Review*, Irving put forth this evaluation of himself: "I feel that I am a very life-affirming person. I mean, of course, I believe in blackness, you would be an idiot not to, you see it everywhere; but at the same time, I believe that literature is a sign of life, not a sign of death. If a novel doesn't say something about human value, there isn't any worth in it."

■ Works Cited

Anderson, Michael, "Casting Doubt on Atheism," *New York Times Book Review*, March 12, 1989, p. 30.

Bannon, Barbara A., "John Irving," *Publishers Weekly*, April 24, 1978, p. 6.

Beatty, Jack, "A Family Fable," *New Republic*, September 23, 1981, p. 37.

Bell, Pearl K., "Family Affairs," *Commentary*, September, 1978, p. 70.

Butler, Robert Olen, "Willed Visions: In a Novel of Religious Faith, John Irving Fails to Convince," *Tribune Books* (Chicago), March 19, 1989, p. 3, section 14.

DeMott, Benjamin, "Guilt and Compassion," *New York Times Book Review*, May 26, 1985, p. 1.

Des Pres, Terrence, in a review of *The World According to Garp*, *New Republic*, April 29, 1978, p. 31.

Graetz, Wendy, "An Author Who'd Rather Run than Write," *Chicago Tribune Book World*, September 13, 1981, p. 1, section 7.

Gray, Paul, "An Orphan or an Abortion," *Time*, June 3, 1985, p. 81.

Grumbach, Doris, "1978's Most Original Novel," *Saturday Review*, May 13, 1978, p. 42.

Haller, Scot, "John Irving's Bizarre World," *Saturday Review*, September, 1981, p. 30.

Irving, John, in an interview conducted by himself, *Washington Post Book World*, April 30, 1978, p. 1.

Irving, John, *The Cider House Rules*, Morrow, 1985.

Irving, John, "Doing Things His Way," an interview with *Time*, April 3, 1989, p. 80.

Japenga, Ann, "The Feminist According to John Irving," *Los Angeles Times*, September 16, 1982, p. V1.

Kendall, Elaine, "Truth and Consequences of Passion and Polemics," *Los Angeles Times*, June 4, 1985, p. V4.

King, Stephen, "The Gospel According to John Irving," *Washington Post Book World*, March 5, 1989, p. 1.

Lehmann-Haupt, Christopher, in a review of *The World According to Garp*, *New York Times*, April 13, 1978.

Lehmann-Haupt, Christopher, in a review of *The Cider House Rules*, *New York Times*, May 20, 1985.

Locke, Richard, "Three Young Writers," *New York Times Book Review*, May 21, 1978, p. 3.

Los Angeles Times, March 20, 1983.

Malone, Michael, "Everything that Rises," *Nation*, June 10, 1978, p. 705.

Marcus, Greil, "John Irving: The World of 'The World According to Garp,'" *Rolling Stone*, December 13, 1979, p. 70.

Markman, Jon D., "Irving's Novel Heroes Are Born to Suffer," *Los Angeles Times*, July 10, 1985, p. VI1.

McCaffery, Larry, "An Interview with John Irving," *Contemporary Literature*, winter, 1982, p. 1.

Miller, Gabriel, *John Irving*, Ungar, 1982.

Priestly, Michael, "An Interview with John Irving," *New England Review*, summer, 1979, p. 498.

Robinson, Phyllis, *Book-of-the-Month Club News*, April, 1989.

Rossner, Judith, "Irving's Bear Deserts Him in New Novel," *Chicago Tribune Book World*, September 13, 1981, p. 1, section 7.

Ruppersburg, Hugh M., "John Irving," *Dictionary of Literary Biography*, Volume 6: *American Novelists since World War II*, Second Series, Gale, 1980, p. 153.

Sheppard, R. Z., "Life into Art" (cover story), *Time*, August 31, 1981, p. 46.

Sheppard, R. Z., "The Message Is the Message," *Time*, April 3, 1989, p. 80.

Weeks, Brigitte, *Book-of-the-Month Club News*, April, 1989.

West, Richard, "John Irving's World after 'Garp,'" *New York*, August 17, 1981, p. 29.

Williams, Thomas, "Talk with John Irving," *New York Times Book Review*, April 23, 1978, p. 26.

■ For More Information See

BOOKS

Bestsellers 89, Issue 3, Gale, 1989.

Contemporary Literary Criticism, Gale, Volume 13, 1980, Volume 23, 1983, Volume 38, 1986.

Dictionary of Literary Biography Yearbook: 1982, Gale, 1983.

Harter, Carol C., and James R. Thompson, *John Irving*, Twayne, 1986.

PERIODICALS

Chicago Tribune, May 12, 1985.

Chicago Tribune Book World, May 11, 1980.

Christian Century, October 7, 1981; March 22, 1989.

Commentary, June, 1982.

Detroit News, August 30, 1981; March 12, 1989.

Esquire, September, 1981.

Globe and Mail (Toronto), March 10, 1984; July 6, 1985.

Los Angeles Times Book Review, March 26, 1989.

Maclean's, June 11, 1979.

Ms., July, 1979.

Newsweek, April 17, 1978; September 21, 1981.

New Yorker, May 8, 1978; October 12, 1981; July 8, 1985.

New York Times, August 31, 1981; March 8, 1989.

New York Times Book Review, March 12, 1989.

People, December 25, 1978.

Prairie Schooner, fall, 1978.

Spectator, June 22, 1985.

Time, April 24, 1978.

Times (London), June 20, 1985.

Times Literary Supplement, October 20, 1978; June 21, 1985.

Village Voice, May 22, 1978.

Wall Street Journal, March 21, 1989.

Washington Post, August 25, 1981.

Washington Post Book World, May 19, 1985.

—Sketch by Janice Jorgensen

Bob Kane

Personal

Born October 24, 1916, in New York, NY; son of Herman (an engraver for the *New York Daily News*) and Augusta Kane; married first wife Beverly, 1949 (divorced, 1957); married Elizabeth Sanders (an actress), 1986; children: (first marriage) Debbie. *Education:* Attended Commercial Art Studio, Cooper Union, and Art Students League.

Career

Artist. Free-lance cartoonist with S. M. Iger's Studio, 1936-37; Fiction House, 1937-39; DC Comics, Inc., New York, NY, cartoonist, creator of "Batman," 1939-1966. Worked for 9 months in the garment industry, c. 1937; Fleischer Animated Film Studio, New York, NY, worked as fill-in animator, inker and painter, c. 1937. Creator of animated syndicated television series "Courageous Cat and Minute Mouse," Trans-Artist Production, 1961, and of "Cool McCool" (aired on NBC-TV, 1966-69); creator of superhero "Negative Man," 1989. *Exhibitions:* Gallerie Internationale (one-man show), New York, NY, 1969; Galerie Michael,

Beverly Hills, CA, "Batman Art Exhibition," July 25-August 25, 1989; many other exhibitions.

Writings

(With Tom Andrae) *Batman and Me*, Eclipse Books, 1989.
Batman: The Dailies, edited by Peter Poplaski, Kitchen Sink Press, Volume 1: *1943-1944*, 1990, Volume 2: *1944-1945*, 1990, Volume 3: *1946-1946*, 1991.

Also author of TV scripts.

Adaptations

"The Batman" (movie serial; fifteen episodes), starring Lewis Wilson as Batman and Douglas Croft as Robin, Columbia Pictures, 1943.
"Batman and Robin" (movie serial; fifteen episodes), starring Robert Lowery as Batman and John Duncan as Robin, Columbia Pictures, 1949.
"Batman" (television series), starring Adam West as Batman and Burt Ward as Robin, originally broadcast on ABC-TV, January 12, 1966-March 14, 1968.
"Batman" (film), starring West and Ward, Twentieth Century-Fox, 1966.
Batman and the Fearsome Foursome (novelization of Twentieth Century-Fox film), Signet, 1966.
Winston Lyon, *Batman versus Three Villains of Doom* (novel), Signet, 1966.
Batman versus the Joker (novel), Signet, 1966.
Batman versus the Penguin (novel), Signet, 1966.

"The Adventures of Batman" (animated television series), featuring the voices of Bud Collyer as Batman and Casey Kasem as Robin, produced by Filmation Studios and broadcast on CBS-TV, September 10, 1966-September 2, 1967.

"The Batman-Superman Hour" (includes rebroadcasts of "The Adventures of Batman"), broadcast on CBS-TV, September 14, 1968-September 6, 1969.

"The New Adventures of Batman" (animated cartoon show), featuring the voices of Adam West and Burt Ward, produced by Filmation Studios and broadcast on CBS-TV, September 10, 1977-September 2, 1978.

"Batman: 40th Anniversary Special," broadcast on NBC-TV, 1979.

"Batman" (film), starring Michael Keaton as Batman and Jack Nicholson as the Joker, Warner Bros., 1989.

"Batman" (cassette), Dove Books on Tape, 1989.

Batman also appeared as a syndicated newspaper comic strip from 1943-45 and from 1966-71.

■ **Sidelights**

Artist Bob Kane is best known for his creation of The Batman, one of the twentieth century's greatest mythic heroes. Inspired by the success of Jerry Siegal and Joe Shuster's *Superman*, Kane and his writer/partner Bill Finger developed a costumed crimefighter who struck a responsive chord in the American psyche. Using dark, grim images developed in part from 30s detective films, they created a hero whose realm was the dark urban underbelly of America.

Kane himself was born in the midst of urban America shortly after World War I. "I lived in a tough East Bronx neighborhood—Freeman Street and Westchester Avenue," Kane writes in *Batman and Me*. "These communities were melting pots composed of different ethnic groups and often one nationality would be pitted against another. In order to survive, if one were a loner like myself, he would have to join his neighborhood gang for protection, believing in the old adage, 'safety in numbers.'

"Each neighborhood club would wear sweatshirts emblazoned with an emblem that identified you with your gang. My cronies and I were shopping around for a name for our club when I suggested 'the Zorros,' adapted from a movie starring the first and greatest swashbuckler of them all, Douglas Fairbanks, Sr., who was my idol.

"My club members agreed with my suggestion and we became known as the Crusading Zorros. Like Zorro, we wore hooded black masks at night to conceal our real identities. Thus, rival gangs wouldn't know who to blame when we fought them during rumbles.

"Those were the days of massive unemployment and widespread poverty, when people who had once worked for a living and been proudly independent were forced to stand idly in bread lines waiting for a handout. Not only the lower classes but the affluent were affected by the stock market crash of 1929 which began the Depression.

"When I was a kid, [my father] bought me books on how to draw cartoons, encouraging me to copy them. This particularly stands out in my mind because in those days, most parents didn't even know what the word cartoonist meant. Indeed, my relatives thought being a comic strip artist was equivalent to being a horse thief and that I should be locked up on the funny farm.

"Dad was the exception, championing my determination to become a cartoonist, even though he wasn't sure that I wouldn't starve trying to make a living in this profession.

"As an engraver in the *New York Daily News* printing department, his job brought him into contact with the plates from which the comics were printed. Upon inquiring about the cartoonists' salaries (which were in the five and six figures), he surmised that his son had chosen a lucrative profession after all. Realizing the possibilities, Dad encouraged me to draw cartoon posters for store merchants. He persuaded them to buy the posters as eye-catchers for window displays.

"I realize that watching Dad's plight was my strongest motivating force, and this compelled me to use my talent for cartooning to its fullest. I wanted the better things in life and poverty didn't fit into my plans. Had my father been wealthy I doubt whether I would have had the incentive to work as hard as I did to become successful at my chosen craft."

"My career as an artist really began at De Witt Clinton High School in the Bronx, where I landed a job as a cartoonist on the school paper, *The Clinton News*. Looking back, I must admit that the cartoons I drew for the paper were pretty stiff and amateurish. Nevertheless, they possessed a creative spark and were considered good enough by the art editor to be published. How thrilled I was to see my work in print for the first time! I felt like I was on my way to becoming a professional cartoonist."

Recognizing Kane's artistic talent, his high school teachers arranged a scholarship for him to the Commercial Art Studios in New York. While attending classes, Kane began to offer his artwork to commercial publishers. In 1936 he was hired by a high-school classmate and former artistic rival, Will Eisner (creator of the comic-book detective *The Spirit*) to work on *Wow! What a Magazine.* Kane drew funny-character strips for Eisner and his partner, Sam Iger. "I used to copy Floyd Gottfredson's 'Mickey Mouse' newspaper strip all the time and my best feature for Eisner-Iger during the late 1930s was done in a kind of Disney style. It was called 'Peter Pupp' and was about a puppy who had a younger, smaller dog for a sidekick called Tinymite. Their relationship prefigured that of Batman and Robin, who came along a few years later." However, Kane found that the techniques he used on strips such as "Peter Pupp" were too costly, especially since he had to provide his own art materials, and he quit the job.

"I was always looking for new ways to get my work published," Kane relates in *Batman and Me.* "After working for *Wow* comics, I tried my hand at drawing one-panel cartoons. There was a burgeoning market for this type of art in general interest magazines like *The Saturday Evening Post, Harper's Weekly,* and *Collier's,* and humor magazines like *Judge* and the old *Life.* Some newspapers, like the *New York Journal American,* also published cartoons." Kane sold a single panel strip to *Journal American,* but proved unable to sell others. Soon his family's relative poverty compelled him to join the work force at his uncle's garment factory. "I received ten dollars a week for working in a sweatshop where the factory squalor and the din of the sewing machines was enough to drive me to a psychiatrist, if I could have afforded one."

Kane left the garment industry after only nine months, bent on continuing his career as an artist. "I could not find an immediate job as a cartoonist in those Depression days of 1937, and began wondering whether I did the right thing in quitting my uncle Sam. But I was determined to forge ahead, and after six months I landed a job with the Fleischer Animated Film Studio in New York City. I did fill-ins, inking, and opaque painting for their 'Betty Boop' cartoons for seven or eight months. I earned twenty-five dollars a week, which wasn't bad for the time, and considerably more than the ten dollars a week I had received at the garment factory, or the five dollars a page [*Wow*] had paid

me." Unfortunately, Kane found the only work he was permitted to do boring, and quit the studios when the Fleischer brothers moved their base of operations to Florida.

Kane soon returned to drawing for comics. He began illustrating humor strips again, this time for DC Comics, one of the leading publishers in the field. At this time—the late 1930s—the comic book industry, which had grown out of the related dime novel and pulp magazine genres, was beginning to establish its own identity. Comic books in the early 1930s were largely reprinted collections of strips that had originally appeared in newspapers—for instance, in 1934 *Famous Funnies* began to reprint the newspaper adventures of "Buck Rogers." Many of them offered a variety of strips or other entertainment in a single issue. In 1935, however, DC introduced *New Fun Comics,* the first comic book to publish original humor stories. In 1937, the same company presented *Detective Comics,* the first title to group similar stories together. And in June, 1938, the premiere issue of DC's *Action Comics* launched the career of the first of the superheroes: Superman.

Superman was the creation of Jerry Siegel and Joseph Shuster, two young men from Cleveland, Ohio, and he was unlike any comic strip hero readers had ever seen. Mixing elements of science fiction with ancient myth, Siegel and Shuster created "a character of almost unequalled appeal. A character who reached into the American psyche and pressed all the right buttons," states John Byrne in his introduction to *The Greatest Superman Stories Ever Told.* The man who, according to his origin story, could "hurdle skyscrapers, leap an eighth of a mile, raise tremendous weights, run faster than a streamline train," and whose skin could not be penetrated by anything "less than a bursting shell," revolutionized the comic book industry and ushered in a Golden Age of comic books.

Superman's success sparked a flood of imitations. Vincent Sullivan, a senior editor at DC Comics in the late 1930s, said to Kane one day, "'There's a character called Superman by Siegel and Shuster, and they are making $800 a week apiece.' I was only making $35-50 a week at the time," Kane reminiscences in *Batman and Me.* "I said, 'My God, if I could make that kind of money!' Sullivan continued. 'We're looking for another superhero. Do you think you could come up with one?' This was on Friday. I said, 'To make that kind of money, I'll have one for you on Monday!'

"So over the weekend I laid out a kind of naked superhero on the page, with a figure that looked like Superman or Flash Gordon. I placed a sheet of tracing paper over him so that I could create new costumes that might strike my fancy. Then, POW! It came to me in a flash—like the old cliche of an electric light bulb lighting up over a cartoon character's head when he has a brainstorm."

What Kane had in mind was a costumed superhero who fought crime like Superman, but was a detective as well. Unlike Superman, the new character was an ordinary mortal whose abilities were developed through years of intensive training and study. "There were three major influences on Batman," Kane tells Michael Alexander in an interview for *People Weekly*. "The first was Zorro." Kane vividly remembered the film *The Mark of Zorro*, which had inspired him as a child in the Bronx. "By day, like Bruce Wayne, he feigned being a bored, foppish count, the son of one of the richest families in Mexico. By night, he became a vigilante. He would disguise himself, wearing a handkerchief mask with the eyes slit out. He exited on a black horse from a cave underneath his home, and that's the inspiration for the Batcave and the Batmobile."

"The second influence was a Leonardo da Vinci book I had seen. The book had a lot of inventions, including a flying machine. It was a man on a sledlike contraption with huge bat wings. Da Vinci had a quote that went something like, 'Your bird will have no model but that of a bat.' There it was—from a book 500 years old!

"The third inspiration was a silent mystery movie called 'The Bat,' in which the bat was a villain." *The Bat* was based on a novel by Mary Roberts Rinehart, a writer whose works mixed elements of Gothic and detective fiction. "I remember his shadowy outline on the wall when he was about to kill somebody," Kane recalls in *Batman and Me*. "They caught up with him in the attic—he wore a costume that looked a little like my early Batman's, with a black robe and a bat-shaped head. This made him look like a bat—very ominous. The film not only helped inspire Batman's costume but also the bat-signal, a prototype of which appeared on the wall when the Bat announced his next victim."

There were several other heroes that influenced Kane's Batman. One was the comic strip *The Phantom*, which first appeared in 1936. It also featured a crime-fighting hero who wore a form-fitting grey suit, covered his face with a mask and cowl, and maintained a secret identity. "The dark menace of the Shadow provided a piece of the puzzle, as did the grim purpose (and weird villains) of detective Dick Tracy," notes Mark Cotta Vaz in *Tales of the Dark Knight*. "The swashbuckling adventure of such films as ... *Robin Hood* was also present at the creation."

"One day I called Bill [Finger]," explains Kane in *Batman and Me*, "and said, 'I have a new character called the Bat-Man and I've made some crude, elementary sketches I'd like you to look at.' He came over and I showed him the drawings. At the time, I only had a small domino mask, like the one Robin later wore, on Batman's face. Bill said, 'Why not make him look more like a bat and put a hood on him, and take the eyeballs out and just put slits for eyes to make him look more mysterious?' At this point, the Bat-Man wore a red union suit; the wings, trunks, and mask were black. I thought that red and black would be a good combination. Bill said that the costume was too bright: 'Color it dark gray to make it look more ominous.' The cape looked like two stiff bat wings attached to his arms. As Bill and I talked, we realized that these wings would get cumbersome when Bat-Man was in action, and changed them into a cape, scalloped to look like bat wings when he was fighting or swinging down on a rope. Also, he didn't have any gloves on, and we added them so that he wouldn't leave fingerprints."

The Bat-Man, as Kane originally styled him, made his debut in *Detective Comics* number 27, published in May, 1939. At this time he was a much more violent and grim figure than he later became. Described as "a mysterious and adventurous figure fighting for righteousness and apprehending the wrongdoer, in his lone battle against the evil forces of society," the Bat-Man used his unique talents to unravel "The Case of the Chemical Syndicate." Four former partners in the Apex Chemical Corporation are being killed by one of their number; the Bat-Man intervenes only just in time to save the last of them. He closes the case by knocking the head criminal into a vat of acid. The Bat-Man's vigilante methods made him "hunted by the police," explains E. Nelson Bridwell in his introduction to *Batman from the 30s to the 70s*, "who resented this mystery man's taking the law into his own hands.... But that was the tradition of the times. Many a superhero killed with no compunction if he felt the victim deserved it. No fooling around with habeas corpus or trial by jury or the fifth amendment. The heroes dealt out their own brand of justice quickly and efficiently."

Kane's early pictures of the Bat-Man echoed the character's grim and forceful ways. His cowl cov-

The Batman swings into action for the first time in *Detective Comics* issue 27, published in 1939. (Copyright © 1939 DC Comics Inc., copyright renewed 1957.)

Lewis Wilson (Batman) and Doug Croft (Robin) star as a slightly disheveled dynamic duo in the 1943 Columbia movie serial *The Batman.*

ered more of the lower part of his face, meeting in a triangular point below his nose, and the "ears" were much longer and more horn-like and were placed on the sides rather than the top of his head. "He had a cape that looked like enormous bat wings, a vestige of the stiff bat wings I had originally given him," Kane recalls in *Batman and Me.* "I occasionally drew these large bat wings in early stories to make Batman look eerie and menacing, but soon abandoned this practice, sticking to the less formidable looking cape he wears now."

To enhance the Bat-Man's formidable appearance, Kane and his associates developed a bat-motif that eventually appeared on all the character's paraphernalia. "At first Batman wore only gloves but soon Bill suggested that we give him gauntlets," Kane states in *Batman and Me.* "Then I added fins to the gauntlets in keeping with the bat symbolism. We changed Batman's belt also. At first it was only an ordinary belt with a round buckle. I gave it a

square buckle and it became a utility belt for the first time when DC writer Gardner Fox created gas pellets for Batman to carry in a story in which he battles the mad scientist Dr. Death. Three issues later, Fox added a boomerang and a helicopter-like airplane called an Autogyro to Batman's arsenal. Designing them according to the bat motif, I created the Batarang and the first Batplane." "Likewise," Kane adds, "Batman drove just an ordinary car at first until I put a bathood on the front and a fin on top, turning it into the Batmobile."

These elements, when combined with Kane's atmospheric backgrounds, presented the reader with a clear and vivid vision of the Batman's realm. "Batman inhabited a world where no one, no matter the time of day, cast anything but long shadows—seen from weird perspectives," states cartoonist Jules Feiffer in his *The Great Comic Book Heroes.* "Kane's strength . . . lay not in his draftsmanship (which was never quite believable), but in his total involvement in what he was doing (which made everything believable)." "Batman's world took control of the reader," Feiffer concludes. "Kane's was an authentic fantasy, a genuine vision, so that however one might nit-pick the components, the end product remained an impregnable whole: gripping and original. Kane, more than any other comic book man . . . set and made believable the terms offered to the reader."

Although Batman's secret identity was revealed to readers at the close of "The Case of the Chemical Syndicate," his origin was left unexplained until *Detective Comics* number 33, published in November, 1939. "The reason for the delay," writes Kane, "was partly because we were too busy at first establishing the character to think up an origin for him and partly because Bill [Finger] was replaced by Gardner Fox on a few of the first stories. As soon as Bill returned to writing Batman we set out to create the missing explanation." In a two-page layout entitled "The Legend of the Batman," Kane and Finger explained how young Bruce Wayne witnessed the murder of his parents and vowed to devote his life to a war on criminals.

Making Bruce Wayne someone who had experienced such great grief made him more accessible than most other superheroes. "At a very early age," writes Mike Gold in his foreword to *The Greatest Batman Stories Ever Told*, "each and every one of us realized that we probably were not born on Krypton, we were unlikely to get bitten by a radioactive spider, and we were not the spawn of mud touched by the gods. We knew, however, that if given the proper motivations, we could become The Batman. More important, we knew that if we had to endure those motivations, becoming The Batman probably was the proper thing to do." Readers could identify with young Bruce and his loss. "We all can understand Bruce's grief, we can all understand his frustration at having to watch helplessly as the lives of the most important people in his young life are taken uselessly, and we all can understand his need to do something to avenge the deaths of his parents," says Dick Giordano in his introduction to *The Greatest Batman Stories Ever Told.* "The origin of The Batman is grounded, therefore, in emotion. An emotion that is primal and timeless and dark." In Finger's words, "And thus is born this weird figure of the dark . . . This avenger of evil: *The Batman!*"

Despite the fact that only Kane's name appeared on the stories, many other people contributed to the Batman's success. Young artists Jerry Robinson and Dick Sprang helped launch the Caped Crusad-

er on his career. The most influential of the early Batman writers, however, was Bill Finger, a former pulp writer. "Bill Finger was a contributing force to 'Batman' right from the beginning," Kane writes in *Batman and Me.* "He wrote most of the great stories and was influential in setting the style and genre other writers would emulate. We called him the 'Cecil B. De Mille of the comics.'" Many of his scripts, writes Bridwell, featured "giant working models of everyday objects. They might be outdoor signs or indoor displays, but they were exact replicas of their smaller originals. His giant sewing machines really sewed; his giant phonographs played; and his giant paint tubes were chock full of real paint." Finger's stories also helped establish the Batman as a reasoning superhero, rather than one who simply crashed through windows and tossed crooks around. "I made Batman a superhero-vigilante when I first created him," Kane concludes. "Bill turned him into a scientific detective."

"Batman departed even further from the vigilante image when I created Robin, the Boy Wonder, to be his partner," Kane adds. Introduced in *Detective Comics* number 38, published in April, 1940—less than a year after Batman's own debut—Robin quickly became an important part of the Batman mythos. "The Batman, that amazing weird figure of night, at last takes under his protecting mantle, an ally in his relentless fight against crime," reads the first panel of Robin's introductory story. "Introducing in this issue . . . an exciting new figure whose incredible gymnastic and athletic feats will astound you . . . a laughing, fighting, young daredevil who scoffs at danger like the legendary Robin Hood whose name and spirit he has adopted . . . Robin the Boy Wonder."

Like Bruce Wayne, Robin—Dick Grayson—was orphaned through criminal activity. His parents, the Flying Graysons, were circus trapeze artists who plunged to their deaths during an evening performance. While listening at the circus owner's door, young Dick discovers that his parents were murdered by gangsters under orders from "Boss" Zucco in order to extort protection money. The Batman, who witnessed the murder, adopts the young orphan and trains him in his fight against crime. Working together, they bring Zucco to justice and discover that they make a terrific team.

"Robin evolved from my fantasies as a kid of fourteen, when I visualized myself as a young boy fighting alongside my idol, Douglas Fairbanks, Sr.," Kane writes. "I imagined that young boys reading about Batman's exploits would project their own images into the story and daydream about fighting alongside the Caped Crusader as junior Batmen. I named him after Robin Hood, whom I loved as a kid, as played on the screen by Fairbanks. Both Robins were crusaders, fighting against the forces of evil.... I even dressed Robin in the tunic, cape, and shoes of Robin Hood's era, and drew his trunks to look like chain mail." Kane adds that Robin's introductory issue "sold almost double what Batman had sold as a single feature."

"The introduction of Robin changed the entire tone of the Batman stories," Kane continues. With Robin by his side the Batman relaxed more often, and the two crimefighters often engaged in word-play as they thrashed their opponents. "In Robin," writes Vaz, "Batman had a lively pupil who seemed far more resilient in responding to the death of his parents than had the young, obsessed Bruce Wayne. Dick Grayson's enthusiasm helped bring a smile to Batman's lips. Robin helped make fighting crime FUN!" "The brightness of Robin's costume also served to brighten up the visuals and served as a counterpoint to Batman's sombre costume," Kane concludes. "More significantly, the addition of Robin gave Batman a permanent relationship, someone to care for, and made him into a fatherly big brother rather than a lone avenger."

"I never consciously intended to change the tone of the strip; this just evolved as we wrote stories involving Robin," says Kane in *Batman and Me.* "I didn't introduce Robin to humanize Batman, but created him because I thought it would make the strip more successful by appealing to two audi-ences. I felt that children wanted a lighter hero and a lighter mood and would identify with a young character like Robin, while adults and teenagers wanted a serious hero and would identify with an adult like Batman."

"These embellishments helped to make Batman and Robin human beings with understandable motives while allowing them to retain an aura of charisma and mystery," Kane concludes. "However, this was not enough. To test their abilities to the fullest, they had to have equally strong and colorful antagonists. Thus we began to create a rogues' gallery for the feature which would consist of a repertory company of continuing villains. Along with Chester Gould's 'Dick Tracy,' 'Batman' has the most bizarre and unique villains in comics. Indeed, it was 'Dick Tracy' which inspired us to create an equally weird set of villains for 'Bat-man.'"

"When we were trying to create a super-villain for Batman to oppose in the first year of the strip," Kane states in *Batman and Me,* "I made a few crude sketches based on the Joker playing card and showed them to Bill. He liked the idea of a compulsive practical joker and we kicked around ideas about a maniacal killer who would play life-and-death jokes on Batman, and that would test his mettle and ability to outwit his foe." "However," Bridwell continues, "when Bill saw Bob's sketch, he decided it looked *too* clownish. He happened to have a movie edition of Victor Hugo's *The Man Who Laughs,* with stills from the 1928 film starring Conrad Veidt." *The Man Who Laughs* is the story of Gynplaine, scion of a noble English family, who is stolen by gypsies and mutilated by having a permanent grin carved on his face. "This, I recall (and it has been fifty years)," writes Kane, "is how the Joker was created."

The Joker made his debut in *Batman* number 1—the Spring, 1940 issue—and quickly established himself as Batman's greatest adversary, making an unprecedented second appearance in the same issue. A warped, yet brilliant murderer and thief, the Joker was the embodiment of everything that Batman fought against. He gained a following among comic book readers, and became "the greatest and most identifiable of comics villains," states Mike Goldin in his introduction to *The Greatest Joker Stories Ever Told.* "Between 1940 and 1956, the Joker made an appearance in one of the various Batman titles nearly every month."

Kane and Finger developed many other adversar-ies for the Dynamic Duo, although few of them ever approached the Joker in popularity. "Bill and I decided to create a somewhat friendly foe who committed crimes but was also a romantic interest in Batman's rather sterile life," Kane states. They introduced a female burglar called The Cat in *Batman* number 1, but they soon rechristened her The Catwoman. She "was a kind of female Batman, except that she was a villainess and Batman was a hero. We figured that there would be this cat and mouse, cat and bat byplay between them—he would try to reform her and bring her over to the side of law and order. But she was never a murderer or entirely evil like the Joker."

"I created one of my most famous characters, the Penguin, after I saw a cute little penguin on a Kool Cigarette pack," Kane recalls in *Batman and Me.* "Penguins always looked like little fat men in tuxedos to me. So this was how I drew the Penguin. Bill invented 'The Man of a Thousand Umbrellas' gimmicks the Penguin used against Batman. The

Penguin debuted in *Detective Comics* #58 in December, 1941. His waddle, pudginess, and short stature made him a more cartoony character than my other villains, but he was a killer and a formidable foe nonetheless." Some of Batman's other chief opponents included Two-Face, once District Attorney Harvey Dent (or Kent—the name varies), who was hideously disfigured by acid thrown on him during a trial in *Detective Comics* number 66 (August, 1942), and the Riddler, introduced in *Detective Comics* number 140 (October, 1948), whose obsession made him send clues to Batman about his crimes.

With the onset of World War II, the humanization of Batman that had begun with the introduction of Robin took a great leap forward. "Given the strategic East Coast location of Gotham City," explains Vaz, "it was only natural that the State Department would be on the phone to Commissioner Gordon to shine the Bat Signal and call the Dynamic Duo into service.... In addition to his regular Gotham crime-busting duties, Batman would have to drum up support for the Allied cause as well as protect the home front from any Nazi invasion."

The crimefighters soon became upstanding, patriotic citizens, who supported bond drives and made public appearances on behalf of the armed services. By January, 1942 (in *Batman* number 8), the man who had been pursued by police only two years before was invited to Washington by the president for a ticker-tape parade. In *Batman* number 14 (January, 1943), the Dynamic Duo broke up a Nazi spy ring intent on turning the White House over to Adolph Hitler. *Detective Comics* number 78 (the August, 1943, issue) contained a feature story called "The Bond Wagon," in which Batman and Robin travelled across the country in support of a war bonds drive. Many covers featured the two crimefighters (and in *World's Finest*, Superman as well) in military situations: making nighttime parachute jumps, firing a machine gun, or simply hawking war bonds. "In retrospect," Vaz writes, "Batman's wartime patriotism probably made him less the eerie figure

Adam West and Burt Ward wreak havoc with a variety of villains in the popular 1960s television show: (from right) Lee Meriwether as the Catwoman, Frank Gorshin as the Riddler, Caesar Romero as the Joker, and Burgess Meredith as the Penguin.

Frank Miller's *Dark Knight* returns to strike terror into the hearts of evildoers in a decaying Gotham City of the future.

of the dark in the eyes of the Gotham public and the comics readership."

Batman was introduced to the film world early in his career. By 1943, Batman and Robin had become so well-known that they were optioned for a motion-picture serial, called "The Batman." Unfortunately, the picture was produced on a very low budget—Batman's costume was somewhat less than skin-tight—and suffered from wartime racism: the villain was an oriental called Dr. Daka who made people into zombies. In 1948 a second serial was made, called "Batman and Robin." It had slightly higher production values, and is noteworthy mainly for its introduction of Vicki Vale, modelled after Lois Lane in *Superman.* Kane had no involvement with either serial, but he did introduce Vicki Vale into the strip as a photojournalist. "Like Lois," Kane says, "she was pushy and out for a scoop, trying to expose Batman's secret identity. She was always a romantic interest of Bruce Wayne's and, later, of Batman's." "I told the colorist to color her hair blonde, because it was Marilyn Monroe I was emulating, but he inadvertently gave her red hair," Kane explains. "Vicki Vale first appeared in 'The Scoop of the Century' in *Batman* #49, October-November, 1948."

By the late 1940s and early 1950s, *Batman* had lost much of its bitter, *noir* edge. The Caped Crusader took on "more of what [*Batman* writer] Denny O'Neil has referred to as a 'benign scoutmaster' personality," writes Vaz. "There he was, the former 'weird figure of the night,' too often waltzing around Gotham in the light of day." As early as February, 1950 (in *Batman* number 57), Batman could be seen delivering lectures against racism and for good citizenship. Batman's cases of the time, Vaz points out, "emphasized his detective qualities, or involved globetrotting adventures." Even the Joker had become less frightening: "His felonies," writes Mark Waid in his afterword to *The Greatest Joker Stories Ever Told,* "became less macabre and more zany, his crimes revolving around gimmicks such as committing bizarre thefts in mysterious patterns or around weird themes."

One contributing factor to this process was the anti-comics feeling that developed in the United States following World War II. In 1954, that feeling was given a voice and a focus in Dr. Frederic Wertham's *Seduction of the Innocent.* Dr. Wertham, a psychiatrist with the New York Department of Hospitals, argued that comic books led American youth into delinquency and perversion. Wertham even went so far as to suggest that Batman and Robin were homosexuals, on no better evidence than that they were two males living under one roof. "The book, heralded as a sensational expose by its publishers," Vaz states, "led to the United States Senate investigating comics in 1954. Suddenly the comic books, once the province of childhood fun and escapism, were being used as fodder for a censorship battle" that resembled the anti-Communist hysteria of the era.

Wertham's report was not based on scientific research and analysis, says Vaz. "Simply because many mentally disturbed youngsters read comic books was enough to suggest to him that the comics themselves were causing juvenile delinquency." Nevertheless, his conclusions were taken seriously, even though the congressional hearings did not result in a ban. Comic book sales plummeted. Many publishers went out of business altogether, and many once-flourishing titles were dropped. The publishers who managed to remain in business banded together and, in a gesture of self-preservation, formed the Comics Code Authority in September, 1954. "The little logo bearing the legend 'Approved by the Comics Code Authority' carried a divine weight until the 1980s, when a new era of creativity would relax such censorship guidelines," Vaz reports.

Despite the fact that DC (then called National Comics Publications) had won the 1949 Medal of Honor from the Woman's National Institute for its role in preventing juvenile delinquency, it too was hard-hit by Wertham's allegations. Batman underwent some specialized changes. Crime-fighting girlfriends were introduced for both Batman and Robin—Batwoman (in reality Kathy Kane, heiress and former circus performer), introduced in *Detective Comics* number 233, July, 1956; and Bat-Girl (in reality Betty Kane, Kathy Kane's niece), introduced in *Batman* number 139, April, 1961. The Dynamic Duo was also joined by Ace, the Bat-Hound, who first appeared in *Batman* number 92, June, 1955, and the mystical imp Bat-Mite, who appeared in *Detective Comics* number 267, May, 1959. In addition, Batman's adventures took a bizarre turn in the late 50s and early 60s. Beginning in December, 1957, with *Detective Comics* number 250, Batman began a series of outer-space adventures, where he and Robin (sometimes joined by other members of the "Batman Family") apprehended law-breakers on other planets or in other dimensions. On other occasions, Batman himself assumed monstrous forms: in February, 1961, he became a giant genie (*Detective Comics* number

332), and in March, 1964 (*Batman* number 162), he became "The Batman Creature!"

By mid-1964, however, Batman had largely passed through the science-fiction/monster phase of his career and had returned to fighting crime in Gotham City. Classic criminals such as the Penguin and the Joker returned to plague the Caped Crusader. When Julius Schwartz took over as editor of the Batman titles that year, he encouraged the "return to basics" approach. "Batman was equipped with a new, streamlined Batmobile and Batplane," writes Vaz. "The old twisting staircase that had descended into the Bat Cave from Wayne Manor was replaced with an automatic elevator. The work area in the Bat Cave itself was modernized with the latest crime-fighting technology. The crowning touch, and Schwartz's own editorial signature, was his enclosing the black bat image on Batman's chest in a yellow moon." Schwartz also killed off faithful Alfred, Wayne's butler, in a last gesture toward Wertham's allegations, and replaced him with Dick Grayson's overprotective Aunt Harriet.

Nonetheless, comic book sales continued to drop. "After a quarter century of continuous publication, 'Batman' started to decline in popularity in 1965," Kane recalls in *Batman and Me*. "My publisher informed me that unless sales picked up the next year, it would mean the demise of the Caped Crusader. This was one of my darkest periods—I had built my whole life on drawing Batman, and it was the only vocation I knew. I felt unqualified to do anything else [and] felt very apprehensive about the future."

Kane went to work developing new comic ideas. He created an animated cartoon superspy, Cool McCool, for the Saturday morning television market. "However, I didn't have to depend on immediately selling the show. Batman was saved from extinction in a most surprising way—by becoming a hit prime-time TV series."

The *Batman* program, with its parodies of 60s trends, its elaborate fight sequences with animated "BatFight Words" sound effects, its "Bat-equipment" and "Holy BatWords," its special cameo appearances by stars of other TV series, and, most of all, its super-serious heroes and wildly flamboyant villains, was an idea whose time had come. Drawing in part on the serials from the late 1940s for inspiration, the show aired two nights a week, with episodes connected by cliffhanger endings and with the memorable injunction to "Tune in next week—Same BatTime, Same BatChannel!"

"The series," writes Joel Eisner in the introduction to his *The Official Batman Batbook*, "was unlike anything else that had ever appeared on prime time television. It was to create one of the biggest 'fads' this country would ever know." The show, Eisner continues, "was constructed so that it appealed to the television audience on two levels. It appealed to the youth of America in that it was a living comic book. It had the action and adventure that the kids just loved. At the same time, it also appealed to adult audiences with its camp humor and well-known celebrities. This was a rare program that parents and children could watch together and enjoy simultaneously."

"I continued to pencil 'Batman' stories in the comics until 1966," Kane reminisces in *Batman and Me*, "always drawing the main characters in the stories I illustrated. At that time I decided to retire from comics. I had been drawing 'Batman' for twenty-eight years and was tired of it. When the TV show became successful, I decided the time was ripe to move on to new horizons."

"My strategy proved successful; gallery showings of my Batman paintings and sales of signed Batman lithographs were greeted with enthusiasm by the public—and I found myself with a second career on my hands. This new career ... has been financially rewarding but, more importantly, it is also a source of great personal satisfaction to me."

The ramifications of the television series image of Batman spilled over into the comic books. When the producers of the show wanted a female-interest character, editor Schwartz put Commissioner Gordon's daughter Barbara into costume and introduced her as the new Batgirl (in *Detective Comics* number 359, January, 1967). When they wanted Alfred back, Schwartz figured out a way to resuscitate the character, who had been declared dead two years before. For a while, the comics featured some of the elements of the TV show: Batman and Robin began to use the "Holy whatever" expressions, and the Bat-Signal was replaced by the red Hot-Line phone.

After the TV show's popularity faded, however, DC writer Denny O'Neil and artist Neil Adams moved to bring The Batman back to his origins. In *Batman* number 217—published in December, 1969—they broke up the Dynamic Duo by sending Dick Grayson off to college. Bruce Wayne and Alfred closed up shop at Wayne Manor, abandoned the Bat Cave, and moved to penthouse accommodations in Gotham City. Villains like the Joker were given new prominence and a fresh perspective (for a time in the mid-70s, the Joker even had his own comic book), and new ones—especially Ra's al Ghul and his lovely daughter Talia—were introduced. Although Bruce Wayne and Alfred would eventually return to Wayne Manor, the quipping, light-hearted Batman was gone, and the Darknight Detective took his place.

In the 1980s, writers and artists returned to the Batman mythos for inspiration. In 1986, comic book artist Frank Miller revitalized the Batman in his four-part graphic novel *The Dark Knight Returns*. Set some time in the future, Miller's grim, bloody epic brings an aging, embittered Batman out of retirement and pits him against street gangs, mindless violence, and classic villains such as Two-Face and the Joker in a nightmare-like, warped Gotham City. Miller portrays Batman/Bruce Wayne as psychically damaged by the murder of his parents. Alan Moore writes in the introduction to *The Dark Knight Returns*, "Depicted over the years as, alternately, a concerned do-gooder and a revenge-driven psychopath, the [Batman] character as presented here managed to bridge both of those interpretations quite easily while integrating them in a much larger and more persuasively realized personality." "*The Dark Knight Returns* redefined Batman for contemporary audiences, turning him once again into the hottest character in comics," declares Howard Wornom in *Premiere*. "He has become darker, a sinister avenger of the night, and he again reflects the fearsome image created by Bob Kane and Bill Finger in 1939: 'a weird menace to all crime.'"

Other changes quickly followed. Dick Grayson left the Robin persona permanently, assuming the identity of Nighthawk for his crimefighting career. He was replaced by Jason Todd, a former juvenile delinquent rehabilitated by the Batman. Todd became Robin in 1987, but was killed off in November, 1988 (*Batman* number 428) after a majority of readers who responded to a telephone poll indicated that they wanted him dead. "That his own 'fans' had sided with the Joker to kill off the Boy Wonder was more proof of the grim, cynical nature of Batman's world in the 1980's," writes Vaz. More recent graphic novels—such as *The Killing Joke*, which explores the origin and psychology of the Joker—continue the process, bringing Batman back to his darkest origins.

Batman's fiftieth anniversary in 1989 was marked by a major media event—the release of the Warner Bros. movie *Batman*. Unlike the TV show of the 60s, the film concentrated on the dark, *noir* images that had marked Batman's introduction in

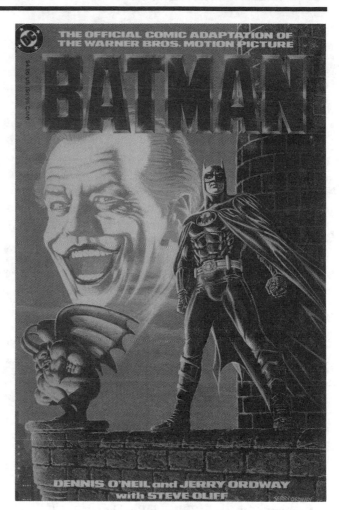

The comic book adaptation of the 1989 Warner Brothers film. (Copyright © 1989 DC Comics Inc.)

1939, and that artists such as Frank Miller had captured in their work. Like the TV show, however, it ushered in a period of Batmania. "Months before the film opened Batman merchandising, with potential sales of hundreds of millions of dollars, began flooding the market, helping to fuel the phenomenon," writes Vaz. Fans flocked into theaters to see it. "*Batman*," Vaz continues, "became the first film in history to sell $100.2 million worth of tickets in just ten days."

Kane served as a creative consultant on the Warner Bros. film. Alan Jones explains in *Cinefantastique* that hiring Kane helped Warner's "to combat the comic book fan backlash against their production." "Hiring Kane was a very intelligent move," says production designer Anton Furst in Jones's article. "He loved what we were doing. We sent over sketches constantly and he kept sending back these little drawings with notes attached saying, 'Well done boys.' He came over once to visit the set and when he was shown around, he was totally awe-inspired. Very clever, because when it comes to the American media, just to have it [the *Batman* film] sanctioned by the creator makes it very difficult for the [audience] to complain. If Kane goes on record saying his concept has been brilliantly interpreted, the ardent fans buckle down."

"Kane had envisioned actor Jack Nicholson in the role of his Joker as far back as 1980, when he drew a likeness of the character over a still of the actor from THE SHINING," Jones continues. "Kane thinks our Joker is better than the original in his strip," Furst tells Jones. "Very early on Bob kept saying, 'Get Jack Nicholson. He is The Joker. Get the man!'"

Although Kane long ago gave up regularly drawing the Batman, he remains a working cartoonist. "Aspiring young cartoonists today should not try to be a ghost or an assistant to a famous cartoonist," Kane told Shel Dorf in an interview for *Amazing Heroes*, "except for a short apprentice period . . . a year or two or three, but not live in the shadow and glory of a famed man. First of all they resent it inwardly, whether they admit it or not. Secondly they're not going anywhere. My name will be remembered when it's all over. No one will ever know the ghost artists' names. There can be 100 on 'Batman,' but Bob Kane's name will prevail. Most of them have had a ghost at one time or another, but somehow the Billy deBecks, the Chester Goulds, the Rube Goldbergs, the Harry Hershfields, the Milton Caniffs . . . their name prevails on the strip even after they die, it's immortalized. The ghosts, they come and go, and yet today, a lot of them still want to capitalize on the coattails of the innovator. So my advice to young cartoonists is innovate, don't imitate."

"Although I've stopped drawing comics, I'm far from retired and am busier than ever," Kane explains in *Batman and Me*. "I've continued to write screenplays and to paint, and have had one-man art shows all over the world.

"I would like to thank you, my faithful fans, for your enthusiastic reception of the Batman movie and for supporting me all these years. I hope that you will continue to be enthralled and entertained by my indomitable superhero for years to come."

■ Works Cited

Alexander, Michael, "Bob Kane," *People Weekly*, July 31, 1989.

Bridwell, E. Nelson, author of introduction, *Batman from the 30s to the 70s*, Crown, 1971, pp. 9-16.

Byrne, John, author of introduction, "The Origins of Superman," *The Greatest Superman Stories Ever Told*, DC Comics, 1987, pp. 6-13.

Dorf, Shel, "Bob Kane: The Man Whose Name Means 'Batman,'" *Amazing Heroes*, June 15, 1989, pp. 26-30.

Feiffer, Jules, *The Great Comic Book Heroes*, Bonanza Books, 1965, pp. 26-32.

Giordano, Dick, author of introduction, "Growing Up with the Greatest," *The Greatest Batman Stories Ever Told*, Warner Books, 1988, pp. 6-11.

Gold, Mike, author of foreword, "Our Darkest Knight," *The Greatest Batman Stories Ever Told*, Warner Books, 1988, pp. 12-16.

Gold, Mike, author of introduction, "The Joker's Dozen," *The Greatest Joker Stories Ever Told*, DC Comics, 1988, pp. 6-10.

Jones, Alan, "Batman: Eccentric Cinema Stylist Tim Burton on Bringing the Comic Book Legend to the Screen," *Cinefantastique*, November, 1989, pp. 48-62.

Kane, Bob, and Tom Andrae, *Batman and Me*, Eclipse Books, 1989.

Vaz, Mark Cotta, *Tales of the Dark Knight: Batman's First Fifty Years, 1939-1989*, Ballantine, 1989.

Waid, Mark, author of afterword, "Stacking the Deck: The *Other* Joker Stories," *The Greatest Joker Stories Ever Told*, DC Comics, 1988, pp. 278-83.

Wornom, Howard, "The Dark Knight: The New Batman Debunks the Campy Stereotypes," *Premiere*, July, 1989, p. 56.

■ For More Information See

BOOKS

Berger, Arthur Asa, *The Comic-Stripped American*, Walker, 1973.

Fleischer, Michael L., *The Encyclopedia of Comic Book Heroes*, Volume 1: *Batman*, Collier Books, 1976.

Horn, Maurice, editor, *The World Encyclopedia of Comics*, Chelsea House, 1976.

Wolfman, Marv, and George Perez, editors, *History of the DC Universe*, DC Comics, 1988.

Zummerman, Dwight Jon, "Bob Kane," *Comics Interview Super Special*, Fictioneer Books, 1989.

PERIODICALS

American Cinematographer, June, 1966, p. 384.
Comics Feature, March, 1984, p. 55.

Comics Journal May, 1989, p. 5.
Daily News Magazine, August 20, 1989.
Los Angeles, May, 1989, p. 22.
Newsweek, June 26, 1989, p. 70.
New York Post, January 9, 1966.
Publishers Weekly, July 14, 1989, p. 51.
Sunday News, October 9, 1966, p. 4.

Time, January 25, 1988, p. 65; June 19, 1989, p. 60.
Variety, May 31-June 7, 1989, p. 5; June 2, 1989, p. 10; June 13, 1989, p. 2; June 14-20, 1989, p. 7; June 28-July 4, 1989, p. 1; July 28, 1989, p. 3.°

—Sketch by Kenneth R. Shepherd

Maxine Hong Kingston

■ Personal

Born October 27, 1940, in Stockton, CA; daughter of Tom (a scholar, manager of a gambling house, and laundry worker) and Ying Lan (a practitioner of medicine and midwifery, field hand, and laundry worker; given name means "Brave Orchid"; maiden name, Chew) Hong; married Earll Kingston (an actor), November 23, 1962; children: Joseph Lawrence Chung Mei. *Education:* University of California, Berkeley, A.B., 1962, teaching certificate, 1965.

■ Addresses

Home—Oakland, CA. *Agent*—Tim Schaffner, Schaffner Agency, 6625 Casas Adobes Rd., Tucson, AZ 85704.

■ Career

Writer. Sunset High School, Hayward, CA, teacher of English and mathematics, 1965-67; Kahuku High School, Kahuku, HI, teacher of English, 1967; Kahaluu Drop-In School, Kahaluu, HI, teacher, 1968; Honolulu Business College, Honolulu, HI, teacher of English as a second language, 1969; Kailua High School, Kailua, HI, teacher of language arts, 1969; Mid-Pacific Institute, Honolulu, teacher of language arts, 1970-77; University of Hawaii, Honolulu, visiting associate professor of English, beginning 1977; Eastern Michigan University, Ypsilanti, Thelma McAndless Distinguished Professor, 1986; University of California, Berkeley, Chancellor's Distinguished Professor, 1989, senior lecturer, 1990—.

■ Awards, Honors

General nonfiction award from National Book Critics Circle, 1976, *Mademoiselle* Magazine Award, 1977, and Ainsfield-Wolf Race Relations Award, 1978, all for *The Woman Warrior: Memoirs of a Girlhood among Ghosts*, which was also named one of the top ten books of the year by *Time* magazine, *New York Times Book Review*, and *Asian Mail*, all 1977, selected as one of the top ten nonfiction works of the decade by *Time* magazine, 1979, and chosen one of New York Public Library's Books for the Teen Age, 1980, 1981, and 1982; National Education Association writing fellow, 1980; named Living Treasure of Hawaii, 1980, by Honpa Hongwanji Temple; American Book Award for general nonfiction, 1981, for *China Men*, which was also named to the American Library Association Notable Books List, 1980, received runner-up for Pulitzer prize, 1981, National Book Critics Circle award nomination, 1981, and chosen one of New York Public Library's Books for the Teen Age, 1981; named Asian/Pacific Women's Network Woman of the Year, 1981; Stockton (Calif.) Arts Commission

Award, 1981; Hawaii Writers Award, 1983; PEN Center U.S.A. West award, 1990, for *Tripmaster Monkey: His Fake Book;* Guggenheim Foundation fellow; honorary Doctoral degrees from Eastern Michigan University, Colby College, and the University of Massachusetts.

■ Writings

(Contributor) Jerry Walker, editor, *Your Reading,* National Council of Teachers of English, 1975.
The Woman Warrior: Memoirs of a Girlhood among Ghosts, Knopf, 1976.
China Men (Book-of-the-Month Club selection), Knopf, 1980.
Hawai'i One Summer, Meadow Press, 1987.
Tripmaster Monkey: His Fake Book, Knopf, 1988.

Contributor to anthologies, including *Wonders: Writings and Drawings for the Child in Us All,* edited by Jonathan Cott and Mary Gimbel, Rolling Stone, 1983; Geoff Hancock and Rikki Ducornet, editors, *Shoes and Shit,* Aya Press, 1984; Mark Schorer, *Harbrace College Reader,* 6th edition, Harcourt, 1984; Sandra Gilbert and Susan Gubar, editors, *The Norton Anthology of Literature by Women,* Norton, 1985; *Hers,* Time-Life, 1985; Scott Walker, editor, *Buying Time,* Graywolf Press, 1985; *Essay 2: Reading with the Writer's Eye,* Wadsworth, 1987. Contributor of stories and articles to periodicals, including *New York Times Magazine, Ms., New Yorker, New West, New Dawn, American Heritage, Iowa Review, New York Times Book Review, Washington Post, Mother Jones,* and *Caliban.*

■ Adaptations

China Men was made into a cassette by American Audio Prose Library; *The Woman Warrior* was made into a recording by Green Island Productions.

■ Sidelights

"An American writer born of Chinese immigrant parents, Maxine Hong Kingston blends myth, legend, history, and autobiography into a genre of her own invention," writes Susan Currier in the *Dictionary of Literary Biography Yearbook: 1980. The Woman Warrior: Memoirs of a Girlhood among Ghosts* and *China Men* are classified as nonfiction, but according to *New Republic* critic Anne Tyler, "in a deeper sense, they are fiction at its best—novels, fairytales, epic poems." Further, Kingston's first novel, *Tripmaster Monkey: His Fake Book,*

"could qualify as densely packed biography, the life of a Berkeley graduate in the psychedelic 1960's," according to *New York Times Magazine* editor Margarett Loke.

Many of the stories included in *The Woman Warrior* are reconstructed from those Kingston's mother related to her as "lessons 'to grow up on,'" writes Currier. Kingston's mother, Ying Lan ("Brave Orchid"), married her father in China, before he immigrated to New York City. For fifteen years her father worked in a laundry and sent part of the money he earned back to China, enabling her mother to study for certifications in medicine and midwifery, which eventually provided her with a good income and respect in what *Ms.* critic Sara Blackburn calls "a starving society where girl children were a despised and useless commodity." She came to the United States when her husband sent for her, having to give up her medical practice because her degree was not recognized in the United States. Her first two children had died in China while she was alone, but within her first year in the United States, at the age of thirty-seven, she gave birth to Maxine in Stockton, California, where the family later settled. Maxine was named after a lucky blonde American gamester in a gambling parlor her father managed. The first of her mother's six American-born children, she grew up surrounded not only by the ghosts of the ancestors and characters who peopled her mother's tales, but also by Americans who, as "foreigners," were considered "ghosts" by ethnic Chinese people. Moreover, in *The Woman Warrior,* Kingston says that the older generation regarded their children as people who "had been born among ghosts, were taught by ghosts, and were ourselves ghostlike. They called us a kind of ghost."

"At one time, *The Woman Warrior* and *China Men* were supposed to be one book," Kingston tells Paula Rabinowitz in an interview for *Michigan Quarterly Review.* "I had conceived of one huge book. However, part of the reason for two books is history. The women had their own time and place and their lives were coherent; there was a woman's way of thinking. My men's stories seemed to interfere. They were weakening the feminist point of view. So I took all the men's stories out, and then I had *The Woman Warrior.*" Both books are based on the history and myth imparted to Kingston by members of her family and other Chinese-American "story-talkers" who lived in her childhood community of Stockton.

The Woman Warrior is described by Currier as "a personal work, an effort to reconcile American and Chinese female identities." Primarily a memoir of Kingston's childhood, The Woman Warrior also concerns itself with the lives of other women in her family, as embellished or imagined by the author. According to Washington Post critic Henry Allen, "in a wild mix of myth, memory, history and a lucidity which verges on the eerie," Kingston describes "their experiences as women, as Chinese coming to America and as Americans." The book is divided into five different sections; Kingston's character is central to the second and fifth sections, in each instance, identifying herself with a legendary warrior woman. The tales Kingston's mother told her about heroines and swordswomen were "especially appealing," writes Currier, since the actual status of females in Chinese culture was so low. Such myths had long coexisted with an ancient tradition of female oppression. New York Review of Books critic Diane Johnson points out that Kingston "has been given hints of female power, and also explicit messages of female powerlessness from her mother, who in China had been a doctor and now toiled in the family laundry." Kingston dreamed of becoming an avenger, "like Fa Mu Lan, the girl of her mother's chants who fought gloriously in battle centuries ago and became a legend to the Chinese people ... and then ... took off her armor to be a perfect, obedient wife in her husband's house," observes Jane Kramer in the New York Times Book Review. In Kingston's version of the myth, before Fa Mu Lan went into battle, her parents carved on her back a motto of vengeance. Kingston uses the Chinese legend to depict her experience in American society when she asserts in The Woman Warrior that "The swordswoman and I are not so dissimilar.... What we have in common are the words at our backs. The idioms for revenge are 'report a crime' and 'report to five families.' The reporting is the vengeance—not the beheading, not the gutting, but the words. And I have so many words—'chink' words and 'gook' words too—that they do not fit on my skin."

The avenger fantasy was impractical in Kingston's childhood community, but, as an adult, she eventually fights a more solitary, unconventional battle by coming to terms with her family through her writing. For example, The Woman Warrior begins with the story of her father's sister whose name was never revealed to her American nephews and nieces. "No Name" aunt became pregnant with an illegitimate child while her husband was in America. Villagers raided and destroyed the family

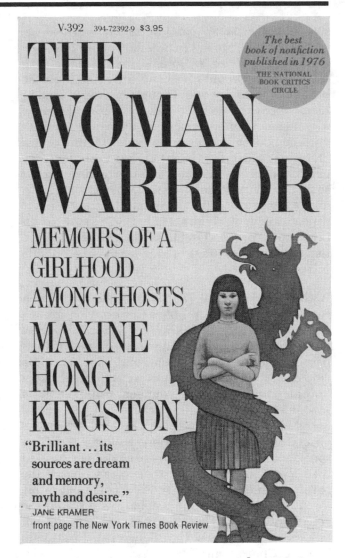

Kingston's 1976 memoir grew out of stories her mother told her as "lessons to grow up on."

compound on the day she bore the child, and she committed "spite suicide" with the baby in the family well. Since the aunt was regarded as a curse to the family, and never discussed, Kingston had to imagine the circumstances of her life, retelling the story in several possible variations. Sympathy for this relative was an act of rebellion. As Currier writes, "Deliberately forgotten by her family, 'No Name' aunt has an avenger in the niece, who, fifty years later, devotes 'pages of paper to her, though not origamied into houses and clothes'" [in the traditional way of caring for spirits of ancestors].

Kingston tells her mother's story in part three, concentrating on the fifteen-year interval between her husband's departure and her own arrival in the United States. Currier asserts that "of the ... women of her generation whose stories are told in this book, she is the most heroic." Brave Orchid's tale stands in sharp contrast to the story of her younger sister, Moon Orchid. As Currier observes, the younger sister is "Fragile, timid, and a little silly." Moon Orchid's husband travels to the United States to find work. Though he keeps sending money back to Moon Orchid, the husband marries a younger, Chinese-American woman. Brave Orchid convinces her sister to come to the United States to reclaim her husband, but he rejects her, and Moon Orchid suffers a nervous breakdown and soon dies. Currier comments, "[Moon Orchid's life] is one story which Brave Orchid does not have to repeat for her children. Live witnesses to its injustice, 'Brave Orchid's daughters decided fiercely that they would never let men be unfaithful to them.'"

In the last chapter of *The Woman Warrior*, Kingston directly narrates problems of growing up as a second-generation Chinese American. Currier notes that "Difficulties with English, which their parents had not taught them, and with American conventions of tone and gesture apparently kept Maxine Hong and her younger sister silent at school for years." Kingston relates, "It was when I found out I had to talk that school became a misery, that the silence became a misery. I did not speak and felt bad each time that I did not speak. I read aloud in first grade, though, and heard the barest whisper with little squeaks come out of my throat. 'Louder,' said the teacher, who scared the voice away again. The other Chinese girls did not talk either, so I knew the silence had to do with being a Chinese girl."

But in Chinese school, conducted in the evenings after American school, most of the Chinese-American students weren't afraid to express themselves. "The boys who were so well behaved in the American school played tricks on [their teachers] and talked back to them. The girls were not mute. They screamed and yelled during recess, when there were no rules; they had fistfights. Nobody was afraid of children hurting themselves or of children hurting school property."

Later, Kingston remarks that her silence was not a feature of Chinese society. "How strange," she writes, "that the emigrant villagers are shouters, hollering face to face." Similarly, she notes that "Normal Chinese women's voices are strong and bossy. We American-Chinese girls had to whisper to make ourselves American-feminine. Apparently we whispered even more softly than the Americans. Once a year the teachers referred my sister and me to speech therapy, but our voices would straighten out, unpredictably normal, for the therapists."

Episodes of silence occur often in *The Woman Warrior*, beginning with the first sentence, a warning given to introduce the story of "No Name" aunt: "'You must not tell anyone,' my mother said, 'what I am about to tell you.'" In the final chapter, Kingston relates another instance of silence: "Our sixth-grade teacher, who liked to explain things to children, let us read our files. . . . I looked at my parents' aliases and their birthdays, which variants I knew. But when I saw Father's occupations I exclaimed, 'Hey, he wasn't a farmer, he was a. . .' He had been a gambler. My throat cut off the word—silence in front of the most understanding teacher. There were immigration secrets never to be said in front of the ghosts, immigration secrets whose telling could get us sent back to China. Sometimes I hated the ghosts for not letting us talk; sometimes I hated the secrecy of the Chinese." In a review for *Time* magazine, Paul Gray notes that during the adaptation of immigrant families to the United States, "a heritage of centuries can die in a generation of embarrassed silence." Gray then declares, "*The Woman Warrior* gives that silence a voice."

Kingston turns to the male side of her family in *China Men*, a book which, like *The Woman Warrior*, uses combinations of myth, memory, and biography to present several generations of the author's family. In *China Men*, writes Allen, Kingston "describes the men slaving for a dollar a week building sugar plantations; smuggling themselves into America in packing crates; building the railroads; adopting new names, such as Edison, Roosevelt and Worldster." Although women are not prominent as characters in *China Men*, Currier observes that it "is women from whom Kingston gathered the stories of these men's lives, and about her sources, she concludes: 'I would never be able to talk with them; I have no stories of equal pain.'"

China Men begins with the story of Kingston's father, who had trained as a scholar in China and now resented his low status and menial laundry job in the United States. "His angriest curses vilify women's bodies. The girl both understands and is bewildered," writes Gray in another review for *Time*. But since her father was not a "story-talker" like Brave Orchid, and was silent about his past, Kingston must "piece together the few facts she has and invent the rest," observes Mary Gordon in *New York Times Book Review*. Not only does the author recreate her father's life in China and provide five different versions of how he entered the United States; she also widely separates the story of "the father from China" from that of the man she knew and refers to as "the American father."

In Kingston's tale, "the father from China" found his skills in calligraphy and poetry useless in the United States. After emigrating, he became part-owner of a laundry in New York City, writes Frederick Wakeman, Jr., in the *New York Review of Books,* "along with three other China Men who spend their salaries on $200 suits, dime-a-dance girls, motorcycles, and flying lessons." Kingston follows this account of idyllic bachelor existence with an ancient Chinese ghost story about a beautiful spirit woman who, writes Wakeman, "beguiles a handsome traveler until he loses nearly all memory of his family back home." Eventually, the man is "released from her spell" and returns to his wife. "In the same way," points out Wakeman, "the father from China turns away from the lure of his three high-living friends, and puts the temptations of bachelorhood behind him after his wife joins him in New York." But soon after Brave Orchid arrived in the United States and weaned her husband away from his companions, the partners cheated the father from China out of his share of the business. The couple then left for California where "the American father" had to struggle to support his family.

In a later section of the book, Kingston presents the story of the father she knew in Stockton, and she ends *China Men* with characters of her own generation, relating the tale of a brother's tour of duty in Vietnam and his attempts to locate relatives in Hong Kong. Rounding out the book are the highly representative, embellished histories of earlier China Men who preceded her father to America. She tells of a great-grandfather who traveled to Hawaii to clear the land and work on a sugar plantation. The overseers forbade talking, she relates, and Gordon maintains that "nowhere is Mrs. Kingston's technique—the close focus, the fascination with the details of survival strategies, the repetitive fixated tone—more successful than in her description of the plantation workers' talking into the earth in defiance of the silence imposed upon them by white bosses. The men dig holes and shout their longings, their frustrations, down the hole to China, frightening their overseers, who leave them alone." "The poignancy of that moment is the fruit of stunning historical reconstruction coupled with the imagination of a novelist," Gray writes.

Originally planned as part of *The Woman Warrior,* this 1980 work tells the story of the men in Kingston's family.

Another grandfather was hired by the Central Pacific Railroad in the 1860s to work in the Sierra Nevada mountains, helping to link the continent by rail. *Los Angeles Times Book Review* critic Phyllis Quan remarks that Kingston portrays this grandfather "as part of that band of migrant workers who fled the white demons' ceremonial photograph sessions held upon the completion of the tracks and were bound to other destinations, leaving a network of steel trails as the only evidence of their presence." Gordon indicates that Kingston's "success at depicting the world of men without women must be the envy of any woman writer who has tried to capture this foreign territory. Her understanding of the lacerations of crushing physical work and the consolations of community is expressed in nearly perfect prose." She adds: "In comparison with these tales of her ancestors, the story of the brother who goes to Vietnam is a disappointment.... Since Mrs. Kingston's particular genius is most suited to illuminating incompre-

hensible lives, the brother's life, being more understandable, does not call up her highest gifts.''

Quan has similar criticisms, commenting that the
second half of the book loses ''the cohesion and
vitality of myth of the first half,'' but she believes
that this discontinuity is due to the fact that
Kingston interrupts her narrative with a section
called ''The Laws,'' ''a somewhat rude but informa-
tive overview of the immigration and naturalization
policies affecting Chinese people.'' Kingston discusses this section with Timothy Pfaff in an interview published in the *New York Times Book
Review*, commenting that ''the mainstream culture
doesn't know the history of Chinese Americans,
which has been written and written well. That
ignorance makes a tension for me, and in [*China
Men*] I just couldn't take it anymore. So all of a
sudden, right in the middle of the stories, plunk—
there is an eight-page section of pure history. It

Kingston's 1988 novel focuses on the fortunes of
Wittman Ah Sing, a fifth-generation Chinese-American who adopts the persona of the Monkey King, a
mythical Chinese figure.

starts with the Gold Rush and then goes right
through the various exclusion acts, year by
year.... It really affects the shape of the book, and
it might look quite clumsy. But on the other hand,
maybe it will affect the shape of the novel in the
future. Now maybe another Chinese-American
writer won't have to write that history.'' Kingston
also asserts that ''the reason the second half of the
book has fewer myths is that our modern daily life
has lost its myths. I am exploring how we live
without nature, how we live with machines and
battleships.''

In her writings, Kingston sometimes alters classical
Chinese myths. Although Wakeman finds *China
Men* generally praiseworthy, he writes that ''as
Kingston herself has admitted, many of the myths
she describes are largely her own reconstructions.
Often, they are only remotely connected with the
original Chinese legends they invoke; and sometimes they are only spurious folklore, a kind of self-
indulgent fantasy that blends extravagant personal
imagery with appropriately *voelkisch* [folk]
themes.'' He adds that ''precisely because the
myths are usually so consciously contrived, her
pieces of distant China lore often seem jejune
[lacking substance] and even inauthentic—especially to readers who know a little bit about the
original high culture which Kingston claims as her
birthright.'' However, in comments provided to
Authors and Artists for Young Adults, Kingston
asserts, ''I do not claim 'high culture.' I claim to be
a peasant and an American—and these myths are
true and ours.'' Similarly, the author relates to
Loke, ''[One Sinologist] said I got my mythology all
wrong, without any realization that I was writing
American mythology. He said I was trying to
elevate my family to the status of high culture by
bringing in all these high-culture Chinese myths.
He had no understanding that I was saying that the
Chinese-American peasant embodied these myths.
They are part of a lower culture. And when I say
'peasant,' I mean 'American peasant.''' Moreover,
Kingston tells Pfaff that the old myths are kept vital
and relevant by adaptation: ''We have to do more
than record myth. That's just more ancestor worship. The way I keep the old Chinese myths alive is
by telling them in a new American way. I can't help
feeling that people who accuse me of misrepre-
senting the myths are looking at the past in a
sentimental kind of way.''

While the biographical *China Men* and *The Woman
Warrior* deal with several generations of Kingston's
family, the novel *Tripmaster Monkey: His Fake Book*
details a few weeks in the life of one character.

Wittman Ah Sing is "a 23-year-old, fifth-generation Chinese-American male, Cal English major, playwright and draft dodger," writes John Leonard in the *Nation*. "The protagonist's name is a play on Walt Whitman's and the poet's 'I sing the body electric,'" notes Loke, who also explains that "'Tripmaster' in the book's title is both a reference to the clearheaded in the 60's who guided people on drug trips safely home and to the monkey in the 16th-century Chinese folk legend 'Journey to the West,' who protects a monk on his pilgrimage to India in search of Buddhist scriptures." Early in the novel, Wittman declares himself to be a present-day incarnation of the Monkey King of the legend. The novel's subtitle refers to the basic written arrangement of chords around which a jazz musician improvises; Wittman muses, "I want so bad to be the first bad-jazz China Man bluesman of America." But Wittman's version of the blues turns out to be a history of the Chinese-American world, staged in the spectacular manner of Chinese opera and drawing on both Chinese literary classics and the experience of Chinese immigrants in the United States.

"Wittman, one year out of college, is in a tough spot, culturally speaking," states Le Anne Schreiber in the *New York Times Book Review*. "His assimilation goes unrecognized, masked by appearances, and he can't be Chinese even if he wants to be. If first-generation Americans, like his author, have to make up China out of silences and ghost stories, imagine what little is left for Wittman to work with." "Most of Wittman's most impassioned monologues, private or public, have to do with his resentment of the way white Americans perceive him," observes Tyler in *New Republic*. After Wittman successfully stages his play, he says to the audience, "The one that drives me craziest is 'Do you speak English?' Particularly after I've been talking for hours, don't ask, 'Do you speak English?' The voice doesn't go with the face, they don't hear it. On the phone I sound like anybody, I get the interview, but I get downtown, they see my face, they ask, 'Do you speak English?'" Summarizing Wittman's difficulties, Schreiber writes, "It only takes one generation to lose China. How many does it take to gain America?"

Though departing from Kingston's previous books in manner of presentation, *Tripmaster Monkey* features some of the same concerns—for example, a certain tension between young Chinese Americans and new immigrants from China. Recalling the young immigrant Chinese men that her parents brought home as potential husbands for her sister and herself, Kingston writes in *The Woman Warrior*, "They were all funny-looking FOB's, Fresh-off-the-Boat's, as the Chinese-American kids at school called the young immigrants. FOB's wear high-riding gray slacks and white shirts with the sleeves rolled up. Their eyes do not focus correctly—shifty-eyed—and they hold their mouths slack, not tight-jawed masculine. They shave off their sideburns. The girls said *they'd* never date an FOB." *Tripmaster Monkey*'s protagonist makes similar remarks when he sees a family newly arrived from China: "Immigrants. Fresh Off the Boats out in public. Didn't know how to walk together. Spitting seeds. So uncool. You wouldn't mislike them on sight if their pants weren't so highwater, gym socks white and noticeable. F.O.B. fashions—highwaters or puddlecuffs. Can't get it right. Uncool. Uncool."

Some reviewers of *Tripmaster Monkey* have commented on the absence of the lyrical style of Kingston's earlier writings. For example, Schreiber declares, "Wittman's maniac monkey talk made me long for the less fevered but more exciting voice of Maxine Hong Kingston speaking for herself, as she did in *The Woman Warrior* and *China Men*." In the *New York Times*, Michiko Kakutani acknowledges that "the reader can grow impatient with [Wittman's] constant digressions, his long-winded style," but she then adds that "such misgivings are quickly forgotten, given Mrs. Kingston's verve for storytelling, her ability to so effortlessly create a distinctive idiomatic voice for her brash young hero."

Other critics note that Wittman is at times contradicted by the novel's narrator. "This omniscient narratorial voice exposes the flimsy underpinnings of the Tripmaster Monkey's delusional Monkey-God fantasies," writes Caroline Ong in *Times Literary Supplement*. Leonard asserts, "a female narrator—usually affectionate, always ironic, occasionally annoyed—looks down on him. Don't ask me how I know the narrator's female. I just do. She's as old as China, and remembers what happened in five dynasties and three religions. She's also foreseen the future." Kingston tells Loke, "the careful reader will see that the omniscient narrator is a woman. Definitely a female voice. She's always kicking Wittman around and telling him to do this and that and making fun of him. She always understands the woman characters. She's Kuan Yin, [Buddhist] goddess of mercy."

Loke reports that *Tripmaster Monkey* is Kingston's tribute to the hopes of the 1960s, when she was a student in Berkeley: "In Maxine Kingston's mind, her time in Berkeley remains magical—'when the values of the time matched mine so well. Comity [harmonious society]. Peace on earth. Friendship. We in Berkeley thought we were going to change the world. People spoke without cynicism. I keep seeing various people try to tell about that time and I think they diminish it, or they dismiss it. Nobody has written a novel about what we were doing back home during the Vietnam War, and I'm doing that.'"

"Now that I have written fiction and two non-fictions," Kingston said to Rabinowitz, "I just don't see why everybody doesn't do both. Each kind of writing draws on other kinds of strengths needed to find new ways to create a literary reality, to get at life. Just playing with another form, I feel that I am in another world." Commenting on the way she blends myth and reality in her writing, Kingston once told *Contemporary Authors:* "I was sorting them out. One of the themes in *The Woman Warrior* was: what is it that's a story and what is it that's life? Sometimes our lives have plots like stories; sometimes we're affected by the stories or we try to live up to them or the stories give a color and an atmosphere to life. So sometimes the boundaries are very clear, and sometimes they interlace and we live out stories." The author also stated, "The China that's in my stories can't be the one that's actually there. The Chinese Americans have a myth of China that we pass around to one another and that we talk about and that hovers over us. I thought it was very important to write that down, that mythic China that influences some people's lives so strongly that they live for it or live *by* it. After capturing the myth, I can go and see what's over there."

■ **Works Cited**

Allen, Henry, *Washington Post,* June 26, 1980.

Blackburn, Sara, *Ms.,* January, 1977.

Currier, Susan, "Maxine Hong Kingston," *Dictionary of Literary Biography Yearbook: 1980,* Gale, 1981.

Gordon, Mary, "Mythic History," *New York Times Book Review,* June 15, 1980, pp. 1, 24-25.

Gray, Paul, "Book of Changes," *Time,* December 6, 1976 p. 91.

Gray, "On the Gold Mountain," *Time,* June 30, 1980, p. 67.

Johnson, Diane, review of *The Woman Warrior* in *New York Review of Books,* February 3, 1977.

Kakutani, Michiko, "Being of 2 Cultures, and Liking and Loathing It," *New York Times,* April 14, 1989.

Kingston, Maxine Hong, comments provided to *Authors and Artists for Young Adults.*

Kingston, *The Woman Warrior: Memoirs of a Girlhood Among Ghosts,* Knopf, 1976.

Kingston, interview in *Contemporary Authors New Revision Series,* Volume 13, Gale, 1984.

Kingston, *Tripmaster Monkey: His Fake Book,* Knopf, 1988.

Kingston, interview with Paula Rabinowitz, in *Michigan Quarterly Review,* Winter, 1987, pp. 177-87.

Kramer, Jane, review of *The Woman Warrior* in *New York Times Book Review,* November 7, 1976.

Leonard, John, *Nation,* June 5, 1989, pp. 768-72.

Loke, Margarett, "The Tao Is Up," *New York Times Magazine,* April 30, 1989, pp. 28-29, 50-51, 55.

Ong, Caroline, "Demons and Warriors," *Times Literary Supplement,* September 15, 1989, p. 998.

Pfaff, Timothy, "Talk with Mrs. Kingston," *New York Times Book Review,* June 15, 1980, pp. 1, 25-27.

Quan, Phyllis, *Los Angeles Times Book Review,* June 22, 1980, p. 6.

Schreiber, Le Anne, "The Big, Big Show of Wittman Ah Sing," *New York Times Book Review,* April 23, 1989, p. 9.

Tyler, Anne, *New Republic,* June 21, 1980.

Tyler, "Manic Monologue," *New Republic,* April 17, 1989, pp. 44-46.

Wakeman, Frederick, Jr., review of *China Men* in *New York Review of Books,* August 14, 1980.

■ **For More Information See**

BOOKS

Contemporary Literary Criticism, Gale, Volume 12, 1980, Volume 19, 1981.

Kingston, Maxine Hong, *China Men,* Knopf, 1980.

PERIODICALS

America, February 26, 1976.

Christian Science Monitor, August 11, 1980.

Harper's, October, 1976, August, 1980.

Horizon, July, 1980.

International Fiction Review, January, 1978.

Los Angeles Times, June 24, 1990.

Los Angeles Times Book Review, April 23, 1989.

Mademoiselle, March, 1977.

Ms., August, 1980; June, 1989.

Newsweek, October 11, 1976; June 16, 1980.

New Yorker, November 15, 1976.

New York Times, September 17, 1976; June 3, 1980.

San Francisco Review of Books, September 2, 1980.
Saturday Review, July, 1980.
Southwest Review, spring, 1978.
Times Literary Supplement, January 27, 1978.

Tribune Books (Chicago), April 16, 1989.
Washington Post Book World, October 10, 1976; June 22, 1980; April 16, 1989, pp. 1-2.

Margaret Mahy

Personal

Born March 21, 1936, in Whakatane, New Zealand; daughter of Frances George (a builder) and May (a teacher; maiden name, Penlington) Mahy; children: Penelope Helen, Bridget Frances. *Education:* University of New Zealand, B.A., 1958. *Politics:* "Anarchist." *Religion:* "Humanist." *Hobbies and other interests:* Reading, gardening.

Addresses

Home—R.D. 1, Lyttelton, New Zealand. *Agent*—Vanessa Hamilton, The Summer House, Woodend, West Stoke Chichester, West Sussex PO18 9BP England.

Career

Writer. Petone Public Library, Petone, New Zealand, assistant librarian, 1958-59; School Library Service, Christchurch, New Zealand, librarian in charge, 1967-76; Canterbury Public Library, Christchurch, children's librarian, 1976-80. Writer in Residence, Canterbury University, 1984, and Western Australian College of Advanced Educa-

tion, 1985. *Member:* New Zealand Library Association.

Awards, Honors

Esther Glenn Medals, New Zealand Library Association, 1969, for *A Lion in the Meadow,* 1973, for *The First Margaret Mahy Story Book,* and 1983, for *The Haunting;* Een Zilveren Griffel, 1978; Best Children's Books of 1982 citation, and *School Library Journal* Best Book citation, both 1982, for *The Haunting;* Carnegie Medals, British Library Association, 1982, for *The Haunting,* 1986, for *The Changeover: A Supernatural Romance,* and 1987 for *Memory;* 1984 Notable Children's Book citation, Association for Library Service to Children (ALSC), Children's Book of the Year citation, and Best Books for Young Adults award, American Library Association (ALA), all 1986, for *The Changeover;* Honor List citation, *Horn Book,* 1985, for *The Changeover,* and 1987, for *The Catalogue of the Universe; 17 Kings and 42 Elephants* was named one of the year's ten best illustrated books in 1987 by the *New York Times Book Review;* Best Books of 1987 citation, Young Adult Services Division (ALA), for *The Tricksters,* and Best Books of 1989 citation for *Memory;* Society of School Librarians International Book award (Language Arts, Science and Social Studies category), and *Boston Globe/Horn Book* award, both 1988, for *Memory;* May Hill Arbuthnot Lecturer, ALSC, 1989.

■ Writings

YOUNG ADULT NOVELS

The Haunting (also see below), illustrations by Bruce Hogarth, Atheneum, 1982.

The Changeover: A Supernatural Romance, Atheneum, 1984.

The Catalogue of the Universe, Atheneum, 1985.

Aliens in the Family, Scholastic, 1986 (first hardcover edition published in England by Methuen, 1986).

The Tricksters, Margaret McElderry Books, 1987.

Memory, Margaret McElderry Books, 1988.

JUNIOR NOVELS

Clancy's Cabin, illustrations by Trevor Stubley, Dent, 1974.

The Bus Under the Leaves, illustrations by Margery Gill, Dent, 1974.

The Pirate Uncle, illustrations by Mary Dinsdale, Dent, 1977.

Raging Robots and Unruly Uncles, illustrations by Peter Stevenson, Dent, 1981.

The Pirates' Mixed-Up Voyage: Dark Doings in the Thousand Islands, illustrations by Margaret Chamberlain, Dent, 1983.

The Blood-and-Thunder Adventure on Hurricane Peak, illustrations by Wendy Smith, Dent, 1989.

Dangerous Spaces, Viking Children's Books, 1991.

PICTURE BOOKS

A Lion in the Meadow (verse; also see below), F. Watts, 1969, new edition with illustrations by Jenny Williams, 1986.

A Dragon of an Ordinary Family, illustrations by Helen Oxenbury, F. Watts, 1969.

Pillycock's Shop, illustrations by Carol Barker, F. Watts, 1969.

The Procession, illustrations by Charles Mozley, F. Watts, 1969.

Mrs. Discombobulous, illustrations by Jan Brychta, F. Watts, 1969.

The Little Witch, illustrations by Mozely, F. Watts, 1970.

Sailor Jack and the 20 Orphans, illustrations by Robert Bartelt, Picture Puffin, 1970.

The Princess and the Clown, F. Watts, 1971.

The Railway Engine and the Hairy Brigands, Dent, 1972.

17 Kings and 42 Elephants (verse), Dent, 1972, 2nd edition edited by Phyllis J. Fogelman with illustrations by Patricia MacCarthy, Dial, 1987.

The Boy with Two Shadows, illustrations by Williams, F. Watts, 1972, Lippincott, 1989.

The Man Whose Mother was a Pirate, illustrations by Brian Froud, Atheneum, 1972, illustrations by Chamberlain, Viking Kestrel, 1986.

Rooms to Let, F. Watts, 1974, published in the United States as *Rooms to Rent*.

The Rare Spotted Birthday Party, F. Watts, 1974.

The Witch in the Cherry Tree, illustrations by Williams, Parents' Magazine Press, 1974, Dent, 1984.

Stepmother, F. Watts, 1974.

Ultra-Violet Catastrophe! Or, The Unexpected Walk with Great-Uncle Mangus Pringle, Parents' Magazine Press, 1975.

David's Witch Doctor, F. Watts, 1975.

The Wind between the Stars, Dent, 1976.

The Boy Who Was Followed Home, illustrations by Steven Kellogg, F. Watts, 1976.

Leaf Magic (also see below), Parents' Magazine Press, 1976.

Jam: A True Story, illustrations by Helen Craig, Little, Brown, 1986.

JUVENILE FICTION

The Great Millionaire Kidnap, illustrations by Brychta, Dent, 1975.

The Nonstop Nonsense Book, illustrations by Quentin Blake, Dent, 1977.

The Great Piratical Rumbustification, and The Librarian and the Robbers, illustrations by Blake, Dent, 1978.

The Birthday Burglar and A Very Wicked Headmistress, Dent, 1984, new edition with illustrations by Chamberlain, Godine, 1988.

The Adventures of a Kite, illustrations by David Cowe, Arnold-Wheaton, 1985.

Sophie's Singing Mother, illustrations by Jo Davies, Arnold-Wheaton, 1985.

The Earthquake, illustrations by Dianne Perham, Arnold-Wheaton, 1985.

The Cake, illustrations by Cowe, Arnold-Wheaton, 1985.

The Catten, illustrations by Davies, Arnold-Wheaton, 1985.

A Vary Happy Bathday, illustrations by Elizabeth Fuller, Arnold-Wheaton, 1985.

Clever Hamburger, illustrations by McRae, Arnold-Wheaton, 1985.

My Wonderful Aunt (four volumes), illustrations by Dierdre Gardiner, Wright Group, 1986, revised edition in one volume, Children's Press, 1988.

When the King Rides By, Thornes, 1988.

Seven Chinese Brothers, illustrations by Jean and Mou-sien Tseng, Scholastic, 1990.

The Great White Man-Eating Shark: A Cautionary Tale, illustrations by Jonathan Allen, Dial Books for Young Readers, 1990.
Making Friends, illustrations by Smith, McElderry Books, 1990.
Keeping House, Macmillan, 1991.
Pumpkin Man and the Crafty Creeper, Greenwillow Books, 1991.
The Queen's Goat, illustrations by Emma Chichester Clark, Dial Books for Young Readers, 1991.

Also author of *Ups and Downs, Wibble Wobble, The Dragon's Birthday*, and *The Spider in the Shower*, all 1984. Author of *Out in the Big Wild World*, 1985, *The Three Wishes*, 1986, and *How Mr. Rooster Didn't Get Married*, illustrations by Fuller, Arnold-Wheaton.

JUVENILE FICTION WITH JOY COWLEY AND JUNE MELSER

Roly-Poly, illustrations by Deirdre Gardiner and others, Shortland (New Zealand), 1982, Arnold-Wheaton, 1985.
Cooking Pot, illustrations by Gardiner and others, Shortland, 1982, Arnold-Wheaton, 1985.
Fast and Funny, illustrations by Lynette Vondrusha and others, Shortland, 1982, Arnold-Wheaton, 1985.
Sing to the Moon, illustrations by Isabel Lowe and others, Shortland, 1982, Arnold-Wheaton, 1985.
Tiddalik, illustrations by Philip Webb, Shortland, 1982, Arnold-Wheaton, 1985.

FOR SCHOOLS; PUBLISHED BY SCHOOL PUBLICATIONS BRANCH, DEPARTMENT OF EDUCATION (WELLINGTON, NEW ZEALAND)

The Crocodile's Christmas Jandals, 1982.
The Bubbling Crocodile, 1983.
Mrs. Bubble's Baby, 1983.
Shopping with a Crocodile, 1983.
Going to the Beach, 1984.
The Great Grumbler and the Wonder Tree, 1984.
Fantail, Fantail, 1984.
A Crocodile in the Garden, 1985.
The Crocodile's Christmas Thongs, 1985.
Horrakopotchin, 1985.

THE "SUNSHINE SERIES"; PUBLISHED BY THE WRIGHT GROUP

The Sunshine Series, Level 6: The Trouble with Heathrow, illustrations by Rodney McRae, *The Pop Group*, illustrations by Madeline Beasley, *Baby's Breakfast*, illustrations by McRae, *The Man Who Enjoyed Grumbling*, illustrations by Wendy Hodder, 1986, revised edition, Heinemann Educational, 1987.
..., *Level 7: Muppy's Ball*, illustrations by Jan Vander Voo, *The Garden Party*, illustrations by McRae, *The Tree Doctor*, illustrations by Hodder, *Feeling Funny*, illustrations by McRae, 1986, revised edition, Heinemann Educational, 1986.
..., *Level 8: A Pet to the Vet, The King's Treasure, The New House Villain, The Funny Funny Clown Face*, illustrations by Miranda Whitford, 1986, revised edition, Heinemann Educational, 1987.
..., *Level 9: Tai Taylor is Born*, illustrations by Nick Price, *Grow Up Sally Sue, Trouble on the Bus*, illustrations by Hodder, *Shuttle 4, Mr. Rumfitt*, illustrations by Price, *The Terrible Topsy-Turvy, Tissy-Tossy Tangle*, 1986, revised edition, Heinemann Educational, 1987.
..., *Level 11: The Mad Puppet; Iris La Bonga and the Helpful Taxi Driver; The Haunting of Miss Cardamon; The Girl Who Washed in Moonlight; Elliott and the Cats Eating Out*, 1987.

NONFICTION

New Zealand: Yesterday and Today, F. Watts, 1975.

Also author of *Look under 'V'*, 1977.

COLLECTIONS

The First Margaret Mahy Story Book: Stories and Poems, Dent, 1972.
The Second Margaret Mahy Story Book: Stories and Poems, Dent, 1973.
The Third Margaret Mahy Story Book: Stories and Poems, illustrations by Shirley Hughes, Dent, 1975.
A Lion in the Meadow and Five Other Favorites, illustrations by Williams, Bartelt, Brychta, Mozley, and Froud, 1976.
The Chewing-Gum Rescue and Other Stories, illustrations by Jan Ormerod, Dent, 1982, Methuen, 1984.
Leaf Magic and Five other Favourites, illustrations by Chamberlain, Dent, 1984.
Mahy Magic: A Collection of the Most Magical Stories from the Margaret Mahy Story Books, illustrations by Shirley Hughes, Dent, 1986.
The Downhill Crocodile Whizz and Other Stories, illustrations by Ian Newsham, Dent, 1986.
The Door in the Air and Other Stories, illustrations by Diana Catchpole, Dent, 1988, Delacorte, 1991.

Chocolate Porridge and Other Stories, illustrations by Hughes, 1989.

Also author of *The Horrible Story and Others*, 1987.

OTHER

(Adaptor) *The Haunting of Barney Palmer* (screenplay based on *The Haunting*), [New Zealand], 1987.

The Tin Can Band and Other Poems, illustrations by Honey De Lacey, 1989.

Author of scripts "A Land Called Happy," "Wooly Valley," "Once upon a Story," and "The Margaret Mahy Story Book Theatre" for Television New Zealand, and scripts for the Gibson Group television series *Cuckooland*.

■ Adaptations

Cassette versions of Mahy's works include *The Haunting*, 1986, *The Chewing Gum Rescue and Other Stories*, 1988, and *The Pirate's Mixed-Up Voyage*, all read aloud by Richard Mitchley, and *Nonstop Nonsense*, read by Kenneth Stanley, all published by G. K. Hall.

■ Sidelights

Fantastical adventures that tell about how people get along in family life have made New Zealand author Margaret Mahy well-known around the world. In more than fifty titles since her first book, *A Lion in the Meadow*, Mahy has written about a world full of surprising possibilities, a world familiar to children, that she insists remains real for adults. Her younger characters help each other to learn about the world of adults; through friendship tested by adventure, teens and preteens wounded by childhood experiences find healing. This healing helps them to continue their journeys into adulthood. Critics place Mahy's work, which appeals to readers of all ages, with the best in the field of young people's literature. Mahy "has deserved her reputation as queen of the light fantastic with stories and picture-book texts which erupt with delightful visions," states *Times Literary Supplement* critic Sarah Hayes. When writing about aliens with unusual powers, intelligent adolescents, or "a primeval New Zealand of immense rain-forests and sulphorous volcanoes, ... she writes with all the force and precision and richness of a poet," Elizabeth Ward observes in the *Washington Post Book World*.

The first of many books concerned with the relationship between fantasy and reality, *A Lion in the Meadow* shows a mother in trouble because she refuses to take her son seriously when he relates a report that seems incredible to her. Annoyed by his warnings that there is a lion in the meadow, and thinking that he is playing an imaginative game with her, the busy mother gives the child a box of matches. Inside it, she says, is a little dragon that can grow large enough to scare the lion away. She soon regrets having lied to the child and vows not to lie to her children again. The fable illustrates that though fantasy is important to children, it is dangerous for adults not to recognize and teach the difference between fantasy and reality.

In addition to being valued for their themes, Mahy's books for children are popular and highly acclaimed because of her skills as a poet. The rhythmic verses in *17 Kings and 42 Elephants* such as "Watchers in the jungle, moist and mistilline, Bibble-bubble-babbled to the bing-bang-bong!" are as memorable as "The Congo" and other masterpieces by American poet Vachel Lindsay. The parade of kings, elephants, tigers, and other jungle animals winds from an un-named beginning to an un-named destination. The journey is enjoy-

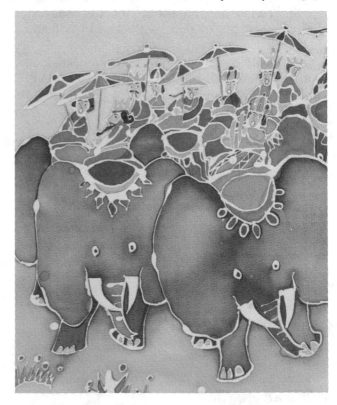

Many of Mahy's picture books for children, such as *The 17 Kings and 42 Elephants*, feature whimsical rhythmic verse.

able for its own sake, say the critics. The book's "language is a miraculous mixture of concision and freedom, joy and mystery, silliness and seriousness, all rolled into one," Arthur Yorinks comments in the *New York Times Book Review.* Patricia MacCarthy's brightly colored batik illustrations make the second edition particularly pleasing to the eye as well as the ear. The *New York Times Book Review* named it one of the year's ten best illustrated books in 1987.

Mahy's sense of the fun that can be had with wordplay is further seen in *The Birthday Burglar and A Very Wicked Headmistress.* Puns and alliterations of the letter B abound in this story of a rich but lonely man who steals birthday parties. Confronted with the family and friends of an elderly woman who intend to reclaim her stolen birthday party, he returns all the stolen birthdays and becomes a bee-keeper. Clever puns also make *Jam,* a picture book for young children, fun to read. The action is centered on an ambitious and thrifty house-husband with a plum tree who becomes obsessed with making jam. Surrounded by his jam-production process for more than a year, his family shudders when he notices that plums are ripening again. Though children under ten find the story delightful, Julia Eccleshare comments in the *Times Literary Supplement* that *Jam* "is largely a book with jokes for the adult reader."

Mahy's artistry as a wordsmith is most noticeable in her collected short stories, writes Mary M. Burns in *Horn Book.* The comic wordplay in *The Great Millionaire Kidnap* helps the plots along, says a reviewer for the *Spectator.* For instance, the two crooks who kidnap a kind rich man are named Scarcely and Hardly Likely, and their mother's name is Pretty. In addition to Mahy's sense of humor, delightful comic names, and a matter-of-fact presentation of improbable sights such as a roller-skating alligator, "her wonderful sense of words and timing" make her one of the best short story writers writing today, a reviewer comments in a *Junior Bookshelf* review of *The Downhill Crocodile Whizz.*

The family relationships of young adults is the focus of Mahy's books for that age group. Though it appears in each book, the theme remains interesting because she uses characters of different age groups from a wide range of backgrounds to demonstrate it. New problems faced by teens everywhere are given special attention in each new book. The author also makes use of many different fictional techniques from fantasy to dramatic dialogue.

Young Barney Palmer is dismayed to discover that he is next in line to inherit psychic powers in this 1982 novel.

In *The Haunting,* a young man finds out he is in line to inherit psychic powers that he feels are a curse more than a blessing. Barney Palmer describes a sequence of meal-time family discussions and ties them together with explanations of his own thoughts and feelings. In the end, Barney needs the help of his older sisters to ward off a series of aunts and uncles who determine to make him accept his inheritance. Critics praise Mahy's ability to develop likable characters and an ambitious theme within this framework. Barney and his family "are beautifully drawn, and perhaps because they care so much for each other, readers care for them, too," Michael Cart comments in *School Library Journal.* Hayes observes in the *Times Literary Supplement,* "*The Haunting* manages to combine a realistic approach to family life—in which how you feel about your parents and yourself is actually important—with a strong and terrifying line in fantasy."

"The book is in fact a powerful demonstration of the perils and rewards of imagination as it works through the Scholar family," Margery Fisher notes in *Growing Point*. Marcus Crouch, writing in a *Junior Bookshelf* review, feels that the book's strength "lies in the way Miss Mahy relates the fantasy to the relationships of ordinary life. The Scholars and the Palmers may be unusual but they are real people, and it matters greatly to the reader that the harmony of their lives should not be destroyed."

Aliens in the Family combines elements of science fiction and drama. The story begins with a broken family group made up of twelve-year-old Jake's father, stepmother, and a new brother and sister who do not accept her. When an alien from outer space, a cataloguer of the universe, appeals to them

Scholastic 0-590-41289-2 $2.50

THE CHANGEOVER

A Supernatural Romance

Margaret Mahy

"...the best supernatural Young Adult fiction around, with Stephen King power and Mahy's own class and polish." — *Kirkus Reviews*

Mahy's 1984 novel revolves around a fourteen-year-old girl's introduction to the world of witchcraft and the supernatural.

for help in his escape from his pursuers the Wirdegen, the children become allies and friends through the process of problem-solving. Unexpected time-travel helps the group to find a new starting point from which they learn to define themselves by looking forward to common goals instead of hanging onto roles that defined them in the past. Penny Blubaugh summarizes in *Voice of Youth Advocates*, "Using Bond and Jake as aliens in their own situations, Mahy has written a story of families learning to accept and believe in each other in spite of, and even because of, their differences."

The Tricksters provides an insightful look at the inner lives of people who celebrate Christmas together at a New Zealand beach house. The Hamiltons share their celebration with their British friend Anthony. During his visit, the seven family members take turns telling him the story of the house and the family who built it (the Cardinals), each giving a new twist to the story of a boy who had died by drowning. Anthony suspects the legends he hears about the boy's death and the house are not completely factual. He discovers as well that the Hamiltons are not what they appear to be. Helen J. Hinterberg remarks in the *Christian Science Monitor* that "Mahy creates an eerie atmosphere worthy of a classic gothic novel and suspense worthy of a first-rate thriller." The group's interactions become even more interesting with the arrival of three young men, the Carnival brothers. Though they claim to be related to the family who built the house, the Hamiltons suspect something more sinister explains their visit. Perhaps they are ghosts, or the ghost of the drowned boy returned, incarnated in three different aspects of his personality. Seventeen-year-old Ariadne fears that she has called them into being by writing a romantic novel that she hides from the rest of the family. The Cardinal brothers' unnerving similarity to her characters helps to convince her that they are tricksters with harmful plans. "Just when it seems evil is going to win, Mahy throws in a surprising ending" which is tidy if not completely satisfying, Kristie A. Hart writes in a *Voice of Youth Advocates* review.

Keeping whimsy "just a step away," here Mahy also offers "the solidity of a robust and affectionate family, with its shared language, its traditional squabbles, accepted rivalries and secrets," Hayes sums up. Hayes also remarks that "The ability to combine a dazzling fantasy with painfully real emotions is a particular gift." According to Robin McKinley, writing in the *New York Times Book*

Review, Ariadne's thoughts in the novel express Mahy's theme that convincing storytellers have a dangerous skill. The complicated plot, the fight between good and evil, and thought-provoking theories about the Carnival brothers' origins, make *The Tricksters* more challenging than the average young adult novel. McKinley observes, "In [Mahy's] hands the matter of living in the world we must share with other people becomes clearer, kinder, more involving, and more exciting." Critics recommend it to adult readers of contemporary fantasy as well as to young adults.

Dangerous Spaces presents one young woman's struggle to control her habit of trying to avoid life's difficulties by escaping to a private world inhabited by her great-uncle's ghost. Anthea's own parents have died suddenly and she lives with relatives whose complicated and noisy lives are no comfort to her. Soon she is retreating to the spacious dream-world Viridian every night, and her trips become so dangerous that her life is threatened. Compared to the dream-worlds in other books, Mahy's Viridian "is unique in its slow slide from . . . a place of beauty to one of menace and danger," writes Patricia Manning in the *School Library Journal*.

Down-to-earth Flora, the cousin who resents the glamorous Anthea at first, charges into Viridian to rescue her and puts an end to the haunting that has plagued the family for generations. Descriptions of Viridian that are challenging at the book's beginning make more sense to the reader when Mahy brings the book to a memorable close. "The skillful weaving of adventure with insights into family relationships for which Mahy is known rewards readers who finish the book," a *Publishers Weekly* reviewer comments.

Family relationships and their importance to young adults is just one of the author's major themes. Hayes writes in the *Times Literary Supplement*, "the double aspect of things—man and beast, [good] and evil, young and old—intrigues Margaret Mahy." *The Catalogue of the Universe* finds a balance between rational thinking and idealistic belief. The main characters are high school seniors working out the problems of identity common to that age group. Angela has lived without a father for many years, and feels that the blessings of beauty, a loving mother, and intelligence have not compensated for his absence. Tycho, her friend since early childhood, who is looking to science and astronomy to provide a rational basis for his life, helps Angela in her search for her missing father. Their quest moves quickly from surprise to

An alien in distress helps a disjointed family grow closer in this science-fiction drama.

surprise until they encounter the lost parent, and a disappointment that leaves Angela to find out who she is apart from family ties. She comes away knowing that heroes are not always found where she had dreamed they would be.

The young adults discover that it takes both faith and facts to survive these experiences and achieve their goals. "Angela and Tycho learn what they have suspected all along, that neither idealism nor rationalism [alone] is the key to coping with an existence that must be made up minute by minute," Colin Greenland notes in the *Times Literary Supplement*. Furthermore, their story shows that while forgiveness can help relationships to survive, it does not always change the imperfections of others, and it is difficult to forgive. Mahy's story makes these points without becoming pessimistic or sentimental. "Angela shares with her friend

Tycho a fascination with matters like the square root of two and the moons of Jupiter which outlast emotional pains and the novel moves lightly,'' Gillian Wilce maintains in the *New Statesman*. Greenland notes that readers who ''know at least a little of what it feels like to be in love'' will appreciate this book more than others.

The Changeover: A Supernatural Romance presents a fourteen-year-old girl's collaboration with adult witches who have told her that magic is the only way to save her three-year-old brother from death. The child's health had begun to fail at about the same time that Laura's divorced mother took a growing interest in a man she does not trust. Soon after, Laura becomes convinced that an evil warlock has cast a spell on her brother, and she determines to break the spell in a ritual that turns her into a witch. Set in contemporary New Zealand, the story copes realistically with Laura's feelings and ''reconciles a number of disparate elements,'' says *Horn Book* reviewer Paul Heins, who relates that Mahy keeps the supernatural and realistic components of the story well-balanced. As Laura grows attracted to the classmate who has introduced her to the witches, she better understands her mother's emotional needs. In turn, the now-more-compassionate Laura helps her classmate to overcome painful childhood memories.

Critics believe the supernatural elements in *The Changeover* are secondary to what it teaches about growing up in a threatening environment. ''The author's insights into the jagged tensions of family life in contemporary New Zealand count for much more than her world of witches,'' Robert Dunbar remarks in the *School Librarian*. ''In the manner of all good supernaturalists, [Mahy's] stories always have a perfectly possible rational explanation,'' Hayes observes in the *Times Literary Supplement*. ''This one could be about the products of a young girl's fevered imagination during a period of physical and emotional turmoil; or about the influence of a boy traumatized by a cruel foster father and years of psychotherapy; or about a miracle cure, a single parent, and a dirty old man.'' The story of entrapment and rescue lends itself to many such interpretations. In addition, Laura's changeover coincides with her passage through puberty. Hayes concludes, ''It is rare to find a novel which captures so well the changeover from child to adult, and from what is real in the mind to what is real outside.'' McKinley declares, ''Ms. Mahy deals with something ... she can handle as no other writer has: the first terrifying awakening of teenage sexuality. She seems to know the delicate

balances of the highly indelicate things that hormones start doing to you around the age of 14, and she describes them in a funny, real, significant and haunting way that no one old enough to write as elegantly as she does should be able to remember.''

Mahy compares the powers and limitations of magic and science in the well-received novel *The Blood-and-Thunder Adventure on Hurricane Peak*. Michael Dirda of the *Washington Post Book World* remarks, ''In my book you can't beat a slapstick novel starring an evil industrialist, a beautiful scientist and a bumbling sorcerer, two talking cats, a supernatural forest and plot mixups right out of [Shakespeare's comedy] *A Midsummer Night's Dream*.'' The threads of the entertainingly tangled plot take as many unexpected turns as the book's roller-skating policemen. *Horn Book* reviewer Nancy Vasilakis added, ''We are also the beneficiaries of some discerning Mahy wisdom regarding the truth of fairy tales and forests, enchanted or otherwise, as well as the meaning of the imagination and art and its application to science.'' *Times Literary Supplement* reviewer John Mole explains, ''There is a romance between the acting principal of the school and the scientist Belladonna Doppler, in which the rival claims of magic and science argue their way towards a happy marriage.'' The scientist sums up near the end that though sorcery had brought them into the forest, they needed science to come back out.

Memory explores how the ability to remember can be both a curse and a blessing. Main character Jonny Dart blames himself for the accidental death of his sister, and the passage of five years has not helped to ease his sense of loss. For the old woman he lives with, however, a better memory would solve problems. Because she suffers from Alzheimer's disease, Sophie forgets where she is, wakes Jonny at night thinking he is someone else, and wears a tea cozy instead of a hat. These challenges bring Jonny's attention to present realities and help him to discover that he is kind-hearted.

Mahy wrote *Memory* while thinking of her own experiences with caring for the elderly. She explains in the May Hill Arbuthnot Lecture published in *Journal of Youth Services in Libraries*, ''For a number of years, I was in charge of my aunt, and though my aunt and Sophie are not the same person, they are similar in many ways. A lot of the happenings, a lot of the conversations, in *Memory* are directly transposed from life with my aunt, and if the story lacks the nastiness, the sheer fatigue of response involved in looking after a demented person, it is partly because, though these elements were present, they were not a commanding part of my life with [my] aunt." Mahy's other experiences relating to the homeless gave her the idea for the book. "Driving home through an empty city at about 2 a.m., I saw an old man coming out of a supermarket car park pushing an empty trolly. The image stayed with me until I found a place for it," she says. While writing the book, she was also told of a group of derelict teens who had moved into a demented old woman's house and were taking care of her.

Like her other books, *Memory* contains material that communicates to adults as well as to children. Doug Anderson sees "a well-defined political context" for the book. He writes in the *Times Literary Supplement,* "it is full of allusions to issues in contemporary New Zealand politics; Maori rights, the social complexities of a racially mixed nation, the disintegration of a traditional culture in the face of rampant commercialism (references that non-New Zealanders are unlikely to understand are carefully footnoted). Above all, Mahy raises the idea that anger at injustice is a good thing, something to be nurtured and focused."

Mahy's ability to combine themes relevant to young adults with fantasy is matched by her consistently non-sexist perspective on roles and relationships. Jan Dalley, writing in the *Times Literary Supplement,* points out that Mahy "continually pushes at the boundaries of [fairy-tale] conventions," and "roots out the sexism that used to be integral" to fiction for young readers. For example, though the roles of rescuer, leader, and problem-solver have been traditionally assigned to males, she gives these roles as often to females of various ages and levels of social status. In Mahy's books, the roles of home economist and nurturer, traditionally assigned to women, are also assigned to men. Growth to sexual maturity is equally exciting and frightening to her male and female adolescents. Adults of both sexes are equally subject to weakness and failure to discern the needs of their children. All her characters face the same challenges to strike a balance between freedom and commitment, reason and emotion. And they all benefit from recognizing the power of the imagination, which they learn to celebrate as well as to contain.

While many of her books explore the need to keep fantasy in its proper proportion to reality, Mahy indulges fantasy most freely in *The Door in the Air and Other Stories.* In "The Bridge Builder," for example, the main character creates bridges that double as bird cages, musical instruments, and

The appearance of three mysterious young men creates problems for a New Zealand family in this 1987 thriller.

aquariums. "Best of all are the quality and texture of her fantasy: vivid, dreamlike, seldom whimsical, with images that last," Dalley comments in the *Times Literary Supplement.* Keeping the collection in perspective as whimsy is the humorous story "A Work of Art," in which two young men exhibit a home-baked birthday cake as a sculpture in a local gallery. There, the fruitcake receives praise for its "passionate equilibrium." The presence of this story suggests that while *A Door in the Air* entertains readers of one age group, it also can be appreciated by older readers as a study of the purpose of art and art criticism.

Stories and storytelling have always held Mahy's attention. She says in her Arbuthnot lecture, "From the time I was very small I was encouraged to listen to stories. I began as a listener, and then, since I wanted to join in that particular dance, I put together stories of my own ... telling them aloud to walls and trees. Because I couldn't write back then, I learned them by heart as a way of containing them, but I went on to become a reader, and very shortly after that learned to write and began to contain them by putting them down in notebooks. I began as a listener, became a teller, then a reader, and then a writer in that order. Later still I became a librarian."

In her work as a librarian, Mahy is called upon to distinguish works of fact from works of fiction by shelving them separately, as if imagined stories somehow do not contain elements of truth about life. Unlike the many fault lines that score the geography of her homeland, she believes the distinction is an imaginary rift. This "dislocation," as she calls it in her lecture, comes from the contrast between the British culture she learned from books and the tropical New Zealand environment in which she lived. The "imaginative truth" seemed to be more true than "the facts and images of my everyday life," she recalls. The celebration of Christmas, for example, which she has always observed in the sunny islands, is not complete for her without stories of England's snow drifts and holly. "The imaginative truth and the factual truth are at odds with one another but I still need those opposites to make Christmas come alive for me," she explains. She finds that the same kind of paradox applies to differences between make-believe and science. Pointing to changes in scientific theories about how the world began, she comments that what we think of as scientific fact sometimes proves to be wrong in the light of new discoveries, "and the truest thing in science is wonder just as it is in story. And I never forget that story is as important to human beings as science, more powerful at times because it is more subversive."

In her lecture, she says, "I have told the children all the truth I know from personal experience." One does not have to impose the truth onto children, she says, because "they demand to be told. When a child writes and asks me 'Do you believe in supernatural things?' they may be asking me to confirm that a story like *The Haunting* is literally true. But mostly they are asking 'Just where am I to fit this story in my view of the world?' ... Part of giving them the truest answer we can give also involves telling stories of desire: once there was a man who rode on a winged horse, once there was a boy who spoke to the animals, and the animals talked back to him, once there was a girl who grew so powerful that she was able not

Mahy drew on her experiences with caring for the elderly when writing this book about both the curse and blessing of memory.

only to overcome her enemy but to overcome the base part of herself. Beware or the wolf will eat you and then you will become part of the wolf until something eats the wolf and so on. . . . It is a gamble because we cannot tell just what is going to happen in the individual head when the story gets there and starts working."

She concludes by explaining that what has always driven her to read and write is a fascination with what can be known through stories, a fascination that she believes has always been an important part of human nature. She emphasizes, "*The mere cadence of six syllables—A Tale of Adventure—instantly conjures up in the mind a jumbled and motley host of memories. Memories not only personal but we may well suspect racial; and not only racial but primeval. Ages before history had learned its letters, there being no letters to learn, ages before the children of men builded the city and the tower called Babel and their language was confounded, the rudiments of this kind of oral narrative must have begun to flourish. Indeed the greater part of even the largest of dictionaries, every page of the most comprehensive atlases consists of relics and records in the concisest shorthand from bygone chapters of the tale whereof we know neither the beginning nor the end—that of Man's supreme venture into the world without and into the world within."*

■ Works Cited

Anderson, Doug, "A Good Anger," *Times Literary Supplement*, October 30, 1987, p. 1205.

Blubaugh, Penny, review of *Aliens in the Family*, *Voice of Youth Advocates*, April, 1987, p. 39.

Burns, Mary M., "Margaret Mahy: *The Door in the Air and Other Stories*," *Horn Book*, March, 1991, p. 201.

Cart, Michael, review of *The Haunting*, *School Library Journal*, August, 1982, p. 119.

Crouch, Marcus, review of *The Haunting*, *Junior Bookshelf*, February, 1983, p. 45.

Dalley, Jan, "Fantastical Flights," *Times Literary Supplement*, November 25, 1988, p. 1323.

Dirda, Michael, "Young Bookshelf," *Washington Post Book World*, January 14, 1990, p. 10.

Dunbar, Robert, review of *The Changeover: A Supernatural Romance*, *School Librarian*, September, 1984, p. 260.

Eccleshare, Julia, "Comforting Corners," *Times Literary Supplement*, December 13, 1985, p. 1435.

Fisher, Margery, review of *The Haunting*, *Growing Point*, November, 1982, p. 3985.

Greenland, Colin, "Ritual Dismembering," *Times Literary Supplement*, November 8, 1985, p. 1274.

Hart, Kristie A., review of *The Tricksters*, *Voice of Youth Advocates*, June, 1987, p. 80.

Hayes, Sarah, "Adding Another Dimension," *Times Literary Supplement*, July 13, 1984, p. 794.

Hayes, "Fantasy and the Family," *Times Literary Supplement*, August 1, 1986, p. 850.

Hayes, "Unearthing the Family Ghosts," *Times Literary Supplement*, September 17, 1982, p. 1001.

Heins, Paul, review of *The Changeover: A Supernatural Romance*, *Horn Book*, November, 1984, p. 764.

Hinterberg, Helen J., "Reading for Tuned-In Teens," *Christian Science Monitor*, January 25, 1989, p. 13.

Mahy, Margaret, *17 Kings and 42 Elephants*, Dent, 1972, 2nd edition, Dial, 1987.

Mahy, Margaret, *The Great Millionaire Kidnap*, Dent, 1975.

Mahy, Margaret, *The Door in the Air and Other Stories*, Dent, 1988, Delacorte, 1991.

Mahy, Margaret, "May Hill Arbuthnot Lecture, A Dissolving Ghost: Possible Operations of Truth in Children's Books and the Lives of Children," *Journal of Youth Services in Libraries*, summer, 1989, p. 313-329.

Manning, Patricia, review of *Dangerous Spaces*, *School Library Journal*, April, 1991, p. 121.

McKinley, Robin, "Falling in Love with a Ghost," *New York Times Book Review*, May 17, 1987, pp. 31, 44.

Mole, John, "Abandoning Reality," *Times Literary Supplement*, April 7, 1989, p. 378.

Review of *Dangerous Spaces*, *Publishers Weekly*, February 1, 1991, p. 80.

Review of *The Downhill Crocodile Whizz*, *Junior Bookshelf*, August, 1986, pp. 144-145.

Review of *The Great Millionaire Kidnap*, *Spectator*, December 6, 1975, p. 732.

Vasilakis, Nancy, "Margaret Mahy: *The Blood-and-Thunder Adventure on Hurricane Peak*," *Horn Book*, November/December, 1989, pp. 772-773.

Ward, Elizabeth, "Space to Dream," *Washington Post Book World*, October 12, 1986, p. 11.

Wilce, Gillian, "Waking Up to the Kid Next Door," *New Statesman*, November 8, 1985, pp. 27-28.

Yorinks, Arthur, "Lots of Pachyderms," *New York Times Book Review*, November 8, 1987, p. 40.

■ For More Information See

BOOKS

Children's Literature Review, Volume 7, Gale, 1984, pp. 176-188.

PERIODICALS

Christian Science Monitor, June 6, 1986, p. B6; November 4, 1988, p. B3.

Fantasy Review, March, 1985, p. 27.

Horn Book, November/December, 1984, p. 764.

Listener, November 8, 1984, p. 27.

New York Times Book Review, July 13, 1986, p. 22.

School Library Journal, April, 1991, p. 98.

Times Literary Supplement, October 9, 1987, p. 1120.

Milton Meltzer

■ Personal

Born May 8, 1915, in Worcester, MA; son of Benjamin and Mary (Richter) Meltzer; married Hilda Balinky, June 22, 1941; children: Jane, Amy. *Education:* Attended Columbia University, 1932-36. *Politics:* Independent.

■ Addresses

Home—263 West End Ave., New York, NY 10023. *Agent*—Harold Ober Associates, 425 Madison Ave., New York, NY 10017.

■ Career

Federal Theatre Project of the Works Projects Administration, New York City, staff writer, 1936-39; Columbia Broadcasting System Inc. (CBS-Radio), New York City, researcher and writer, 1946; Public Relations Staff of Henry A. Wallace for President, 1947-49; Medical and Pharmaceutical Information Bureau, New York City, account executive, 1950-55; Pfizer Inc., New York City, assistant director of public relations, 1955-60; Science and Medicine Publishing Co. Inc., New York City, editor, 1960-68; full-time writer of books, 1968—;

historian; biographer. Consulting editor, Thomas Y. Crowell Co., 1962-74, Doubleday & Co. Inc., 1963-73, and Scholastic Book Services, 1968-72; University of Massachusetts, Amherst, adjunct professor, 1977-80; lecturer at universities in the United States and England and at professional meetings and seminars; writer of films and filmstrips. *Military service:* U.S. Army Air Force, 1942-46; became sergeant. *Member:* Authors Guild, PEN, Organization of American Historians.

■ Awards, Honors

Thomas Alva Edison Mass Media Award for special excellence in portraying America's past, 1966, for *In Their Own Words: A History of the American Negro*, Volume 2, *1865-1916*; Children's Literature Award of the National Book Award, finalist, 1969, for *Langston Hughes: A Biography*, 1975, for *Remember the Days: A Short History of the Jewish American* and *World of Our Fathers: The Jews of Eastern Europe*, and 1977, for *Never to Forget: The Jews of the Holocaust*; Christopher Award, 1969, for *Brother, Can You Spare a Dime? The Great Depression, 1929-1933*, and 1980, for *All Times, All Peoples: A World History of Slavery; Slavery: From the Rise of Western Civilization to the Renaissance* was selected one of *School Library Journal's* Best Books, 1971; Charles Tebeau Award from the Florida Historical Society, 1973, for *Hunted Like a Wolf: The Story of the Seminole War*; Jane Addams Peace Association Children's Book Award Honor Book, 1975, for *The Eye of Conscience: Photographers and Social Change.*

Boston Globe-Horn Book Nonfiction Honor Book, 1976, for *Never to Forget: The Jews of the Holocaust,* and 1983, for *The Jewish Americans: A History in Their Own Words, 1650-1950;* Association of Jewish Libraries Book Award, 1976, Jane Addams Peace Association Children's Book Award, 1977, Charles and Bertie G. Schwartz Award for Jewish Juvenile Literature from the National Jewish Book Awards, 1978, Hans Christian Andersen Honor List, 1979, and selected by the American Library Association as a "Best of the Best Books 1970-1983," all for *Never to Forget: The Jews of the Holocaust; Dorothea Lange: A Photographer's Life* was selected on the *New York Times* Best Adult Books of the Year, 1978; Washington Children's Book Guild Honorable Mention, 1978 and 1979, and Nonfiction Award, 1981, all for his total body of work; American Book Award finalist, 1981, for *All Times, All Peoples: A World History of Slavery.*

Carter G. Woodson Book Award from the National Council for Social Studies, 1981, for *The Chinese Americans;* Jefferson Cup Award from the Virginia State Library Association, 1983, for *The Jewish Americans: A History in Their Own Words, 1650-1950;* Children's Book Award special citation from the Child Study Children's Book Committee, one of *School Library Journal's* Best Books for Young Adults, both 1985, and Olive Branch Award from the Writers' and Publishers' Alliance for Nuclear Disarmament, Jane Addams Peace Association Children's Book Award, and New York University Center for War, Peace, and the News Media, all 1986, all for *Ain't Gonna Study War No More: The Story of America's Peace-Seekers;* John Brubaker Memorial Award from the Catholic Library Association, 1986; Golden Kite Award for nonfiction, Society of Children's Book Writers, 1987, for *Poverty in America;* Jane Addams Peace Association Children's Book Award Honor Book, 1989, for *Rescue: The Story of How Gentiles Saved the Jews in the Holocaust.*

Many of Meltzer's books have been selected as Library of Congress' Best Children's Books of the Year, Notable Children's Trade Book in Social Studies from the National Council for Social Studies, and *New York Times* Outstanding Children's Books of the Year.

■ Writings

NONFICTION FOR YOUNG READERS, EXCEPT AS NOTED

(With Langston Hughes) *A Pictorial History of the Negro in America* (adult), Crown, 1956, 5th revised edition, with C. Eric Lincoln, published as *A Pictorial History of Black Americans,* 1983, revised as *African American History: Four Centuries of Black Life,* Scholastic Textbooks, 1990.

Mark Twain Himself (adult), Crowell, 1960.

(Editor) *Milestones to American Liberty: The Foundations of the Republic* (adult), Crowell, 1961, revised edition, 1965.

(Editor, with Walter Harding) *A Thoreau Profile* (adult), Crowell, 1962.

(Editor) *Thoreau: People, Principles and Politics* (adult), Hill & Wang, 1963.

A Light in the Dark: The Life of Samuel Gridley Howe (ALA Notable Book), Crowell, 1964, Modern Curriculum Press, 1991.

In Their Own Words: A History of the American Negro, Crowell, Volume 1, *1619-1865* (ALA Notable Book), 1964, Volume 2, *1865-1916* (ALA Notable Book), 1965, Volume 3, *1916-1966* (ALA Notable Book), 1967, abridged edition published as *The Black Americans: A History in Their Own Words, 1619-1983,* Crowell, 1984, Trophy, 1987.

Tongue of the Flame: The Life of Lydia Maria Child, Crowell, 1965.

(With August Meier) *Time of Trial, Time of Hope: The Negro in America, 1919-1941* (with teacher's guide), illustrated by Moneta Barnett, Doubleday, 1966, Modern Curriculum Press, 1991.

Thaddeus Stevens and the Fight for Negro Rights, Crowell, 1967.

(With L. Hughes) *Black Magic: A Pictorial History of the Negro in American Entertainment* (adult), Prentice-Hall, 1967, revised as *Black Magic: A Pictorial History of the African-American in the Performing Arts,* introduction by Ossie Davis, Da Capo Press, 1990.

Bread—and Roses: The Struggle of American Labor, 1865-1915, Knopf, 1967, Facts on File, 1991.

Langston Hughes: A Biography (ALA Notable Book), Crowell, 1968.

Brother, Can You Spare a Dime? The Great Depression, 1929-1933 (ALA Notable Book), Knopf, 1969, Facts on File, 1991.

(With Lawrence Lader) *Margaret Sanger: Pioneer of Birth Control,* Crowell, 1969.

Freedom Comes to Mississippi: The Story of Reconstruction, Follet, 1970.

Slavery: From the Rise of Western Civilization to the Renaissance, Cowles, 1971, Volume 2, *Slavery: From the Renaissance to Today*, Cowles, 1972.

To Change the World: A Picture History of Reconstruction, Scholastic Book Services, 1971.

Underground Man (novel), Bradbury Press, 1972, Harcourt, 1990.

Hunted Like a Wolf: The Story of the Seminole War, Farrar, Straus, 1972.

The Right to Remain Silent, Harcourt, 1972.

(With Bernard Cole) *The Eye of Conscience: Photographers and Social Change*, Follett, 1974.

World of Our Fathers: The Jews of Eastern Europe, Farrar, Straus, 1974.

Remember the Days: A Short History of the Jewish American, illustrated by Harvey Dinnerstein, Doubleday, 1974.

Bound for the Rio Grande: The Mexican Struggle, 1845-1850, Knopf, 1974.

Taking Root: Jewish Immigrants in America, Farrar, Straus, 1974.

Violins and Shovels: The WPA Arts Projects, Delacorte, 1976.

Never to Forget: The Jews of the Holocaust (Horn Book honor list; with teacher's guide), Harper, 1976, Trophy, 1991.

Dorothea Lange: A Photographer's Life (adult), Farrar, Straus, 1978, reprinted, 1985.

The Human Rights Book, Farrar, Straus, 1979.

All Times, All Peoples: A World History of Slavery (Horn Book honor list), illustrated by Leonard Everett Fisher, Harper, 1980.

The Chinese Americans, Crowell, 1980.

(Editor with Patricia G. Holland and Francine Krasno) *The Collected Correspondence of Lydia Maria Child, 1817-1880: Guide and Index to the Microfiche Edition* (adult), Kraus Microform, 1980.

The Truth about the Ku Klux Klan, F. Watts, 1982.

The Hispanic Americans, illustrated with photographs by Morrie Camhi and Catherine Noren, Crowell, 1982.

The Jewish Americans: A History in Their Own Words, 1650-1950 (ALA Notable Book), Crowell, 1982.

(Editor with P. G. Holland) *Lydia Maria Child: Selected Letters, 1817-1880* (adult), University of Massachusetts Press, 1982.

The Terrorists, Harper, 1983.

A Book about Names: In which Custom, Tradition, Law, Myth, History, Folklore, Foolery, Legend, Fashion, Nonsense, Symbol, Taboo Help Explain How We Got Our Names and What They Mean, illustrated by Mischa Richter, Crowell, 1984.

Ain't Gonna Study War No More: The Story of America's Peace-Seekers, Harper, 1985.

Mark Twain: A Writer's Life, F. Watts, 1985.

Betty Friedan: A Voice for Women's Rights (part of the "Women of Our Time" series), illustrated by Stephen Marchesi, Viking, 1985.

Dorothea Lange: Life through the Camera (part of the "Women of Our Time" series), illustrated by Donna Diamond and with photographs by Dorothea Lange, Viking, 1985.

The Jews in America: A Picture Album, Jewish Publication Society, 1985.

Poverty in America, Morrow, 1986.

Winnie Mandela: The Soul of South Africa (part of the "Women of Our Time" series), illustrated by S. Marchesi, Viking, 1986.

George Washington and the Birth of Our Nation, F. Watts, 1986.

Mary McLeod Bethune: Voice of Black Hope (part of the "Women of Our Time" series), illustrated by S. Marchesi, Viking, 1987.

The Landscape of Memory, Viking, 1987.

The American Revolutionaries: A History in Their Own Words, 1750-1800, Crowell, 1987.

Starting from Home: A Writer's Beginnings, Viking, 1988, Puffin, 1991.

Rescue: The Story of How Gentiles Saved Jews in the Holocaust, Harper, 1988, Trophy, 1991.

Benjamin Franklin: The New American, F. Watts, 1988.

American Politics: How It Really Works, illustrated by David Small, Morrow, 1989.

Voices from the Civil War: A Documentary History of the Great American Conflict, Crowell, 1989.

The Bill of Rights: How We Got It and What It Means, Harper, 1990.

Crime in America, Morrow, 1990.

Columbus and the World around Him, F. Watts, 1990.

The American Promise: Voices of a Changing Nation, 1945-Present, Bantam, 1990.

Thomas Jefferson: The Revolutionary Aristocrat, F. Watts, 1991.

The Amazing Potato, HarperCollins, 1992.

Andrew Jackson and his America, F. Watts, in press.

Lincoln: In His Own Words, illustrated by Stephen Alcorn, Harcourt, in press.

Editor of "Women of America" series, Crowell, 1962-74, "Zenith Books" series, Doubleday,

1963-73, and "Firebird Books" series, Scholastic Book Services, 1968-72. Author of introduction for *Learning about Biographies: A Reading-and-Writing Approach,* by Myra Zarnowski, National Council of Teachers of English, 1990.

Also author of documentary films, including *History of the American Negro* (series of three half-hour films), Niagara Films, 1965; *Five,* Silvermine Films, 1971; *The Bread and Roses Strike: Lawrence, 1912* (filmstrip), District 1199 Cultural Center, 1980; *The Camera of My Family,* Anti-Defamation League, 1981; *American Family: The Merlins,* Anti-Defamation League, 1982. Authors of scripts for radio and television.

Contributor to periodicals, including *New York Times Magazine, New York Times Book Review, English Journal, Virginia Quarterly Review, Library Journal, Wilson Library Bulletin, School Library Journal, Microform Review, Horn Book, Children's Literature in Education, Lion and the Unicorn, Social Education, New Advocate,* and *Children's Literature Association Quarterly.* Member of U.S. editorial board of *Children's Literature in Education,* beginning in 1973, and of *Lion and the Unicorn,* beginning in 1980.

■ Sidelights

As a child Milton Meltzer had little interest in his family's cultural origins and history. America of the 1920s offered many avenues for the young boy to explore—movies, radio, and dime novels to name a few. But as the carefree days of post-World War I society evaporated into widespread economic hardship during the Great Depression of the 1930s, Meltzer and his family struggled to survive. His experiences during this difficult era initiated his curiosity in his lineage and in the issue of basic human rights. As his interest grew, Meltzer began chronicling the histories of oppressed peoples. His comprehensive studies have earned him critical recognition as one of the country's most highly regarded authors of nonfiction books and biographies for both children and young adults.

Well-known for his works concerning the injustices that have and continue to afflict humankind, especially those common in America, Meltzer has written more than sixty comprehensive volumes on themes ranging from poverty, crime, peace, and the labor movement, to slavery, anti-semitism, and other forms of discrimination based on race, religion, or sex. His popular biographies have featured historical figures like nineteenth-century abolitionists and social reformers Lydia Maria Child, Samuel

Gridley Howe, and Thaddeus Stevens, as well as twentieth-century women's rights reformers Margaret Sanger and Betty Friedan. Meltzer is often praised by reviewers for the respect he shows his young readers through the tone of his narratives, and he is frequently lauded for his honest and sensitive presentation of uncomfortable history.

"In each of his books, Meltzer shows a piece of the world and allows the reader to enter it and experience both the devastation of injustice and the heroism of those who battle it," surmised Judith Weedman in an article for *Children's Literature Association Quarterly.* "In all his work, Meltzer draws for us a picture of individuals and groups acting out their values, influencing events, and in turn being affected by the events taking place around them. The person who reads his books sees a world in which ethical decisions are of the utmost importance. The experience of history and the present through Milton Meltzer's eyes allows readers to take that step aside from self and in so doing to expand their worlds."

Meltzer's interest in social reform took root during his childhood, although he was unaware of its occurrence. His experiences as a first-generation American in the 1920s and 1930s and his circumstances during the Great Depression greatly influenced his attitudes and later work. Meltzer was born in an era when scores of people left Eastern Europe, relocating to the United States full of hope that they could make better lives for themselves in the West. As multitudes of foreigners entered America's shores, the nation was dubbed a vast "melting pot." The majority, however, arrived in America poor—the expense of resettling exhausted what little money these immigrants had worked years to save in order to make the journey. Primarily moving into urban areas, these foreigners sought jobs in factories. Most were optimistic that they could find prosperity through hard, honest work.

Among the thousands of immigrants from the Austro-Hungarian Empire were Meltzer's parents, Benjamin Meltzer and Mary Richter, as well as parts of their respective families. Both journeyed to America around the turn of the century, meeting for the first time in New York City. After a brief courtship, they married and eventually had three sons. Meltzer was the middle child, born May 8, 1915, in Worcester, Massachusetts. The family had moved further east prior to Meltzer's birth because Benjamin heard that jobs for window cleaners were available. He was eager to obtain such

The first of Meltzer's many histories of oppressed people, *A Pictorial History of Black Americans*, was originally published just before the civil rights movement in 1956.

Meltzer utilizes his own recollections along with the personal accounts of children to explain the Jewish Holocaust in this award-winning 1976 work.

employment, as little training was needed to enter the trade.

Many immigrants felt the need to shed their ethnicity and assimilate into American society as quickly as possible. Meltzer's parents shared this notion and strongly encouraged the Americanization of their children. "I was born during World War One—the war to end all wars, the war to make the world safe for democracy," Meltzer told readers of *Catholic Library World*. "A sign of how my parents felt . . . is a yellowed photograph I still have. It shows my older brother and me, runts trying to stand tall in [U.S.] army uniforms, with campaigner's hats on, and each of us clutching not a gun but a small American flag." Meltzer has theorized in autobiographical accounts that his parents' endeavors to conform were probably linked to a desire to fit into their new surroundings, as immigrants were frequently ridiculed because of their foreign customs and languages. The

Meltzers also spoke very little Yiddish and rarely commented on their pasts in Eastern Europe—a fact Meltzer believes may be the result of his parents' need to forget their former lives or his own initial lack of interest in his heritage.

The necessity to cast aside ethnicity was also stressed in the classroom. School administrators and teachers "were hell-bent on Americanizing us," Meltzer explained in an essay for *Something about the Author Autobiographical Series (SAAS)*. "A great many of the students were first-generation Americans like me. Yet implicit in the way we were taught was the belief that we should drop whatever made us different, forget where our parents came from, what they brought with them, their own feelings and experience, their own beliefs and values. Our job was to become one hundred percent Americans. That was the only way to make it here, we understood. So while I diligently studied the history of ancient Greece and Rome (and enjoyed it!), I learned nothing about the Eastern Europe where my roots lay. I identified far more with England; that was the literature and the history we studied. Anglo-Saxon culture was everything; where we came from was nothing."

In *SAAS* Meltzer recalls that anti-semitism, which was prevalent in Austria-Hungary, was also present in America. Although the Meltzers were Jewish, they were not strict adherents to the faith. Of his limited early exposure to his heritage, he wrote: "I learned what it was to be a Jew mostly in the negative sense: the insults voiced, the jobs denied, the neighborhoods restricted, the club doors closed, the colleges on quotas. And our history as Jews—anniversaries of catastrophes, expulsions, wholesale murder. No wonder an alarm bell rang when I heard the word 'Jew' in an unexpected setting. . . . When we studied Walter Scott's *Ivanhoe* in school I was captivated by the marvelous story he told. But jolted by his many references to Jews as usurers, liars, hypocrites, as covetous, contemptible, inhuman. Most readers remember his sympathetic portrayal of Rebecca, and forget the rest."

Nevertheless, Meltzer developed a deep love for reading in his teenage years. He worked a variety of odd jobs to help his family with finances—such as delivering newspapers and milk—and was allowed to keep a small portion of his earnings, which he used to purchase nickel and dime novels. He especially enjoyed the tales of Frank Merriwell, Nick Carter, Horatio Alger, and Deadwood Dick. "What I liked most were adventure stories that took me out of my skin," the author explained in a

Children's Book Council bulletin. "And biographies. I was always trying on a new hero for size—explorer, tennis star, reporter, detective."

As a result, Meltzer frequented the library on Saturdays, combing the shelves for new books to devour. Then he would escape into the movies, following the jungle escapades of Tarzan, the slapstick comedy of Charlie Chaplin, and the suspense-filled adventures of serial queen Pearl White. Meltzer, like his father, enjoyed radio, especially the comedic routines of Jack Benny, Ed Wynn, and Lou Holtz. He also delighted in reading the newspaper, which often contained stories of exotic lands and amazing human endeavors. He was fascinated by comic strips, particularly one called *Gasoline Alley.*

But the excitement of novels, movies, radio, and comics paled following the stock market crash of October, 1929—a disaster which plummeted the nation into the worst economic depression in its history. The Great Depression, as it came to be called, lasted well into the 1930s and was compounded by severe drought. For many, work and food were scarce. Some schools and once-thriving businesses closed. The numbers of homeless people soared to tremendous heights, and breadlines became a common sight. The destitute constructed small shacks of scrap materials such as tar paper, cardboard, and tin cans. Many of these shelters were built together in communities, named "Hoovervilles" after then-president Herbert Hoover. As poverty increased, optimism waned. In the early years of the Depression, the government did not offer much in the way of relief. Many impoverished people had to rely on donations from private citizens to survive.

Meltzer later chronicled these hard times in books like *Brother, Can You Spare a Dime? The Great Depression, 1929-1933* and *Violins and Shovels: The WPA Arts Projects.* He described the impact of the Depression on his family in the latter work: "The stock market crash in the fall of 1929 was no signal of disaster to the family of a window cleaner. My father washed the windows of factories, stores, offices, and homes. Their owners held some of the stocks that tumbled so disastrously—$26 billion—in the first month of the Depression. But we owned no stocks and didn't even know what they were. All we owned were our clothes and the furniture of the tenement we lived in. Our family did not 'go broke' in the Depression. We started broke."

His recollections about others in Worcester during the Depression include numerous instances of suicide, the mayor's attempt to offer more relief to the destitute by cutting his staff's pay, and desperate robberies for bare necessities such as bread and milk. Meltzer, himself, wondered if he would be able to finish his education. During Meltzer's senior year of high school, many Worcester students feared that their schools would close because the funds needed to pay teachers were running low. Meltzer was able to graduate, however, and accepted a full scholarship to an experimental teachers' college at Columbia University in New York City. He secured a job in exchange for meals and received a meager allowance from his father. Less than a year after Meltzer began college, Franklin Delano Roosevelt took over the presidency of the United States and promised government-sponsored relief—part of the complex policy which he called the "New Deal."

The FDR Administration devised a number of relief measures, including public works projects, which offered jobs to those in need. Meltzer would later obtain such employment. Times were still bleak, but began to improve slowly. During his sophomore year of college, Meltzer returned to Worcester to work in a factory for one year. He took the position in order to fulfill part of his degree requirements. As Meltzer continued college, he hoped for a career as a writer when an essay of his was published in a magazine. He also became interested in the labor movement and unions after a group tried to organize at Columbia. On campus, the current political scene was hotly debated. Some students supported FDR's programs, while others looked to communism, socialism, or ultra-conservatism. Meltzer, himself, advocated pacifism and participated in "No More War" rallies and parades.

During his senior year at Columbia, Meltzer became more and more aware of the odds against finding a teaching job after graduation. Making a difficult decision, he dropped out of school to seek other employment. Meanwhile, his father died of cancer at age fifty-seven. Meltzer, unable to find a job, applied for relief and received $5.50 biweekly, plus $3 per week for rent. Within several months, Meltzer obtained a position as a staff publicity writer with the government-sponsored Federal Theatre Project of the Works Projects Administration (WPA).

"I spent over three years in that job, the first decent one I ever had," explained Meltzer in *SAAS.* "And one that did more good than most jobs people find themselves in because they have to make a living somehow. The New Deal [one of

Roosevelt's relief measures] not only provided work for thousands of unemployed people in the arts, it also satisfied the hunger of America's millions for plays, books, music, art. It was a revolutionary idea, to decide that concertos, poems, novels, sculpture, paintings were not just luxuries for the rich to enjoy, but a vital part of popular education and culture. I was glad to be part of that great enterprise, and I look back proudly on those years. Long after, I worked that personal experience into a book I wrote called *Violins and Shovels: The WPA Arts Projects.*"

Often criticized by the press, the WPA budget was periodically cut by Congress. As a result, Meltzer and others lost their jobs, picketed, and were subsequently rehired again and again. His unpredictable job status rekindled his fascination with labor and unions. He eventually pursued that interest in books like *Bread—and Roses: The Struggle of American Labor, 1865-1915.* His belief in pacifism was tested in the mid-1930s with the onset of the Spanish Civil War—a three-year conflict which pitted the newborn Spanish Republic against General Francisco Franco's forces backed by German fuhrer Adolf Hitler and Italian dictator Benito Mussolini. He later explored the subject of pacifism in his book *Ain't Gonna Study War No More: The Story of America's Peace-Seekers.*

As political unrest in Europe escalated and a second world war seemed inevitable, Congress abolished the Federal Theatre Project in 1939 and Meltzer lost his job. Certain he would be drafted into the armed services in the event of war, Meltzer decided to wait to find other employment. Instead, he set out with two friends on a car tour of the United States, only to return home after Hitler began World War II in Poland. Once back in New York, Meltzer met his future wife, Hilda Balinky, on a blind date. He worked various journalistic jobs while awaiting the draft—the United States did not officially enter the conflict until December 7, 1941, when its naval base at Pearl Harbor in Hawaii was bombed by the Japanese Air Force in a surprise attack. Meltzer, meanwhile, married Balinky in June, 1941. In August of the following year, he was drafted into the U.S. Army Air Force.

"I went into the Air Force, a 27-year-old now, and called an old man by my barracks mates, most of them 18 or 19," Meltzer noted in *Catholic Library World.* "I spent 42 months in the control tower, helping to train fighter and bomber pilots." Meltzer's service spanned some three-and-a-half years in places such as Arkansas and Alabama. During his stint with the Air Force he wrote for service

newspapers and lectured on democracy. Meanwhile, his wife gave birth to a daughter, Jane.

After his discharge from service, Meltzer worked for CBS radio on a documentary show about the problems soldiers faced after their return from war. He then began a series of jobs with public relations firms. Some time after the birth of his second daughter Amy, Meltzer decided to expand his career in his spare time with a book of nonfiction. He began the book, in part, because he wanted to leave behind something permanent in the world. "Writing was my way to make a living," he told Geraldine DeLuca and Roni Natov in *The Lion and the Unicorn.* "But I didn't think of writing a book until I got to that perilous time when I was nearing forty. Nothing is more ephemeral than yesterday's newspapers or last week's magazine and I began to wonder whether anything I did would last, even a little while. I came up with the idea for my first book, the *Pictorial History of [the Negro in America]*, which I did with Langston Hughes. It appeared in 1956, just ahead of the public attention to civil rights issues."

Meltzer attempted to assemble the comprehensive volume alone but felt uncomfortable with the project, because he was a novice at writing books and was not black himself. His concerns led him to approach acclaimed black poet and writer Hughes about a collaborative effort, and the pair subsequently established a friendship that lasted until the poet's death in 1967. Meltzer continued to explore black history and racism in a number of books published in the 1960s, including the three-volume *In Their Own Words: A History of the American Negro; Time of Trial, Time of Hope: The Negro in America, 1919-1941*; and *Black Magic: A Pictorial History of the Negro in American Entertainment* (in collaboration with Langston Hughes). *In Their Own Words: A History of the American Negro* signalled the start of a trend for Meltzer, who went on to describe the histories of other minorities through the personal experiences they voiced themselves. Meltzer's work won the Thomas Alva Edison Mass Media Award—the first of many honors to follow for his books.

"Many of my books have had something to say about minorities in American life," Meltzer said in an essay for *Children's Literature in Education.* "They deal with that question which is at the heart of our history—racism. More and more of us are now coming to see the centrality of racism in the United States. The black experience is what it is because of white racism." He continued: "My aim [with *In Their Own Words: A History of the*

American Negro] was twofold: to help the reader understand what blacks felt, thought, and did, and to make whites see themselves in the light blacks had seen them, down through the centuries of racism."

Generally, Meltzer's early volumes on black history were praised by reviewers as coherent, powerful, and exciting. In a review of *In Their Own Words: A History of the American Negro* for *New York Times Book Review*, Donald Barr deemed there was "no better book for awakening and informing" children about the issue of black rights. Zena Sutherland and May Hill Arbuthnot echoed Barr's sentiment in their review of Meltzer's history for *Children and Books.* "The three books are an excellent source of information on what living conditions have been for black people through American history." *Black Magic,* in turn, was called "an impressive and comprehensive chronicle," by Gilbert Chase in *Quarterly Journal of The Music Library Association.*

Meltzer also began writing biographies early in his career as an author. His first subjects were nineteenth-century writers like Mark Twain and Henry David Thoreau. After several books for adults, he turned to writing for children at the suggestion of one of his daughters and has continued this type of work throughout his career. Among his first books for young readers were biographies of nineteenth-century abolitionists and social reformers Samuel Gridley Howe, Lydia Maria Child, and Thaddeus Stevens.

"My first children's book, the life of Samuel Gridley Howe, . . . came from two things," Meltzer told DeLuca and Natov. "It developed out of my earlier work on the *Pictorial History of [the Negro in America].* That research revealed a vast untapped field of source material. There were thousands of marvelous people in our history, black and white abolitionists whom people knew nothing about." Meltzer added that the publisher asked for a second biography after the Howe book proved successful, and he suggested a book on Child. "And that's how it began," he recalled.

Critical response to his early biographies was positive. His books on Howe and Child—*A Light in the Dark: The Life of Samuel Gridley Howe* and *Tongue of the Flame: The Life of Lydia Maria Child*—are "imbued with enthusiasm for the causes to which the subjects were dedicated," wrote Sutherland and Arbuthnot. Sophia B. Mehrer in *School Library Journal* also noted the importance of Meltzer's biographies in light of the then-

present civil rights movement, calling the Child book "timely and exciting."

As Meltzer continued his writings, he also garnered critical praise for his narrative style, which related events and other information from the perspective of "ordinary" people. "I decided not to use the traditional approach of the historian," he explained in *Children's Literature in Education.* Historians usually tell "what the King, the President, the General did, the men who ruled. But what about the people on the bottom? How did the strange new land look to kidnapped Africans carried in chains across the Atlantic? What was life like for the slave picking cotton or cutting cane? For the despised free black living on the fringe of a slave society? For the preacher plotting an uprising in the piney woods? For the mother standing with her child on the auction block? For the fugitive hiding in the swamps?"

The hardships facing Chinese immigrants and their succeeding generations are honestly and sensitively presented in another of Meltzer's histories.

The author also established a solid reputation for effectively incorporating eyewitness accounts and personal documents, such as diaries, letters, and speeches, into his work. "The use of original sources ... is a giant step up and out of the textbook swamp," wrote Meltzer in *School Library Journal.* "Working with the living expression of an era ... you get close to reliving those experiences yourself. And the challenge of discovering a pattern in them and the meaning they held for millions who lived those lives, is endlessly exciting." He said that recording history through the words of those who lived through a specific event or era helps children understand what is needed to "make this a freer and more peaceful world."

Of such books for children, Mary Ann Heffernan noted in the *Dictionary of Literary Biography* (*DLB*): "Meltzer sees an immense need for intriguing historical documentation for children because there is so little outside of the textbook genre for them to read; he feels textbook treatment of history often does little for the imagination or interest of the student." She added that Meltzer carefully presents his case, providing information to both instruct and intrigue "without overly glorifying the struggle of the oppressed." Although "his first concern is to plant seeds in an inquisitive mind by establishing a scenario from which to expand his issue," Heffernan continued, "his conclusions often explore the ways in which the problem at hand can be rectified, or offer an evaluation of the positive aspects of the social reformer he is portraying. Often in his conclusions Meltzer does not hesitate to involve the reader as a responsible agent for social change."

Writing histories of the oppressed and their struggle to overcome adversity was not Meltzer's aim when he began his career as an author. He told DeLuca and Natov that he concentrated on subjects of personal interest, hoping to bring new insights to his readers. Focusing on social reform and its crusaders was "something I wasn't aware I was doing initially," Meltzer asserted. "It wasn't until some ten books had been published that one reviewer observed that I was known for my books dealing with social issues, with the necessity for social change, and that I always took the side of the underdog. That's when it dawned on me it was what I had been doing, without any conscious plan."

Of his biographies, which have mainly featured people who have tried to reverse unfair treatment and practices, Meltzer told *SAAS:* "All these people share one quality: they never say there is

nothing they can do about an injustice or a wrong they encounter. They are not victims of apathy, that state people get themselves into when they believe there's no way to change things. My subjects choose action.... Action takes commitment, the commitment of dedicated, optimistic individuals. Our American past is full of examples of people like these who tried to shape their own lives."

Furthering his study of the black experience with a biography about his friend Langston Hughes, which appeared after the poet's death, Meltzer resigned from editorship of a medical publication in 1968 to concentrate on writing books. He followed with *Freedom Comes to Mississippi: The Story of Reconstruction; Slavery: From the Rise of Western Civilization to the Renaissance; Slavery: From the Renaissance to Today;* and *To Change the World: A Picture History of Reconstruction.* He also found time to lecture and prepare scripts for radio and television documentaries based on some of his books. In addition, he ventured into historical fiction with *Underground Man,* a book which uses the issue of slavery to show a young man's awakening to social reform in the first half of the nineteenth century. Charting the life of Northern farmer Joshua Bowen, the work follows the character as he helps slaves escape via the Underground Railroad and is subsequently imprisoned.

"The question of means and ends is always deeply troubling," Meltzer explained in *Children's Literature in Education.* "Many times during the 1960s I was struck by the parallel between the decisions faced by the young civil rights activists in the South and the choices confronting the abolitionists of more than a hundred years ago. I took my first foray into fiction with this parallel in mind. The political and ethical issues that troubled Joshua Bowen ... are those troubling today's youth. When if ever is one justified in deliberately breaking the law? Is it right for an abolitionist to use violence in helping slaves escape bondage?.... What do you do when you are so wearied by an unending struggle for justice that you want to give it up?"

A number of critics lauded Meltzer for incorporating period slave songs, advertisements, and narratives into *Underground Man.* His inclusion of various accounts from the era creates a story that is "consistently suspenseful as well as historically accurate," explained a critic in *Kirkus Reviews.* The "fine novel" captures the times with "authority and ease," declared Barbara Ritchie of *New York Times Book Review,* adding that the author provides "an extra measure for the thoughtful who read between the lines."

The themes of women's rights and the achievements of notable women have also been explored in Meltzer's writings. In addition to the Lydia Maria Child book in 1965, Meltzer wrote about the work of birth control movement founder Margaret Sanger in 1969. He furthered his study of prominent women with his adult biography of twentieth-century photographer Dorothea Lange in 1978. He followed with four books in Viking's "Women of Our Time" series, including a second book on Lange, and biographies of twentieth-century activists and civil rights reformers Betty Friedan, Winnie Mandela, and Mary McLeod Bethune.

In the meantime, he also edited the "Women of America" series for Crowell, which featured notable women who had been previously ignored by biographers. "We wanted to find subjects who had, for the most part, never been treated before but who were just as important as those who had been," explained Meltzer to DeLuca and Natov. "Women generally have been so grossly neglected that if we did do a subject who had been written about before, we would only do it if, in our considered opinion, the previous biographer had done a bad job."

The lack of adequate coverage in textbooks, coupled with his interest in his ancestry, prompted Meltzer to branch out in the 1970s and write various books about Jewish history. His first attempts, all issued in 1974, were *Remember the Days: A Short History of the Jewish American*, *World of Our Fathers: The Jews of Eastern Europe*, and *Taking Root: Jewish Immigrants in America*. He followed up these works with the multi-award-winning *Never to Forget: The Jews of the Holocaust* in 1976. "Why did I want to write it?," Meltzer considered in *Children's Literature in Education*. "The impulse came from a pamphlet reporting a study of American high school textbooks, which found that racism, anti-Semitism, and the Holocaust were either ignored in these influential books or dismissed in a few brief lines. Nor were college textbooks much better. It was appalling to realize that as far as young people's books were concerned, nothing of great consequence had happened."

Meltzer had difficulty starting *Never to Forget*, a book that deals with the genocide of more than six million Jews at the hands of German fuhrer Adolf Hitler and the Nazis during World War II. Recalling some of the anti-semitism he observed during

A pacifist himself, Meltzer fills a gap in history textbooks by chronicling the history of anti-war movements and their leaders in this 1985 work.

the era, he began the work with his first remembrance of the Nazis' brand of anti-semitism: "I was fifteen years old when I first noticed the strange words 'Nazi' and 'Hitler' in the newspaper.... I used to read the papers, but not very thoroughly. Sports, the funnies, stories about local people, rarely any foreign news. But on this day something caught my eye in a report datelined from Germany. A hundred-odd members of Adolf Hitler's Nazi party had just been elected to the German legislature ... and they had shown up for the first session wearing brown uniforms and shouting, 'Deutschland erwache! Jude verrecke!' The paper obligingly explained what those foreign words meant: Germany awake! Jew perish!"

Throughout the book Meltzer employs personal accounts, especially testimony of children, to explain concepts and themes. While his overall goal was to fill a void in children's literature about the Holocaust, he hoped to explain how humanity

Published in 1990, *Crime in America* explores the ethical and moral dilemmas youths have faced in the past and those they are facing today.

could execute such a vast atrocity. "Could we learn enough from it to be able to predict its repetition in the future?" Meltzer queried in *Children's Literature in Education.* "Not, I think, where it might happen, or when, or to whom, but only that it *could* happen again. And, I am afraid I have to say, that it is all the more likely to happen again because it has *already* happened."

The critical response to *Never to Forget* was overwhelming. "Meltzer's book is an act of desperation—an act of piety and pity, wrath and love, despair and homage; but the motive force, the terrible sense of urgency which drives and animates it, is desperation," asserted Saul Maloff in *New York Times Book Review.* Calling the book "deeply felt and trenchantly written," he concluded that *Never to Forget* "is an act of mourning and a

call to remember. For our own souls' sake it is indispensable." In a review for *Interracial Books for Children Bulletin* Lyla Hoffman agreed that *Never to Forget* is an "excellent book." She added that the work will help children "gain a greater understanding of history, of racism and of individual responsibility."

Completing more award-winning books in the 1980s on black and Jewish history, Meltzer also looked at the experiences of other minorities in the United States in works like *The Chinese Americans* and *The Hispanic Americans.* He also furthered his study of abolitionist Child by heading a team that assembled and edited her letters under a grant from the National Historical Publications and Records Commission. His other works during this time concerned the white supremacist terrorism of the Ku Klux Klan and "in their own words" treatments of both the American Revolution and the Civil War.

He also published the much-honored *Ain't Gonna Study War No More: The Story of America's Peace-Seekers* in 1985. Charting the role of pacifists from the Revolutionary War-era to the present day, the book highlights anti-war movements and their crusaders. In an article for *Catholic Library World,* Meltzer noted that he wrote the work because so many history books focus mainly on war, primarily handling the subject in a positive manner. He felt the need to "begin correcting that imbalance."

Acknowledging that Meltzer's book sheds light on "startling facts unavailable in history textbooks," Cathi Edgerton in *Voice of Youth Advocates* praised the author's "clear, provocative interpretation," which "will disturb many, frighten some, inspire others." Lyla Hoffman in *Interracial Books for Children Bulletin* called *Ain't Gonna Study War No More* a "superb resource" and lauded the work as "illuminating, exciting and inspiring." "Meltzer is openly partisan," wrote Hazel Rochman in *Booklist,* adding that the book will likely "stimulate discussion" amongst its readership.

Another of Meltzer's works in the 1980s that received much critical praise was *Poverty in America.* The book delves into the causes of deprivation in the United States, the various forms that indigence takes, and the inadequate attempts made to combat it. "Meltzer has written a compelling brief advocating constructive change," explained a critic in *Kirkus Reviews.* Others found the book "well-written," "well-researched," and "compassionate." Told with "clarity and authority," *Poverty in America* "is a marvel of succinct writing," noted

Patty Campbell in *Wilson Library Journal*. Jane Campbell Thornton echoed in *School Library Journal* that the book "imparts a vast amount of information in a concise and precise form."

In the 1990s, Meltzer continues to offer works for young readers—books like *The Bill of Rights: How We Got It and What It Means, Crime in America, Thomas Jefferson: The Revolutionary Aristocrat, The Amazing Potato*, and *Lincoln: In His Own Words*. He has continued writing for children and young adults as he believes these audiences are often more receptive to the ideas and themes he explores. "Meltzer does not offer passive accounts of history for the sake of archival interest alone," said Heffernan in *DLB*. "His body of work presents the past with the intention of influencing the future."

"I try to make my readers understand that history isn't only what happens to us," Meltzer asserted in *SAAS*. "History is also what we *make* happen. Each of us. All of us. And history isn't only the kings and presidents and generals and superstars. If we search the records deep and wide enough we find ample evidence of what the anonymous, the obscure ones have done—and continue to do—to shape history, to make America realize its promise." But he warned in *Beyond Fact: Nonfiction for Children and Young People* that negative history often repeats itself. "The greatest sin is indifference," he concluded. "It is a sign of how dehumanized we have become. It is what can make us cogs in the machinery of destruction."

■ Works Cited

Barr, Donald, review of *In Their Own Words: A History of the American Negro, 1865-1916, New York Times Book Review*, January 23, 1966, p. 26.

Campbell, Patty, review of *Poverty in America, Wilson Library Journal*, April, 1987, p. 51.

Chase, Gilbert, review of *Black Magic: A Pictorial History of the Negro in American Entertainment, Quarterly Journal of the Music Library Association*, December, 1968, p. 244.

DeLuca, Geraldine, and Roni Natov, interview with Milton Meltzer, *The Lion and the Unicorn*, summer, 1980, pp. 95-107.

Edgerton, Cathi, review of *Ain't Gonna Study War No More: The Story of America's Peace-Seekers, Voice of Youth Advocates*, August, 1985, pp. 199-200.

Heffernan, Mary Ann, "Milton Meltzer," *Dictionary of Literary Biography*, Volume 61: *American Writers for Children since 1960: Poets, Illustrators, and Nonfiction Authors*, edited by Glenn E. Estes, Gale, 1987, pp. 214-223.

Hoffman, Lyla, review of *Ain't Gonna Study War No More: The Story of America's Peace-Seekers, Interracial Books for Children Bulletin*, Volume 16, number 4, 1985, p. 19.

Hoffman, Lyla, review of *Never to Forget: The Jews of the Holocaust, Interracial Books for Children Bulletin*, Volume 7, number 6, 1976, pp. 16-17.

Maloff, Saul, review of *Never to Forget: The Jews of the Holocaust, New York Times Book Review*, May 2, 1976, pp. 25, 42.

Mehrer, Sophia B., review of *Tongue of the Flame: The Life of Lydia Maria Child, School Library Journal*, May, 1965, p. 116.

Meltzer, Milton, "American Bicentennial Reading," *Children's Book Council*, 1975.

Meltzer, Milton, "Beyond Fact," *Beyond Fact: Nonfiction for Children and Young People*, compiled by Jo Carr, American Library Association, 1982.

Meltzer, Milton, "The Fractured Image: Distortions in Children's History Books," *School Library Journal*, October, 1968, pp. 107-111.

Meltzer, Milton, "Freedom and Peace: A Challenge," *Catholic Library World*, July-August, 1984, pp. 21-26.

Meltzer, Milton, "Milton Meltzer," *Something about the Author Autobiography Series*, Volume 1, Gale, 1986, pp. 203-221.

Meltzer, Milton, *Never to Forget: The Jews of the Holocaust*, Harper, 1976, p. xiii.

Meltzer, Milton, "The Possibilities of Nonfiction: A Writer's View," *Children's Literature in Education*, autumn, 1980, pp. 110-116.

Meltzer, Milton, *Violins and Shovels: The WPA Arts Projects*, Delacorte, 1976.

Meltzer, Milton, "Who's Neutral?," *Children's Literature in Education*, Volume 14, 1974, pp. 24-36.

Review of *Poverty in America, Kirkus Reviews*, July 1, 1986, pp. 1026-1027.

Review of *Underground Man, Kirkus Reviews*, November 15, 1972, p. 1313.

Ritchie, Barbara, review of *Underground Man, New York Times Book Review*, March 18, 1973, p. 12.

Rochman, Hazel, review of *Ain't Gonna Study War No More: The Story of America's Peace-Seekers, Booklist*, May 1, 1985, p. 1248.

Sutherland, Zena, and May Hill Arbuthnot, *Children and Books*, seventh edition, Scott, Foresman, 1986, pp. 467-68, 497.

Thornton, Jane Campbell, review of *Poverty in America*, *School Library Journal*, August, 1986, p. 104.

Weedman, Judith, "'A Step aside from Self': The Work of Milton Meltzer," *Children's Literature Association Quarterly*, Spring, 1985, pp. 41-42.

■ For More Information See

BOOKS

Carter, Betty, and Richard F. Abrahamson, *Nonfiction Books for Adults: From Delight to Wisdom*, Oryx, 1990.

Children's Literature Review, Volume 13, Gale, 1987.

Contemporary Literary Criticism, Volume 26, Gale, 1983.

Cullinan, Bernice E., with Mary K. Karrer and Arlene M. Pillar, *Literature and the Child*, Harcourt, 1981.

Donelson, Kenneth L., and Alleen P. Nilsen, *Literature for Today's Young Adults*, 3rd edition, Scott, Foresman, 1989.

Otten, Charlotte F., and Gary D. Schmidt, editors, *The Voice of the Narrator in Children's Literature: Insights from Writers and Critics*, Greenwood, 1989.

Something about the Author, Volume 50, Gale, 1988.

PERIODICALS

American Jewish Historical Quarterly, December, 1977.

American Scholar, winter, 1978-79.

Antioch Review, winter, 1979.

Best Sellers, January, 1975; August, 1976; February, 1980; February, 1984; July, 1985.

Black Books Bulletin, Volume 7, number 3, 1981.

Booklist, February 15, 1981; November 1, 1982; January 1, 1983; August, 1985; October 1, 1985; October 15, 1985.

Book World, January 21, 1968; February 2, 1969.

Bulletin of the Center for Children's Books, June, 1975; September, 1976; January, 1981; October, 1983; December, 1985; December, 1986.

Children's Book Review Service, June, 1974.

Children's Literature: Annual of the Modern Language Association Seminar on Children's Literature and The Children's Literature Association, Volume 4, 1975.

Curriculum Review, February, 1978.

English Journal, September, 1977.

Horn Book, October, 1972; December, 1972; February, 1975; April, 1975; June, 1976; August, 1982; October, 1982; January-February, 1986; April-March, 1987.

Interracial Books for Children Bulletin, Volume 10, number 6, 1979; Volume 12, number 1, 1981; Volume 14, numbers 1 and 2, 1983; Volume 17, number 2, 1986.

Kirkus Reviews, January 1, 1969; October 1, 1969; October 1, 1970; June 15, 1972; August 15, 1972; October 15, 1972; May 1, 1974; December 15, 1974; January 1, 1975; August 15, 1976; September 1, 1976; October 1, 1979; October 15, 1980; January 15, 1981; March 15, 1982; September 1, 1982; November 1, 1983; May 15, 1985.

Language Arts, March, 1981; November, 1985.

Library Journal, February 15, 1968; May 15, 1971; December 15, 1979.

Los Angeles Times Book Review, April 23, 1989.

Nation, June 3, 1968.

Negro Digest, February, 1968.

Negro History Bulletin, October, 1967.

New Directions for Women, November-December, 1984.

New Yorker, October 30, 1978.

New York Times, August 4, 1978.

New York Times Book Review, November 1, 1964; July 18, 1965; May 7, 1967; January 28, 1968; November 3, 1968; March 23, 1969; July 25, 1971; August 25, 1974; November 14, 1976; August 6, 1978; February 20, 1983.

Publishers Weekly, August 22, 1966; January 13, 1975; July 5, 1976; July 5, 1985; April 25, 1986; October 31, 1986; November 10, 1989.

Religious Studies Review, April, 1984.

Saturday Review, November 9, 1968.

School Library Journal, February, 1968; January, 1969; December, 1969; December, 1972; October, 1974; December, 1976; October, 1980; April, 1982; November, 1982; January, 1983; December, 1984; September, 1985; December, 1985; October, 1986; December, 1986.

Social Education, October, 1977.

Social Studies, November, 1968; March-April, 1985.

Washington Post Book World, September 24, 1978.

Western Historical Quarterly, October, 1975.

Young Adult Cooperative Book Review Group of Massachusetts, October, 1976.

—*Sketch by Kathleen J. Edgar*

Nicholasa Mohr

■ Personal

Born November 1, 1935, in New York, NY; daughter of Pedro and Nicolasa (Rivera) Golpe; married Irwin Mohr (a clinical child psychologist), October 5, 1957 (deceased); children: David, Jason. *Education:* Attended Art Students' League, 1953-56, Taller de Grafica, Mexico City, c. 1956, New School for Social Research, c. 1957, Brooklyn Museum of Art School, 1959-66, and Pratt Center for Contemporary Printmaking, 1966-69.

■ Addresses

Home—727 President St., Brooklyn, NY 11215.

■ Career

Fine arts painter in New York, California, Mexico, and Puerto Rico, 1952-62; printmaker in New York, Mexico, and Puerto Rico, 1963—; teacher in art schools in New York and New Jersey, 1967—. Art instructor, Art Center of Northern New Jersey, 1971-73; writer in residence, MacDowell Colony, Peterborough, NH, 1972, 1974, and 1976; artist in residence, New York City public schools, 1973-74; lecturer in Puerto Rican studies, State University of New York at Stony Brook, 1977; distinguished visiting professor at Queens College of the City University of New York, 1988-90; also visiting lecturer in creative writing for various educator, librarian, student, and community groups. Head creative writer and co-producer of videotape series *Aqui y Ahora* (title means "Here and Now"). Member of New Jersey State Council on the Arts; member of board of trustees, and consultant, of Young Filmmakers Foundation; consultant on bilingual media training for Young Filmmakers/Video Arts. *Member:* Authors Guild, Authors League of America.

■ Awards, Honors

Outstanding book award in juvenile fiction, *New York Times,* 1973, Jane Addams Children's Book Award, Jane Addams Peace Association, 1974, citation of merit for book jacket design, Society of Illustrators, 1974, and *School Library Journal's* "Best of the Best 1966-78" citation, all for *Nilda;* outstanding book award in teenage fiction, *New York Times,* 1975, best book award, *School Library Journal,* 1975, and National Book Award finalist for "most distinguished book in children's literature," 1976, all for *El Bronx Remembered;* best book award, *School Library Journal,* best book award in young adult literature, American Library Association, and Notable Trade Book Award, joint committee of National Council for the Social Studies and Children's Book Council, all 1977, all for *In Nueva York;* Notable Trade Book Award, joint committee of National Council for the Social Studies and Children's Book Council, 1980, and

American Book Award, Before Columbus Foundation, 1981, both for *Felita*; commendation from the Legislature of the State of New York, 1986, for *Rituals of Survival: A Woman's Portfolio*; honorary doctorate of letters, State University of New York at Albany, 1989.

■ Writings

JUVENILE

(And illustrator) *Nilda* (novel), Harper, 1973, 2nd edition, Arte Publico, 1986.
(And illustrator) *El Bronx Remembered: A Novella and Stories*, Harper, 1975, 2nd edition, Arte Publico, 1986.
In Nueva York (short stories), Dial, 1977.
(And illustrator) *Felita* (novel), Dial, 1979.
Going Home (novel; sequel to *Felita*), Dial, 1986.

OTHER

Rituals of Survival: A Women's Portfolio (adult fiction), Arte Publico, 1985.

Also author, with Ray Blanco, of *The Artist*, a screenplay. Contributor of stories to textbooks and anthologies, including *The Ethnic American Woman: Problems, Protests, Lifestyles*. Contributor of short stories to *Children's Digest*, *Scholastic Magazine*, and *Nuestro*. Member of board of contributing editors, *Nuestro*.

■ Work in Progress

A novel; a screenplay.

■ Sidelights

Nicholasa Mohr draws upon her own childhood and adolescence to create novels and short stories that offer realistic and uncompromising portraits of life in New York City's Puerto Rican barrio. Her first book, *Nilda*, for instance, contains many autobiographical elements as it presents the story of a young girl struggling to mature and succeed despite living with poverty and prejudice. Nilda's drive to become an artist mirrors Mohr's own career, which has taken her from creating noteworthy paintings and prints to writing critically acclaimed novels and stories.

Mohr was born to Puerto Rican parents who had moved to New York City during the Depression. She was the youngest child and only girl, so "growing up in a household with six older brothers, and being part of a family who still held old-fashioned Puerto Rican concepts about the male and female role, was often a struggle for me,"

Mohr related in her *Something about the Author Autobiography Series (SAAS)* essay. She was expected to help more with the housework, and had less freedom to go out with friends. She spent much of her time at home, and occupied herself by drawing and painting.

Art had been an important part of Mohr's life ever since she was a young child. "From the moment my mother handed me some scrap paper, a pencil, and a few crayons, I discovered that by making pictures and writing letters I could create my own world . . . like 'magic,'" Mohr related in *SAAS*. "In the small crowded apartment I shared with my large family, making 'magic' permitted me all the space, freedom, and adventure that my imagination could handle." Mohr's artistic talents also made her stand out in school, where teachers and

Nilda, which Mohr wrote and illustrated, relates a young Puerto Rican girl's determination to become an artist despite the poverty and prejudice she encounters in New York City's barrio.

classmates would admire her drawings—even if some of them were otherwise prejudiced against her because she was Hispanic.

Drawing and painting comforted Mohr when times were difficult. Her father had died when she was only eight, and her mother struggled to support the family even though she was often ill. Her determination to provide for her children and her frequent words of encouragement to her daughter motivated Mohr. She died before Mohr started high school, however, and the young artist was left with an aunt who was distant and concerned more with her own family than with caring for her orphaned niece. Despite this lack of support, Mohr continued excelling in her artistic studies, inspired by her mother's instructions to keep a close hold on her talent: "My mother, who died in poverty, managed to leave me a rich legacy," the artist related in her *SAAS* entry. This legacy gave Mohr "the strength to continue to follow my own star, even under the worst of circumstances."

A guidance counselor's prejudice almost thwarted Mohr's further education. It was time to select which one of New York City's specialized high schools might best serve Mohr, and her counselor decided that a Puerto Rican girl didn't need an academic education. Although she was one of the most talented artists in her class, Mohr was selected to attend trade school to learn sewing skills. "I remember pleading with [the counselor] to let me at least apply to a better high school," the author recalled in *SAAS*. "Her response was that Puerto Rican women were by nature good seamstresses. Therefore, I should follow a natural career and be able to earn a living after graduation." Mohr was lucky and found a school that had a major in fashion illustration; there she was at least able to practice drawing, although she found the repetitious nature of illustrating fashion designs tedious.

After graduation, Mohr attended the Arts Students' League in New York City, where she could study painting and drawing in earnest. Working her way through art school, Mohr intended to save enough money to eventually study art in Europe. But her reading in the local library had drawn her to the work of Mexican muralists and artists such as Diego Rivera, Jose Clemente Orozco, and Frida Kahlo. By the time she had enough money to study abroad, she decided to go to Mexico City. There she saw firsthand the strong, powerful artwork which had impressed her, especially in the way the paintings made strong personal and political statements without using propaganda. "In a profound way their work spoke to me and my experiences as a

Mohr discusses such controversial topics as teenage pregnancy and homosexuality in this 1975 award-winning collection of short stories.

Puerto Rican woman born in New York," the artist said in her autobiographical essay. "The impact was to shape and form the direction of all my future work."

After returning to New York, Mohr entered classes at the New School for Social Research, where she met her future husband. She continued polishing her extremely revealing, almost story-like, artistic style. "My experiences were developed in my work," Mohr explained to Paul Janeczko in *From Writers to Students*. "You could see them in my figurative work and the way I use colors. Sometimes I told a story through the visual interpretation and, hopefully, evoked feelings from the viewer." The artist elaborated in her *SAAS* entry: "Instead of just rendering literal scenes ... or becoming aesthetically abstract and interpreting my mastery of techniques, my prints and painting were filled with bold figures, faces, and various symbols of the city. These symbols were numbers, letters, words, and phrases ... a kind of graffiti.''

The graffiti-like elements of Mohr's art especially appealed to one of her collectors, a publishing executive. Through Mohr's art agent, he asked if she would be willing to try her hand at writing. The artist was reluctant at first, but her agent soon convinced her that a story of a young Puerto Rican girl could fill a gap in children's literature. "When I was growing up, I'd enjoyed reading about the adventures of many boys and girls, but I had never really seen myself, my brothers, and my family in those books," she wrote in her essay. "We just were not there.... Finally, I agreed to write fifty pages of short stories doing the best I could."

Through hard work and perseverance Mohr produced several stories based on her childhood experiences in the barrio. Much to her disappointment and puzzlement, the publisher turned them down. Her agent explained that because there were no tales of gangs, sex, drugs, and crime, the

Mohr's 1979 story features a young Puerto Rican girl who must adjust to a new neighborhood and the problems she faces there.

work didn't seem to be genuine. Mohr was angered by his stereotyping, as she related in her *SAAS* essay: "I knew then that I did not exist for him as the person I really was, but rather as the model for a Puerto Rican female protagonist who would be featured in a sensational book that he fantasized would net us a fortune." Disillusioned, Mohr put her manuscript aside and returned to her artwork.

A short time after, however, Mohr met an editor who agreed to review her stories even though she was more interested in Mohr as an illustrator. The editor soon offered Mohr a contract, and the artist set out to write her first novel. Accompanied by eight illustrations and a jacket by the author, *Nilda* was published in 1973 and gave Mohr a new perspective on her creativity. "It was almost like a catharsis, the first book," Mohr told Janeczko. "I was even thinking of going into sculpture, but all of a sudden I found a medium where I was really comfortable. I could draw a picture with words, and it was extremely stimulating and eye-opening.... Everything I [had] done as an artist [was] transferable to a new craft."

In *Nilda*, the author portrays a Puerto Rican girl as she grows from a child to a teenager during the years of World War II. At home, young Nilda is faced with her family's struggle to survive poverty, while outside that loving circle she is confronted with prejudice from teachers, social workers, police, and classmates. But the novel is not merely a catalog of the problems Nilda encounters; it also describes her experiences at a summer camp, her discovery of a secret garden, and the pleasure she finds in inventing stories and drawing pictures. The entire novel is related "through a child's vision—questioning, resigned, furious, joyful," Edith Blicksilver comments in *Biographical Directory of Hispanic Literature in the United States*. The result is "a powerful story of the hardships of being Puerto Rican and of the barriers facing women," Myra Pollack Sadker and David Miller Sadker state in *Now upon a Time*.

While many children's books have attempted to explore the problems of poor, minority children, *New York Times Book Review* contributor Marilyn Sachs observes that "few come up to 'Nilda' in describing the crushing humiliations of poverty and in peeling off the ethnic wrappings so that we can see the human child underneath." But Miguel A. Ortiz faults the book as undramatic, due to its superficial characters; Nilda "seems to be living through events which have no effect on her," he writes in *The Lion and the Unicorn*. Other reviewers, however, praise Mohr for her characterization;

Sachs notes that "what makes the book remarkable is the richness of detail and the aching sense of a child's feelings." "There is no pity here, for the author is too much aware of the humanity of her characters and of the other implications of pity to be in any way condescending," Donald B. Gibson comments in *Children's Literature. Nilda*, he concludes, is "what I would call a significant book, a touchstone by which others may be judged."

El Bronx Remembered, Mohr's second book, is a collection of stories set in Nilda's New York City neighborhood, after the war. The narratives vary from stories of teenagers dealing with death, prejudice, and feelings of embarrassment, to the tale of an elderly Jewish man who is befriended by a Puerto Rican family. *El Bronx Remembered* also contains such potentially controversial topics as teenage pregnancy and homosexuality; one story, "Herman and Alice," tells of the doomed marriage between a pregnant teenager and a older homosexual man. Despite such weighty topics, however, Mohr also shows the optimism and humor of the neighborhood, and "her stories focus upon the universal emotions of pride, nostalgia, hope, love, and fear with Chekovian narrative skill," Blicksilver writes.

"In her earlier outstanding novel *Nilda,* it was apparent that if any author could make you hear pulses beating from the pages, Nicholasa Mohr was the one," Sachs similarly remarks. "In *El Bronx Remembered,* she has done it again." The critic continues: "If there is any message at all in these stories, any underlying theme, it is that life goes on. But Nicholasa Mohr is more interested in people than in messages." The reviewer notes that the stories are without "complicated symbolism ..., trendy obscurity of meaning ... hopeless despair or militant ethnicity. Her people endure because they are people." "Much has been written about Spanish-speaking communities, but it its rare to find such delicate insight combined with such deliberate detail," Anne M. Flynn maintains in a *Best Sellers* review. "Miss Mohr has the ability to describe quite commonplace situations, dissect them, relate them to the reader, and then allow her interpretations to be savored." "At their best," Paul Heins notes in *Horn Book,* "the short Chekhov-like narratives reveal universal emotions hovering beneath an urban, ethnic casing." A critic for the *Bulletin of the Center for Children's Books* agrees, concluding that Mohr's characters "ring true, having both universality and the special quality of the vitality and warmth of the Puerto Rican community."

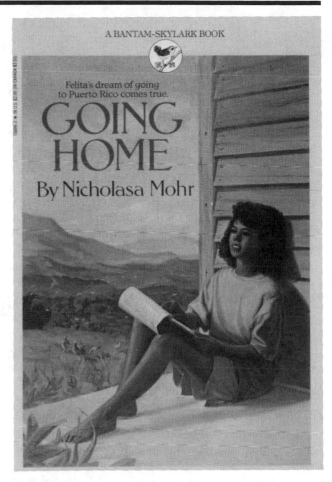

A BANTAM-SKYLARK BOOK

Felita's dream of going to Puerto Rico comes true.

GOING HOME
By Nicholasa Mohr

Felita, now eleven years old, deals with her first boyfriend and a trip to Puerto Rico in this 1986 sequel.

In Nueva York is similar to *El Bronx Remembered* in that it contains several stories and novellas set in the Puerto Rican neighborhoods of New York City. *In Nueva York,* however, features several recurring characters: Old Mary, a fiftyish woman whose search for a better life on the mainland often led to heartache; her sons, one of whom she hasn't seen since she left Puerto Rico; and a bedraggled alley cat. Mohr's characters have many problems, often battling "rats, dirt, junkies, street gangs, ruthless landlords, hostile building inspectors, greedy politicians, prejudiced teachers, and racist police," as Blicksilver summarizes. Nevertheless, the critic adds, "they are sustained through their crises by family and community support, by their religious faith, and by loving concern for their children. They do more than survive—they fight back."

In populating the neighborhood of *In Nueva York,* "Mohr creates a remarkably vivid tapestry of community life as well as of individual characters," Zena Sutherland writes in her *Bulletin of the Center for Children's Books* review. The critic adds:

"Tough, candid, and perceptive, the book has memorable characters, resilient and responsive, in a sharply-etched milieu." Georgess McHargue, however, faults the stories as "too obviously intended as slice-of-life fiction" with unrealistic characters, as she states in the *New York Times Book Review*. But because many individuals appear in more than one story, Aileen Pace Nilsen suggests in *English Journal*, "the effect is an intimate look into the most interesting parts of several people's lives without the artificial strain of having them all squeezed into a single plot." The result, she continues, is "an excellent book to help people see beyond the stereotypes." "Mohr's characters are warm and believable," Jack Forman similarly notes in *School Library Journal*, "and she succeeds admirably in involving readers in what happens to them."

Mohr turns to a younger audience in *Felita*, a novel about a young girl whose parents move to a more upscale area in hopes of providing a better life for their children. But Felita is unhappy in their new home; she misses her old friends, and prejudice intrudes when her new friends are kept away by their parents and her family is harassed by neighbors. When the family returns to the old neighborhood, Felita is happy again, but she must still confront problems with school and classmates. With the aid of her grandmother, Felita begins to readjust. "The episodic story is usually engaging," Denise M. Wilms writes in *Booklist*, "and Felita's presence is lively and strong."

Mohr continues Felita's story in the 1986 novel *Going Home*. Now eleven years old, Felita has her first boyfriend and is looking forward to a trip to Puerto Rico with her parents. These happy events have a down side, however, for her friends are jealous of Vinnie, her new sweetheart, and her vacation in Puerto Rico is marred by homesickness and the taunts of local children. Felita gradually makes friends, however, and by the time the summer is over she is sad to leave.

Going Home is "a charming sequel to the author's *Felita*," Sutherland claims in *Bulletin of the Center for Children's Books*. The author's narration "is colloquial and exuberant, and Mohr has a particularly sharp eye for the friendships (as well as the downright meanness) of pre-teen girls." As Wilms writes in another *Booklist* review, *Going Home* "is deftly written and lively—an enjoyable story for any reader." "Felita is a vivid, memorable character, well realized and well developed," Christine Behrmann remarks in *School Library Journal*. "It is a pleasure to welcome her back."

Although Mohr's works have enjoyed popularity with teenagers, "I don't write for young people, per se," she related to Janeczko. "I write for people. Some of them are young and some of them are old. I don't like this division that young people sort of have a place; they're people," the author continued. Nevertheless, she is pleased that her work appeals to younger readers, "because I feel that's part of life, that's part of being alive. But good writing is writing that someone picks up and says, 'Okay, I want to go on with this, not because it's for a teenager or adolescent, but because the writer is saying something that I want to get involved with."

Although Mohr found writing a way to heighten the artistic energies she had previously expressed through painting, she has no plans to abandon it for yet another creative outlet. "I see fiction as an art form which I don't see myself leaving," the author revealed to Janeczko. "As a writer I have used my abilities as a creative artist to strengthen my skills and at the same time in small measure have ventured to establish a voice for my ethnic American community and our children," Mohr explained in her *SAAS* essay. But more important to her is retaining that "magic" that using her imagination brought her as a young child—that ability her mother instructed her to hold on to at all costs. "Because of who I am," Mohr concluded, "I feel blessed by the work I do, for it permits me to use my talents and continue to 'make magic.' With this 'magic' I can recreate those deepest of personal memories as well as validate and celebrate my heritage and my future."

■ Works Cited

Behrmann, Christine, review of *Going Home*, *School Library Journal*, August, 1986, p. 105.

Blicksilver, Edith, "Nicholasa Mohr," *Biographical Directory of Hispanic Literature in the United States*, edited by Nicolas Kanellos, Greenwood Press, 1989, pp. 199-213.

Review of *El Bronx Remembered*, *Bulletin of the Center for Children's Books*, June, 1976, p. 161.

Flynn, Anne M., review of *El Bronx Remembered*, *Best Sellers*, December, 1975, p. 266.

Forman, Jack, review of *In Nueva York*, *School Library Journal*, April, 1977, p. 79.

Gibson, Donald B., "Fiction, Fantasy, and Ethnic Realities," *Children's Literature*, Volume 3, 1974, pp. 230-234.

Heins, Paul, review of *El Bronx Remembered*, *Horn Book*, February, 1976, p. 57.

Janeczko, Paul, interview with Nicholasa Mohr, in *From Writers to Students: The Pleasures and Pains of Writing*, edited by M. Jerry Weiss, International Reading Association, 1979, pp. 75-78.

McHargue, Georgess, review of *In Nueva York, New York Times Book Review*, May 22, 1977, p. 29.

Mohr, Nicholasa, *Something about the Author Autobiography Series*, Volume 8, Gale, 1989, pp. 185-194.

Nilsen, Aileen Pace, review of *In Nueva York, English Journal*, February, 1978, p. 100.

Ortiz, Miguel A., "The Politics of Poverty in Young Adult Literature," *The Lion and the Unicorn*, fall, 1978, pp. 6-15.

Sachs, Marilyn, review of *Nilda, New York Times Book Review*, November 4, 1973, pp. 27-28.

Sachs, Marilyn, review of *El Bronx Remembered, New York Times Book Review*, November 16, 1975.

Sadker, Myra Pollack, and David Miller Sadker, *Now upon a Time: A Contemporary View of Children's Literature*, Harper, 1977, pp. 210-230.

Sutherland, Zena, review of *In Nueva York, Bulletin of the Center for Children's Books*, July-August, 1977, p. 178.

Sutherland, Zena, review of *Going Home, Bulletin of the Center for Children's Books*, May, 1986, p. 178.

Wilms, Denise M., review of *Felita, Booklist*, December 1, 1979, p. 559.

Wilms, Denise M., review of *Going Home, Booklist*, July, 1986, p. 1615.

■ For More Information See

BOOKS

Children's Literature Review, Volume 22, Gale, 1991.

Contemporary Literary Criticism, Volume 12, Gale, 1980.

PERIODICALS

Horn Book, April, 1974.

Interracial Books for Children Bulletin, Volume 7, number 4, 1976.

Kirkus Reviews, October 1, 1973; September 1, 1975; April 1, 1977; February 1, 1980.

Newsweek, March 4, 1974.°

Ouida Sebestyen

■ Personal

Name is pronounced "WEE-da See-best-yen"; born February 13, 1924, in Vernon, TX; daughter of James Ethridge (a teacher) and Byrd Grey (a teacher; maiden name, Lantrip) Dockery; married Adam Sebestyen, December 22, 1960 (divorced, 1966); children: Corbin. *Education:* Attended University of Colorado. *Hobbies and other interests:* "Gardening, travel, hiking, all crafts, building new things and restoring old ones."

■ Addresses

Home and office—115 South 36th St., Boulder, CO 80303.

■ Career

Writer; lecturer. Worked variously at a training school for military pilots and as a day-care provider, housekeeper, gardener, seamstress, carpenter, mason, and handyperson.

■ Awards, Honors

Words by Heart was selected as one of the best books of the year by *New York Times* and *School Library Journal,* both 1979, named one of the best books for young adults and a notable children's book by American Library Association and a Library of Congress Children's Book, both 1979, and received International Reading Association Children's Book Award, 1980, and American Book Award, 1982; *Far from Home* was named one of the best books for young adults by American Library Association and one of the best books of the year by *School Library Journal,* both 1980, received American Book Award nomination and was a Child Study Association recommended title, both 1981, was included on William Allen White master list, 1982-83, and received Zilveren Griffel (Silver Pencil) Award, 1984; *IOU's* was named a National Council of Teachers of English Teacher's Choice-*Parents' Choice* Remarkable Book, and one of the best books for young adults by American Library Association, both 1982, was included on Child Study Children's Book Committee list, 1983, received Texas Institute of Letters Children's Book Award, 1983, and was a Mark Twain Award nominee, 1985; *The Girl in the Box* was nominated for the Colorado Blue Spruce Young Adult Award.

■ Writings

NOVELS FOR YOUNG ADULTS

Words by Heart, Little, Brown, 1979.
Far from Home, Little, Brown, 1980.
IOU's, Little, Brown, 1982.

On Fire, Atlantic, 1985.
The Girl in the Box, Little, Brown/Joy Street Books, 1988.

Some of Sebestyen's novels have been translated into French, Dutch, Japanese, Danish, Norwegian, Spanish, and Swedish.

OTHER

Contributor of stories to magazines and anthologies under pseudonym Igen Sebestyen.

■ Adaptations

Words by Heart was adapted as a dramatic special under the same title for PBS-TV, 1985; the program received two Emmy nominations.

■ Work in Progress

"A boy-and-dog novel for young adults"; a play.

■ Sidelights

Ouida Sebestyen is internationally known for her award-winning novels for young adults. Highly regarded as realistic and multi-dimensional, Sebestyen's works, which include *Words by Heart, On Fire, IOU's,* and *The Girl in the Box,* are appreciated for their convincingly drawn characters, thought-provoking themes, and touches of humor. Although her work is directed toward young adults, Sebestyen aspires to reach a broader audience. She told *Something about the Author (SATA)* that "I hope I write for readers of all ages, because I want to nourish the child's idealism and delight in life that we all have in us." The main characters in Sebestyen's novels are usually spirited teenagers who overcome barriers such as prejudice, poverty, and the death of loved ones on their road to maturity. Sebestyen also focuses on families, particularly on relationships between parents and children. In the *ALAN Review* Sebestyen reflected that she likes to express all the joys, difficulties, and responsibilities inherent in being a part of a family; for her, a family, or lack thereof, not only shapes the lives of young people but is full of dramatic potential: "Certainly every family is a world, teeming with life, symbiotic, ancient and futuristic, sending little spaceships out, first to visit grandma, then off to college, and finally out to people other colonies."

The author's own family encouraged creativity and provided inspiration for her successful novels. Her parents were both schoolteachers, and though she was an only child, she was surrounded by plenty of aunts, uncles, and cousins. She often spent summers at her Aunt Martha's busy Texas home. "One of my joys on those trips was to discover my aunts and mother reminiscing," Sebestyen noted in *Something about the Author Autobiography Series (SAAS).* "They peppered their talk with quotes from the Bible, Shakespeare, the English poets, old songs. Aunt Eula had been a promising artist before she detoured into her hard, lonely life on the farm. My quiet, withdrawn mother had a medal in oratory. Aunt Martha had dreams of being a writer.... I listened to them, storing the seeds [my novel] *Words by Heart* would come from." Sebestyen fondly recalled in *SAAS* how she and her cousins used to entertain themselves during those summers: "We would divide into two groups. One group would quickly make up a play, devise

After moving to an all-white neighborhood in 1910, twelve-year-old Lena faces injustice and racial prejudice yet chooses to live by the Christian values of her father in this award-winning novel.

costumes for it, and present it to the other group waiting out in the yard. Characters would pop from behind privet hedges and declaim from porch steps. Sometimes the drama got so enticing that both groups simply played it out to its conclusion, as fireflies and finally streetlamps lit the summer dark. It was magic, sheer magic that no amount of chigger and mosquito bites could diminish."

Sebestyen likens her memories of growing up in the farming community of Vernon, Texas, to a series of picture slides: she remembers sitting in a sunny kitchen eating toast, her first glimpse of mountains on a trip to Oklahoma, the anxiety that accompanied her first day of school, heating bath-water on the kitchen stove, the lean, dusty days of the Great Depression, the gardens her family planted in the vacant lot next to their house, watching a harvest moon rise over a ridge while picnicking, and performing in school plays. Such are the images Sebestyen recalls from her youth; she explained in *SAAS*, "Events that should have endured—birthdays and Christmases, momentous decisions and life-changing meetings—have curled up their toes and melted like the Wicked Witch of the West. (Or was it the East?—you see how my mind works.) Everyone of appropriate age, I'm told, remembers what he or she was doing when Pearl Harbor was bombed [during World War II] or [President John F.] Kennedy was shot. Not me."

Her memory of her love of books, however, is one that especially endures. "Oh those books!," she told *SAAS*. "It was almost worth the discomfort of catching every known childhood disease, including a nearly fatal bout of pneumonia, to be able to lie in bed and read, or be read to. . . . I still give secret thanks to the authors and illustrators who melted my bedroom walls and let in their worlds." When she read Sir Walter Scott's *Ivanhoe*, she recalled in *SAAS* being "so engrossed that I [ate] a large box of raisins without noticing." Her interest in writing also came early. Sebestyen remembers writing her first play when she was seven, adapting it from a story she found in a children's magazine. According to the author's article collected in *Innocence and Experience: Essays and Conversations on Children's Literature*, writing "seemed like reasonable work for a shy, delicate type. . . . I wrote little half-baked stories and plays in blank verse."

Although she liked books and earned good grades, Sebestyen disliked school. She worked on the school newspaper and was in the honor society, "but a photo of that group shows me squashed nearly sideways in a row of sturdier types. I was a misfit and loner who loved learning, but was intimidated by the process," she told *SAAS*. Nevertheless, Sebestyen recalls two memorable events from her high school years. "The first occurred as I was sitting in a long, empty corridor one day, acting as hall monitor and scribbling away as usual. I quietly and firmly decided that I would be a writer. . . . Surely it would be a wonderful way to spend a life. . . . Anywhere in the world, under any circumstances, at my very own pace, without a boss, I could unpack my toolbox of words and build books." She continued, "The second important event was making friends with a girl named Peggy who wrote poetry. . . . Knowing her made school easier to take." After their senior year of high school, Peggy and Sebestyen "had bright plans for writing The Great American Novel and wallowing in fame and fortune, preferably within a few months."

Although they had grand hopes, nothing went quite as planned. For a while other endeavors occupied the pair's time; during World War II Peggy worked at an airfield in Oklahoma and Sebestyen took a job at a training school for military pilots. The author would repair holes torn in planes, "work that seemed off-the-wall, patriotic, and enlarging enough for a budding writer," she told *SAAS*. "I loved every day of my years there—the rough men, the hard dirty work, the night shift, the contrasts." She and Peggy eventually wrote a novel together, and although it was rejected by publishers, Sebestyen recalled in *SAAS* that "we learned a lot, specifically that we weren't natural collaborators." Sebestyen, then twenty, wrote her own novel that was also never published. She continued writing, however, commenting in *SAAS* that "if I couldn't be an instant novelist, there was always The Theater. I remember adapting [French writer Guy de] Maupassant's 'Necklace' for our local radio station. . . . No one actually told me it was awful."

Theater continued to be an interest for Sebestyen; at one point she and Peggy attempted to start a production company in Vernon. Sebestyen recalled in *SAAS* that their venture was "funnier than a French farce." They did manage to put on one play with, as Sebestyen remembered, "a mismatched collection of stagehands, ham actors, and advice-givers." The pair also incorporated theater into their summer travels, joining the stage crew of the Shakespeare Festival in Colorado, where Sebestyen's father was pursuing his master's degree. Sebestyen enjoyed working backstage because, as she explained in *SAAS*, it "always rivals what is going on out front." She continued, "Our infatua-

Sebestyen's 1980 story about a young boy coming to terms with a father who refuses to acknowledge him was praised for its blend of humor and seriousness.

tion with plays and acting led us one summer to moviemaking country in Arizona. We got so adept at sneaking in to watch westerns being filmed on location in Sedona's dramatic red rocks that once we were practically powdering James Stewart's nose for a close-up before we were thrown out.''

During this time, Sebestyen continued to write and continued to receive discouraging rejections from publishers. But then came a glimmer of hope: she sold her first story to a women's magazine in 1950. "I couldn't believe it," she told *SAAS*. "I was really and truly a Published Author at last." Though two more of her stories were published, Sebestyen was headed for another long dry spell. Her spirits were buoyed, however, when a writer from New York wanted to adapt one of her stories as a television drama. Sebestyen went to New York to discuss the adaptation, and although the television play was never produced, she made friends who invited her to visit them in Iceland. "Girls from Vernon didn't do that in the '50s," she remarked in *SAAS*, "but I went."

She visited Ireland at the end of her Iceland trip and was so inspired by the country and its people that she sent a Dublin newspaper a thank-you note "to Ireland in general," she said in *SAAS*. When the note was published in the newspaper, Adam Sebestyen, a visiting Hungarian student, saw it and wrote her a letter. Their correspondence flowered into a romance; he moved to the United States and they were married in 1960. "Naturally we had mutual interests in music, art, literature, psychology, philosophy, travel," explained Sebestyen in *SAAS*, admitting that the way she and her husband met seemed straight out of a soap opera. The couple moved to California, where Ouida's retired parents eventually established themselves as well. After the Sebestyens built a house and settled in, the author began writing again, but the birth of her son, Corbin, the death of her father, and the subsequent breakup of her marriage provided yet more interruptions. In *SAAS* Sebestyen commented on her divorce from her Hungarian husband: "Budapest and Vernon, Texas, kept colliding.... When we began to hurt each other constantly with our opposing expectations, we knew our marriage had been a tragic mistake."

So Sebestyen, her mother, and Corbin moved to Boulder, Colorado. Sebestyen started a new novel while supporting her three-generation family by taking on a variety of odd jobs, from day-care to trimming bushes. She remembered in *SAAS:* "We were keeping a dear little girl named Lisa whose mother wanted to resume her teaching career. I took jobs at church nurseries, rocking babies and chasing terrible-twos, not knowing I was collecting mood and material for [the novel] *IOU's* years later. In it, Lisa has become a child called Yetta." While the novel she was working on at the time was never published, Sebestyen sold a story, her first in fifteen years. "It was about a young black girl who wins a contest for reciting Bible verses, and it was based on something my aunt Martha had remembered from her childhood," she explained. Sebestyen was painting the outside of her house when she learned that the story would be published; she wrote in *SAAS* that she was so excited that "I think I walked into the house without getting down from my ladder."

After that success, Sebestyen sold only two more stories, not enough, according to friends and family, to justify keeping odd jobs in favor of a permanent one. One friend, Sebestyen said in *SAAS*, told her that "it was not possible to make a living from something as chancy and competitive as writing fiction." Yet Sebestyen persisted, writing and doing odd jobs, her family barely squeaking by. She said in *Innocence and Experience:* "I wasn't about to give up just because I couldn't write!" Sebestyen admitted that this attitude was impractical, but writing, with its freedom, flexibility, and creative outlet, was what she most wanted to do. Failure was frustrating, but supported emotionally by her mother and son, Sebestyen kept her morale up with inspiring quotations tacked to her bulletin board. Her goal in writing, she noted in *Innocence and Experience*, was derived from a quote from American historian Will Durant: "To seek, beneath the universal strife, the hidden harmony of things." And a quotation by poet Henry Wadsworth Longfellow helped Sebestyen start the words flowing: "Give what you have. To some one it may be better than you dare to think."

Since she had failed at writing adult novels, poetry, plays, articles, and true confessions, Sebestyen opted for a new approach. She had not yet tried to write books for children, but she found she did not feel comfortable writing about their simple, fairy-tale world. Sebestyen recalled in *SAAS*, "The talking animals and retold tales and jolly nonsense left me feeling adult and exiled." She then began

reading books for young adults and remembered that "I came alive.... I didn't know all those skillful, pertinent, moving books were out there."

Sebestyen realized that she had already written a story with a young protagonist (the one about the Bible-verse contest) and sent it to a publishing company that had encouraged her in the past. The editor in the children's department of that company read Sebestyen's story and expressed interest in seeing a longer version. Sebestyen explained in *Innocence and Experience* that after years of frustrating rejections, the encouragement she received "absolutely electrified me. If she had asked me to write a sequel to [Leo Tolstoy's] *War and Peace*, I would have tried." So Sebestyen expanded her story to novel length. After weeks of waiting for a response to the book, titled *Words by Heart*, Sebestyen received a phone call from her editor. She recounted the call in *Innocence and Experience:* "A soft voice said, 'Did you know you've written a beautiful book?... I sobbed when I read it. The

Two brothers mature and overcome adversity to look toward a brighter future in this 1985 novel.

assistant editor sobbed. That doesn't happen very often in this business. And we want your book.'"

Finally a published novelist at age fifty-five, Sebestyen received enthusiastic praise for *Words by Heart*. The author commented in *SATA* that after thirty-five years of writing, "I finally got the hang of it." Set in 1910, *Words by Heart* is about a black family who moves to an all-white Western town in search of opportunity and a better life. The novel focuses on the relationship between Ben Sills and his twelve-year-old daughter Lena. Ben is a hard-working man who teaches Lena Christian ethics—forgiveness, especially—through Bible study. During the course of the book Lena learns that to know Bible verses "by heart" means not only to memorize them but to live by them, even in the face of injustice and racial prejudice. When Ben takes over the job of a lazy sharecropper and is shot and killed by the sharecropper's spiteful son, Tater, Lena makes the difficult choice to live by the values her father instilled in her; she decides to save the life of Tater, who was also shot in the scuffle with Ben. Though hailed by reviewers as a story showing the triumph of good over evil and regarded as a novel of literary merit, *Words by Heart* was nevertheless a controversial book. Some reviewers questioned the values Sebestyen promotes in the novel, claiming that her characterizations of Ben and Lena perpetuate the stereotype of meek, passive blacks who "turn the other cheek" when they encounter violence and racism. Still, Sebestyen commented in *Innocence and Experience* that the favorable reviews of *Words by Heart* "took my breath away."

For the first time, success began to come regularly for Sebestyen. Her second novel, *Far from Home*, was published in 1980. The story begins with the death of thirteen-year-old Salty's deaf-mute mother. Salty, who has never known his father, is left with his great-grandmother, Mam. He is also left with a note from his mother instructing him to visit Tom Buckley, who she says will take Salty in. Salty gets a job at Tom's boarding house and rooms there with Mam, later discovering that Tom, who is married, is his father. This finding does not make life easier for Salty, for he must face the pain of having a father who will not acknowledge him. *Far from Home* was critically acclaimed; reviewers especially noted that Sebestyen's sense of humor serves to counteract the seriousness of the novel. In a *Bulletin of the Center for Children's Books* review, Zena Sutherland commented that "all of the characters are drawn in depth, in a moving story in which several of them change believably in

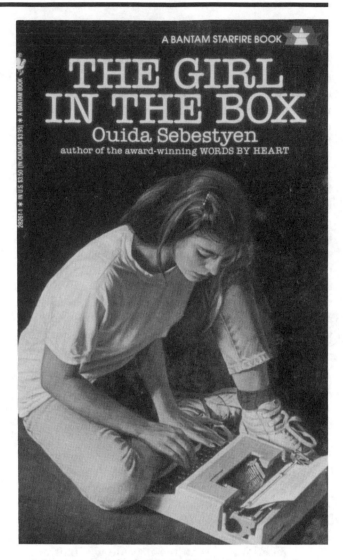

A BANTAM STARFIRE BOOK

THE GIRL IN THE BOX
Ouida Sebestyen
author of the award-winning WORDS BY HEART

Sebestyen uses the letters Jackie McGee writes when she is inexplicably kidnapped and locked in a cellar to structure this powerful 1988 story.

response to the others. . . . [*Far from Home* is] a fine novel."

Reflecting on the roles her parents played in her first two published novels, Sebestyen noted that *Words by Heart* turned out to be a farewell to her father, who had died when she was thirty-eight. Although they had a close relationship, Sebestyen acknowledged in the *ALAN Review* that "last things are never fully said." Writing was cathartic for the author, who continued, "As my characters worked through their losses I worked through mine." Sebestyen's mother lived to see her daughter's first published book, dying the day after Sebestyen finished the second. The novelist declared in the *ALAN Review* that "if my father's spirit shines out of *Heart*, my mother's brave last days are echoed in the indomitable Mam of [*Far from Home*]."

The author's next novel, *IOU's*, traces a relationship between an unorthodox mother and son that parallels Sebestyen's relationship with her own son. The mother, Annie, is divorced and is estranged from her father; she struggles to support her son, Stowe, by taking in day-care children. The two share a strong bond that endures poverty and other adversities only to become stronger. "This is a powerful story," remarked Hazel Rochman in the *New York Times Book Review*. "The young protagonist, strengthened by the love and integrity of a parent, takes on moral responsibility in a harsh world." Mary M. Burns, writing in the *Horn Book Magazine*, praised *IOU's*, "With feeling, but not without humor, the novel works on many levels. The characters, developed in action and dialogue, are remarkably well rounded, and the theme . . . is a substantial one."

Like the character Annie, Sebestyen shared a close relationship with her son. In the *ALAN Review* she noted: "Motherhood was the turning point of both my life and my career. I couldn't have written my . . . books before my son was born." Motherhood, for Sebestyen, brought about ideas and instincts that were later incorporated into her novels. The urge to guide, nurture, and relate her past to her son gave her a new enthusiasm for childhood that spilled over into her writing. The author expressed in the *ALAN Review* that she had finally found her niche: "It was wonderful to be, without apology, as upbeat and idealistic and silly and uncertain about life as my readers. My high-heeled attempts at sophistication had never felt right."

Sebestyen followed *IOU's* with *On Fire*, a novel that tells the story of Tater Hanley, the boy who shot Ben Sills in *Words by Heart*. *On Fire* is told from the perspective of Sammy, Tater's younger brother who worships Tater and is unaware of his crime. When their father is imprisoned for drunkenness, Tater takes a hazardous position as a strikebreaker in the local mines to support their family. Both Tater and Sammy mature in the novel: Sammy forms a more realistic portrait of his brother's character, and Tater voices remorse for his wrongdoings. Their father's suicide in jail eventually brings the Hanleys closer together, giving them the strength to face the future with hope. Sebestyen was again praised by critics for her vivid characterizations and for presenting her characters with difficult choices and questions. In *Interracial Books for Children Bulletin* Rudine Sims praised *On Fire* as "a provocative book, worth reading, worth thinking about, worth discussing with young people."

In her next book, *The Girl in the Box*, Sebestyen deviates from the pattern of her earlier novels. Rather than focusing on families who weather adversity and eventually look toward a brighter future, Sebestyen tells the story of an isolated teenager whose future is at best uncertain. Jackie McGee is kidnapped on her way home from school one day. She is given no explanation and is left in a cellar with little food and water and the typewriter and paper she was carrying. The novel is structured as a series of letters that Jackie writes and slips out through the crack in the door, hoping someone will find them and rescue her. Through her letters, the reader experiences Jackie's panic, learns about the state of her personal relationships before her kidnapping, and witnesses a philosophical transformation that comes from hours of meditation. Whether or not Jackie is ever rescued cannot be determined—a departure from Sebestyen's typically optimistic endings. Like her earlier works, though, Sebestyen was praised for her powerful story and remarkable characterization. Sebestyen remarked in *SAAS* that a friend "said that *The Girl in the Box* had slammed her into her own box of self-examination, and that the strange view from it had given her new insights. I was so pleased, because that's the gift I wanted the book to give its readers."

Sebestyen commented further on the effect she hopes to produce through her writing in the *ALAN Review*: "I hope one out of every ten words in [my books] conjures up love, because in my mind love, and the miracles of acceptance and connection it generates, are the ultimate things to write about." Love and family are themes evident throughout Sebestyen's life as well as her works. The author commented in *SAAS* that "as I try to form a picture of my life-so-far, I see how much a love of family and home has shaped it." She continued, "Maybe each of my books is a home, too, where I come to stay a year or so, unpacking the baggage from my past and growing to love the family I move in with."

Given her love for family and her affinity for portraying parent-child relationships in her novels, it is not surprising that Sebestyen often compares writing to parenthood. She noted in the *ALAN Review* that, like bearing a child, writing a book "looks easy until you try it"; she added, "both [are] acts of faith and giving." Emphasizing further the connection between parents and writers, Sebestyen stated in the *ALAN Review* that both writers and parents have an obligation "to do more than hold the mirror up to life for [children]. They need to tilt the mirror so it catches light, and suggests not only how life is, but how it ought to be."

Reflecting upon her writing career, Sebestyen remarked in *Innocence and Experience* that "sometimes writing fiction is a struggle, sometimes a joy. Most of the time it's like a chronic backache or a ringing in the ears that won't go away." Her persistence, however, has led her to produce award-winning novels. Commenting on the numerous awards she has won for her books, Sebestyen noted in *SAAS*, "I am grateful for their encouragement, although books have no more business being ranked than people do—how can we judge a book's worth as it touches mind after mind?" The awards are, however, an indication of Sebestyen's achievements. Indeed, Sebestyen has likened her success story to that of the magical rags-to-riches tale of Cinderella. Marvelling at her accomplishments, she hopes that her perseverance will be an inspiration to other writers; in *SATA* Sebestyen expressed that if her story "can keep another writer trying—never, never giving up—that will be frosting on the cake."

Looking toward the future, Sebestyen disclosed in *SAAS* that "the dream of my life was (and still is) to have a dear place where I could have the space to grow vegetables, fruit and nut trees, grapes, herbs, grains, flowers, and the time to enjoy pets, grandchildren, crafting pottery, baskets, models—and, oh yes—write a lot of books. I will have it. It's waiting out there. A dream that lovely can't go unfulfilled forever." Sebestyen declared in *SAAS* that she has cleared a shelf on her bookcase for her future volumes "and will fill it if I can." The author continued, "There is so much to do and learn. Where do I start? I feel great changes ahead. An old house to restore? Briar patches waiting to become gardens? I'm writing a play—could that be the beginning of something lovely?"

■ Works Cited

Burns, Mary M., review of *IOU's, Horn Book Magazine*, August, 1982, p. 418.

Rochman, Hazel, review of *IOU's, New York Times Book Review*, September 19, 1982, p. 41.

Sebestyen, Ouida, "Family Matters," *ALAN Review*, spring, 1984, pp. 1-3.

Sebestyen, Ouida, "On Being Published," *Innocence and Experience: Essays and Conversations on Children's Literature*, edited by Barbara Harrison and Gregory Maguire, Lothrup, 1987, pp. 440-42.

Sebestyen, Ouida, *Something about the Author Autobiography Series*, Volume 10, Gale, 1990, pp. 289-303.

Sims, Rudine, review of *On Fire, Interracial Books for Children Bulletin*, Volume 17, numbers 3 & 4, 1986, pp. 34-5.

Something about the Author, Volume 39, Gale, 1985, p. 187.

Sutherland, Zena, review of *Far from Home, Bulletin of the Center for Children's Books*, September, 1980, p. 21.

■ For More Information See

BOOKS

Children's Literature Review, Volume 17, Gale, 1989.

Contemporary Authors, Volume 107, Gale, 1983.

Contemporary Literary Criticism, Volume 30, Gale, 1984.

PERIODICALS

ALAN Review, spring, 1983.

Horn Book, November, 1988.

Times Literary Supplement, November 3, 1989.

—*Sketch by Michelle M. Motowski*

Steven Spielberg

■ Personal

Born December 18, 1947, in Cincinnati, OH; son of Arnold (an electrical engineer) Spielberg and Leah (a pianist and restaurant owner; maiden name, Posner) Adler; married Amy Irving (an actress), November 27, 1985 (divorced), married Kate Capshaw, October 12, 1991; children: (first marriage) Max Samuel; (second marriage) Sasha. *Education:* Attended California State College (now University), Long Beach.

■ Addresses

Office—Amblin Entertainment, 100 Universal City Plaza, Universal City, CA 91608.

■ Career

Writer, director, and producer. Founder of Amblin Entertainment, 1984. *Member:* British Academy of Film and Television Arts (fellow).

■ Awards, Honors

Received awards at Atlanta Film Festival and Venice Film Festival for *Amblin'*; Academy Award nomination for best director, Academy of Motion Picture Arts and Sciences, 1977, for *Close Encounters of the Third Kind;* Directors Guild award for best director, 1985, and Image Award for best picture, National Association for the Advancement of Colored People (NAACP), 1986, both for *The Color Purple;* Scopus Award, American Friends of the Hebrew University, 1986; National Board of Review awards for best director and best picture, 1987, for *Empire of the Sun;* Irving G. Thalberg Award, Academy of Motion Picture Arts and Sciences, 1987; honored at the Moving Picture Ball, American Cinematheque, 1989.

■ Films

DIRECTOR

The Sugarland Express, Universal, 1974.
Jaws, Universal, 1975.
(And author of screenplay) *Close Encounters of the Third Kind,* Columbia, 1977.
1941, Universal, 1979.
Raiders of the Lost Ark, Lucasfilm Ltd., 1981.
(And coproducer) *E.T. the Extra-Terrestrial,* Universal, 1982.
(And coproducer) *Twilight Zone—The Movie,* Warner Brothers, 1983.
Indiana Jones and the Temple of Doom, Lucasfilm Ltd., 1984.
(And coproducer) *The Color Purple,* Guber-Peters, 1985.
(And coproducer) *Empire of the Sun,* Amblin Entertainment, 1987.
(And coproducer) *Always,* Universal, 1989.

Indiana Jones and the Last Crusade, Lucasfilm Ltd., 1989.
Hook, Amblin Entertainment, 1991.

Also director of television films, including *Duel,* 1971. Director and author of screenplays, including *Escape to Nowhere, Firelight,* and *Amblin'.*

COPRODUCER

I Wanna Hold Your Hand, 1978.
(And author of screenplay with Michael Grais and Mark Victor) *Poltergeist,* Metro Goldwyn Mayer/United Artists, 1982.
Back to the Future, Universal, 1986.
Who Framed Roger Rabbit?, Walt Disney Productions/Amblin Entertainment, 1988.
The Land before Time, 1988.
An American Tail, Amblin Entertainment, 1986.

OTHER

Close Encounters of the Third Kind (novel; adapted from screenplay of the same title), Delacorte, 1977.
(Editor) *The New Illustrated Disney Songbook,* Abrams, 1986.

Also author of stories, including *The Sugarland Express, Ace Eli and Rodger of the Skies,* and *The Goonies.* Director of episodes of television series, including *Night Gallery, Marcus Welby, M.D., Owen Marshall, The Name of the Game,* and *Columbo.* Producer and segment director of television series *Amazing Stories,* 1985; producer of television series *Tiny Toon Adventures.*

■ Adaptations

Ace Eli and Rodger of the Skies was adapted for film by Chips Rosen and released by Twentieth Century-Fox, 1973; *The Sugarland Express* was adapted for film by Hal Barwood and Matthew Robbins and released by Universal, 1974; *The Goonies* was adapted for film by Chris Columbus and released by Warner Bros., 1985.

■ Sidelights

Motion picture producer, director, and writer Steven Spielberg, creator of such immensely popular films as *Jaws, Close Encounters of the Third Kind, E.T. the Extra-Terrestrial,* and *Raiders of the Lost Ark,* is considered one of the most gifted and successful filmmakers of all time. With a powerful appeal among moviegoers of all ages, most of Spielberg's highest-grossing films examine the effects of horror or fantasy on mainstream, middle-class Americans. In *Jaws,* for example, a concerned police chief patrols the waters, stalking a killer shark that has been terrorizing swimmers from a once serene resort community. And in the enchanting *E.T. the Extra-Terrestrial,* a loveable little alien who is accidentally left on Earth befriends a young boy living in a typical suburban neighborhood who then helps him return home. "Everything I do in my movies," remarked Spielberg in *Time,* "is a product of my homelife in suburban U.S.A. I can always trace a movie idea back to my childhood."

Spielberg was born in Cincinnati, Ohio, in 1947 and was raised with his three younger sisters. His father, who worked in the computer industry in the late 1940s and early 1950s, was often forced to relocate the family to follow promising job leads. "Just as I'd become accustomed to a school and a teacher and a best friend," Spielberg related in *Time,* "the FOR SALE sign would dig into the front lawn and we'd be packing and off to some other state. I've often considered Arizona, where I was from [age] nine to sixteen, my real home. For a kid, home is where you have best friends and your first car, and your first kiss; it's where you do your worst stuff and get your best grades." The Spielberg family moved from Phoenix, Arizona, to northern California when Steven was sixteen, and soon after, his parents separated. "They hung in there to protect us until we were old enough," the filmmaker wrote in *Time.* "But I don't think they were aware of how acutely we were aware of their unhappiness.... When the separation finally came, we were no better off for having waited six years for it to occur. I have two wonderful parents; they raised me really well. Sometimes parents can work together to raise a wonderful family and not have anything in common with each other. That happens a lot in America."

As a young child, Spielberg experienced many of the same fears that other youngsters have; he thought that monsters lived under his bed and in the crack in his bedroom wall. "I remember lying there, trying to go to sleep," he told Michiko Kakutani in the *New York Times,* "and I always used to imagine little [Dutch painter] Hieronymus Bosch-like creatures inside, peeking out and whispering to me to come into the playground of the crack and be drawn into the unknown there, inside the wall of my home in New Jersey." To alleviate his anxieties, the boy told his sisters scary stories and came up with various ways of terrifying them. "This removed the fear from my soul and transferred it right onto theirs," Spielberg noted in *Time.* The filmmaker's mother recalled in *People* that "he used to stand outside [his sisters'] window

Elliot befriends and protects a stranded alien in this touching story that became the top-grossing film of all time in 1982, *E.T. the Extra-Terrestrial.*

at night, howling, '1 am the moon! I am the moon!'.... And he cut off the head of his sister Nancy's doll and served it to her on a bed of lettuce.''

Because Spielberg was easily frightened by horror scenes in movies, his parents attempted to limit the youngster's exposure to films to what they thought were harmless, nonviolent Walt Disney movies. "When I came screaming home from *Snow White* when I was eight years old, and tried to hide under the covers,'' Spielberg told David Breskin in *Rolling Stone,* "my parents did not understand it, because Walt Disney movies are not supposed to scare but to delight and enthrall. Between *Snow White, Fantasia* and *Bambi,* I was a basket case of neurosis.'' But his parents' restrictions had another effect on Spielberg—he became increasingly interested in the world of cinema that was closed to him. "I often think that depravity is the inspiration for an entire career,'' he noted in *Rolling Stone.* "I feel that perhaps one of the reasons I'm making

movies all the time is because I was told not to. I was *ordered* not to watch television.''

Discovering an eight millimeter movie camera in his house when he was twelve years old was a particularly pivotal event in Spielberg's life. It began an ardent interest in filmmaking that was encouraged by his very patient mother who even let Steven miss school on most Mondays to finish short films he had begun over the weekend. The boy had a strong distaste for schoolwork that was reflected in his average grades, and he was, as he expressed in *Time,* a "skinny, acne-faced wimp who gets picked on by big football jocks all the way home from school.'' Once safe at home, which Spielberg's mother described in *People* as containing "white walls, blue carpeting and tripods'' in order to accommodate the young movie director, Spielberg escaped the hardships of adolescence by making short films that often involved the participation of his entire family. "It was creative and chaotic at our house,'' remarked Spielberg's father to Richard Corliss in *Time*. "I'd help Steven construct sets for his 8-mm movies, with toy trucks and paper mache mountains." In addition, the family would sometimes dress in costumes and drive to the desert so Steven could film "on location."

At the age of seventeen, Spielberg went on a tour of Universal Studios where he had his first meeting with someone in the motion picture industry. "The tram wasn't stopping at the sound stages," Spielberg told Corliss. "So during a bathroom break I snuck away and wandered over there, just watching. I met a man who asked what I was doing, and I told him my story. Instead of calling the guards to throw me off the lot, he talked to me for about an hour.... He said he'd like to see some of my little films, and so he gave me a pass to get on the lot the next day. I showed him about four of my 8-mm films. He was very impressed. Then he said, 'I don't have the authority to write you any more passes, but good luck to you.'" Spielberg, however, soon found a way to get back onto the movie sets. "I walked past the guard every day," he related to Lynn Hirschberg in *Rolling Stone*,

"waved at him, and he waved back. I always wore a suit and carried a briefcase, and he assumed I was some kid related to some mogul, and that was that."

By the time Spielberg was out of high school, he had already won student awards for his short films. One of them, *Firelight*, premiered at a local movie theatre. Since his high school grades were not good enough for acceptance into film school, Spielberg became a student at California State College (now University), Long Beach; he still found time, however, to spend three days a week on the Universal Studios lot, asking executives to view his films. "They were embarrassed when I asked them to remove their pictures from the wall so I could project my little silent movies," he acknowledged in *Time*. "They said, 'If you make your films in 16-mm or, even better, 35-mm, then they'll get seen.' So I immediately went to work in the college commissary to earn the money to buy 16-mm film and rent a camera. I had to get those films seen."

Spielberg's persistence was finally recognized. Universal executives agreed to view one of his short films titled *Amblin'*, and he was offered a

Scatman Crothers offers the residents of a rest home the Fountain of Youth in the form of a children's game in Spielberg's segment from the 1983 fantasy *Twilight Zone—The Movie*.

seven-year contract as a television director by Sid Sheinberg. "I was still several months shy of my twenty-first birthday," he pointed out to Hirschberg. "And I hadn't graduated [from] college. But Sheinberg said, 'Do you wanna graduate college or do you wanna be a film director?' I signed the papers a week later." Journeyman work in several weekly series—including a *Night Gallery* episode starring Joan Crawford—led to Spielberg's first television movie, *Duel.* The story of a motorist pursued by an unseen driver in a menacing truck, the film gained much critical attention. In fact, it was eventually released as a feature in Europe and Japan and became a worldwide success.

After a story he wrote titled *Ace Eli and Rodger of the Skies* was made into a 1973 film that failed at the box office, Spielberg embarked on his first feature project as a director, *The Sugarland Express.* Goldie Hawn and William Atherton star in this tale of parents who defy authority to regain custody of their child. In this case, defying authority manifests itself in a number of car chases and other action scenes, which prompted critic Pauline Kael of the *New Yorker* to note that the movie "is mostly about cars; Spielberg is a choreographic virtuoso with cars. He patterns them; he makes them dance and crash and bounce back. He handles enormous configurations of vehicles; sometimes they move so sweetly you think he must be wooing them." And yet Kael also saw in the filmmaker a gift for "very free-and-easy, American" humor, speculating in those early days that Spielberg "could be that rarity among directors, a born entertainer." *New York Times* reviewer Stephen Farber, however, maintained that in *The Sugarland Express* "everything is underlined; Spielberg sacrifices narrative logic and character consistency for quick thrills and easy laughs."

This mixed critical response, which characterizes virtually every film Spielberg has directed, has not affected the commercial success of his projects. That became apparent early in Spielberg's career, after his second picture—about a great white shark whose attacks on swimmers cause a panic among citizens and tourists of the fictional Amity Island—was released in the summer of 1975. Based on a best-selling novel, cast with mostly unknown actors, and filmed with a daunting (for 1975) $8 million budget, *Jaws* exploded into American theatres and instantly became the most talked-about movie of its time—making its twenty-six-year-old director a star.

The filming of *Jaws* on Martha's Vineyard in Massachusetts presented Spielberg with many un-

forseen challenges. The director was quoted in *Time* as saying "nobody thought much about the currents or anything at all about the waves." A strong Atlantic tow "would cause equipment boats to drift away," Spielberg continued. "Water color would change, the rhythm of the waves would fluctuate." What problems Mother Nature neglected, the mechanical shark, nicknamed "Bruce," readily provided. There were, in fact, three mechanical sharks, each created to perform differently, and all "fairly programmed for mishap," as Spielberg noted in *Time.* "Bruce sank when he made his debut. During his second test on water his hydraulic system exploded.... A special makeup man in scuba gear would plunge into the ocean to add more blood to Bruce's teeth and gums or administer a touch-up to his tender plastic tissue. Bruce's skin tended to discolor and deteriorate in the salt water."

These filming difficulties were forgotten after millions of moviegoers helped *Jaws* shatter the record for box office earnings. As pointed out by a reviewer in *Time,* this achievement is especially notable considering that the film was released during a season full of adventure and disaster movies. "What sets *Jaws* apart from most of the other ceiling busters and makes it a special case," declared the reviewer, "is that it is quite a good movie. For one thing, it is mercifully free of the padding—cosmic, comic, cultural—that so often mars 'big' pictures. In that sense, the movie is very like its subject. If the great white shark that terrorizes the beaches of an island summer colony is one of nature's most efficient killing machines, *Jaws* is an efficient entertainment machine."

Though the film received some negative reviews, many critics applauded the high level of suspense that Spielberg created with the help of special effects experts. "The right things certainly happen in *Jaws,*" remarked Gordon Gow in *Films and Filming.* "At given moments, the images before us lead to ... dread anticipation. The pulses pound. Excitement escalates. And by climax time, when it is impossible to disbelieve that one of the leading actors ... is actually being swallowed alive by a gigantic shark in an unnerving series of gulps, we are watching movie magic of the highest order. Trickery has mastered the illusion of truth."

After the huge success of *Jaws,* Spielberg enjoyed a newfound clout within the Hollywood community. He even endured what he termed a "*Jaws* backlash. The same people who had raved about [the movie] began to doubt its artistic value as soon as it began to bring in so much money," he explained in

Michael J. Fox as Marty McFly, and Christopher Lloyd as Dr. Emmett Brown, travel back in time and accidentally alter the future in the 1986 comedy adventure *Back to the Future*.

Newsweek. The most apparent aspect of the controversy occurred when Spielberg did not receive a nomination for best director from the Academy of Motion Picture Arts and Sciences. "It hurt me because I felt [*Jaws*] was a director's movie," the filmmaker continued in *Newsweek*. Still, *Jaws* remains number four on the list of top-grossing motion pictures in Hollywood's history.

Even while praising his directorial success, many wondered how the young filmmaker could produce another work to match the commercial appeal of *Jaws*. Spielberg answered the challenge in 1977 with another blockbuster, *Close Encounters of the Third Kind*. The title, at first a meaningless phrase to most Americans, soon became synonymous with making physical contact with alien life forms. Although mainstream films had long portrayed aliens as threatening monsters, Spielberg believed coexistence with creatures from other planets held a much more peaceful promise. The movie tells the story of how a series of Unidentified Flying Object

(UFO) sightings in Indiana leads to revelation and awe. The mysterious spaceships lure several people, including a group of scientists, a family man, and a five-year-old boy and his mother, to Devil's Tower in Wyoming. There the aliens' brightly colored mother ship lands and is able to communicate a message of hope and goodwill to the humans. This uplifting conclusion helped make *Close Encounters of the Third Kind* one of the top ten highest-grossing films.

At the time of its release, many critics and moviegoers considered *Close Encounters of the Third Kind* Spielberg's most poignant film. Commenting on the roles of plot and special effects in the movie, the filmmaker told Chris Hodenfield in *Rolling Stone* that "you need good storytelling to offset the amount of technique the audience demands, the amount of spectacle audiences demand before they'll leave their television sets. And I think people will leave their television sets for a good story before anything else.... That was the reason

I spent so much time on the story of *Close Encounters,* because I didn't just want to make a UFO movie, where something lands, people get on, and it takes off again. I figured I had to write a mystery story. As opposed to just a special effects movie."

Spielberg again utilized a unique combination of mystery and special effects for the first movie in his adventure trilogy with *Star Wars* director George Lucas, titled *Raiders of the Lost Ark.* "Raiders [*of the Lost Ark*] is, in fact, an exemplary film," proclaimed Richard Schickel in *Time,* "an object lesson in how to blend the art of storytelling with the highest levels of technical know-how, planning, cost control and commercial acumen." Ranked number five on the list of the highest-grossing films of all time, the movie recounts the myriad adventures of Indiana Jones, an archaeologist recruited by the U.S. Government to find the lost Ark of the Covenant, described in the Bible's Old Testament as a wooden chest which contains the original tablets of the Ten Commandments and promises great power to its beholder. Indiana's mission—to locate the Ark before the evil, power-seeking German Nazis—takes him to several countries where he obtains clues to the Ark's whereabouts and fends off the attacks of a number of sinister people. Schickel praised the film and found that "so strong is the imagery, so compelling the pace, so sharply defined are the characters, that one leaves . . . [*Raiders of the*] *Lost Ark* with the feeling that, like the best films of childhood, it will take up permanent residence in memory."

The filming of Spielberg's next movie, *E.T. the Extra-Terrestrial*—which became the top-grossing film of all time—was clouded in secrecy; no publicity photographs of its alien star were released prior to the movie's premiere in 1982. The idea for the story, according to Jim Calio in *People,* came to Spielberg in 1980 when he was in the Tunisian desert making *Raiders of the Lost Ark.* "I was kind of lonely at the time," Spielberg told Calio. "My girlfriend was back in Los Angeles. I remember saying to myself, 'What I really need is a friend I can talk to—somebody who can give me *all* the answers.'" The friend Spielberg imagined would eventually be cast as *E.T.*'s main character, a visitor from the heavens who is left stranded on Earth when his spaceship inadvertently leaves without him. Finding his way into a suburban American neighborhood, the little alien—"a squat-looking creature with an expandable neck that sort of looks like an eggplant on a stick," according to *Chicago Tribune* contributor Gene Siskel—meets a lonely boy, Elliott, who names the creature E.T. and offers shelter, friendship, and an education in human culture and language.

Elliott initially manages to keep E.T.'s presence a secret, but when the alien's existence soon becomes known to the community, maleficent government scientists quarantine the family's house in order to perform life-threatening studies on the creature. Meanwhile, the distraught boy, his siblings, and their friends attempt to find a way to help the ailing E.T. contact his native planet, resulting in the most famous line of the film, "E.T. phone home." E.T. and Elliott escape from the scientists after a tense chase scene, and E.T. is ultimately rescued by his fellow aliens. Spielberg shared in the characters' triumph, though on a more personal level: "Action is wonderful," he remarked in *People,* "but while I was doing *Raiders [of the Lost Ark]* I felt I was losing touch with the reason I became a moviemaker—to make stories

Released in 1988, the innovative *Who Framed Roger Rabbit?* combines cartoon and human characters in a humorous detective adventure.

In 1989's *Indiana Jones and the Last Crusade*, Sean Connery and Harrison Ford, as father and son, encounter danger and adventure from Nazi Germany to the Near East as they search for the Holy Grail.

about people and relationships. [*E.T.*] is the first movie I ever made for myself."

Despite drawing huge crowds and garnering critical acclaim, *E.T.* still did not generate an Academy Award nomination for best director for Spielberg. The film, declared Gary Arnold in the *Washington Post,* "is essentially a spiritual autobiography, a portrait of the filmmaker as a typical suburban kid set apart by an uncommonly fervent, mystical imagination. It comes out disarmingly funny, spontaneous, big-hearted." And *New York Times* contributor Vincent Canby proclaimed that *E.T.* "may become a children's classic of the space age."

Ironically, the same year that brought the gentle, life-affirming extraterrestrial also brought a Spielberg horror film—one that he wrote and produced, but did not direct. *Poltergeist,* directed by Tobe Hooper, dispenses with friendly, otherworldly visitors in favor of malicious ghosts tormenting a typical, middle-class family. As the filmmaker told Kakutani, "*Poltergeist* is what I fear and *E.T.* is what I love. One is about suburban evil and the

other is about suburban good. I had different motivations in both instances: in *Poltergeist* I wanted to terrify and I also wanted to amuse—I tried to mix the laughs and the screams together. *Poltergeist* is the darker side of my nature—it's me when I was scaring my younger sisters half to death when we were growing up—and *E.T.* is my optimism about the future and my optimism about what it was like to grow up in Arizona and New Jersey."

Spielberg revisited a proven formula in 1984 when he again teamed with Lucas and directed a sequel to *Raiders of the Lost Ark, Indiana Jones and the Temple of Doom.* Containing even more hair-raising scenes than its predecessor, the film follows Indiana Jones on his mission to recover a mysterious stone missing from the shrine of a village in India. The story finds Indiana in a seemingly endless series of life-threatening and often gruesome predicaments, including a bizarre ritual in which a man's beating heart is ripped from his chest. "They're going to have to scrape youngsters out from under the seats like old chewing gum with this one," insisted *Los Angeles Times* film critic Sheila Benson. Some reviewers faulted Spielberg for his excessive reliance on special effects to hold the audience's attention, but the film was a commercial success and managed to gross $180 million at the box office.

Despite Spielberg's string of successes, he has not been immune to criticism. He suffered his first box office failure in 1979 with the slapstick comedy *1941,* which examines the mayhem arising in Southern California from a fear of invasion after the Japanese attack on Pearl Harbor. The film was deemed tasteless and unfunny by critics, and although it made $23 million at the box office, *1941* failed to match its production costs. In 1986, however, Spielberg responded to critics with his most controversial film, *The Color Purple.* Based on Alice Walker's Pulitzer Prize-winning novel, the plot concerns African-American life in the South. Some questioned the appropriateness of a white, male director at the helm of this powerful story which tackles such issues as race relations and sexism, while others charged that Spielberg had tampered with the intent of the novel.

The Color Purple chronicles a woman's coming of age in the rural South in the early twentieth century. Celie, with the triple burdens of being black, female, and poor in a racist society, endures a brutal marriage and continual heartache until she meets singer Shug Avery, a woman who is everything Celie is not. In the novel, Celie and Shug's

Spielberg giving directions on the set of his 1987 epic *Empire of the Sun*.

friendship turns into a homosexual relationship, an aspect Spielberg intentionally avoids in his film version. In a *Film Comment* article, Marcia Pally remarked, "Sadly, Spielberg did not let his actors preserve the voice Walker gave black women who love women." His "empathy," continued the reviewer, "doesn't extend that far."

The Color Purple was nominated for eleven Academy Awards, but failed to win any. However, the film did earn some praise for its epic sweep and fine performances. Whoopi Goldberg received a best actress nomination for her portrayal of Celie and *New York* contributor David Blum recognized that the movie provided another example of "conflict between the little people and the big, evil forces of society that has dominated all [Spielberg's] movies." Blum found Celie's dilemma similar to that of E.T.: "Both are outsiders in a strange, cruel world, struggling for freedom." The reviewer also lauded the director's handling of many complicated social issues, concluding that "as with all his movies, Spielberg managed to bring *The Color Purple* to a rousing, uplifting conclusion in the simplest way possible."

Spielberg directed another film of epic proportions in 1987, *Empire of the Sun.* The film centers on Jim Graham, a nine-year-old British boy living with his aristocratic family in Shanghai, China, during the 1940s. When Japanese troops invade China in a campaign during World War II, British citizens—fearing for their lives—try to flee the city. In the turmoil of the streets, Jim is separated from his family and must try to take care of himself. He befriends an older man, but the two are soon rounded up and placed in a prison camp where Jim, free of parental guidance and initially oblivious to the horrors of war, has many adventures. Eventually, however, the boy is psychologically affected by the situation. When the war ends, the now thirteen-year-old Jim is reunited with parents he doesn't recognize. The film earned fair reviews, and critics especially praised the performance of Christian Bale, the actor who portrayed Jim Graham. And in the same year *Empire of the Sun* was released, the Academy of Motion Picture Arts and Sciences finally recognized Spielberg's directorial talent, bestowing upon him the Irving J. Thalberg Award.

Spielberg's next project, *Always,* released in 1989, was a remake of the 1943 romance movie *A Guy Named Joe.* The director presents the tale of a hotshot Montana pilot killed while fighting a forest fire who becomes the guardian angel of one of his fellow fliers. Pete, though now invisible, wishes to continue his romance with his love in life, Dorinda. He ultimately realizes, however, that their union is impossible, and he must relinquish his feelings for Dorinda so she can pursue a new relationship. The film received mixed reviews and critics complained about the its sentimentality and melodramatic cinematic effects. Though she ultimately assessed its elaborate "visual style" as "powerfully distracting" for the viewer, *New York Times* contributor Janet Maslin found that *Always* has a "stirring, inspirational tone."

Also in 1989 Spielberg released *Indiana Jones and the Last Crusade,* the final segment of the Indiana Jones trilogy. Spielberg cast Sean Connery as Indiana's archaeologist father, Henry Jones. After Indiana rescues Henry from a Nazi fortress, the twosome embark on a quest to find the Holy Grail, the centuries-old chalice believed to hold magical powers. "Though it uses some of the same characters that appeared in the earlier two [Indiana Jones] films," commented a reviewer in the *New York Times,* "it also explores new narrative territory—as usual, the geographic territory is the globe." The critic proclaimed that *Indiana Jones and the Last Crusade,* "an endearing original, attests to the filmmaker's expanding talent."

Further cultivating his creativity, Spielberg has also taken on the role of producer for film and television, and beginning in 1984 he has served as the head of his own production company, Amblin Entertainment. His movie production credits include such commercial successes as the *Back to the Future* trilogy, about a boy's adventures with a brilliant scientist who invents a time machine; *Who Framed Roger Rabbit?,* a $45 million movie combining human actors and cartoon characters in a 1940s Hollywood setting; and *The Land before Time,* an animated story focusing on dinosaurs that Hal Hinson described in the *Washington Post* as "entertaining" and "emotionally rich." In television Spielberg produced a short-lived anthology series titled *Amazing Stories* as well as *Tiny Toon Adventures,* an animated show with characters reminiscent of Bugs Bunny and his friends. Commenting in a 1990 advertisement in *Fortune* on his involvement with animated films and television programs, Spielberg said, "Animation is the most fun I have right now.... As the dollar shrinks and movies cost more, my imagination is becoming less and less affordable. So I've turned to animation as a way to free it up. In animation, anything can happen."

Spielberg's longstanding popularity as a producer, director, and writer for film and television stems perhaps from his appeal to a child's sensibility that attracts viewers among both youngsters and adults. "I use my childhood in all my pictures, and all the time," he told David Breskin in *Rolling Stone*. "I go back there to find ideas and stories. My childhood was the most fruitful part of my entire life. All those horrible, traumatic years I spent as a kid became what I do for a living today, or what I draw from creatively today."

■ Works Cited

Benson, Sheila, "Temple of Doom? Indy's 'Temple of Doom' Desecrated by Too Much Worship of Special Effects," *Los Angeles Times*, May 23, 1984.

Bernstein, Fred A., "Present at the Creation," *People*, May 5, 1986, pp. 95-99.

Blum, David, "Steven Spielberg and the Dread Hollywood Backlash," *New York*, March 24, 1986, pp. 52-64.

Breskin, David, "Steven Spielberg," *Rolling Stone*, October 24, 1985, pp. 22-24 and 70-80.

Calio, Jim, "Director Steven Spielberg Takes the Wraps Off E.T., Revealing His Secrets at Last, *People*, August 23, 1982, pp. 81-88.

Canby, Vincent, "Enchanted Fantasy," *New York Times*, June 11, 1982.

Corliss, Richard, "'I Dream for a Living," *Time*, July 15, 1985, pp. 54-61.

Gow, Gordon, "Jaws," *Films and Filming*, January, 1976, pp. 30-31.

Hinson, Hal, "'Land Before Time': A Touching Parable," *Washington Post*, November 18, 1988.

Hirschberg, Lynn, "Will Hollywood's Mr. Perfect Ever Grow Up?," *Rolling Stone*, August 2, 1984, pp. 32-38.

Hodenfield, Chris, "The Sky is Full of Questions: Science Fiction in Steven Spielberg's Suburbia," *Rolling Stone*, January 26, 1978, pp. 33-37.

Kael, Pauline, "Sugarland and Badlands," *New Yorker*, March 18, 1974.

Kakutani, Michiko, "Steven Spielberg—Horror vs. Hope," *New York Times Biographical Service*, May, 1982, pp. 654-657.

Maslin, Janet, "'Always,' Love and Death in a Wilderness," *New York Times*, December 22, 1989.

"Meet the Tiny Toons," *Fortune*, May 7, 1990, p. F24.

Pally, Marcia, "Women in Love," *Film Comment*, April, 1986, pp. 35-39.

Review of *Indiana Jones and the Last Crusade*, *New York Times*, June 18, 1989.

Schickel, Richard, "Slam! Bang! A Movie Movie," *Time*, June 15, 1981, pp. 74-76.

Spielberg, Steven, "The Autobiography of Peter Pan," *Time*, July 15, 1985, pp. 62-63.

"Summer of the Shark," *Time*, June 23, 1975, pp. 42-50.

■ For More Information See

BOOKS

Collins, T., *Steven Spielberg, Creator of E.T.*, Dillon, 1983.

Contemporary Literary Criticism, Volume 20, Gale, 1982.

Farber, S., *Outrageous Conduct*, Arbor House, 1988.

Kael, Pauline, *Reeling*, Little, Brown, 1974.

Kael, Pauline, *When the Lights Go Down*, Holt, 1980.

Leather, M., *The Picture Life of Steven Spielberg*, Watts, 1984.

Mabery, D. L., *Steven Spielberg*, Lerner, 1986.

Monaco, James, *American Film Now: The People, the Power, the Money, the Movies*, Oxford University Press, 1979.

Mott, D. R., *Steven Spielberg*, Twayne, 1982.

PERIODICALS

American Film, June, 1988.

Business Week, May 29, 1989.

Chicago Tribune, December 23, 1979, June 4, 1982, June 11, 1982, December 11, 1987, January 10, 1988.

Commonweal, June 20, 1975.

Film Comment, January, 1978, July-August, 1981, May-June, 1982, September-October, 1985, July-August, 1989.

Journal of Popular Film, Volume 6, no. 4, 1978.

Los Angeles Times, June 4, 1982, May 21, 1984, December 16, 1986, November 20, 1989, November 22, 1989, December 3, 1989.

Maclean's, June 4, 1984.

Monthly Film Bulletin, July, 1974.

New Republic, December 10, 1977, September 6, 1980.

Newsweek, April 8, 1974, June 23, 1975, November 21, 1977, June 4, 1984, June 27, 1988, October 15, 1990.

New York, November 7, 1977, January 7, 1980, June 15, 1981, June 4, 1982.

New Yorker, November 28, 1977, September 1, 1980.

New York Times, April 28, 1974, November 13, 1977, December 23, 1979, June 7, 1981, May 30, 1982, June 4, 1982, January 10, 1988, November 22, 1989.

North American Review, fall, 1978.

People, July 20, 1981, November 1, 1982, March 10, 1986, December 5, 1988.

Rolling Stone, July 22, 1982.

Saturday Review, June, 1981.

Sight and Sound, winter, 1972, summer, 1978.

Take One, January, 1978.

Time, May 31, 1982, June 4, 1984.

Washington Post, May 31, 1975, June 6, 1982, February 9, 1987, December 18, 1987, November 22, 1989, November 24, 1989, December 22, 1989.

Mary Stolz

■ Personal

Full name, Mary Slattery Stolz; born March 24, 1920, in Boston, MA; daughter of Thomas Francis and Mary Margaret (a nurse; maiden name, Burgey) Slattery; married Stanley Burr Stolz (a civil engineer), January, 1940 (divorced, 1956); married Thomas C. Jaleski (a doctor), June, 1965; children: (first marriage) William. *Education:* Attended Birch Wathen School, NY, 1929-36, Columbia University, 1936-38, and Katharine Gibbs School, NY, 1938-39. *Politics:* "Liberal Northern Democrat." *Hobbies and other interests:* "Writing letters to editors as to the many matters in society that infuriate me—neglect of the sick, the poor, the jobless, the homeless, and the helpless by the last two administrations, indifference to the environment, to the creatures of the earth, to children, to the future of this poor little planet. I love ballet, baseball, cats. Like to play hard games of Scrabble. And, of course, I read constantly."

■ Addresses

Home—P.O. Box 82, Longboat Key, FL 34228. *Agent*—Roslyn Targ Literary Agency, Inc., 105 West Thirteenth St., Suite 15E, New York, NY 10011.

■ Career

Worked at various jobs, including R. H. Macy's (department store), New York City, book salesperson, 1938, and Columbia University, New York City, secretary at Teachers College, 1938; writer of books for children and young adults. *Member:* Authors League.

■ Awards, Honors

American Library Association (ALA) Notable Book citation, for *The Sea Gulls Woke Me;* Child Study Children's Book Award, Child Study Children's Book Committee at Bank Street College, 1953, for *In a Mirror;* Spring Book Festival Older Honor Award, *New York Herald Tribune,* 1953, for *Ready or Not,* and 1956, for *The Day and the Way We Met;* Spring Book Festival Older Award, *New York Herald Tribune,* 1957, for *Because of Madeline;* ALA Notable Book citation, for *Belling the Tiger;* Newbery Award Honor Books, ALA, 1962, for *Belling the Tiger,* and 1966, for *The Noonday Friends;* Junior Book Award, Boys' Club of America, 1964, for *The Bully of Barkham Street; Horn Book* Honor List citation, and National Book Award nomination, Association of American Publishers, 1975, both for *The Edge of Next Year;* Recognition of Merit Award, George G. Stone Center for Children's Books, 1982, for entire body of work; ALA Notable Book citation, for *Quentin Corn;* Children's Science Book Younger Honor Award,

New York Academy of Sciences, 1986, for *Night of Ghosts and Hermits;* German Youth Festival Award; numerous other ALA Notable Book citations.

■ Writings

FOR YOUNG ADULTS

To Tell Your Love, Harper, 1950.
The Organdy Cupcakes, Harper, 1951.
The Sea Gulls Woke Me, Harper, 1951.
In a Mirror, Harper, 1953.
Ready or Not, Harper, 1953.
Pray Love, Remember, Harper, 1954.
Two by Two, Houghton, 1954, revised edition published as *A Love, or a Season,* Harper, 1964.
Rosemary, Harper, 1955.
Hospital Zone, Harper, 1956.
The Day and the Way We Met, Harper, 1956.
Good-by My Shadow, Harper, 1957.
Because of Madeline, Harper, 1957.
And Love Replied, Harper, 1958.
Second Nature, Harper, 1958.
Some Merry-Go-Round Music, Harper, 1959.
The Beautiful Friend and Other Stories, Harper, 1960.
Wait for Me, Michael, Harper, 1961.
Who Wants Music on Monday?, Harper, 1963.
By the Highway Home, Harper, 1971.
Leap before You Look, Harper, 1972.
The Edge of Next Year, Harper, 1974.
Go and Catch a Flying Fish, Harper, 1979.
What Time of Night Is It?, Harper, 1981.

FOR CHILDREN

The Leftover Elf, illustrated by Peggy Bacon, Harper, 1952.
Emmett's Pig, illustrated by Garth Williams, Harper, 1959.
A Dog on Barkham Street (also see below), illustrated by Leonard Shortall, Harper, 1960.
Belling the Tiger, illustrated by Beni Montresor, Harper, 1961.
The Great Rebellion (also see below), illustrated by Montresor, Harper, 1961.
Fredou, illustrated by Tomi Ungerer, Harper, 1962.
Pigeon Flight, illustrated by Murray Tinkelman, Harper, 1962.
Siri, the Conquistador (also see below), illustrated by Montresor, Harper, 1963.
The Bully of Barkham Street (also see below), illustrated by Shortall, Harper, 1963.
The Mystery of the Woods, illustrated by Uri Shulevitz, Harper, 1964.

The Noonday Friends, illustrated by Louis S. Glanzman, Harper, 1965.
Maximilian's World (also see below), illustrated by Shulevitz, Harper, 1966.
A Wonderful, Terrible Time, illustrated by Glanzman, Harper, 1967.
Say Something, illustrated by Edward Frascino, Harper, 1968.
The Story of a Singular Hen and Her Peculiar Children, illustrated by Frascino, Harper, 1969.
The Dragons of the Queen, illustrated by Frascino, Harper, 1969.
Juan, illustrated by Glanzman, Harper, 1970.
Land's End, illustrated by Dennis Hermanson, Harper, 1973.
Cat in the Mirror, Harper, 1975.
Ferris Wheel, Harper, 1977.
Cider Days, Harper, 1978.
Cat Walk, illustrated by Erik Blegvad, Harper, 1983.
Quentin Corn, illustrated by Pamela Johnson, David Godine, 1985.
The Explorer of Barkham Street (also see below), illustrated by Emily Arnold McCully, Harper, 1985.
Night of Ghosts and Hermits: Nocturnal Life on the Seashore, illustrated by Susan Gallagher, Harcourt, 1985.
The Cuckoo Clock, illustrated by Johnson, David Godine, 1986.
Ivy Larkin, Harcourt, 1986.
The Scarecrows and Their Child, illustrated by Amy Schwartz, Harper, 1987.
Zekmet, the Stone Carver: A Tale of Ancient Egypt, illustrated by Deborah Nourse Lattimore, Harcourt, 1988.
Storm in the Night, illustrated by Pat Cummings, Harper, 1988.
Pangur Ban, illustrated by Johnson, Harper, 1988.
Barkham Street Trilogy (contains *A Dog on Barkham Street, The Bully of Barkham Street,* and *The Explorer of Barkham Street*), Harper, 1989.
Bartholomew Fair, Greenwillow, 1990.
Tales at the Mousehole (characters' names have been changed; contains *The Great Rebellion, Siri, the Conquistador,* and *Maximilian's World*), illustrated by Johnson, David Godine, 1990.
Deputy Shep, illustrated by Johnson, Harper, 1991.
King Emmett the Second, illustrated by Williams, Greenwillow, 1991.
Go Fish, illustrated by Cummings, Harper, 1991.

OTHER

Truth and Consequence (adult), Harper, 1953.

Contributor of fiction to periodicals, including *Seventeen, Ladies' Home Journal, Woman's Day, Good Housekeeping, McCall's, Redbook,* and *Cricket.*

Stolz's works have been published in nearly thirty languages, and some have been issued in Braille. Her manuscripts are housed in the Kerlan collection at the University of Minnesota, Minneapolis.

■ Adaptations

"Baby Blue Expression" (short story; first published in *McCall's*) was adapted for television by Alfred Hitchcock.

■ Work in Progress

A book that features Thomas, a black child who appears in both *Storm in the Night* and *Go Fish,* publication expected by HarperCollins; *Cezanne Pinto, Cowboy,* a book "about Thomas's ancestor, who was a runaway slave who eventually became a cowboy. Not many people know there were any."

■ Sidelights

Mary Stolz is well known to young readers ranging in age from children just learning to read to teenagers on the brink of adulthood. As evidenced by such popular works as *To Tell Your Love* and *The Edge of Next Year,* she has achieved success among her older readers, who enjoy her candid examinations of such topics as young love, family conflicts, death, and maturity. And she has also gained a wide following among her younger readers, who favor works like her Newbery Honor Book *Belling the Tiger* and her tales about growing up, such as her "Barkham Street" stories. In 1982 she was recognized for her entire body of work with the George G. Stone Recognition of Merit Award, and in her acceptance speech, as quoted in *Something about the Author Autobiography Series* (*SAAS*), she summed up the reasons she writes for young people. "From my mail, I know that there are many children still looking for answers in books. I used to, as a child. I still think something reassuring is to be found in them. If we read hard enough they can offer us at least part of a perspective to *What are we going to do about it?* With even that part of a perspective we could, possibly, still save our world. . . . The children are, at present, all we can hope through. Which is why I write for them."

Born in Boston, Massachusetts, in 1920, Stolz grew up in an unstable family environment. In her *SAAS*

article, she recalled that her mother and aunt, both barely in their twenties, had been sent during World War I to serve as nurses in France. There "they encountered men wild to find love, or something like love, some warmth and light in the flinty icy night of the First World War." Her aunt found Bill, and they eventually established a successful marriage. But her mother found Thomas Francis Slattery, and the two "hurled themselves headlong into love, as if it were a foxhole. Little was the luck they had," Stolz continued in *SAAS*. "Our father was . . . handsome, intelligent, and had 'the failing.'" Because he drank so heavily, neither Stolz nor her sister Eileen ever really knew him— or loved him. Instead, they were afraid of him. "Any child who's lived with a drunken father knows fear," Stolz explained in *SAAS*, "and, in my opinion, grows up slightly daft from uncertainty. If it had not been for Aunty and Unk, the dear knows we might have become daft entirely."

"Aunty and Unk"—Margaret Mary and Bill—not only provided Stolz and Eileen with a sense of security, they also introduced the girls to books.

Franny and Simone try to sustain their lunchtime friendship in Stolz's 1965 Newbery Honor Book.

"My Uncle Bill," Stolz remembered in *Something about the Author* (SATA), "bought me *Silver Pennies* when I was eight. *This Singing World* when I was ten, [American poet] Emily Dickinson and [British poet John] Keats when I was twelve. Marvelous selections." From these, Stolz developed both a tremendous love of reading and an intense fascination with writing. "I made the dazzling discovery," she wrote in *SAAS*, "that not only could I read the words in the books that my Uncle Bill was already buying for me, . . . but that I could also put words on paper in any order that pleased me. I can still recall the shivery joy of having a sheet of blank paper, a pencil, a notion, and realizing nothing else was needed."

Attending Birch Wathen School, then, was a pleasure for the young Stolz. Since it was a private, progressive school, its staff encouraged the students to study only those subjects they liked best. "In my case," Stolz recalled in *SATA*, "it worked out very well because all I bothered about was literature; and history. That was about it." So she put aside her studies of science or math—she never did master her multiplication tables—and instead dabbled in writing verses, essays, and short stories. She even completed her first novel when she was eleven and sent it to Hollywood, California, hoping it would be made into a movie. In time, Birch Wathen recognized Stolz's writing talents by naming her part-time reporter for its newspaper and assistant editor for its magazine, *Birch Leaves*. "The reason I did not make editor," she confessed in *SAAS*, "was that I was expelled for my sophomore and junior years as being disruptive, discourteous, boy-crazy, inattentive, and, excepting what was considered a real talent for writing, an all-round undesirable."

Fortunately, Birch Wathen eventually overlooked these offenses and accepted Stolz back for her senior year. She then graduated and entered Columbia University, where she continued her study of English. A few years later she also attended New York's Katharine Gibbs School, and there, she noted in *More Junior Authors*, "I learned to type, which is wonderful because I'm afraid I'd be too lazy to write an entire novel by hand, and would skip words, paragraphs, whole sections, just to have fewer words to pen."

In 1940 Stolz's writing career came to a halt. She married Stanley Burr Stolz, a civil engineer, and later had a son, Bill—named after her favorite uncle. For the next few years she busied herself as a homemaker and mother and rarely thought about writing. However, she was soon drawn back to her craft in quite a peculiar way. While in her early twenties, she fell ill. Then she began to ache. "And the ache increased," she remembered in *SAAS*, "and after several months it was so painful to move that I actually was afraid to cross a street for fear of not making it to the other side before the light changed. This, to a young woman . . ., seemed to me monstrous, unfair, and not to be *believed*. I kept thinking it would go away. It did not."

Stolz went to a handful of doctors and even had an operation, but the ache persisted. Then she saw Thomas C. Jaleski, a doctor whom she recalled in *SAAS* as being not only a wonderful physician but also an exceptional psychologist. Thinking that she might need something to engage her mind as well as heal her body, he asked her what she enjoyed doing—besides reading. "At length," she recalled in *SAAS*, "I told him that when I was in school . . . I'd liked to write. 'Well, that's excellent,' he said. 'My advice is that you write something that will take you a long time. Write a novel.' By then I was so in love with the doctor (never mind that we were both married, *or* that I never told my love, at least not then) that anything he suggested was, to me, a privilege, a joy, to accede to. I guess I took it as a prescription."

So arming herself with a used typewriter and a pile of yellow paper, Stolz wrote her first novel, *To Tell Your Love*, about a young girl who is abandoned by her first love. "It is sometimes said that the first novel is written some ten years back in a writer's life," Stolz suggested in *SAAS*. "This probably isn't a rule, but I followed it, writing about a fifteen-year-old girl who falls in love and loses her love, which probably should, or anyway does, happen to most fifteen-year-old girls. It had happened to me, and it was easy to recall the disbelief, the *pain* of having to accept that a boy who had seemed to love me, who had *said* he loved me, no longer did."

Stolz sent *To Tell Your Love* to Harper and Brothers (now Harper), though she never thought her novel would be published. She was wrong. After a few months, she received an invitation to meet with Ursula Nordstrom, Harper's children's book editor. Stolz calmly drove to the meeting. "'[Take] one minute at a time,'" she remembers telling herself, as she wrote in *SAAS*. "[I was] so happy to be able to walk and drive and be free of the house after years of pain and what I considered imprisonment, that it seemed to me I'd never ask anything more of life. (I wanted the doctor, but that seemed unreasonable.)"

As it turned out, Harper wanted to publish *To Tell Your Love* as a novel for young adults. Stolz was shocked. It seemed that her years of physical suffering had resulted somehow in a positive outcome. "I would not not have had those few years of pain for anything else life could offer me," she reflected in *SAAS*. "They led me to Dr. Jaleski, he led me back to writing, and ten years after that—never mind how—I could say, with Jane Eyre [the title character of a famous novel by Charlotte Bronte], 'Reader, I married him.'"

Since the publication of *To Tell Your Love* in 1950, Stolz has alternated between writing for children and writing for teenagers, though at the start of her career she concentrated primarily on composing young adult books. Among the earliest of these is *In a Mirror*, which won the Child Study Association Children's Book Award in 1953. Revolving around Bessie, a college junior, the story unfolds through journal entries, which reveal her innermost thoughts about college life, dates, and parties. The entries also reveal her emerging sense of self-understanding. When she finally admits that she has a weight problem, for example, she recognizes that she overeats to compensate for other problems in her life. The story "is a work of art," wrote a reviewer in *Horn Book*.

Stolz examines young love and its aftereffects in both *Pray Love, Remember* and *Wait for Me, Michael*. In the first story, Dody is a dreamy young girl who falls in love with Stephen Roth, a Jewish boy. When he suddenly dies, she is left to reassess and reformulate her ideas about religion, work, and values. In *Wait for Me, Michael*, Anny is a fifteen-year-old girl who is infatuated with Michael, an older man. However, he falls in love with Anny's widowed mother, and Anny is left to deal with her own heartache. *Wait for Me, Michael* is an "excellent novel," asserted Mary K. Eakin in *Good Books for Children*.

In 1957's *Because of Madeline* and 1963's *Who Wants Music on Monday?*, Stolz portrays heroines whose appeal lies in their intellect and ambition, not their physical beauty or popularity. In the former story, the title character is an underprivileged student who earns a scholarship to an exclusive, private school. With no desire to be accepted by the school's "in" crowd, she instead concentrates on her strong academic abilities, which enable her to achieve scholastic success. In the latter story, Cassie is an intelligent but awkward fourteen-year-old who resents the charm and grace of her attractive sister, Lotta. As the narrative develops, however, Lotta's shallowness and

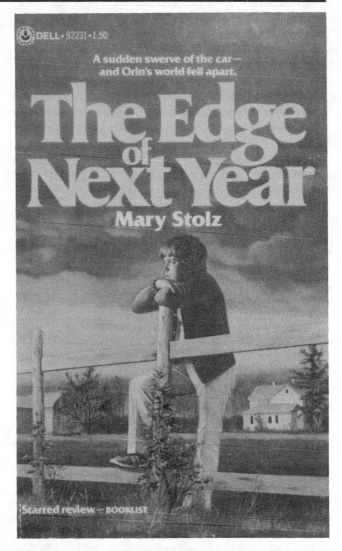

In this 1974 novel, Orin's tranquil life is destroyed when his mother is killed and he is forced to take on the responsibility of running the household.

arrogance are revealed, and she is rejected by the man she loves. The same man, though, welcomes a new friendship with Cassie. *Who Wants Music on Monday?* is a "wonderful book," judged Eakin in *Good Books for Children*.

During the 1960s Stolz concentrated on writing for children, not completing her next young adult novel, *By the Highway Home*, until 1971. The story features the Reed family, whose young son has been killed more than a year earlier while fighting in the Vietnam War. Throughout the course of the narrative the Reeds deal with economic misfortune—Mr. Reed loses his job—and an unsettling move to Vermont. But the sorrow they continually suffer over their son's tragic death overshadows all their daily events. In *By the Highway Home*, "Stolz [exhibits] remarkable insight into that long, aching grief that settles down to live with a family," concluded Jean Fritz in the *New York Times Book Review.*

In *The Edge of Next Year,* which was nominated for the National Book Award in 1975, Stolz again focuses on a family that has suffered an immediate death. In the story, fourteen-year-old Orin Woodward lives a serene and almost idyllic life on a rustic farm. Days are happily spent both with his parents, who read poetry aloud and gaze at the moon, and his younger brother, Victor, who collects bugs and snakes. Orin's security is shattered, though, the day his mother is struck by a motorist. Her death plummets Orin's father into alcoholism and forces Orin to assume sole responsibility for not only Victor but for the management of the entire household. As the story progresses, Orin increasingly becomes not only emotionally isolated but also terrified that his father is abandoning him forever. "The shock and numbness of sudden tragedy are sharply drawn," noted a critic in *Kirkus Review.*

Following *The Edge of Next Year,* Stolz wrote two other young adult novels, *Go and Catch a Flying Fish* and its sequel, *What Time of Night Is It?* Then she again turned her talents to composing children's books. In a 1974 article, Linda Giuca, a *Hartford Courant* reporter, proposed that Stolz has gradually shifted her focus to a younger audience because she feels more comfortable writing for children rather than teenagers. "The Stolz name will be added to more children's books," Giuca wrote in the article, as reprinted in *Authors in the News,* "but the successful author doubts that she will pen more books for high school students. 'I don't understand the drug culture of today,' [Stolz] said thoughtfully. 'You can't write about what you don't know.'" In comments Stolz provided to *Authors and Artists for Young Adults (AAYA),* she further elaborated on her decision to direct her writings toward a younger audience: "Teenagers seem to me already beyond rescue, having had their emotions warped, their minds and vision smeared by the violence and vulgarity that society now accepts with little murmur. But I am positive that young children are still to be reached, that many of them will still listen to voices raised in defense of beauty, civility, regard for others, and for the well-being of this trembling planet on which we live and depend, and which we, the adults, seem determined to destroy.

"That's why I write for children. I cannot share their lives because I am too old, but I try to fly over their encampments, dropping leaflets saying, 'When you are grown, remember what you were in childhood, remember what you thought was important, and what you dreamed of doing and of being. Then do it, and be it. Confront the destroyers with passion, with fury, with all your might. You *might* just bring them down and save the rest of us.'"

Among Stolz's most popular works for children are her "Barkham Street" books, which include *A Dog on Barkham Street, The Bully of Barkham Street,* and *The Explorer of Barkham Street.* The first of these revolves around ten-year-old Edward Frost, who is terrified of Martin Hastings, the bully who lives next door. As the story evolves, Edward continually flees from Martin's abuse—until Martin dares to insult Edward's favorite uncle. *Bully* and *Explorer,* on the other hand, focus on Martin. In the first, Martin retells the events of *Dog* from his own point of view and gradually exposes his loneliness and unhappiness. In *Explorer,* set a few years later, Martin resolves to make amends with Edward and redeem himself in the eyes of his neighbors. Through a successful baby-sitting venture and a memorable vacation to the country, he slowly gains self-confidence. The "sensitivity to the feelings which may lie beneath the armor of a young ruffian mark a fine book," declared a reviewer in *Horn Book.*

During the 1960s, Stolz received Newbery Honor Book awards for both *Belling the Tiger* and *The Noonday Friends.* The first begins a series of adventures about Asa and Rambo, two timid cellar mice who are selected to fasten a belled collar on a cat. During the course of the story, they find themselves transported to a tropical island, where they not only ward off an elephant, but ultimately bell a tiger. *The Noonday Friends* features Franny and Simone, two schoolmates so burdened with after school chores that they only see each other during lunch. Although the narrative also chronicles the events of their individual families—Franny's family deals with her father's unemployment, for example—the story focuses primarily on Franny and her determination to maintain her new friendship. *The Noonday Friends* "is warm, convincing," declared a reviewer in the *Bulletin of the Center for Children's Books,* while a critic in *Booklist* called the novel "delightful" and "perceptively written."

In other children's books Stolz delves into such topics as animal fantasies and historical fiction. In *Quentin Corn,* for instance, a smart pig escapes a butchering by disguising himself as human. Since he has learned to speak "people," he secures a job and becomes friends with the neighborhood children, the only ones who know his true identity. In *Bartholomew Fair*, set in sixteenth-century London, six people ranging from a town orphan to the Queen of England attend the final day of the Bartholomew Fair. The story is "a compelling tale brimming with ... traditions [and] pageantry," declared a reviewer in *Publishers Weekly*.

Throughout the years, as evidenced by 1988's *Storm in the Night* and 1991's *Go Fish,* Stolz has decided to write stories that are for and about black children. "It is my opinion that black children do not have enough books written for them," she told *AAYA*. "They don't have enough of anything done for them, of course." She also added that she "care[s], deeply, about the future of this earth, about all that part of it that cannot speak to us or defend itself—the creatures we term the 'lower animals,' the rivers and forests, the oceans, the *land*. I do not think we will save ourselves, or

the planet, and aside from sending as much money as I can to organizations trying to balance out the kinds of human beings who can't see beyond the next lottery ticket, my aim until I am out of all this is to write for young children, specifically black children."

In addition to working on her books, Stolz indulges her love for her family—she has several grandchildren, nieces, and nephews—and she especially enjoys spending time with her husband. "He's never been less than I guessed him to be the first day I walked into his office," she proclaimed in *SAAS*. At home she also takes care of the cooking, washing, and shopping. But each morning she makes sure she devotes several hours to writing, a vocation she has never regretted choosing. "As I look back," she decided in *SAAS*, "and back and back, over the years of writing, as a child and a girl, and then—to my stunned surprise—as a professional, the disappointments are slight, weighed against the rewards. I *always* wanted to be a writer, a real, published writer—the way other girls at school wanted to become actresses. A few of them did become actresses, and here am I, a writer."

■ Works Cited

Eakin, Mary K., reviews of *Wait for Me, Michael* and *Who Wants Music on Monday?, Good Books for Children,* 3rd edition, University of Chicago Press, 1966, pp. 318-319.

Review of *The Edge of Next Year, Kirkus Review,* October 15, 1974, pp. 111-112.

Review of *The Explorer of Barkham Street, Horn Book,* January, 1986, p. 61.

Fritz, Jean, review of *By the Highway Home, New York Times Book Review,* October 24, 1971, p. 8.

Giuca, Linda, "Author's 'Recipe': Add Talent to Volumes of Reading, Writing," *Hartford Courant,* June 2, 1974, reprinted in *Authors in the News,* Volume 1, Gale, 1976, p. 454.

Review of *In a Mirror, Horn Book,* December, 1953, pp. 469-470.

Review of *The Noonday Friends, Bulletin of the Center for Children's Books,* November, 1965, pp. 50-51.

Something about the Author, Volume 10, Gale, 1976, pp. 165-167.

Stolz, Mary, in comments provided to Denise E. Kasinec for *Authors and Artists for Young Adults.*

Stolz, Mary, "Mary Stolz," *More Junior Authors,* edited by Muriel Fuller, H. W. Wilson, 1963, pp. 195-196.

Set in sixteenth-century London, Stolz's 1990 historical children's story describes the various people attending the last day of a country fair.

Stolz, Mary, "Mary Stolz," *Something about the Author Autobiography Series*, Volume 3, Gale, 1986, pp. 281-292.

■ For More Information See

BOOKS

Contemporary Literary Criticism, Volume 12, Gale, 1980.

Hopkins, Lee Bennett, *More Books by More People: Interviews with Sixty-five Authors of Books for Children*, Citation, 1974.

PERIODICALS

Atlantic Monthly, December, 1953.

Booklist, September 15, 1974; January 1, 1976; November 1, 1988.

Bulletin of the Center for Children's Books, May, 1969; December, 1969; July, 1979; July, 1981; July, 1983; October, 1985; May, 1988.

Chicago Sunday Tribune, August 23, 1953; November 6, 1960.

English Journal, September, 1952; September, 1955.

Horn Book, April, 1957; October, 1957; October, 1965; December, 1975; April, 1981; November, 1985.

Los Angeles Times Book Review, July 28, 1985; April 20, 1986; May 3, 1987.

New York Herald Tribune Book Review, October 28, 1951; December 13, 1953; November 14, 1954; November 28, 1954; November 13, 1955; December 30, 1956.

New York Times Book Review, May 13, 1951; August 30, 1953; September 26, 1954; April 22, 1956; May 18, 1958; November 13, 1960; May 14, 1961; November 12, 1961.

Publishers Weekly, July 12, 1985; August 9, 1985; September 20, 1985; September 26, 1986; October 9, 1987; January 15, 1988; February 12, 1988; August 26, 1988; August 31, 1990.

School Library Journal, April, 1964; September, 1985; November, 1985; January, 1986; December, 1986; April, 1987; January, 1988; November, 1990.

Times Literary Supplement, November 26, 1954.

Washington Post Book World, May 10, 1987; February 10, 1991.

Writer, October, 1980.

—Sketch by Denise E. Kasinec

Maia Wojciechowska

■ Personal

Surname pronounced Voi-che-*hov*-skah; born August 7, 1927, in Warsaw, Poland; came to United States in 1942; naturalized U.S. citizen, 1950; daughter of Zygmunt (wartime chief-of-staff, Polish Air Force) and Zofia (Rudakowska) Wojciechowski; married Selden Rodman (a writer), December 8, 1950 (divorced, 1957); married Richard Larkin (a poet and antique restorer), January 9, 1972 (divorced, 1981); children: (first marriage) Oriana (daughter); Leonora (adopted daughter). *Education:* Attended schools in Poland, France, and England; attended Immaculate Heart College, 1945-46. *Politics:* "Jeffersonian Christian Anarchist." *Religion:* Roman Catholic.

■ Addresses

Home—122 North Railroad Ave., Mahwah, NJ 07430. *Agent:* Gunther Stuhlmann, P.O. Box 276, Becket, MA 01223.

■ Career

Poet, translator, and writer of children's fiction. Has worked at a variety of jobs (seventy-two in one year), including undercover detective, poll taker, and ghost writer. Translator for Radio Free Europe, 1949-51; *Retail Wholesale and Department Store Union Record,* New York City, assistant editor, 1953-55; *Newsweek,* New York City, copy girl, 1956; *RWDSU Record* (labor newspaper), New York City, assistant editor, 1957; *American Hairdresser* (trade publication), New York City, assistant editor, 1958-60; Kurt Hellmer, New York City, literary agent, 1960-61; independent literary agent, 1960-61; Hawthorn Books, Inc., New York City, publicity manager, 1961-65. Professional tennis player and instructor, 1949—. Founder and president of Maia Productions, Inc., Independent Books, 1975—, and ENOUGH!!!, 1986—.

■ Awards, Honors

New York Herald Tribune Children's Spring Book Festival Awards honor book, 1964, and John Newbery Medal, 1965, both for *Shadow of a Bull;* awarded Deutscher Jugendbuchpries, 1968; named to New Jersey Literary Hall of Fame, 1985.

■ Writings

UNDER NAME MAIA RODMAN

Market Day for Ti Andre (juvenile), Viking, 1952.
The Loved Look: International Hairstyling Guide, American Hairdresser, 1960.
The People in His Life (novel; Book-of-the-Month Club alternate selection), Stein & Day, 1980.

UNDER NAME MAIA WOJCIECHOWSKA

Shadow of a Bull, Atheneum, 1964.

Odyssey of Courage: The Adventure of Alvar Nunez Cabeza de Vaca (juvenile biography), Atheneum, 1965.

A Kingdom in a Horse, Harper, 1966.

The Hollywood Kid, Harper, 1967.

A Single Light, Harper, 1968.

Tuned Out, Harper, 1968.

Hey, What's Wrong with This One?, Harper, 1969.

Don't Play Dead Before You Have To, Harper, 1970.

(Translator) Monika Kotowska, *The Bridge to the Other Side,* Doubleday, 1971.

The Rotten Years, Doubleday, 1971.

The Life and Death of a Brave Bull, Harcourt, 1972.

Through the Broken Mirror with Alice (includes parts of *Through the Looking Glass* by Lewis Carroll), Harcourt, 1972.

Winter Tales from Poland, Doubleday, 1972.

Till the Break of Day: Memories, 1939-1942, Harcourt, 1973.

How God Got Christian into Trouble, Westminster/John Knox, 1984.

Contributor of poetry to anthologies; writer of humorous pieces for *Sports Illustrated.* Contributor of articles and reviews to numerous periodicals. Translator from the Polish of a play by Slawomir Mrozek, performed Off-Broadway in 1962, and on British Broadcasting Corp. Radio in 1963 and 1964.

■ Adaptations

Tuned Out was adapted for film and released as *Stoned: An Anti-Drug Film* by Learning Corp. of America, 1981; *A Single Light* was adapted for film and released by Learning Corp. of America, 1986; the movie rights to *The People in His Life* and *Shadow of a Bull* have been optioned.

■ Sidelights

Maia Wojciechowska is a Polish-born novelist, biographer, poet, and translator who has long been considered an influential and respected figure in young adult and juvenile literature. Once described by John R. Tunis in the *New York Times Book Review* as "a magnificent writer," Wojciechowska's skill for writing accurately and with sensitivity about the various problems facing young people today in their search to find their own identity is admired and appreciated by her many loyal readers. Awarded the prestigious Newbery Medal in 1965 for *Shadow of a Bull,* Wojciechowska has created many unique and unforgettable characters who courageously confront and resolve their problems.

One has only to look at Wojciechowska's interesting and adventurous life to understand the inspiration behind many of her popular works of fiction. Born in Warsaw, the capital of Poland, in 1927, Wojciechowska was a middle child—a resourceful and capable girl sandwiched between her two energetic brothers and surrounded by many colorful relatives. Wojciechowska's father was a pilot in the Polish Air Force and her mother often raised the family alone for the periods of time her father was stationed away from home. Definitely a daredevil, Wojciechowska was constantly challenging herself with some dangerous feat. "I liked to do things I could feel were individualistic or strange," Wojciechowska told Justin Wintle in *The Pied Pipers.* For example, before her eleventh birthday, Wojciechowska had already parachuted three times from an airplane.

In this 1965 Newbery Medal-winner, a young man must choose between loyalty to his deceased father and his own desires and aspirations.

But all her childhood adventures paled when compared to Wojciechowska's dangerous escape from her homeland following the Nazi invasion of Poland at the outbreak of World War II in 1939. This historic event would dramatically change her life and force Wojciechowska to grow up quickly and face unimaginable challenges.

Witnessing the horrible and vicious behavior of the Nazi invading troops towards the Polish people, especially those of Jewish descent, and fearing for her family's safety, Maia's mother decided to leave their home and join her husband, who was stationed in France. Mrs. Wojciechowska bravely guided Maia and her two brothers out of war-torn Poland. Often travelling on foot and desperately trying to avoid both the German and Soviet invaders, the Wojciechowska family made their way through Rumania and Italy, finally reaching France.

While the entire family found life in France very difficult, the Wojciechowski children found the abrupt and stressful flight to a new country, culture, and language especially tough. For example, in one year alone, the family moved so many times Maia attended seventeen different schools. "I would often sit for hours on end looking at the Seine and think of the emptiness that I felt and of what we were doing in this limbo of a place," Wojciechowska wrote in her autobiography, *Till the Break of Day: Memories 1939-1942.* "We had lost our roots—that much I knew—and I worried about what this would do to all of us. For once I gave a lot of thought to the five of us, to the family.... Suspended in space, that's what we were, and there was nothing happening but much to feel."

In 1940, when the French government surrendered to the power of the German occupation forces, Colonel Wojciechowski left for England while his family remained in France. The family would later seek refuge in Spain, Portugal, and England before deciding that the United States would make the safest and best home. At the end of 1942, Colonel Wojciechowski, who had been chief-of-staff of the Polish Air Force in Great Britain, accepted an assignment as air attache to the Polish Embassy in Los Angeles and the family started their new life in America.

Wojciechowska discusses this intriguing and fascinating time of her life in *Till the Break of Day.* Mary M. Burns writes in *Horn Book* of Wojciechowska's book in this manner: "Confession may be good for the soul, but confessional writing may not be good reading unless the penitent is blessed, as is the author of this remarkable document, with an understanding of life's absurdities, a sense of the dramatic, and a felicitous talent for precise, vivid description. Because of these qualities, her reminiscences of a turbulent adolescence during the Second World War are both intensely personal and yet recognizable as a universal statement on the tragicomic conditions which are a necessary part of maturation.... The book is a dazzling blend of emotional pyrotechnics and disciplined structure."

In her review of *Till the Break of Day* published in *Best Sellers* Shirley Weinstein remarks: "With great candor, humor, and vividness, Maia Wojciechowska gives an autobiographical account of how she lived through the years 1939-1942." Weinstein goes on to note that "many of Maia's escapades and lucky breaks will make the reader gasp. In describing herself Maia gives a true picture of the adolescent. Her obsession with ideals, death, love, self-hatred will strike a responsive chord. This is a book for everyone."

Life and freedom in the United States was vastly different from anything Wojciechowska had ever experienced. Although she learned the English language very quickly, Maia felt different and out of sync with her peers at Los Angeles' Sacred Heart Academy. At times Wojciechowska seemed to rebelliously distance herself from her fellow classmates and teachers, possibly because she was having a difficult time adjusting to her new life in America.

After graduation from high school in Los Angeles, Wojciechowska attended Immaculate Heart College for a year before leaving school in 1946. Although she always wanted to write for a living, Wojciechowska's first novel was rejected by over thirty publishers. Unable to survive as a writer and unsure of what other career she wanted to pursue, Wojciechowska tried her hand at a myriad of professions and amused herself with numerous adventures, such as motorcycle racing and downhill skiing. In one year, Maia worked at an unbelievable seventy-two jobs—including waitress, masseuse, and undercover detective. During this time Wojciechowska also maintained a career as a professional tennis player and instructor.

"During what seems like an extremely long and adventurous life," Maia remarked, "I have parachuted, fought bulls, won a few tennis championships, motorcycle raced, snuck into almost every Broadway theater in an attempt to stimulate applause even for mediocre plays, bid at numerous auctions and have been caught a few times, jay-walked out of a sense of duty to preserve some right to self determination ... tried periodically and always unsuccessfully to be 'like everybody else'." Perhaps it is Wojciechowska's constant and life-long search to find inner peace and happiness that has made her so sensitive to the same search for identity in her young readers.

In 1952, Wojciechowska finally discovered a vent for her sense of adventure and her passion for the unorthodox—writing. With the help and encouragement of her then husband, Selden Rodman, Wojciechowska wrote a story to accompany the artwork of a Haitian artist whose work she admired. Maia's first book, *Market Day for Ti Andre*, was published, launching what would become a very successful and rewarding writing career for Wojciechowska.

Although never really losing her daredevil ways and her thirst for excitement, writing brought

THE HOLLYWOOD KID

by Maia Wojciechowska
Winner of the 1965 Newbery Medal

Wojciechowska's 1967 book chronicles a fifteen-year-old boy's search for identity and rejection of his empty life as the son of a famous movie star.

more stability to Wojciechowska's life. "Becoming a full-time writer 'for a living' was my way, I think, of growing up," explains Wojciechowska in her essay for *Something about the Author Autobiography Series (SAAS)*. "That I began to write children's books was perhaps my way of not cutting away from the childhood too drastically."

It is perhaps Wojciechowska's childlike spirit of adventure as well as her still vivid memories of her own adolescence that have made her stories for young people so appealing and popular. Her award-winning book *Shadow of a Bull*, for example, is an exciting tale involving bullfighting set in a colorful city located in Spain. Manolo, the son of a famous bullfighter who lost his life in a bullfight, feels immense pressure to follow in his father's footsteps. Manolo is unhappy and confused and does not understand why he is feeling these emotions. Manolo finally realizes that he is training to be a bullfighter out of loyalty to his late father and not because it is what he really wants. For the first time in his life, Manolo is free to look within himself to discover what he wants to do with his life. He decides he wants to become a doctor. "In this somber tale, the author captures the rhythm of the Spanish people and the personal conflict of a young boy," writes John Gillespie and Diane Lembo in *Juniorplots: A Book Talk Manual for Teachers and Librarians*. "Wojciechowska's style reflects the austere grandeur of the Andalusian countryside. It is reminiscent of Hemingway, both in the knowledge of bullfighting and in the deceptively spare construction."

Some people were surprised that a book about bullfighting set in Spain would be so well received by young readers in America and elsewhere in the world. But, as a number of reviewers point out, *Shadow of a Bull* is much more than a tale about bullfighting. Wojciechowska writes of a boy's search for happiness and fulfillment for himself no matter what pressures or demands are placed on him. It is a book about a universally understood theme that is merely set in a somewhat unfamiliar setting.

Ruth Hill Viguers explains in *Horn Book* that this book is "no manifesto for or against bullfighting. [*Shadow of a Bull*] is a perceptive story, with a perfectly realized setting, of a boy torn between loyalty and the need to be himself. Rarely in a book for any age does one find such understanding of bullfighting background and the symbolic role of the *torero* (the 'killer of death'), of the agonies of an adolescent boy longing to be understood and recognized for himself, and of the phenomenon of the oneness of viewpoint of all the people of a village."

Wojciechowska shared her thoughts on writing *Shadow of a Bull* in her acceptance speech upon receiving the Newbery Medal in 1965. She told the audience attending the awards ceremony that "*Shadow [of a Bull]* was mostly about pride and being locked in. I say pride rather than self-respect, because in Spain the word *pride* encompasses so much—honor and dignity and self-esteem. You'll find that sort of pride in others, more often in the poor than in the rich, and you'll find it in yourself. Because you are you, you'll respect it wherever you find it in spite of what others may say about it. That sort of pride, sometimes—most of the time—makes life harder than it needs to be. But without pride, life is less.

"About being locked in. Sometimes one lives in a prison without a key, without hope of a pardon. Sometimes one never gets out. And sometimes, when one gets out, it is at a cost in pride, and sometimes at a cost in success. It all depends on who built the prison. If you've built the prison yourself, you should never pay in pride. If others have built it, I hope you'll pay them in success. So, you see, *Shadow of a Bull* is not a book about bullfighting after all." Wojciechowska's entire speech was printed in *Newbery and Caldecott Medal Books: 1956-1965.*

This philosophy of self-respect or self-realization or searching for identity is a favorite theme of Wojciechowska's and is the focal point of most of her books. Wojciechowska believes in order to find happiness with themselves young people must first develop their own sense of self or identity. Critics often point to such Wojciechowska books as *The Hollywood Kid, A Single Light,* and *Tuned Out* as examples how gifted Wojciechowska is at portraying the emotions experienced by many of today's youths as they move closer to adulthood.

For example, in *The Hollywood Kid,* fifteen-year-old Bryan finds himself lonely, emotionally empty, and confused. As the only son of a famous Hollywood movie star, Bryan was given all the material advantages money could buy, but none of the good things a stable, supportive family would provide. After several failed attempts to find happiness, Bryan finally discovers that what really matters in life is learning to accept and be content with who he is. Bryan rejects his old, shallow lifestyle and works hard to find his true self and achieve inner peace and fulfillment. "[In *The Hollywood Kid*] Bryan must choose between psychic independence

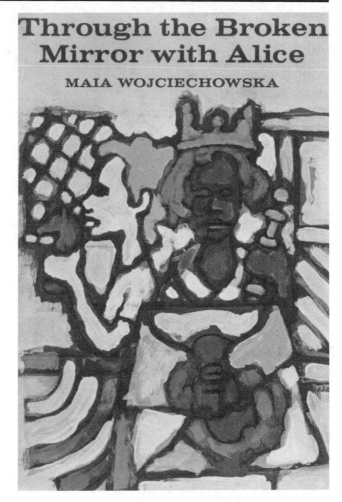

Through the Broken Mirror with Alice

MAIA WOJCIECHOWSKA

This 1972 work presents a modern-day black Alice who uses the fantasy of Wonderland to escape the harsh realities of her life.

or a relationship in which he is his mother's prop," explains Zena Sutherland in the *Bulletin of the Center for Children's Books.* "This is a problem faced by many adolescents, a problem not always recognized by the parental instigator; for this reason, the book has value."

"The strength of the book is in the fact that it doesn't touch up the basic problem of any youngster's accommodation to adults who are what they are and who will stay that way, and it reads with the greatest of ease," notes a critic for *Kirkus Service.* And A. H. Weiler states in the *New York Times Book Review* that "Maia Wojciechowska again illustrates, through *The Hollywood Kid,* her sensitive insight into the enigma of a genuinely troubled juvenile born to the purple of picture royalty.... Bryan's anxieties and confusion are not contrivances for plot purposes. Miss Wojciechowska's taut, precise prose makes it plain that she knows the heart and mind of an unusual lad

Maia Wojciechowska

Till the Break of Day
Memories: 1939-1942

Wojciechowska describes her emotional adolescence spent in France as a refugee from Poland during World War II in this acclaimed memoir.

struggling to free himself from a tinseled world he never made or wanted." In correspondence with *Authors and Artists for Young Adults* (AAYA), Wojciechowska explains that she wrote *The Hollywood Kid* "because I was obsessed with the thought that I knew what it would be like to be Marilyn Monroe's child."

In *A Single Light*, Wojciechowska once again draws on the starkly beautiful countryside of Spain to set her story of a deaf and nonverbal girl who was abandoned by her family and ostracized by the villagers confused by her handicap. Treated meanly and called a witch because of her inability to communicate and to hear properly, the young child takes a priceless religious statue she has grown attached to and hides in the nearby woods. Finally the townspeople come to their senses and accept the girl for who she is and give her the love and understanding she has desired for so long. "I wanted to see whether I was any good as a writer,"

Wojciechowska writes *AAYA*, "so I picked the most difficult character, a mute-deaf girl. I am strongest at dialogue, you see, so it was working uphill. But it's probably my best book."

John R. Tunis states in the *New York Times Book Review* that *A Single Light* "is a short book, not more than 30,000 words. (How often good books are short!) I read it twice, to see whether it was as fine as it seemed. It was even better.... The unnamed girl's story is told in the simplest terms. As it moves to its climax, we see how her presence changes the lives of those around her.... The overtones in Maia Wojciechowska's book defy synopsis. The finale, in the hands of a less skillful craftsman, could have seemed overdone, even spurious. Here, it is both austere and moving. The whole tale moves and flows, like life. Hope for the future of man is its essence."

In a *Library Journal* review of *A Single Light*, Bernice Levine tells why she was impressed with Wojciechowska's book: "Told with controlled pathos, the plight of a young deaf and dumb girl, who grew up unwanted in an Andalusian village, and the impact of her presence on the villagers ... makes a strong story. The themes are the overwhelming human need for love and the possibility for even the meanest persons to change. Because of the appeal that these universal themes have for young people and the smooth and unobtrusive quality of the writing, the book should have a wide readership."

Three other books that contain the same themes of self-realization and the need for love as Wojciechowska's earlier works are *Tuned Out, Don't Play Dead Before You Have To*, and *The Rotten Years*. However, these novels for young people are different because they deal with very modern and serious problems—such as drug abuse in *Tuned Out*, depression and suicide in *Don't Play Dead Before You Have To*, and passionate political activism in *The Rotten Years*.

In general these books have been praised for their realistic and straightforward treatment of their sensitive subject matter. In her *New York Times Book Review* article discussing Wojciechowska's *Tuned Out*, Anita Macrae Feagles writes, "A hopeful trend in teen-age fiction is the increase in titles dealing with current, serious and often unpleasant situations." Feagles goes on to state that she believes *Tuned Out* "is certainly worthwhile reading for young people, for whom fictionalized material is likely to be more meaningful."

Zena Sutherland remarks in the *Bulletin of the Center for Children's Books* that *Tuned Out* is "a story of intensity and bleak honesty.... At times the writing slows, but this seems curiously appropriate in a story in which the stunned protagonist is fighting against time. [The book is candid], with no melodrama except the terrible melodrama of what is happening, and with a lack of didacticism that makes the message all the more effective."

Of Wojciechowska's book dealing with suicide, *Don't Play Dead Before You Have To*, John Neufeld comments in the *New York Times Book Review* that there are several positive elements: "Here is an attempt to write about the kid in-between—neither college nor slumbound, neither bright nor deadeningly dumb, not ambitious but aware—the middle achiever who is too frequently ignored. There is an honest, moving, yet oddly oblique look at the depression and attempted suicide of a very bright child whose parents are separating. And there is a lovely *coup de theatre* as an old man, a once-famous philosopher, allows a television interview knowing he will die on camera."

Benjamin DeMott remarks in his review of Wojciechowska's book about political activism, *The Rotten Years*, in the *New York Times Book Review* that "the strength of the book ... is the author's fine enthusiasm for great moral and political undertakings. *The Rotten Years* doesn't stand back from 'causes' and commitment: it embraces them with a quickness and force that's the best kind of answer to the question, Does injustice matter?"

Summing up Wojciechowska's work for young adults, I. V. Hansen states in *Children's Literature in Education* that "Wojciechowska moralizes to a point where we as older readers become impatient. Classroom experience suggests to me that this impatience is an adult phenomenon.... In the affairs of people, animals and even things, the young teenager is still attracted by the bald contrast between good and evil, beauty and ugliness, calm and convulsion, courage and fear, all part of [Wojciechowska's] novels. For these novels breathe a myth-quality that makes some sense of a violent world of pain, uncertainty and rejection. Young readers want to feel that, after all, people are just. All too soon they will learn bitterly that this is not so."

Throughout her years writing, Wojciechowska has always taken her responsibility as a writer very seriously. So committed was she to publishing quality literature that would stimulate the intelligence of young readers that Wojciechowska found-

ed her own publishing company, Independent Books, in 1975. She has also conducted many workshops on writing for young adult and juvenile readers during writers' conferences.

In her Newbery acceptance speech, Wojciechowska directed the following statement of her purpose as a writer to her readers: "I want to give you a glimpse of the choices you have before you, of the price that will be asked of you.... When you know what life has to sell, for how much, and what it can give away free, you will not live in darkness. I hope that in books you'll find your light, and that by this light you may cross from one shore of love to another, from your childhood into your adulthood. I hope that some of the light will come from my books and that, because of this light, life will lose its power to frighten you."

Wojciechowska shares some of her thoughts on what she feels makes a good writer of books for

Christian, who is able to hear the voice of God, befriends the optimistic neighborhood gardener in Wojciechowska's 1984 novel, *How God Got Christian into Trouble.*

young people in *The Writer*. She notes: "First of all, you must be a natural *admirer* of children. You must be one of those people who *instinctively* knows that children are the truly beautiful people. You must be aware of the magnificent beginning that is the lot of every human being, a beginning that is invariably loused up by people who don't recognize children as a superior breed. Children are more intelligent than adults. The directness of their thought processes must be the delight of logicians. They can write any adult under the table as readily as they can put to shame any painter. So you owe them *respect*."

■ Works Cited

Burns, Mary M., review of *Till the Break of Day*, *Horn Book*, December, 1972, p. 609.

DeMott, Benjamin, review of *The Rotten Years*, *New York Times Book Review*, November 7, 1971, pp. 3, 22.

Feagles, Anita Macrae, review of *Tuned Out*, *New York Times Book Review*, November 24, 1968, p. 42.

Gillespie, John, and Diane Lembo, *Juniorplots: A Book Talk Manual for Teachers and Librarians*, Bowker, 1967, p. 54.

Hansen, I. V., "The Spanish Setting: A Re-appraisal of Maia Wojciechowska," *Children's Literature in Education*, winter, 1981, pp. 186-91.

Kingman, Lee, editor, "Shadow of a Kid," *Newbery and Caldecott Medal Books: 1956-1965*, Horn Book, 1965, pp. 140-52.

Levine, Bernice, review of *A Single Light*, *Library Journal*, Bowker, July, 1968, p. 2738.

Neufeld, John, review of *Don't Play Dead Before You Have To*, *New York Times Book Review*, August 16, 1970, p. 22.

Review of *The Hollywood Kid*, *Kirkus Service*, August 1, 1966, pp. 757-58.

Sutherland, Zena, review of *The Hollywood Kid*, *Bulletin of the Center for Children's Books*, March, 1967, p. 116.

Sutherland, Zena, review of *Tuned Out*, *Bulletin of the Center for Children's Books*, February, 1969, p. 104.

Tunis, John R., "That Day in Almas," *New York Times Book Review*, May 5, 1968 (Part 2), p. 3.

Viguers, Ruth Hill, review of *Shadow of a Bull*, *Horn Book*, June, 1964, pp. 293-94.

Weiler, A. H., review of *The Hollywood Kid*, *New York Times Book Review*, November 6, 1966 (Part 2), p. 8.

Weinstein, Shirley, review of *Till the Break of Day*, *Best Sellers*, April 15, 1973, p. 47.

Wintle, Justin, and Emma Fisher, *The Pied Pipers*, Paddington Press, 1975.

Wojciechowska, Maia, in comments provided for *Authors and Artists for Young Adults*.

Wojciechowska, Maia, acceptance speech at the Newbery and Caldecott Awards Ceremony, 1965, published in *Newbery and Caldecott Medal Books: 1956-1965*.

Wojciechowska, Maia, *Something about the Author Autobiography Series*, Volume 1, Gale, 1986, pp. 307-325.

Wojciechowska, Maia, *Till the Break of Day: Memories 1939-1942*, Harcourt, 1973.

Wojciechowska, Maia, "Who Should Write for Young Readers?," *The Writer*, April, 1971, p. 3.

■ For More Information See

BOOKS

Children's Literature Review, Volume 1, Gale, 1976.

Contemporary Authors New Revision Series, Volume 4, Gale, 1981.

Contemporary Literary Criticism, Volume 26, Gale, 1983.

Current Biography 1976, H. W. Wilson, 1977.

Hopkins, Lee Bennett, *More Books by More People*, Citation, 1974.

PERIODICALS

Library Journal, July, 1968.

National Observer, December, 1968.

New York Times Book Review, November 5, 1972.

Saturday Review, March 27, 1965.

The Writer, July, 1987; September, 1990.

Tom Wolfe

■ Personal

Full name Thomas Kennerly Wolfe, Jr.; born March 2, 1930, in Richmond, VA; son of Thomas Kennerly (a scientist and business executive) and Helen (Hughes) Wolfe; married Sheila Berger (art director of *Harper's* magazine), 1978; children: Alexandra. *Education:* Washington and Lee University, B.A. (cum laude), 1951; Yale University, Ph.D., 1957.

■ Addresses

Home—New York, NY. *Agent*—Lynn Nesbit, 598 Madison Ave., New York, NY 10022.

■ Career

Writer, journalist, social commentator, and artist. *Springfield Union*, Springfield, MA, reporter, 1956-59; *Washington Post*, Washington, D.C., reporter and Latin American correspondent, 1959-62; *New York Herald Tribune*, New York City, city reporter, and *New York* Sunday magazine (now *New York* magazine), New York City, writer, both 1962-66; *New York World Journal Tribune*, New York City, writer, 1966-67; *New York* magazine,

New York City, contributing editor, 1968-76; *Esquire* magazine, New York City, contributing editor, 1977—; *Harper's* magazine, New York City, contributing artist, 1978-81. Has exhibited drawings in one-man shows at Maynard Walker Gallery, 1965, and Tunnel Gallery, 1974.

■ Awards, Honors

Washington Newspaper Guild awards for foreign news reporting and for humor, both 1961; Society of Magazine Writers award for excellence, 1970; D.F.A., Minneapolis College of Art, 1971; Frank Luther Mott research award, 1973; D.Litt., Washington and Lee University, 1974; named Virginia Laureate for literature, 1977; American Book Award, 1980, for *The Right Stuff;* Harold D. Vursell Memorial Award for excellence in literature, American Institute of Arts and Letters, 1980; Columbia Journalism Award, 1980; citation for art history from National Sculpture Society, 1980; L.H.D. from Virginia Commonwealth University, 1983, and Southampton College, 1984; John Dos Passos Award, 1984; Gari Melchers Medal, 1986; Benjamin Pierce Cheney Medal from Eastern Washington University, 1986; Washington Irving Medal for literary excellence from Nicholas Society, 1986.

■ Writings

(Self-illustrated) *The Kandy-Kolored Tangerine-Flake Streamline Baby* (essays), Farrar, Straus, 1965, recent edition, 1987.

(Contributor) Alan Rinzler, editor, *The New York Spy*, David White, 1967.

The Electric Kool-Aid Acid Test, Farrar, Straus, 1968, recent edition, 1987.

The Pump House Gang (essays), Farrar, Straus, 1968 (published in England as *The Mid-Atlantic Man and Other New Breeds in England and America*, Weidenfeld & Nicolson, 1969).

Radical Chic and Mau Mauing the Flak Catchers (two essays), Farrar, Straus, 1970, recent edition, 1987.

(Editor with E. W. Johnson and contributor) *The New Journalism* (anthology), Harper, 1973.

(Self-illustrated) *The Painted Word*, Farrar, Straus, 1975.

(Self-illustrated) *Mauve Gloves & Madmen, Clutter & Vine, and Other Short Stories* (essays), Farrar, Straus, 1976.

(Contributor) Susan Feldman, editor, *Marie Cosindas, Color Photographs*, New York Graphic Society, 1978.

The Right Stuff (Book-of-the-Month-Club selection), Farrar, Straus, 1979.

(Self-illustrated) *In Our Time* (essays), Farrar, Straus, 1980.

From Bauhaus to Our House, Farrar, Straus, 1981.

(Self-illustrated) *The Purple Decades: A Reader* (collection), Farrar, Straus, 1982.

The Bonfire of the Vanities (novel), Farrar, Straus, 1987.

Contributor of numerous articles to periodicals. Co-founder of literary quarterly *Shenandoah*.

■ Adaptations

The Right Stuff (film), directed by Phil Kaufman, starring Sam Shepard, Ed Harris, and Dennis Quaid, Warner Bros., 1983.

The Bonfire of the Vanities (film), directed by Brian De Palma, starring Tom Hanks, Melanie Griffith, and Bruce Willis, 1990.

■ Sidelights

"Those of you who are not aware of Tom Wolfe should—really—do your best to acquaint yourselves with him," writes William F. Buckley in the *National Review*. "He is probably the most skilful writer in America. I mean by that he can do more things with words than anyone else." Satirist, caricaturist, social critic, coiner of phrases ("Radical Chic," "The Me Decade"), and novelist, Wolfe has become known as a leading chronicler of American trends. His painstaking research and detailed accounts have made him a widely respect-

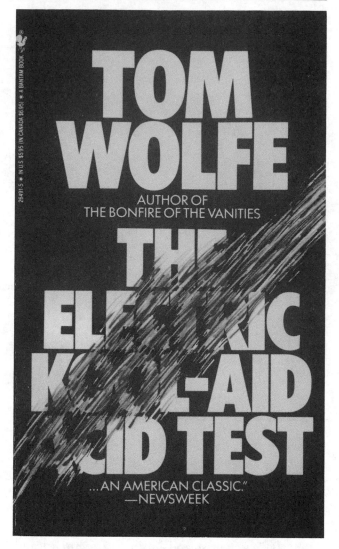

In this 1968 expose, Wolfe applies his unique brand of journalism to a group of people who seek happiness and knowledge through the use of hallucinogenic drugs.

ed reporter; at the same time, his unorthodox style and frequently unpopular opinions have resulted in a great deal of controversy. Leslie Bennetts of the *Philadelphia Bulletin* calls him "a professional rogue," who has "needled and knifed at the mighty of every description, exposing in print the follies and foibles of superstars from Leonard Bernstein to the Hell's Angels. Gleefully ripping off every shred of disguise from anyone's pretensions, Wolfe has performed his dissections in *New York* magazine, *Esquire*, and *Rolling Stone*, not to mention his earlier years on the *New York Herald Tribune* and the *Washington Post*."

Wolfe is generally recognized as one of the leaders in the branch of writing known as "New Journalism." Bennetts says that while Wolfe did not invent the movement, "he at least became its stentorian spokesman and most flamboyant practitioner.'' *Fort Lauderdale Sun-Sentinel* writer Margo Harakas believes that there is ''only a handful of standouts among [New Journalists]—Jimmy Breslin, Gay Talese, Hunter Thompson, and of course, Wolfe, with his explosive punctuation, name brand detailing, and kaleidoscopic descriptions.'' In a *Writer's Digest* article, Wolfe defines New Journalism as ''the use by people writing nonfiction of techniques which heretofore had been thought of as confined to the novel or to the short story, to create in one form both the kind of objective reality of journalism and the subjective reality that people have always gone to the novel for.'' The techniques employed in New Journalism, then, include a number of devices borrowed from traditional fiction writing: extensive dialogue; shifting point of view; scene-by-scene construction; detailed descriptions of setting, clothes, and other physical features; complex character development; and, depending on the reporter and on the subject, varying degrees of innovation in the use of language and punctuation.

Wolfe's association with New Journalism began in 1963, when he wrote his first magazine article, a piece on custom automobiles. He had become intrigued with the strange subculture of West Coast car customizers and was beginning to see these individuals as folk artists worthy of serious study. He convinced *Esquire* magazine to send him to California, where he researched the story, interviewed a number of subjects, and, says Harakas, ''racked up a $750 tab at the Beverly Wilshire Hotel (picked up by *Esquire,* of course).'' Then, having returned to New York to write the article, he found that standard journalistic techniques, those he had employed so successfully during his years of newspaper work, could not adequately describe the bizarre people and machines he had encountered in California.

Stymied, he put off writing the story until, finally, he called Byron Dobell, his editor at *Esquire,* and admitted that he was unable to finish the project. Dobell told him to type up his notes so that the magazine could get another writer to do the job. In the introduction to *The Kandy-Kolored Tangerine-Flake Streamline Baby,* Wolfe writes: ''About 8 o'clock that night I started typing the notes out in the form of a memorandum that began, 'Dear Byron.' I started typing away, starting right with the first time I saw any custom cars in California.'' In an attempt to provide every possible detail for the writer who was to finish the piece, he wrote in a stream-of-consciousness style, including even some of his most garbled notes and random thoughts. ''I wrapped up the memorandum about 6:15 A.M., and by this time it was 49 pages long. I took it over to *Esquire* as soon as they opened up, about 9:30 A.M. About 4 P.M. I got a call from Byron Dobell. He told me they were striking out the 'Dear Byron' at the top of the memorandum and running the rest of it in the magazine.''

It is the style developed during the writing of the custom car article—his unique blend of ''pop'' language and creative punctuation—that for many years remained Wolfe's trademark. He was a pioneer in the use of what several reviewers refer to as an ''aural'' style of writing, a technique intended to make the reader come as close as possible to experiencing an event firsthand. Wilfrid Sheed, in the *New York Times Book Review,* says that Wolfe tries to find ''a language proper to each subject, a special sound to convey its uniqueness''; and *Newsweek*'s Jack Kroll feels that Wolfe is ''a genuine poet'' among journalists, who is able ''to get under the skin of a phenomenon and transmit its metabolic rhythm. . . . He creates the most vivid, most pertinent possible dimension of his subject.'' F. N. Jones, in a *Library Journal* article, describes Wolfe's prose as ''free-flowing colorful Joycean, quote-slang, repetitive, cult or class jargon with literary and other reverberations.''

In a interview with Brant Mewborn for *Rolling Stone,* Wolfe confesses that the development of New Journalism was not what he originally intended for himself as a writer: ''For years, I thought about writing a novel. In fact, when I was in college, if you were going to write, it was just *assumed* that's what you'd write. If you were serious, you'd write a novel. I went into newspaper work the way a lot of people did, with the idea that I'd work on the newspaper for a while and get a little experience, maybe work some of the fat off my prose style—and yes, I believed that mystical stuff about immersing yourself in life—and then leave the newspaper business and write a novel. Instead, I began to get more and more excited about what was being done in nonfiction as a literary form. That became my great passion.''

Wolfe's style, combined with solid reporting and a highly critical eye, quickly gained a large audience for his magazine pieces. When his first book, *The Kandy-Kolored Tangerine-Flake Streamline Baby,* a collection of twenty-two of his best essays, was published in 1965, William James Smith wrote in *Commonweal:* ''Two years ago [Tom Wolfe] was unknown and today those who are not mocking him are doing their level best to emulate him.

Magazine editors are currently flooded with Zonk! articles written, putatively, in the manner of Wolfe and, by common account, uniformly impossible.... None of his parodists—and even fewer of his emulators—has successfully captured much of the flavor of Wolfe.... They miss the spark of personality that is more arresting than the funny punctuation. Wolfe has it, that magical quality that marks prose as distinctively one's own."

In *The Kandy-Kolored Tangerine-Flake Streamline Baby* Wolfe analyzes, caricaturizes, and satirizes a number of early-sixties American trends and pop culture heroes. His essays zero in on the city of Las Vegas, the Peppermint Lounge, demolition derbies, fashion, art galleries, doormen, nannies, and such personalities as Murray the K, Phil Spector, Baby Jane Holzer, and Muhammed Ali (then Cassius Clay). "He knows everything," writes Kurt Vonnegut in the *New York Times Book Review*. "I do not mean he *thinks* he knows everything. He is loaded with facile junk, as all personal journalists have to be—otherwise, how can they write so amusingly and fast?.... Verdict: Excellent book by a genius who will do anything to get attention."

What Wolfe has done, according to *Commonweal's* Smith, "is simply to describe the brave new world of the 'unconscious avant-garde' who are shaping our future, but he has described this world with a vividness and accuracy that makes it something more than real." In a *New Republic* article, Joseph Epstein expresses the opinion that "Wolfe is perhaps most fatiguing when writing about the lower classes. Here he becomes Dr. Wolfe, Department of American Studies, and what he finds attractive about the lower orders, as has many an intellectual slummer before him, is their vitality. At bottom, what is involved here is worship of the Noble Savage.... Wolfe is much better when he writes about New York City. Here he drops his studied spontaneity, eases up on the rococo, slips his doctorate, and takes on the tone of the reasonably feeling New Yorker who has not yet been knocked insensate by the clatter of that city." A *Newsweek* writer concludes that "partly, Wolfe belongs to the old noble breed of poet-journalists, like Ben Hecht, and partly he belongs to a new breed of supereducated hip sensibilities like Jonathan Miller and Terry Southern, who see the complete human comedy in everything from a hair-do to a holocaust. Vulgar? A bit. Sentimental? A tick. But this is the nature of journalism, with its crackling short waves transmitting the living moment."

In *The Electric Kool-Aid Acid Test*, Wolfe applies his distinctive brand of journalism to novelist Ken Kesey and his "Merry Pranksters," a West Coast group dedicated to LSD and the pursuit of the psychedelic experience. Joel Lieber of the *Nation* says that in this book Wolfe "has come as close as seems possible, with words, at re-creating the entire mental atmosphere of a scene in which one's understanding is based on feeling rather than verbalization.... [The book] is nonfiction told as experimental fiction; it is a genuine feat and a landmark in reporting style." Lawrence Dietz, in a *National Review* article, calls *The Electric Kool-Aid Acid Test* "the best work Wolfe has done, and certainly the most profound and insightful book that has been written about the psychedelic life.... [He] has elicited a history of the spread of LSD from 1960 (when Kesey and others got their first jolts in lab experiments) to 1967, when practically any kid with five dollars could buy some kind of trip or other." Dietz feels that Wolfe displays "a willingness to let accuracy take the place of the hysterical imprecations that have passed for reportage in most magazine articles and books" on this subject.

The Electric Kool-Aid Acid Test caught the imagination of an entire generation. In his interview with Mewborn, Wolfe explains that Kesey was representative of the emerging youth culture of the sixties, so his was "*the* right story of the whole psychedelic hippie movement. All of the changes that movement brought to the country generally—which we're still feeling—can be felt and traced in his story.... I insist that the way the young people changed life in this country was the big news of the Sixties. It overshadows, in importance, Vietnam, the riots, the racial collisions, the space program. Any of the big historical events of the Sixties are overshadowed by what young people did. And they did it because they had money. For the first time in the history of man, young people had the money, the personal freedom and the free time to build monuments and pleasure palaces to their own tastes. And they created styles. That's what the psychedelic, or hippie, world did."

Wolfe's 1970 book, *Radical Chic and Mau Mauing the Flak Catchers*, was made up of two lengthy essays. The first, "Radical Chic," elicited by far the most critical commentary; it deals with a fund-raising party given by Leonard Bernstein in his Park Avenue apartment on January 14, 1970, to raise money for the Black Panthers. Wolfe was at the party, and he became aware of the incongruity of the scene, distinguished, according to Melvin Maddocks of the *Christian Science Monitor*, by "white liberals nibbling caviar while signing checks for the revolution with their free hand." Thomas R. Edwards writes in the *New York Times Book Review:* "For Wolfe, the scene in the Bernsteins' living room demonstrates his pet sociological thesis, here called *nostalgie de la boue*, the aristocrat's hankering for a proletarian primitivism. He shows us cultivated parvenu Jews, torn between cherished new 'right wing' lifestyles and the 'left wing' politics of their own oppressive history, ludicrously confused about how to take the black revolution. Though there's a touch of ugliness in his determination to let us know, without seeming to do so, that certain socialites with gentile names weren't born that way, 'Radical Chic' is sometimes brilliant and telling in its dramatization of this case."

Many readers were not happy with *Radical Chic and Mau Mauing the Flak Catchers.* As William F. Buckley explains in the *National Review,* "[Wolfe] has written a very very controversial book, for which he has been publicly excommunicated from the company of the orthodox by the bishops who preside over the *New York Review of Books.*" Buckley continues: "What Mr. Wolfe did in this book was MAKE FUN of Bernstein et al., and if you have never been told, you MUST NOT MAKE FUN of Bernstein et al., when what hangs in the balance is Bernstein's moral prestige plus the integrity of Black Protest; learn the lesson now." Edwards feels that Wolfe "humiliates and degrades everyone concerned, his pre-potent but child-like and shiftless blacks no less than his gutless, time-serving, sexually-fearful white bureaucrats." Timothy Foote, in a *Time* article, notes: "When a *Time* reporter recently asked a minister of the Panther Party's shadow government about the truthfulness of Wolfe's *Radical Chic* account, the reply was ominous: 'You mean that dirty, blatant, lying, racist dog who wrote that fascist disgusting thing in *New York* magazine?'" Yet, despite the objections to the book, Foote insists, the fact remains that "it is generally so accurate that even some of the irate guests at the Bernsteins later wondered how Wolfe—who in fact used shorthand—managed to smuggle a tape recorder onto the premises."

Christopher Lehmann-Haupt of the *New York Times,* noting that "Radical Chic" first appeared as a magazine article, writes: "When the news got out that it would be published as a book eventually, one began to prepare a mental review of it. One had certain questions—the usual Tom Wolfe questions: Where exactly was Wolfe located when all those things occurred? Just how did he learn Leonard Bernstein's innermost fantasies? At exactly what points did Wolfe's imagination impinge on his inferences, and his inferences on his facts?... Still, one was prepared to forget those questions. The vision of the Beautiful People dos-a-dosing with black revolutionaries while white servants passed out 'little Roquefort cheese morsels rolled in crushed nuts' was too outrageous. Shivers of malice ran up and down one's spine. Wolfe's anatomy of radical chic would have to be celebrated." The book, Lehmann-Haupt concludes, "represents Wolfe at his best, worst, and most. It has his uncanny eye for life-styles; his obsessive lists of brand names and artifacts; his wicked, frequently cruel, cartoon of people's physical traits; his perfect mimicry of speech patterns. Once again, Wolfe proves himself the complete chameleon, capable of turning any color. He understands the human animal like no sociologist around."

The Painted Word was another of Wolfe's more controversial works. T. O'Hara, in a *Best Sellers* review, sums up the book's thesis: "About 10,000 people constitute the present art world. Artists, doing what they must to survive, obey orders and follow the gospel as written by the monarchs." Among these monarchs, in Wolfe's opinion, are three of our most influential and well-respected art critics: Clement Greenberg, Harold Rosenberg, and Leo Steinberg (the "kings of cultureburg," he calls them). In a *Time* article, Robert Hughes says that "the New York art world, especially in its present decay, is the easiest target a pop sociologist could ask for. Most of it is a wallow of egotism, social climbing and power brokerage, and the only thing that makes it tolerable is the occasional reward of experiencing a good work of art in all its richness, complexity and difficulty. Take the art from the art world, as Wolfe does, and the matrix becomes fit for caricature. Since Wolfe is unable to show any intelligent response to painting, caricature is what we get.... Wolfe seems to know virtually nothing about the history of art, American or European."

New York Times art critic John Russell, writing in the *New York Times Book Review,* states: "If someone who is tone-deaf goes to Carnegie Hall every night of the year, he is, of course, entitled to his opinion of what he has listened to, just as a eunuch is entitled to his opinion of sex. But in the one case, as in the other, we on our side are entitled to discount what they say. Given the range, the variety and the degree of accomplishment represented by the names on Mr. Wolfe's list [including artists such as Pollock, de Kooning, Warhol, Newman, Rauschenberg, and Stella], we are entitled to think that if he got no visual reward from any of them, . . . the fault may not lie with the art."

As Ruth Berenson of the *National Review* points out, however, response to the book is generally dependent on the extent to which an individual is involved in the world of modern art. She maintains that *The Painted Word* "will delight those who have long harbored dark suspicions that modern art beginning with Picasso is a put-on, a gigantic hoax perpetrated on a gullible public by a mysterious cabal of artists, critics, dealers, and collectors aided and abetted by *Time* and *Newsweek*. Those who take modern art somewhat more seriously will be disappointed."

In *From Bauhaus to Our House,* published in 1981, Wolfe does to modern architecture what he did to modern art in *The Painted Word,* and the response

Wolfe's 1980 history of the early days of America's space program was a favorite with both critics and the public.

has been similar: Readers close to the subject tend to resent the intrusion by an "outsider," while those with a more detached point of view often appreciate the author's fresh perspective. *New York Times* architecture critic Paul Goldberger, in a *New York Times Book Review* article, writes: "Mr. Wolfe wants to argue that ideology has gotten in the way of common sense. Beginning half a century ago with the origins of the International Style in Europe, he attempts to trace the development of that style, which for many, including Mr. Wolfe, is a virtual synonym for modern architecture. . . . We are told how the International Style became a 'compound'—a select, private, cult-like group of ideologues [including Walter Gropius, Mies van der Rohe, Marcel Breuer, and Josef Albers] whose great mission, as Mr. Wolfe sees it, was to foist modern design upon an unwilling world. . . . The problem, I think . . . is that Tom Wolfe has no eye. He has a wonderful ear, and he listens hard and long, but he does not seem to see. . . . He does precisely what he warns us against; he has listened to the words, not looked at the architecture."

And in a *Washington Post Book World* review, *Post* architecture critic Benjamin Forgey says that "the book is a case of crying Wolfe for one more time. *Bauhaus* is distinguished by the same total loathing of modern culture that motivated *The Painted Word*. . . . Wolfe's explanation is that modernism has been a conspiracy. In place of the New York critics who foisted abstract art upon us, we have the European giants of architecture . . . and their abject American followers. In Wolfe's view the motivation was pretty much the same, too. They were all playing the hypocritical bohemian game of spitting on the bourgeois." Forgey feels that "there is some truth in this, but it makes for a thin book and a narrow, limited history of architecture in the 20th century."

On the other hand, *New York Times* literary critic Christopher Lehmann-Haupt makes the point that even many architects have been unhappy with the structures created by proponents of the Bauhaus school. This style of architecture (distinguished by what is often referred to as a "glass box" appearance) was, for instance, denigrated by architect Peter Blake in his 1977 book, *Form Follows Fiasco.* According to Lehmann-Haupt, Blake "anathematized modern architecture for being sterile, functionless and ugly"; thus Wolfe "has not really come up with anything very startling when he laments the irony that four-fifths of the way into the American Century, when what we ought to be expressing with our building is 'exuberance, pow-

America's first astronauts as depicted in the acclaimed 1983 film adaptation of *The Right Stuff.*

er, empire, grandeur, or even high spirits and playfulness,' what we still see inflicted upon us is the anti-bourgeois, socialist, pro-worker ideas that arose from 'the smoking rubble of Europe after the Great War.' But the explication of this notion is done with such verve and hilarity by Mr. Wolfe that its substance almost doesn't seem to matter.... It flows with natural rhetorical rhythm.... And often it is enough to laugh right out loud." John Brooks, in a *Chicago Tribune Book World* review, calls the book "a readable polemic on how in our architecture over the past few decades things have gone very much as they have in the other visual arts—a triumph of conformity over true innovation, of timidity over uninhibited expression, of irony over straightforwardness, of posing over real accomplishment.... *From Bauhaus to Our House* is lucidly and for the most part gracefully written."

In 1979 Wolfe published the book that many critics consider his finest: *The Right Stuff,* an award-winning study of the early years of the American space program. At one point in the book Wolfe attempts to define the "ineffable quality" from which the title is taken: "It obviously involved bravery. But it was not bravery in the simple sense of being willing to risk your life ...

any fool could do that.... No, the idea ... seemed to be that a man should have the ability to go up in a hurtling piece of machinery and put his hide on the line and then have the moxie, the reflexes, the experience, the coolness, to pull it back in the last yawning moment—and then to go up again *the next day*, and the next day, and every next day."

The main characters in the book are Chuck Yeager, the famous Air Force test pilot who first broke the sound barrier, and the seven members of the first U.S. astronaut team: Scott Carpenter, Gordon Cooper, John Glenn, Gus Grissom, Wally Schirra, Alan Shepard, and Deke Slayton. Wolfe assiduously chronicles their early careers as test pilots, their private lives, their selection for the astronaut program and the subsequent medical processing and training. But, as *Commonweal*'s Thomas Powers points out, *The Right Stuff* "is not a history; it is far too thin in dates, facts and source citations to serve any such pulse. It is a work of literature which must stand or fall as a coherent text, and its subject is not the Mercury program itself but the impulse behind it, the unreflecting competitiveness which drove the original astronauts to the quite extraordinary lengths Wolfe describes so vividly." That the author goes beyond mere reportage of historical fact is confirmed by Mort Sheinman in a *Chicago Tribune* article: "Wolfe tells us what it's like to go 'shooting straight through the top of the sky,' to be 'in a king's solitude, unique and inviolate, above the dome of the world.' He describes what happens when someone is immolated by airplane fuel, and he talks about the nightmares and hallucinations experienced by the wives.... [*The Right Stuff*] is a dazzling piece of work, something that reveals much about the nature of bravery and celebrity and—yes—patriotism."

Time writer R. Z. Sheppard says that the book "is crammed with inside poop and racy incident that 19 years ago was ignored by what [Wolfe] terms the 'proper Victorian gents' of the press. The fast cars, booze, astro groupies, the envies and injuries of the military caste system were not part of what Americans would have considered the right stuff. Wolfe lays it all out in brilliantly stated Op Lit scenes: the tacky cocktail lounges of Cocoa Beach where one could hear the *Horst Wessel Song* sung by ex-rocket scientists of the Third Reich; Vice President Lyndon Johnson furiously cooling his heels outside the Glenn house because Annie Glenn would not let him in during her husband's countdown; Alan Shepard losing a struggle with his full bladder moments before lift-off; the overeager press terrifying Ham the chimp after his proficient flight; the astronauts surrounded by thousands of cheering Texans waving hunks of raw meat during an honorary barbecue in the Houston Coliseum."

Christopher Lehmann-Haupt of the *New York Times* writes: "What fun it is to watch Mr. Wolfe put the antiseptic space program into the traces of his inimitable verbal cadenzas. It's a little like hearing the story of Jesus of Nazareth through the lips of the Chicago nightclub comedian Lord Buckley." Lehmann-Haupt says that in this book Wolfe undertakes "the restoration of the zits and rogue cilia of hair to the face of the American space program" and reveals a good deal of the gossip that was denied the public by a hero-worshipping press in the early sixties, gossip "about how the test-pilot fraternity looked down on the early astronauts for being trained monkeys in a capsule ('spam in a can') instead of pilots in control of their craft; about the real feelings of the original seven for one another and the tension that arose between the upright John Glenn and some of the others over their after-hours behavior, particularly with the 'juicy little girls' who materialized wherever they trained; and about what National Aeronautical and Space Administration engineers really felt about

the flight of Gus Grissom and Scott Carpenter and the possibility that they had secretly panicked."

Former test pilot and astronaut Michael Collins (a member of the Gemini 10 flight and command module pilot on the Apollo 11 moon flight), writes in a *Washington Post Book World* review: "I lived at Edwards [Air Force Base, site of the Air Force Flight Test Center] for four years, and, improbable as some of Tom's tales seem, I know he's telling it like it was. He is the first gifted writer to explore the relationship between test pilots and astronauts—the obvious similarities and the subtle differences. He's obviously done a lot of homework—too much in some cases. Some of this stuff could only be interesting to Al Shepard's mother. While the first part of the book is a paean to guts, to the 'right stuff,' it is followed by a chronology—but one that might have profited from a little tighter editing. But it's still light-years ahead of the endless drivel [Norman] Mailer has put out about the Apollo program, and in places the Wolfe genius really shines." Collins feels that at times Wolfe allows himself to get too close to his subject: "He's almost one of the boys—and there's too much to admire and not enough to eviscerate." As a result "*The Right Stuff* is not vintage, psychedelic Tom Wolfe, but if you ... have ever been curious about what the space program was really all about in those halcyon Kennedy and Mercury years, then this is your book."

In a review of *The Right Stuff* for the *Lone Star Book Review*, Martha Heimberg says that, for the most part, "Wolfe's reporting, while being marvelously entertaining writing, has also represented a telling and trustworthy point of view. His is one of those finely critical intelligences that can detect the slightest pretention or falsification in an official posture or social pose. And, when he does, he goes after the hypocrisy—whether large or small, left or right—with all the zeal of the dedicated reformer." Like Collins, Heimberg feels that *The Right Stuff* "represents a departure for the satirist whose observant eye and caustic pen have impaled on the page a wide range of American social phenomena" in that Wolfe "clearly likes his subjects—none are treated as grist for the satirist's mill, but put down with as great a skill and detail as an observer could possibly muster." She concludes that "the book represents a tremendous accomplishment and a new direction for a writer who figures among the top stylists of his generation."

Independent producers Robert Chartoff and Irwin Winkler purchased the movie rights to *The Right Stuff* in 1979. When Wolfe indicated that he was not interested in adapting his own work for the screen, the producers asked highly esteemed screenwriter William Goldman to handle the screenplay. Goldman's version concentrated on the astronauts' heroics rather than their human side, and he ended up quitting the project when Chartoff and Winkler were not satisfied with this approach. The director, Phil Kaufman, eventually rewrote the screenplay, and in 1983 *The Right Stuff* was released as a movie starring Sam Shepard as Chuck Yeager, Ed Harris as John Glenn, and Dennis Quaid as Gordon Cooper. The production took over eight months and cost approximately $27 million. Since the film's release coincided with Senator John Glenn's 1984 presidential campaign, there even was some speculation in Washington, D.C., about whether it might influence voters (Glenn did not receive the Democratic party nomination).

The adaptation received many enthusiastic reviews. As David Ansen comments in *Newsweek*, "Kaufman has done a prodigious job of literary adaptation. He seems to have swallowed the book whole: it's extraordinary how much of Wolfe he gets on the screen, not just the events of the space race and the multilayered story lines but the double-edged, hyperbolic tone, which zig-zags in the blink of an eye from awe to archness, from savage satire to outright idolatry." He also praises the film for its factual accuracy and realistic flight sequences, noting that "when *The Right Stuff* takes to the skies, it can't be compared with any other movie, old or new: it's simply the most thrilling flight footage ever put on film."

Like the book, the film covers the period between 1947, when Chuck Yeager secretly broke the sound barrier, and 1963, when Gordon Cooper completed the last solo flight in the NASA space program. Yeager served as a technical consultant for the film, further refining Kaufman's careful attention to detail. Ansen says that Yeager "stood by as a daily reminder of the rightest of the right stuff. He took the actors flying, beat them at pool, played a bit part as bartender at Pancho's, studied the story boards and the special effects and pointed out the errors." Describing the importance of the movie, Ansen concludes: "In the end, what's most special about Kaufman's big, jaunty, generous epic is that it asks us not merely to contemplate the transformation of seven flyboys into national heroes, but the nature of America itself. It's about nothing less than our brash, tenacious, straining-at-the-bit soul. It recaptures, with all its rough edges

exposed, a vibrant chunk of our heritage, and shows the grace hidden beneath the flimflam."

By the mid-1980s Wolfe had a new ambition for his writing. As he told the *New York Times:* "I was curious, having spouted off so much about fiction and nonfiction, and having said that the novelists weren't doing a good job, to see what would happen if I tried it. Also, I guess I subconsciously had the suspicion that maybe, what if all this to-do I've made about nonfiction is because I really, secretly think I can't do a novel. So I said, well, I've got to prove this to myself." The result was *The Bonfire of the Vanities,* a novel that exposes the greed and hate seething in modern New York City. In the book, an arrogant Wall Street bond trader named Sherman McCoy is reduced to a political pawn when he is implicated in the hit-and-run traffic death of a young black man in the South Bronx. McCoy's downfall is hailed and accelerated by an opportunistic black activist preacher and a sensation-seeking tabloid journalist. A *Publishers Weekly* reviewer comments, "Erupting from the first line with noise, color, tension and immediacy, this immensely entertaining novel accurately mirrors a system that has broken down: from the social code of basic good manners to the fair practices of the law." *Washington Post Book World*'s Jonathan Yardley calls *Bonfire* "a superb human comedy and the first novel ever to get contemporary New York, in all its arrogance and shame and heterogeneity and insularity, exactly right." After his novel became a major bestseller, Wolfe issued what he called a "literary manifesto" in *Harper's* magazine. He urged fellow novelists to abandon the esoteric literary experiments that have characterized fiction for much of the twentieth century and use realism to chronicle the bizarre and astounding world around them. The author's peers reacted with both praise and condemnation. "Ever the provocateur," reported *Time*, "Wolfe is enjoying the controversy."

In 1990 *The Bonfire of the Vanities* was released as a movie directed by Brian De Palma and starring Tom Hanks as Sherman McCoy. Most reviewers were disappointed with De Palma's adaptation. A *Newsweek* writer comments, "De Palma, a smart guy, isn't wrong in seeing Wolfe's ferocious portrait of '80s New York in satirical terms—the dark humor is there. But it's built upon a base of journalistically precise details: just what De Palma discards." *Time* movie critic Richard Schickel maintains that "director Brian De Palma has succeeded in the more difficult task of finding a cinematic equivalent for the novelist's singular

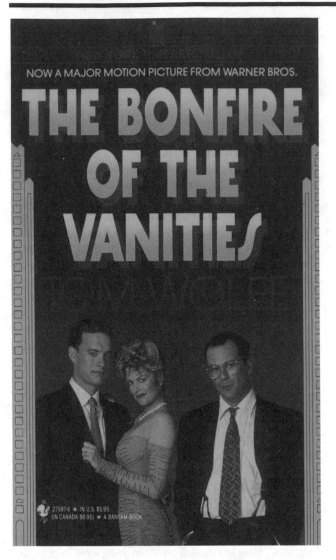

This controversial 1987 best-seller first appeared in serialized form in *Rolling Stone* magazine.

style. Using unconventional angles, lenses and light, he accomplishes on the screen what Wolfe achieved on the page through deliciously exaggerated dialogue and deadpan parody." But Schickel concludes that the film, and in particular its modified ending, "manages to travesty all the tough-minded things Wolfe tried to say, and everything a movie unafraid of its own subject matter should have said."

Although there can be no question that Tom Wolfe has achieved a reputation as a superb stylist and skillful reporter, no discussion of Wolfe would be complete without some mention of his famous wardrobe. *Philadelphia Bulletin* writer Leslie Bennetts tells of an encounter with the author when he lectured at Villanova University: "The legendary sartorial splendors were there, of course: the gorgeous three-piece creamy white suit he has

been renowned for . . . (how many must he have, do you suppose, to appear in spotless vanilla every day: rows upon rows of them hanging in shadowed closets, a veritable army of Gatsby ghosts waiting to emerge?). Not to mention the navy suede shoes, dark as midnight, or the jaunty matching suede hat, or the sweeping midnight cashmere coat of the exact same hue, or the crisp matching tie on which perched a golden half-moon pin to complement the glittering gold watch chain that swung gracefully from the milky vest. Or the navy silk handkerchief peeking out from the white suit pocket, or the white silk handkerchief peeking out from the navy coat pocket."

Wolfe told Bennetts that he began wearing the white suits in 1962: "That was when I had a white suit made, started wearing it in January, and found it annoyed people tremendously. Even slight departures in dress at that time really spun people out. So I liked it. It's kind of a harmless form of aggression, I guess." But Wolfe's mode of dress has also been an important part of his journalism, serving as a device to distance him from his subject. He told Susan Forrest of the *Fort Lauderdale News*: "A writer can find out more if he doesn't pretend to be hip. . . . If people see you are an outsider, they will come up and tell you things. If you're trying to be hip, you can't ask a lot of naive questions." This technique has been effective for Wolfe in interviewing stock car racers, Hell's Angels, and—particularly—astronauts. He feels that at least part of the success of *The Right Stuff* is due to the fact that he did not try to get too close to that inner circle. Wolfe told Janet Maslin of the *New York Times Book Review*: "I looked like Ruggles of Red Gap to them, I'm sure. . . . But I've long since given up on the idea of going into a situation trying to act like part of it. . . . Besides, it was useless for me to try to fit into the world of pilots, because I didn't know a thing about flying. I also sensed that pilots, like people in the psychedelic life, really dislike people who presume a familiarity with the Lodge."

A writer for *Time* calls Wolfe's form of dress "a splendiferous advertisement for his individuality. The game requires a lot of reverse spin and body English but it boils down to antichic chic. Exclaims Wolfe proudly: 'I own no summer house, no car, I wear tank tops when I swim, long white pants when I play tennis, and I'm probably the last man in America to still do the Royal Canadian Air Force exercises.'"

■ For More Information See

BOOKS

Authors in the News, Volume 2, Gale, 1976.

Bellamy, Joe David, editor, *The New Fiction: Interviews with Innovative American Writers,* University of Illinois Press, 1974.

Bestsellers 89, Issue 1, Gale, 1989.

Contemporary Literary Criticism, Gale, Volume 1, 1973; Volume 2, 1974; Volume 9, 1978; Volume 15, 1980; Volume 35, 1985; Volume 51, 1989.

PERIODICALS

America, February 5, 1977; April 2, 1988.

Atlantic, October, 1979; December, 1987.

Best Sellers, August, 1975.

Books and Art, September 28, 1979.

Books in Canada, April, 1988.

Business Week, November 23, 1987.

Chicago Tribune, September 9, 1979; September 15, 1979; January 16, 1983; November 4, 1987.

Chicago Tribune Book World, December 7, 1980; October 25, 1981; January 16, 1983.

Christian Science Monitor, November 17, 1970; November 3, 1987.

Commentary, March, 1971; May, 1977; February, 1980; February, 1988.

Commonweal, September 17, 1965; December 20, 1968; March 3, 1978; October 12, 1979; February 26, 1988.

Detroit News, October 14, 1979; November 9, 1980.

Encounter, September, 1977.

Fort Lauderdale News, April 22, 1975.

Fort Lauderdale Sentinel, April 22, 1975.

Globe and Mail (Toronto), December 5, 1987.

Guardian Weekly, February 21, 1988.

Harper's, February, 1971; November, 1989; January, 1990.

Library Journal, August, 1968.

Listener, February 11, 1988.

London Review of Books, February 18, 1988.

Lone Star Book Review, November, 1979.

Los Angeles Times, October 19, 1979; November 22, 1987; October 12, 1989.

Los Angeles Times Book Review, November 2, 1980; October 25, 1981; October 17, 1982; January 23, 1983; October 25, 1987.

Nation, March 5, 1977; November 3, 1977.

National Review, August 27, 1968; January 26, 1971; August 1, 1975; February 19, 1977; December 18, 1987.

New Leader, January 31, 1977.

New Republic, July 14, 1965; December 19, 1970; November 23, 1987.

New Statesman, February 12, 1988.

Newsweek, June 28, 1965; August 26, 1968; June 9, 1975; September 17, 1979; October 3, 1983; October 26, 1987; December 23, 1990.

New York, September 21, 1981; March 21, 1988.

New Yorker, February 1, 1988.

New York Review of Books, August 26, 1965; December 17, 1970; June 26, 1975; January 20, 1977; October 28, 1979; November 4, 1982; February 4, 1988.

New York Times, November 25, 1970; May 27, 1975; November 26, 1976; September 14, 1979; October 9, 1981; December 20, 1981; October 13, 1987; October 22, 1987; November 21, 1987; December 31, 1987; January 3, 1988; March 11, 1988.

New York Times Book Review, June 27, 1965; August 18, 1968; November 29, 1970; December 3, 1972; June 15, 1975; December 26, 1976; October 28, 1979; October 11, 1981; October 10, 1982; November 1, 1987.

Observer (London), February 7, 1988.

Partisan Review, Number 3, 1969; Number 2, 1974.

People, December 24, 1979; November 23, 1987.

Philadelphia Bulletin, February 10, 1975.

Punch, February 12, 1988.

Rolling Stone, August 21, 1980; November 5-December 10, 1987.

Saturday Review, September 15, 1979; April, 1981.

Spectator, February 13, 1988.

Time, September 6, 1968; December 21, 1970; June 23, 1975; December 27, 1976; September 29, 1979; November 9, 1987; February 13, 1989; November 27, 1989; December 23, 1990.

Times (London), February 11, 1988; February 13, 1989; April 22, 1989.

Times Literary Supplement, October 1, 1971; November 30, 1979; November 26, 1980; March 18, 1988.

Tribune Books, August 2, 1987; October 18, 1987.

U.S. News and World Report, November 23, 1987.

Village Voice, September 10, 1979.

Wall Street Journal, October 29, 1987.

Washington Monthly, March, 1988.

Washington Post, September 4, 1979; October 23, 1980; March 27, 1988; October 17, 1989.

Washington Post Book World, September 9, 1979; November 23, 1980; November 15, 1981; November 7, 1982; October 25, 1987.

Writer's Digest, January, 1970.°

Patricia C. Wrede

■ Personal

Surname is pronounced "Reedy"; born March 27, 1953, in Chicago, IL; daughter of David Merrill (a mechanical engineer) and Monica Marie (an executive; maiden name, Buerglar) Collins; married James M. Wrede (a financial consultant), July 24, 1976 (divorced, 1992). *Education:* Carleton College, A.B., 1974; University of Minnesota, M.B.A., 1977. *Politics:* Independent. *Religion:* Roman Catholic.

■ Addresses

Home and office—4900 West 60th St., Edina, MN 55424-1709. *Agent*—Valerie Smith, Route 44-55, RR Box 160, Modena, NY 12548.

■ Career

Minnesota Hospital Association, Minneapolis, MN, rate review analyst, 1977-78; B. Dalton Bookseller, Minneapolis, MN, financial analyst, 1978-80; Dayton-Hudson Corporation, Minneapolis, MN, financial analyst, 1980-81, senior financial analyst, 1981-83, senior accountant, 1983-85; full-time writer, 1985—. Laubach reading tutor. *Member:* Science Fiction Writers of America, Novelists, Inc.

■ Awards, Honors

"Books for Young Adults" Recommended Reading List citation, 1984, for *Daughter of Witches,* and 1985, for *The Seven Towers;* Minnesota Book Award for Fantasy and Science Fiction, 1991, and ALA "Best Book for Young Adults" citation, both for *Dealing with Dragons.*

■ Writings

Shadow Magic, Ace Books, 1982.
Daughter of Witches, Ace Books, 1983.
The Seven Towers, Ace Books, 1984.
Talking to Dragons, Tempo/MagicQuest Books, 1985.
The Harp of Imach Thyssel, Ace Books, 1985.
(Contributor) Will Shetterly and Emma Bull, editors, *Liavek,* Ace Books, 1985.
(Contributor) Shetterly and Bull, editors, *Liavek: The Players of Luck,* Ace Books, 1986.
Caught in Crystal, Ace Books, 1987.
(Contributor) Jane Yolen, editor, *Spaceships and Spells,* Harper & Row, 1987.
(With Caroline Stevermer) *Sorcery and Cecelia,* Ace Books, 1988.
(Contributor) Bruce Coville, editor, *The Unicorn Treasury,* Doubleday, 1988.
(Contributor) Shetterly and Bull, editors, *Liavek: Spells of Binding,* Ace Books, 1988.
Snow White and Rose Red ("Fairy Tales" series), Tor Books, 1989.

(Contributor) Shetterly and Bull, editors, *Liavek: Festival Week*, Ace Books, 1990.

(Contributor) Andre Norton, editor, *Tales of the Witch World 3*, Tor Books, 1990.

Dealing with Dragons ("Chronicles of the Enchanted Forest" series, Volume 1; prequel to *Talking to Dragons*), Harcourt, 1990.

Mairelon the Magician, Tor Books, 1991.

Searching for Dragons ("Chronicles of the Enchanted Forest" series, Volume 2), Harcourt, 1991.

■ Work in Progress

The Raven Ring, a Lyra novel; a third volume in the "Chronicles of the Enchanted Forest"; a revised version of *Talking to Dragons*, which is the fourth volume of the "Chronicles of the Enchanted Forest."

■ Sidelights

Patricia C. Wrede is one of the most innovative writers working in fantasy today. Her novels and stories, ranging from modern versions of traditional fairy-tales to comic fantasy, break new ground in the genre. Much fantasy uses a pseudo-medieval, vaguely Celtic setting, but Wrede, while she occasionally makes use of these, expands the boundaries of fantasy to include Renaissance and Regency-era England in *Snow White and Rose Red*, *Sorcery and Cecelia*, and *Mairelon the Magician*. She also is the author of several volumes of related works, including the "Lyra" cycle of novels (which take place on her own created world of the same name) and the "Enchanted Forest" books, which are comic variations on fairy-tale motifs.

"I was an omnivorous reader as a child," Wrede said in an interview for *Authors and Artists for Young Adults (AAYA)*. "I don't think I ever read anything only once. I read the Oz books, and I still treasure a set of those that I collected over the years. *Mrs. Piggle Wiggle* and *The Borrowers*, the Walter Farley horse books, Robert Lawson animal stories, the Narnia Chronicles—practically everything I could get my hands on. They knew me very well down at the library. I also told stories to my younger siblings (I am the eldest of five) and to any of my friends who would listen.

"I started writing fiction in the seventh grade, and never really stopped in spite of the fact that for many years I did not really expect writing to be more than a hobby. The novel (quote unquote) that I started was wildly improbable. It involved a couple of children who were my age, who had just moved into a house with secret passages, smugglers and a castle in the backyard that someone had imported from England. I worked on it during class when I was supposed to be studying and brought it home every day. My mother aided and abetted me by typing out the pages and my father read them and told me they were great (he still thinks I should try to publish the book).

"I grew up around Chicago, in the Chicago suburbs, but I went to school at Carleton College which is in Minnesota. It is about 45 minutes south of the Twin Cities, where I live now, and when I graduated I just stayed. In college, I placed out of the required Freshman English class and never got around to taking any others. Instead, I majored in biology and filled in the college distribution requirement with history and art. I'd always been

Alethia, princess of Alkyra, unites the four races of her land for a final climactic battle against the Shadowborn in Wrede's 1982 novel.

interested in science. In fact, I thought at the time that was probably going to be my profession. And of the sciences I liked biology the best because it dealt on a personal level with living things, as opposed to physics and chemistry, which deal with things in abstract—little molecules you can't even see. With biology you can pick up a plant and look at the roots and know what you've got.

"I took one semester's worth of art of the Far East, because I didn't know anything at all about it, and I thought 'Well, here's the chance to find out something. I have to take a distribution course anyway. I might as well take this.' And I enjoyed it tremendously. That was how I filled in most of my distribution requirements: I'd pick something that I didn't know anything at all about, and I'd take a class in it to see if it turned out to be interesting. That seems to be kind of a characteristic of writers. They'll find a subject that they don't know anything about and deliberately choose to write a book about it. I know a number of writers who work that way.

"I can't point to any specific facts or bits and pieces of classes that I used in my stories. Far more important were the research skills I learned: the ability to walk into a library and say, 'I want to know something about the way they treated horses in the 13th century, or the way they built galleys during the Roman Empire, and how those worked. What kinds of books do I want, and what kinds of articles? or, I need to know something about Elizabethan England. Where do I start?' When you've got a very broad topic and you want to get enough information to do the book, those skills are infinitely valuable.

"I graduated from college in 1974, and I had two choices in mind. One was to get an M.B.A.—my parents are self-employed and I knew that that would be a good thing to do—and the other was to go on in biology. I took a year off to try and make up my mind what I wanted to do. During that year I worked at the University of Minnesota as a secretary and took night school classes, concentrating on the classes I would need for admission into the business school. I didn't have those courses and I wanted to see just how interested I was. I decided it was pretty interesting. In some ways I have a very tidy mind; I like to set things in order, and accounting and finance is something that appeals to that aspect of me. I also find money infinitely fascinating, even if it belongs to other people. So about a year and a half later I quit my job and went back to school." Wrede obtained her M.B.A. in 1977 and, although she no longer works in finance,

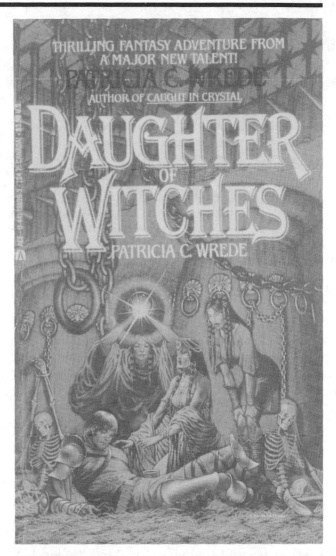

In Wrede's 1983 continuation of the Lyra series, bondservant Ranira is sentenced to death and must escape from the prison city of Drinn.

continues to apply her business knowledge in her writing. "An awful lot of writers seem to overlook the fact that this is a business. It needs to be handled and treated like a business.

"After I graduated, I began work on my first novel, *Shadow Magic.* It took me five years to finish it." *Shadow Magic*, published by Ace Books in 1982, tells the story of Alethia, daughter of a noble house of the nation of Alkyra. Alethia is of mixed blood— her mother is one of the magic-using Shee, and magic runs in her blood. She is kidnapped from her home in the city of Brenn by the Lithmern, agents of a rival nation. To carry out their plan, the Lithmern have unbound the evil Shadowborn, spirits who inhabit men's bodies and slowly destroy their minds. Alethia escapes the Lithmern with the aid of the Wyrds, a forest-dwelling, cat-like race of people, and meets her mother's folk, who train her in the use of magic. Alethia unites the four races of Alkyra—the Wyrds, the Shee, the sea-living Neira, and the humans—against the threat of the aroused Shadowborn. Finally, she discovers the lost magic treasures of the kings of Alkyra, uses them to defeat the Shadowborn, and is proclaimed queen of the land by the four reunited races.

Shadow Magic introduced the world of Lyra, an alternate earth that many of Wrede's novels share. Lyra is a land literally shaped by magic and by the threat of the Shadowborn. Its history is dated from the end of the Wars of Binding, the conflict in which the Shadowborn were finally restrained by the power of the gifts of Alkyra. The land itself was broken, however, and many of its original inhabitants were left homeless, forced to wander across the oceans in ships or over the lands in caravans. The ultimate result was a kaleidoscope of different cultures, from the warrior Cilhar nation to the older and more cultured society of Kith Alunel. The Kulseth sailors were left homeless when their island sank in the Wars of Binding; Varna, the island of wizards, was destroyed in a later conflict, and survivors from both places mingled with other peoples, adding to the variety and occasionally causing friction. The events of *Shadow Magic* take place more than three thousand years after the Wars of Binding, and other Lyra novels examine other eras in the world's history.

Lyra grew out of the stories Wrede had told her siblings. "I told bedtime stories to my sisters when I was at home. I told myself bedtime stories, too, and over time I built up this world in which to tell stories. When I started writing a book, that was what I used. But the stories that I told my younger sisters did not develop directly into *Shadow Magic.* They were more exercises in learning about story telling. *Shadow Magic* was a story that I told myself, yet in a sense it did evolve out of all of those things. I had to make certain changes because of the constraints of telling the story on paper, and Lyra grows and changes with every book I do. But my sisters would undoubtedly be surprised to hear that I had told them *Shadow Magic* as a bedtime story.

"For me the process of turning the story into a novel is a process of asking questions. The two most useful tend to be: 'All right, what are the characters doing now?' and 'Why on earth are they doing *that?*' *What are they doing now* applies not so much to the people who are 'on stage' as to the people who are 'off stage.' For instance, if I've written a scene in which the characters are all sitting around playing cards, I ask myself, 'What are the bad guys doing? That guy who was running away from the Indians—what's he doing? Did he get away, and if so, how did he do it? Where did he go? Did he have any help? Has he run into anybody interesting? Is he going to show up any minute? If so, why did he decide to break up this particular card game?' It's a whole process of asking questions—starting with the basic idea and asking, 'What does this mean?'

"The smallest details turn out to have some resonance. I was working with a young woman who was describing a scene in a bar, and I said, 'Put in some details.' She came back with a description of some moth-eaten, overstuffed chairs. And I said, 'This is a great detail. You know what this implies? This implies that this society can produce overstuffed chairs in such quantities that nobody cares if they put the old ones down in a bar. They don't bother to repair them.' That hadn't even occurred to her. She was just interested in the one detail, but it implied a lot of things about the society, and it made it much more interesting. You have to follow up on a lot of things like that, where you write something down, then stop and look at it and think, 'Oh, well, if it's like this, then that means...,' and work your way back.

"When you're starting out to write, one of the things people tell you is, 'Write short stories and learn your craft. When you're selling short stories, then go on to the novel.' Like a good little girl I followed directions and I started off writing short stories, but I never got anywhere. Finally I started on what became my first novel. I wrote four more novels before I ever sold a short story.

"The kinds of rejections I got back on short stories were things like: 'This sounds like chapter three of a novel. Why don't you do chapters 1 and 2, and 4 through 20 and we'll buy it.' That actually happened to me. Once I got to the point where editors were *telling* me things about my short stories instead of simply sending me a form rejection slip, what they were telling me was, 'These aren't short stories. These are really pieces of novels that you're trying to do.'

"Pieces of novels just don't work well as short stories—the pacing of the novel is too different, and the kinds of ideas I get are generally more suited to novels. I have to work to come up with short fiction, but I wake up all the time thinking, 'Oh, Lord, I don't *need* another novel idea. I've got six of them, and now it's seven.' I have friends that don't have that problem. One of them sold ten or fifteen short stories right away, but she wrote three novels before she finally got the hang of it and started selling them. Her natural length was the short story. It took her a while to figure out how to expand into novel length.

"In 1980, three months before *Shadow Magic* sold, I joined a group of friends who were starting a critique group which later became known as the Scribblies. It turned out to be very successful; of the seven members, none of whom had been professionally published when the group began, all seven eventually sold something, and at least four members, as of this writing, are supporting themselves writing fiction. The group taught me a great deal about good writing, and I remain infinitely grateful to them all."

Shadow Magic was followed in 1983 by *Daughter of Witches,* another Lyra book, which tells of the sentencing of bondservant Ranira to death on suspicion of sorcery and her escape from the prison city of Drinn. "I had an extremely elaborate background world worked out for my first book," Wrede explains, "and it seemed very natural to me to continue using that background rather than try and make up another one. But I didn't want to use the same country; I wanted to explore some different aspects of this world. One of my complaints about a great deal of fantasy and science fiction is that a planet is generally a very large place, and you don't often get a sense of that. It tends to be much more like a country than a planet; frequently there's not a lot of diversity in terms of culture and history. I wanted to make it very clear that although I'm going to write a number of books about this planet, it's big. I'm going to take you to another place that's nothing like where the first book started off, and I'm going to do something there, and you're only going to know it's the same place because they've got the same kinds of moons, or somebody heard a rumor of what was going on back in that other book. But other than that, there's no connection. People seem to like that. They like putting the puzzle pieces together and getting a better and better picture of the world, so I've just kept doing it. I can keep doing that for a long time."

The Seven Towers, Wrede's third book, was published in 1984. The book is not part of the Lyra cycle, but nevertheless introduces several of Wrede's most memorable characters. One of these is Amberglas, a powerful sorceress who speaks in a sort of stream-of-consciousness pattern. Another is Carachel, the wizard-king of Tar-Alem, whose struggle against the magic-devouring Matholych

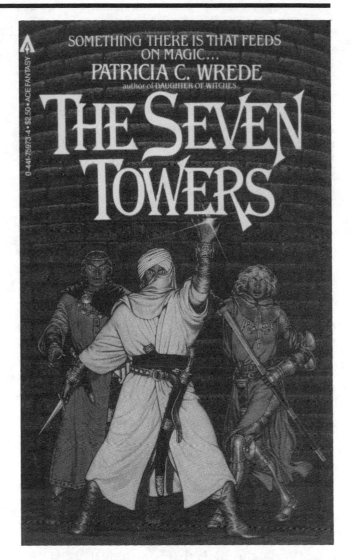

SOMETHING THERE IS THAT FEEDS ON MAGIC...
PATRICIA C. WREDE
author of DAUGHTER OF WITCHES
THE SEVEN TOWERS

An outlaw, a swordswoman, and a desert rider unite as Jermain, Vandaris, and Ranlyn face the magic-devouring Matholych in Wrede's 1984 novel.

has led him to practice black magic. Wrede states, "I've had people tell me they thought I gave Carachel a raw deal. Those kind of people scare me a little bit. He was the villain, and one of the things I wanted to do in *The Seven Towers* was to do a villain who was understandable, who was not all black and white. Apparently I made him a little too sympathetic. 'No, no, you don't understand, he's the bad guy.'"

Talking to Dragons, Wrede's fourth book, was published in 1985 by Tempo Books under their MagicQuest imprint. It mixes elements of traditional fairy tales with modern wit, and tells the story of Daystar, a young man of sixteen who has lived the whole of his life on the outskirts of the Enchanted Forest with his mother, Cimorene. One day a wizard appears at his home, and the consequences of that wizard's arrival send Daystar into the Enchanted Forest alone with a magic sword and no idea what he's supposed to be doing. In the Forest he meets a variety of memorable characters, including Shiara, the young fire witch who can't quite control her magic; Morwen the witch, who lives with her umpteen cats in a cottage that is bigger on the inside than it is on the outside; and Kazul, the female King of the Dragons. The story reaches its climax as Daystar and Shiara confront the Society of Wizards at the castle of the rulers of the Enchanted Forest.

"The Enchanted Forest books did not start off as a series," Wrede told *AAYA*. "Just after I finished *Daughter of Witches*, we were having trouble with the title: the publisher didn't like the title I had originally come up with. I was complaining to one of my friends that either I wrote a book and had to change the title because I didn't have a very good title to start out with—something along the lines of *What I Did on My Summer Vacation*—or I had a really good title, and no book to go with it. My friend said to me, 'What are some of the good titles with no books?' I listed out a few for him, and the last one I mentioned was *Talking to Dragons*. He said, 'That sounds good. *Talking to Dragons* sounds like a good book; you should write that book some day.' I said, 'That's the whole problem. I've got the title; I don't have any book.'

"So we finished our talk, and I started home. I was driving along the freeway thinking, '*Talking to Dragons, Talking to Dragons*, yeah, that *is* a good title. I really should do that book someday. "Mother taught me to be polite to dragons." Yeah, that's the first line of that book. I gotta write that down when I get home.' So I got home and I wrote it down, and by the time I had finished writing down the first sentence I had written a paragraph. And I looked at it, and thought, 'That's very odd. Well, okay, I've got the first paragraph, not just the first sentence. That's fine.' I woke up the following morning, and said, 'I know what the next paragraph is. I better sit down and write it quick.' So I wrote the next paragraph and kept on going, and by the time I had done half a page, I figured I had better just do this book."

Talking to Dragons "was supposed to be just one book," Wrede states. "A number of years later Jane Yolen was putting together an anthology and asked me if I would contribute a short story. I had had a wonderful time writing *Talking to Dragons*, and I had been thinking for years about doing a sequel or prequel, but I had shied off because I didn't know that I could do a good job. But I said

that I could do a short story that just put together the little pieces. So I wrote a short story, 'The Improper Princess,' about Daystar's mother, Cimorene, running away from home because she can't stand being a fairy-tale princess and going to live with the dragons. Jane loved it. She bought it, and then she said to me the same thing that editors have been saying to me for years: 'This isn't a short story, this is the beginning of a novel.' I said, 'Jane, you asked me for a short story, I wrote you a short story. That's all.' She said, 'Yeah, but Harcourt Brace Jovanovich just asked me to edit a line of books. And now I want the rest of this to put it out as a book.' I said, '*Jaaane!*'

"Well, one thing led to another, and she talked me into it. So I wrote *Dealing with Dragons*." *Dealing with Dragons* tells how Cimorene, refused the right to pursue her own interests (fencing, Latin lessons, and the like), and being forced into a marriage not to her liking, flees to the lair of the dragon Kazul and becomes her princess. Eventually Cimorene becomes instrumental in securing Kazul's succession as King of the Dragons and helps defeat the Society of Wizards. "I fully intended for it to be one book," Wrede told *AAYA*. "I turned it in, and Jane called me up and said, 'I love this book. It's really good. We really like this a lot. I just read *Talking to Dragons*. We want to buy that one, too, and we want you to write the book in the middle.' I said, '*Jaaaaane*, I don't *want* to write the book in the middle.' She said, 'But I *want* you to write the book in the middle.' So it's all her fault.

"The Enchanted Forest books are so loopy—one of the things I love about the Enchanted Forest is that anything can happen. Of *course* if you go into the forest you run into a squirrel who can give you just exactly the directions you need. Of *course* there is a back way into the dragon's cave; there is *always* a way for the hero to succeed in whatever his quest is. These things always happen in fairy tales. That allows me to do things that I simply couldn't get *away* with doing in any other kind of writing, simply because I can be as outrageous as I want to. I can sit around thinking *Now what outrageous thing can I do today?*, which is really how the Enchanted Forest books grow: 'Now, what outrageous thing am I going to do. . . no, no, that's not outrageous enough. Let's do something else outrageous. . . . This is too much like the last outrageous thing. . . *OH*, let's try this instead!' It's amazing the kinds of things I think are mildly amusing, but which cause other people to roll around on the floor. There's humor in the Lyra books, too, but it's not the main point. They are adventure stories; given the premise of the world, this really could happen. People would behave this way. Whereas with the Enchanted Forest, *nobody* would behave that way.

"I can be as screwy as I want to in the Enchanted Forest. Most of the humor in the Enchanted Forest books comes from taking for granted the fact that really outrageous things are perfectly normal and coming up with a very mundane solution: 'Well, of *course* these particular streams are either lemon flavored or lime flavored. That's how the world works.' There's a scene in *Searching for Dragons,* the book published in September, 1991, where Cimorene and Mendanbar, the king of the Enchanted Forest, are having a discussion with a giant who is getting tired of going out and ravaging villages and pillaging, but he doesn't know what else to do. Right off the top of his head, Mendanbar says, 'Consulting!' A great many of my friends find this scene incredibly funny because of the idea of a giant consultant teaching other giants how to ravage villages better. It takes concepts that you're used to seeing and turns them upside down.

"*Searching for Dragons* is from Mendanbar's viewpoint. In some ways he is a lot like Daystar. There is certainly a family resemblance. In fact, when I was starting to work on the book I had to keep reminding myself, 'This is not Daystar, this is Mendanbar. This is his father. They are not the same person.' But they have the same very matter-of-fact, low-key approach. Nothing really quite gets them wild very often.

"The next Enchanted Forest book, not *Searching for Dragons*—it turns out that there's going to be four of them, because the middle book turned out to be two books—but the one that I am just beginning to work on, is from Morwen's point of view. You get to meet all of her cats and understand what they are saying. And, of course, Morwen is presently the only one who knows what all the cats are saying; so you get both sides of the conversation. It's going to be a lot of fun to do, I think.

"I am a cat person. When I was young I wanted a cat. That was my choice of pet. But it wasn't until I was in high school that my parents broke down and let me get one. So, I had a cat for a couple of years and I couldn't take her off to college because she was a cat that lived in a large house. I couldn't confine her to my dorm room, so to speak. She was very set in her ways and she would not have liked the move at all. A very established cat; this was her turf and she knew it. She graciously condescended

Young hero Daystar, his fire-witch friend Shiara, and their draconine companion must make their way through the Enchanted Forest guided only by Daystar's magic sword.

to let the rest of us live in her house. So she stayed and I left. Now I have two cats, Merlin and Brisen.

"Cats are traditionally associated with witches and magic—it's something about the way those eyes sort of glow in dim light. Also, they're quiet and they sneak up on you. But if you stop and think about it, practically every animal is associated with magic. Horses are associated with magic in many ways and birds, hawks in particular, fish—the salmon of knowledge in Celtic mythology. But cats do seem to have a certain special something.

"Cats and dragons seem to go together. I see them anyway as having similar personalities. It's just that dragons are much bigger. But cats have the same attitude: 'Well, I'm going to do what I want to do, and if you want it too, that is very nice, and if you don't, well, too bad.' Cats and dragons can both get away with that for different reasons.

"I don't have a particular concept of what a witch or a wizard is like. I think the whole point of the way that I portray witches, wizards, sorcerers, etc., in my books is that magic-using is like any other job. In some sense, anybody could do this. Being a witch doesn't automatically mean you're intelligent or evil or that you like cats, or whatever. In a way it's sort of anti-stereotyping.

"I like writing about strong female characters, possibly because there haven't been a lot of them that I could identity with. If my strong female characters come from anything it's essentially from the women that I know: My mother, my aunts, my grandmothers, the bosses, the women that I have worked for, or professors that I had in college.

Evil enchantress and social climber Miranda Griscomb confronts Regency heroine Katherine Talgarth in Wrede's 1988 collaborative novel-of-letters.

They were all very determined, active women. I hadn't seen a whole lot of that particular type in fantasy.

"Female characters just happen to be the people that I'm interested in. I've tried a couple of times to do male-viewpoint characters, but I've come to the conclusion that mostly I tell a better story with the female characters. There are some stories where a male character's is the only possible viewpoint, or the only right one for the story, and then I'll use that. I don't see any reason why I should be limited to only doing women or only doing men.

"These characters are important as well because they have to be real people. If you have cardboard people moving around a really interesting landscape you can get away with it for a little while, but not for a whole book. You've got to have real characters. Part of what shapes those characters, however, is the cultural background from which they come. When you first see your character standing there in the fog, everything about him implies something about the culture that he comes from—whether he's carrying a gun or a sword or two daggers, whether he is dressed in leather or chain or plate armor or green homespun... One little detail will lead you back to a whole implication about the culture.

"What usually happens when I'm writing the Lyra books, on the other hand, is that I have this basic understanding of the world, so I say, 'All right, now I want to write a book that involves this particular place. I want to write a book about the Cilhar.' I know what this culture is like, so somewhere in this culture (it's a country, it's a big place) I'm going to find a character, a person who is the kind of person I want to tell a story about. Once I've got my character, I build forward and backward from that point: 'All right, now that I know who she is and where she is from, what is she like? and, in these particular ways she is typical of her culture and in these other ways she's not, because she is an individual. Now what happens?'

"Names are very important to me. I can't do a character without also having a name for him. I know there are people who can write pages and pages about 'A said' and 'B said' and then go back later and fill in the names when they know the people, but I can't do that. I have to have a name up front and sometimes it takes me a while to figure it out. I'll get to the point in the story where a new character comes on and I don't know what his or her name is, so I'll have to stop and spend half an hour or so figuring out a name. When I'm just beginning a story and I'm coming up with the names for the main characters, that can sometimes take a day or two. It used to take me much longer to come up with a good name for a character. When I was working as a secretary one of my jobs was cleaning the mailing list and it's amazing the peculiar names that real people in real places have. Every time I ran across a very interesting one I'd copy it down, and I'd also make use of my typos. So I ended up with a long list of names that I could go and look at when I needed one. And that was kind of where it started."

Wrede started a very different type of fantasy writing with *Sorcery and Cecelia,* her seventh book. Written with Caroline Stevermer, a friend, *Sorcery and Cecelia* is set in an alternate England in which magic is systematized and taught in the public schools just after the Napoleonic Wars. The book consists of a series of letters written between two cousins, one of whom has gone down to London to be introduced to the social life. The two become entangled in a power struggle between wizards, but overcome their adversaries and, in true Regency fashion, marry their respective beaus. Her next book, *Snow White and Rose Red,* is also set in an alternate England, but during Tudor times. It is a retelling of an ancient *Grimm's Fairy Tale,* but mixes in historical characters such as Dr. John Dee, mathematician and astrologer to the court of Queen Elizabeth. Blanche and Rosamund, the title characters, are daughters of the widow Arden. They live on the edges of a forest near the river Thames that marks the boundary of the magical realm of Faerie. Because of their isolation and occasional odd behavior the widow and her daughters are suspected of using magic—a serious crime in Elizabethan England, punishable by death. Through the machinations of the villagers, the Faerie Queen's court, and the magical experiments of Dr. Dee, the girls become involved with the half-human sons of the Queen of Faerie.

"*Mairelon the Magician* is more like *Sorcery and Cecelia* or *Snow White and Rose Red,* which are set in an alternate England," Wrede told *AAYA.* "*Mairelon the Magician* is set in this England in about 1816-1817, shortly after the Napoleonic Wars ended. The main character, Kim, is a street waif who has grown up in the slums who is hired to burgle the wagon of a performing magician. He turns out to be a real magician, however, and she gets caught. Since he's a rather eccentric magician, instead of turning her over to the constable, he decides to take her under his wing. He had, it turns

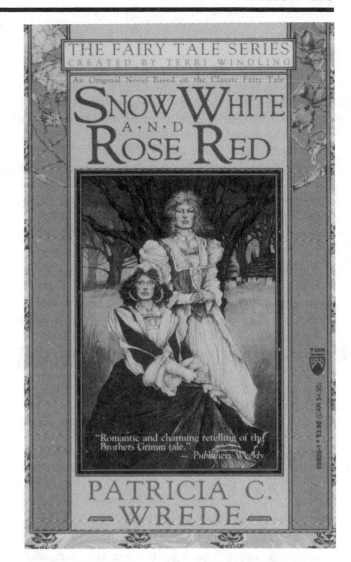

Wrede's version of the fairy tale by the Brothers Grimm takes place in Elizabethan England, but is set on the borders of the realm of Faerie.

out, five years before, been framed for theft and has come back trying to find all of the various things that were stolen so he can clear his name. It turns into very much a lunatic romp. You've got a lot of character types that people who read Regency romances will recognize, although it's not a romance.

"I like Regency because it's got so many levels and so much possibility. Nobody in fantasy has dealt very much with this time, and not just in young adult novels, but in fantasy, period. I have something of a quarrel with labeling all fantasy writing as 'young adult' because I don't consider myself a young adult writer. I don't write my books aimed at any particular market other than *this is stuff I would like to read,* and I don't really consider myself as a young adult anymore. I would like to, but no.

"When you're writing fantasy you're writing about magic, and magic is not something that exists in the real world, like rocks. Essentially magic is a metaphor for something else, and I've had a lot of fun sitting down with other writers and discussing what magic is a metaphor for in their books. It varies from writer to writer and frequently from book to book. Some writers consciously adapt the metaphor of magic in their books, but for me, magic tends to be a metaphor for power.

"Magic for me is the essence of the ability to make things happen, to get things done. When you're the CEO of a corporation you can say, 'I want this to happen' and people will go out and make it happen. You have the power to make it happen. And in my books the fundamental question is, if you can do anything, what do you do? If you've got the power to make stuff happen, good stuff or bad stuff, what do you do with it?

"It's a fascinating concept once you start looking at fantasy novels in that fashion. It's fascinating and it's also very interesting to talk to other authors and to see what they're doing consciously or unconsciously. *The Harp of Imach Thyssel* was definitely the book of mine in which that was front-and-center the most. But it's pretty much there in all my work—the choices that you make in dealing with power: how do you use it.

"Coming up with all these ideas is the easy part of writing. The hard part is finding the time and energy to put them down on paper. Nobody who doesn't actually write believes this, but every writer I know who has done more than one or two books has a stack of ideas that could keep them busy for the next ten years. Sitting down and putting words on paper is the hardest part. So you play tricks on yourself. You turn on the computer. Once the computer is on, you think, 'Wow, geez, I can't just turn it off without *doing* something.' So, if you get into 'zombie mode' and pick up your morning tea and go down to the computer, you're sitting there thinking, 'Oh. Oh, I turned it on. Now I guess I have to do something.' You get it turned on before you start thinking about it. Then you're kind of stuck.

"I'm currently in the process of writing another Lyra book. I do have to write the third of the 'Enchanted Forest' chronicles yet this year, and then revise *Talking to Dragons*. But I have to finish the next Lyra book first, which will be titled *The Raven Ring*, and then (as soon as I'm done with the

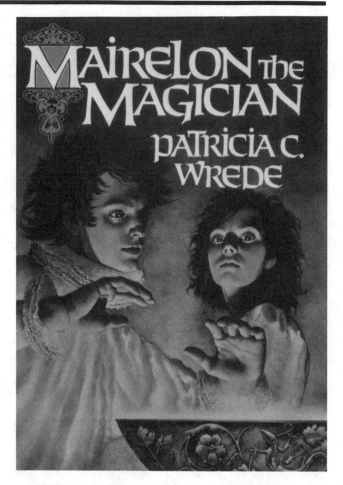

Mairelon, a well-born magician sought for a crime he did not commit, gains the trust and assistance of street waif Kim in Wrede's Dickensian comedy set in an alternate early Victorian England.

'Enchanted Forest' books) I'm supposed to do a sequel to *Mairelon*. After that, I don't know. There are so many possibilities.... I've had people ask for a sequel to practically every book I've ever written and there are a couple of them that could use a sequel. I've been toying with those ideas. I would love to do a Lyra book about the Traders, or a Lyra pirate novel; that would be great fun. I try not to get too far ahead of myself, though. I just want to get finished with the stuff that I'm working on now, because I've got ideas that will keep me busy until the year 2000 and past.

"I have two fundamental patterns for my work day. One is when I get up in the morning and eat, read the paper, come down and spend the morning at the computer working, and then spend the afternoon doing errands and chores—mow the lawn, do the dishes, go to the library, go to the health club, or what have you. In the evening, depending on what's going on, I may do some socializing. The other pattern, which is somewhat more common, is to get up in the morning and tear frantically around trying to find this, that, or the other thing that I absolutely, positively have to have, and then go tearing through whatever chores absolutely, positively have to be done that particular day—the lawn is six inches long and has got to be mowed, the tomatoes that I bought last week are beginning to wilt in their little pots and it's time to plant them, the bills are sitting on the desk and they have got to be paid because it's the last day before they will come out and get me—and spend my day doing what comes up (on an ad hoc basis) and then work in the evening. That works for me partly because when I had a day job, evenings were the only time I had to write, so I can do it either way. Once in a while I really get on a roll and I spend all day at the typewriter and the heck with the lawn.

"My brother, David, reads science fiction and fantasy, and my youngest sister, Carol, does also. They both grab everything hot off the typewriter. David is particularly good at untangling difficult plot points and so sometimes if I'm stuck we sit down and talk. He says the best parts of my books are the ones where he told me what to do. Susan has them all, and she reads them, but she does it because I'm her sister. Peg had never read any of them until she got engaged and her fiance said, 'You mean you haven't...' and immediately went out and got all the books and sat her down with them. Afterwards Peg looked at me and said, 'Yep, and they were pretty good,' with great surprise in her voice. My dad reads them. My mother reads them all, even though fantasy is not her first choice of reading material. I figure that if she likes them, I must be doing something right."

"I still tell stories to my young nieces, and to any of my friends who will listen (though most of them have learned to say sternly, 'Go home and write that down! I don't want to hear it, I want to read it.')"

■ Works Cited

Wrede, Patricia C., interview with Kenneth R. Shepherd for *Authors and Artists for Young Adults*, conducted June 10, 1991.

■ For More Information See

PERIODICALS

Collings, Michael, "Pleasant Fantasy on Serious Themes" (review of *The Seven Towers*), *Fantasy Review*, September, 1984, pp. 35-36.

"*Daughter of Witches*" (review), *English Journal*, December, 1981, p. 67.

"*The Harp of Imach Thyssel*" (review), *Publishers Weekly*, March 8, 1985, p. 89.

Margolis, Sally T., review of *Dealing with Dragons*, *School Library Journal*, December, 1990, p. 25.

Mutter, John, review of *Caught in Crystal*, *Publishers Weekly*, February 27, 1987, p. 159.

"*The Seven Towers*" (review), *English Journal*, December, 1985, p. 58.

Steinberg, Sybil, review of *Mairelon the Magician*, *Publishers Weekly*, April 19, 1991, p. 60.

Steinberg, Sybil, review of *Snow White and Rose Red*, *Publishers Weekly*, April 21, 1991, p. 79.

Strain, Paula M., "A Writer Develops" (review of *Caught in Crystal*), *Fantasy Review*, May, 1987, p. 49.

Acknowledgments

Acknowledgments

Grateful acknowledgment is made to the following publishers,
authors, and artists for their kind permission to reproduce copyrighted material.

VIVIEN ALCOCK. Cover of *Travelers by Night*, by Vivien Alcock. Dell Publishing, 1983. Copyright © 1983 by Vivien Alcock. Cover illustration by Vincent Natale. Reprinted by permission of Dell Publishing Co., Inc., a division Bantam Doubleday Dell Publishing Group, Inc./ Cover of *The Mysterious Mr. Ross*, Vivien Alcock. Lions, 1988. Copyright © 1987 by Vivien Alcock. Reprinted by permission of HarperCollins Publishers./ Cover of *The Monster Garden*, by Vivien Alcock. Dell Publishing, 1988. Copyright © 1988 by Vivien Alcock. Cover illustration by Frank Morris. Reprinted by permission of Dell Publishing Co., Inc., a division of Bantam Doubleday Dell Publishing Group. Inc./ Photograph courtesy of Vivien Alcock.

SUE ELLEN BRIDGERS. Cover of *Permanent Connections*, by Sue Ellen Bridgers. Harper Keypoint, 1988. Copyright © 1987 by Sue Ellen Bridgers. Cover art copyright © 1988 by Eric Velasquez. Cover © 1988 by Harper & Row, Publishers, Inc. Reprinted by permission of HarperCollins Publishers./ Cover of *Notes for Another Life*, by Sue Ellen Bridgers. Bantam Books, 1989. Copyright © 1981 by Sue Ellen Bridgers. Cover art copyright © 1989 by Frederick Ribes. Reprinted by permission of Bantam Doubleday Dell Publishing Group./ Cover of *All Together Now*, by Sue Ellen Bridgers. Bantam Books, 1990. Copyright © 1979 by Sue Ellen Bridgers. Cover artwork copyright © 1984 by Joseph Cellini. Reprinted by permission of Bantam Books, a division of Bantam Doubleday Dell Publishing Group./ Photograph by Ben Bridgers, courtesy of Sue Ellen Bridgers.

BRUCE BROOKS. Jacket of *The Moves Make the Man*, by Bruce Brooks. Harper & Row, Publishers, 1984. Copyright © 1984 by Bruce Brooks. Jacket art © 1984 by Wayne Winfield. Jacket © 1984 by Harper & Row, Publishers, Inc. Reprinted by permission of HarperCollins Publishers./ Jacket of *Midnight Hour Encores*, by Bruce Brooks. Harper & Row, Publishers, 1986. Copyright © 1986 by Bruce Brooks. Jacket art © 1986 by Janet Wentworth. Jacket © 1986 by Harper & Row, Publishers, Inc. Reprinted by permission of HarperCollins Publishers./ Jacket of *No Kidding*, by Bruce Brooks. Harper & Row, Publishers, 1989. Copyright © 1989 by Bruce Brooks. Jacket art © 1989 by Fred Marcellino. Jacket © 1989 by Harper & Row, Publishers, Inc. Reprinted by permission of HarperCollins Publishers./ Jacket of *Everywhere*, by Bruce Brooks. HarperCollins, 1990. Copyright © 1990 by Bruce Brooks. Jacket art © 1990 by Kam Mak. Jacket © 1991 by Harper & Row, Publishers, Inc. Reprinted by permission of HarperCollins Publishers./ Photograph by Penelope Winslow Brooks.

ALICE CHILDRESS. Cover of *Rainbow Jordan*, by Alice Childress. Avon Books, 1981. Copyright © 1981 by Alice Childress. Reprinted by permission of Avon Books, New York./ Cover illustration by David Brown from *A Hero Ain't Nothin' but a Sandwich*, by Alice Childress. Copyright © 1973 by Alice Childress. Reprinted by permission of Coward, McCann & Geoghegan./ Photograph courtesy of Alice Childress.

PAT CONROY. Cover of *The Water Is Wide*, by Pat Conroy. Avon Books, 1972. Copyright © 1972 by Pat Conroy. Cover illustration by Charles Lilly. Reprinted by permission of Avon Books, New York./ Jacket of *The Prince of Tides*, by Pat Conroy. Houghton Mifflin Company, 1986. Copyright © 1986 by Pat Conroy. Jacket illustration copyright © 1986 by Wendell Minor. Reprinted by permission of Wendell Minor./ Cover of *The Great Santini*, by Pat Conroy. Bantam Books, 1987. Copyright © 1976 by Pat Conroy. Cover art copyright © 1987 by Franco Accornero. Reprinted by permission of Bantam Books, a division of Bantam Doubleday Dell Publishing Group, Inc./ Cover of *The Lords of Discipline*, by Pat Conroy. Bantam Books, 1989. Copyright © 1980 by Pat Conroy. Cover art copyright © 1987 by Franco Accornero. Reprinted by permission of Bantam Books, a division of Bantam Doubleday Dell Publishing Group, Inc./ Photograph © Jerry Bauer./ Movie still, copyright © by Warner Bros. Inc.

JIM DAVIS. Cover drawing by Jim Davis from his *U.S. Acres Rules the Roost*. Topper Books, 1988. Copyright © 1988 by United Feature Syndicate, Inc. Reprinted by permission of Topper Books, an imprint of Pharos Books./ Illustration by Jim Davis from his *Garfield Takes up Space*. Ballantine Books, 1991. Copyright © 1990 United Feature Syndicate, Inc. Illustrations copyright © 1989, 1990 by United Feature Syndicate, Inc. Reprinted by permission of United Feature Syndicate, Inc./ Garfield characters, copyright © 1978 by United Feature Syndicate, Inc. Reprinted by permission of United Feature Syndicate, Inc.

LEON GARFIELD. Cover of *Black Jack*, by Leon Garfield. Pantheon Books, 1968. Copyright © 1968 by Anthony Maitland. Reprinted by kind permission of Penguin Books, UK./ Jacket of *Jack Holborn*, by Leon Garfield. Puffin Books,

1983. Copyright © 1964 by Leon Garfield. Cover photograph by TV60/Georgefilm. Reprinted by permission of Penguin Books Ltd./ Cover of *Mr. Corbett's Ghost and Other Stories*, by Leon Garfield. Puffin Books, 1987. Copyright © 1968 by Leon Garfield. Cover photograph by David James, from VIP Film Production. Reprinted by permission of Penguin Books Ltd./ Jacket of *The Apprentices*, by Leon Garfield. Copyright © by Leon Garfield. Jacket design by Stefen Bernath. Reprinted by permission of William Heinemann Limited./ Photograph, Winant, Towers Limited, courtesy of Leon Garfield.

JEAN CRAIGHEAD GEORGE. Cover of *Julie of the Wolves*, by Jean Craighead George. Harper & Row, Publishers, 1972. Copyright © 1972 by Jean Craighead George. Illustrations copyright © 1972 by John Schoenherr. Reprinted by permission of HarperCollins Publishers./ Cover of *My Side of the Mountain*, by Jean Craighead George. E.P. Dutton, 1988. Copyright © 1959, 1988 by Jean Craighead George. Cover art copyright © 1988 by Michael Garland. Reprinted by permission of Michael Garland./ Cover of *On the Far Side of the Mountain*, by Jean Craighead George. Puffin Books, 1991. Copyright © 1990 by Jean Craighead George. Cover illustration copyright © by Lino Saffioti. Reprinted by permission of Penguin USA./ Photograph, Ellan Young Photography./ Movie stills from *My Side of the Mountain* copyright © 1968 by Paramount Pictures Corp.

MATT GROENING. Cover of *Animation Magazine*, volume 3, issue 2, Fall 1989. Reprinted by permission of Expanded Entertainment./ Illustration by Matt Groening from his *School Is Hell*. Copyright © 1987. All rights reserved. Reprinted by permission of Pantheon Books, a division of Random House, NY./ Illustration by Matt Groening from his *Greetings from The Simpsons™*. Copyright © 1990 by Matt Groening Productions, Inc. All rights reserved. Reprinted by permission of HarperCollins Publishers, NY. The Simpsons TM and © 1990 Twentieth Century-Fox Film Corp./ Photograph reprinted by permission of Expanded Entertainment.

RON HOWARD. Movie stills from *Parenthood* copyright © 1989 by Universal City Studios Inc./ Movie still from *Willow* copyright © 1988 by Lucasfilms Ltd. Photograph by Keith Hamshere./ Photograph A/P Wide World Photos.

JOHN IRVING. Cover of *The Cider House Rules*, by John Irving. Bantam Books, 1985. Copyright © 1985 by Garp Enterprises, Ltd. Copyright design by Honi Werner. Reprinted by permission of Bantam Doubleday Dell Publishing Group, Inc./ Cover of *A Prayer for Owen Meaney*, by John Irving. William Morrow and Company, 1989. Copyright © 1989 by Garp Enterprises, Ltd. Reprinted by permission of William Morrow and Company, Inc./ Photograph © Joyce Ravid.

BOB KANE. Cover of *Detective Comics #27*, May 1939. Copyright © 1939 by DC Comics Inc. Copyright renewed 1957. Reprinted by permission of DC Comics Inc./ Illustration from *Batman: The Dark Knight Returns*, by Frank Miller. Art by Klaus Janson, Frank Miller, and Lynn Varley. Copyright © 1986 by DC Comics Inc. Reprinted by permission of DC Comics Inc./ Cover of *Batman: The Official Comic Adaptation of the Warner Bros. Motion Pictures*, by Dennis O'Neil. Art by Jerry Ordway and Steve Oliff. Copyright © 1989 by DC Comics Inc. Reprinted by permission of DC Comics Inc./ Photograph reprinted by permission of Eclipse Books and DC Comics Inc.

MAXINE HONG KINGSTON. Cover of *The Woman Warrior: Memoirs of a Childhood Among Ghosts*, by Maxine Hong Kingston. Vintage Books, 1977. Copyright © 1975, 1976 by Maxine Hong Kingston. Reprinted by permission of Random House, Inc./ Cover of *China Men*, by Maxine Hong Kingston. Vintage Books, 1989. Copyright © 1977, 1978, 1979, 1980 by Maxine Hong Kingston. Cover design by Marc J. Cohen. Reprinted by permission of Random House, Inc./ Cover of *Tripmaster Monkey: His Fake Book*, by Maxine Hong Kingston. Vintage Books, 1990. Copyright © 1987, 1988, 1989 by Maxine Hong Kingston. Art design by Marc J. Cohen. Photograph by Barnaby Hall and Ken Skalski. Reprinted by permission of Random House, Inc./ Photograph © Jerry Bauer.

MARGARET MAHY. Jacket of *17 Kings and 42 Elephants*, by Margaret Mahy. Dial Books for Young Readers, 1972. Text copyright © 1972 by Margaret Mahy. Pictures copyright © 1987 by Patricia MacCarthy. Reprinted by permission of Penguin USA./ Cover of *The Changeover: A Supernatural Romance*, by Margaret Mahy. Scholastic, Inc., 1974. Copyright © 1974 by Margaret Mahy. Reprinted by permission of Scholastic, Inc./ Jacket of *The Haunting*, by Margaret Mahy. Atheneum, 1982. Copyright © 1982 by Margaret Mahy. Jacket painting by Michele Chessare. Reprinted by permission of Margaret K. McElderry Books, an imprint of Macmillan Publishing Company./ Cover of *Aliens in the Family*, by Margaret Mahy. Scholastic, Inc., 1985. Copyright © 1985 by Margaret Mahy. Reprinted by permission of Scholastic, Inc./ Jacket of *Memory*, by Margaret Mahy. Margaret K. McElderry Books, 1988. Copyright © 1987 by Margaret Mahy. Jacket painting © 1987 by Alun Hood. Reprinted with permission of the David Lewis Illustration Agency./ Cover of *The Tricksters*, by Margaret Mahy. Scholastic, Inc., 1988. Copyright © 1986 by Margaret Mahy. Reprinted by permission of Macmillan Publishing Company./ Photograph courtesy of Margaret Mahy.

MILTON MELTZER. Jacket of *The Chinese Americans*, by Milton Meltzer. Crowell, 1980. Copyright © 1980 by Milton Meltzer. Reprinted by permission of HarperCollins Publishers./ Jacket of *A Pictorial History of Black Americans*, by Milton Meltzer. Crown Publishers, 1983. Copyright © 1983 by Crown Publishers. Jacket design by One Plus One Studio. Reprinted by permission of Random House, Inc./ Jacket of *Ain't Gonna Study War No More: The Story of America's Peace Seekers*, by Milton Meltzer. Harper & Row, Publishers, 1985. Copyright © 1985 by Milton Meltzer. Jacket by Barbara A. Fitzsimmons. Jacket © 1985 by Harper & Row, Publishers, Inc. Reprinted by permission of HarperCollins Publishers./ Illustration from *Crime in America*, by Milton Meltzer. Morrow Junior Books, 1990. Copyright © 1990 by Milton Meltzer. Reprinted by permission of William Morrow and Company, Inc./ Cover of *Never to Forget: The Jews of the Holocaust*, by Milton Meltzer. Harper Trophy, 1991. Copyright © 1976 by Milton Meltzer.

Cover photo © 1991 by UPI/Bettmann. Cover © 1991 by HarperCollins Publishers. Cover design by Martha E. Sedgwick. Reprinted by permission of HarperCollins Publishers./ Photograph by Catherine Noren, courtesy of Milton Meltzer.

NICHOLASA MOHR. Illustration by Nicholasa Mohr from her *Nilda*. Harper & Row, 1973. Copyright © 1973 by Nicholasa Mohr. Reprinted by permission of HarperCollins Publishers./ Cover of *Felita*, by Nicholasa Mohr. Bantam Books, 1979. Copyright © 1979 by Nicholasa Mohr. Illustrations copyright © 1979 by Ray Cruz. Cover art copyright © 1990 by Rick Mujica. Reprinted by permission of Bantam Books, a division of Bantam Doubleday Dell Publishing Group, Inc./ Cover of *El Bronx Remembered*, by Nicholasa Mohr. Arte Publico Press, 1986. Copyright © 1986 by Nicholasa Mohr. Cover design by Narciso Pena. Reprinted by permission of Arte Publico Press./ Cover of *Going Home*, by Nicholasa Mohr. Bantam Books, 1986. Copyright © 1989 by Rick Mujica. Reprinted by permission of Bantam Books, a division of Bantam Doubleday Dell Publishing Group, Inc./ Photograph courtesy of Nicholasa Mohr.

OUIDA SEBESTYEN. Cover of *Words by Heart*, by Ouida Sebestyen. Bantam Books, 1979. Copyright © 1968, 1979 by Ouida Sebestyen. Cover art copyright © 1981 by Bantam Books. Reprinted by permission of Bantam Books, a division of Bantam Doubleday Dell Publishing Group, Inc./ Cover of *Far from Home*, by Ouida Sebestyen. Published by Little, Brown and Company. Jacket painting and design copyright © 1980 by Wendell Minor. Reprinted by permission of Wendell Minor./ Jacket of *On Fire*, by Ouida Sebestyen. Little, Brown and Company in conjunction with The Atlantic Monthly Press. Copyright © 1985 by Ouida Sebestyen. Jacket painting © 1985 by Richard Williams./ Cover of *The Girl in the Box*, by Ouida Sebestyen. Bantam Books, 1988. Copyright © 1988 by Ouida Sebestyen. Cover art copyright © 1989 by Derek James. Reprinted by permission of Bantam Books, a division of Bantam Doubleday Dell Publishing Group, Inc./ Photograph courtesy of Ouida Sebestyen.

STEVEN SPIELBERG. Movie still from *Who Framed Roger Rabbit* copyright © 1988 Touchstone Pictures and Amblin Entertainment, Inc./ Movie still from *Indiana Jones and the Last Crusade* courtesy of Movie Star News./ Movie still from *Twilight Zone—The Movie* copyright © 1983 by Warner Bros. Inc.

MARY STOLZ. Cover of *The Noonday Friends*, by Mary Stolz. Harper Trophy Books, 1971. Text copyright © 1965 by Mary Stolz. Pictures copyright © 1965 by Louis S. Glanzman. Reprinted by permission of HarperCollins Publishers./ Cover of *The Edge of Next Year*, by Mary Stolz. Copyright © 1974 by Mary Stolz. Used by permission of Bell Books, a division of Bantam Doubleday Dell Publishing Group, Inc./ Jacket of *Bartholomew Fair*, by Mary Stolz. Greenwillow Books, 1990. Copyright © 1990 by Mary Stolz. Jacket illustration © 1990 by Pamela Johnson. Reprinted by permission of Greenwillow Books, a division of William Morrow and Company, Inc./ Photograph courtesy of Mary Stolz.

MAIA WOJCIECHOWSKA. Cover of *Shadow of a Bull*, by Maia Wojciechowska. Aladdin Books, 1964. Copyright © 1964 by Maia Wojciechowska. Cover design by Lisa Hollander. Cover illustration copyright © 1987 by Ed Martinez. Reprinted by permission of Maia Wojciechowska./ Cover of *The Hollywood Kid*, by Maia Wojciechowska. Harper & Row, Publishers, 1966. Copyright © 1966 by Maia Wojciechowska Rodman. Cover painting by Seymour Leichman. Reprinted by permission of Maia Wojciechowska./ Jacket of *Through the Broken Mirror with Alice*, by Maia Wojciechowska. Copyright © 1972 by Maia Wojciechowska. Jacket painting by John Steptoe. Reprinted by permission of Maia Wojciechowska./ Jacket of *Till the Break of Day: Memories, 1939-1942*, by Maia Wojciechowska. Copyright © 1972 by Maia Wojciechowska. Jacket design by Carl Smith. Reprinted by permission of Maia Wojciechowska./ Illustration from *How God Got Christian into Trouble*, by Maia Wojciechowska. The Westminster Press, 1984. Copyright © 1984 by Maia Wojciechowska. Illustration by Les Gray. Reprinted by permission of Maia Wojciechowska./ Photograph courtesy of Maia Wojciechowska.

TOM WOLFE. Cover of *The Electric Kool-Aid Acid Test*, by Tom Wolfe. Bantom Books, 1969. Copyright © 1968 by Tom Wolfe. Front cover photographs by Bill Cadge. Reprinted by permission of Bantam Books, Inc., a division of Bantam Doubleday Dell Publishing Group, Inc./ Cover of *The Right Stuff*, by Tom Wolfe. Bantam Books, 1980. Copyright © 1979 by Tom Wolfe. Cover copyright © 1980 by Bantam Books. Reprinted by permission of Bantam Books, Inc., a division of Bantam Doubleday Dell Publishing Group, Inc./ Cover of *The Bonfire of the Vanities*, by Tom Wolfe. Bantam Books, 1988. Copyright © 1987 by Tom Wolfe. Cover photograph copyright © 1990 by Warner Bros. Inc. Cover art copyright © by Nick Giciano. Reprinted by permission of Bantam Books, Inc., a division of Bantam Doubleday Dell Publishing Group, Inc./ Movie still from *The Right Stuff* John Bryson/Sygma./ Photograph by Thomas Victor.

PATRICIA C. WREDE. Jacket of *Mairelon the Magician*, by Patricia C. Wrede. Jacket art by Dennis Nolan. Jacket design by Carol Russo. Used with permission of TOR Books./ Cover of *The Seven Towers*, by Patricia C. Wrede. Reprinted by permission of the Berkley Publishing Group./ Cover of *Shadow Magic*, by Patricia C. Wrede. Ace Books, 1982. Copyright © 1982 by Patricia C. Wrede. Cover art by Walter Velez. Reprinted by permission of the Berkley Publishing Group./ Cover of *Daughter of Witches*, by Patricia C. Wrede. Ace Books, 1983. Copyright © 1983 by Patricia C. Wrede. Cover art by Walter Velez. Reprinted by permission of the Berkley Publishing Group./ Cover of *Sorcery and Cecelia*, by Patricia C. Wrede. Ace Books, 1988. Copyright © 1988 by Patricia C. Wrede and Caroline Stevermer. Cover art by David Heffernan. Reprinted by permission of the Berkley Publishing Group./ Cover of *Talking to Dragons*, by Patricia C. Wrede. Ace Books, 1985. Copyright © 1985 by Patricia C. Wrede. Cover art by David Heffernan. Reprinted by permission of the Berkley Publishing Group./ Cover of *Snow White and Rose Red*, by Patricia C. Wrede. Tom Doherty Associates, Inc., 1989. Copyright © 1989 by Patricia C. Wrede. Cover painting and design by Thomas Canty. Copyright © 1989, 1990 by Thomas Canty. Reprinted by permission of Tom Doherty Associates, Inc./ Photograph by David Dyer-Bennet, courtesy of Patricia C. Wrede.

Cumulative Index

Author/Artist Index

The following index gives the number of the volume
in which an author/artist's biographical sketch appears.